QUICKBOOKS® 2007 FINANCE SOFTWARE FOR SMALL BUSINESS
QuickSteps

CINDY FOX

New York Chicago San Francisco
Lisbon London Madrid Mexico City
Milan New Delhi San Juan
Seoul Singapore Sydney Toronto

The McGraw-Hill Companies

Cataloging-in-Publication Data is on file with the Library of Congress

McGraw-Hill books are available at special quantity discounts to use as premiums and sales promotions, or for use in corporate training programs. For more information, please write to the Director of Special Sales, Professional Publishing, McGraw-Hill, Two Penn Plaza, New York, NY 10121-2298. Or contact your local bookstore.

QUICKBOOKS® 2007 FINANCE SOFTWARE FOR SMALL BUSINESS QUICKSTEPS

34567890 CCI CCI 01987

ISBN-13: 978-0-07-148767-2
ISBN-10: 0-07-148767-0

SPONSORING EDITOR / Megg Morin

EDITORIAL SUPERVISOR / Patty Mon

PROJECT MANAGER / Samik Roy Chowdhury

SERIES CREATORS AND EDITORS / Marty and Carole Matthews

ACQUISITIONS COORDINATOR / Carly Stapleton

TECHNICAL EDITOR / Daniel Hodge

COPY EDITOR / Robert Campbell

PROOFREADER / Joette Lynch

INDEXER / Valerie Perry

PRODUCTION SUPERVISOR / Jim Kussow

COMPOSITION / International Typesetting and Composition

ILLUSTRATION / International Typesetting and Composition

SERIES DESIGN / Bailey Cunningham

ART DIRECTOR, COVER / Jeff Weeks

COVER DESIGN / Pattie Lee

COVER ILLUSTRATION / Tom Willis

Contents at a Glance

1 2 3 4 5 6 7 8 9 10

Contents

3

4

5

9

10

To Mark, who always believed in me.
Thank you.

About the Author

Cindy Fox (www.cindyfox.com) has been working with computers in some form—hardware, software, networking, programming, management, writing, and teaching—since 1986. Cindy owns Butterfly Consulting LLC, which provides database and Web design, hosting, programming, training, and writing services to a diverse client base. A certified college instructor, she has taught SCUBA and Philosophy in addition to a variety of computer courses. She also writes and teaches online courses for companies such as HP and CNET with up to 25,000 students in each class. In addition, she is always learning, most currently with her two boys, as they play with science, art, building, experiments, music, stories, and more through Life Learning. Cindy lives with her husband, Mark, sons Richie and Lane, and three cats in Mesa, Arizona.

Acknowledgments

Thanks once again to **Megg Morin** for taking this book through the process! Special thanks to **Daniel Hodge**, my technical editor, **Samik Roy Chowdhury**, my project manager and **Robert Campbell**, my copy editor for checking up on everything and making excellent suggestions that improved the final product!

The Credits page in the front is filled with real people full of real talent! Thank you, all!

Introduction

QuickSteps books are recipe books for computer users. They answer the question "how do I…" by providing a quick set of steps to accomplish the most common tasks with a particular operating system or application.

The sets of steps are the central focus of the book. QuickSteps sidebars show how to quickly perform many small functions or tasks that support the primary functions. QuickFacts sidebars supply information that you need to know about a subject. Notes, Tips, and Cautions augment the steps, presented in a separate column to not interrupt the flow of the steps. The introductions are minimal rather than narrative, and numerous illustrations and figures, many with callouts, support the steps.

QuickSteps books are organized by function and the tasks needed to perform that function. Each function is a chapter. Each task, or "How To," contains the steps needed for accomplishing the function along with the relevant Notes, Tips, Cautions, and screenshots. You can easily find the tasks you need through:

- The table of contents, which lists the functional areas (chapters) and tasks in the order they are presented
- A How To list of tasks on the opening page of each chapter
- The index, which provides an alphabetical list of the terms that are used to describe the functions and tasks
- Color-coded tabs for each chapter or functional area with an index to the tabs in the Contents at a Glance (just before the Table of Contents)

Conventions Used in This Book

QuickBooks 2007 Finance Software for Small Business QuickSteps uses several conventions designed to make the book easier for you to follow:

- A in the table of contents and in the How To list in each chapter references a QuickSteps sidebar in a chapter, and a references a QuickFacts sidebar.
- **Bold type** is used for words or objects on the screen that you are to do something with—for example, "click the **Start** menu, and then click **My Computer**."
- *Italic type* is used for a word or phrase that is being defined or otherwise deserves special emphasis.
- Underlined type is used for text that you are to type from the keyboard.
- **SMALL CAPITAL LETTERS** are used for keys on the keyboard such as **ENTER** and **SHIFT**.
- When you are expected to enter a command, you are told to press the key(s). If you are to enter text or numbers, you are told to type them.

How to...

- *Use the Start Menu to Open QuickBooks*
- *Open a Sample Company File*
- *Updating Older Company Files to Work with QuickBooks 2007*
- *Registering QuickBooks*
- *Use the Home Page*
- *Use the Icon Bar*
- *Explore the Menu Bar*
- *Use the View Menu to Customize Your Desktop*
- *Opening Other Company Files (.QBW)*
- *Edit the Icon Bar*
- *Delete an Icon*
- *Edit an Icon*
- *Rearrange the Order of Icons*
- *Add a Separator Between Icon Buttons*
- *Add an Icon to the Icon Bar*
- *Ask a Help Question*
- *Use the How Do I? Drop-Down Menu*
- *Use the Help Menu*
- *Use Keyboard Shortcuts*
- *Close the Company File*
- *How to Exit QuickBooks*

Chapter 1

Stepping into QuickBooks 2007

QuickBooks is a powerful yet easy-to-use accounting program that keeps the finances of your business in shape and at your fingertips. This book uses QuickBooks Premier 2007, which includes features from Simple Start and QuickBooks Pro, plus a few additional features. This chapter explains how to open QuickBooks and your company file (if you have one) or the sample file included with QuickBooks. You'll use this sample file to learn how to move around the program, get help, and close QuickBooks. Creating a new QuickBooks file will be covered in Chapter 2.

NOTE

The term "version" refers to the release of QuickBooks, such as 2007, and "edition" refers to the level of features within the program, such as QuickBooks Simple Start, Pro, and Premier.

TIP

While this book will show you *how* to do things, to determine *what* to do, consult your accountant. Your accountant (who hopefully knows QuickBooks) can help you with local laws and industry-specific advice. He or she can also help you set up new processes or evaluate your options.

NOTE

The QuickBooks company file always ends in a .qbw extension. QuickBooks backup files always end with a .qbb extension. Backups will be covered in Chapter 2.

Learn about the QuickBooks Family

QuickBooks is a family of programs that includes three primary editions: QuickBooks Simple Start, QuickBooks Pro, and QuickBooks Premier, as well as a variety of business-specific editions. The core of these QuickBooks programs is the same, and Tips and Notes will be used to point out special features of some editions. This book is here to help you get started, understand important features, run your business, and give you step-by-step directions on the features most businesses need to use, such as creating invoices and sales receipts, making deposits, paying bills, running reports, and managing inventory.

Table 1-1 compares the three most popular QuickBooks editions. A complete list of all features is available online at www.intuit.com or on the back of any QuickBooks package.

QuickBooks Pro is the best overall solution for most businesses, since it includes payroll, job costing, and multiuser capabilities. QuickBooks Premier is also popular and comes in business-specific editions, which include specialized reports for specific industries, such as construction, manufacturing, and retail.

Three other editions of QuickBooks are also available: QuickBooks Enterprise Solutions, QuickBooks Pro 2007 for Mac, and QuickBooks Online Edition. You'll find that many chapters will apply to these editions as well, but your computer screen will not always look like the illustrations in this book.

Start QuickBooks

QuickBooks stores all your financial data in a single file called a *company file*. You may have multiple company files if you have multiple companies or locations.

In this chapter, you will open a sample file and examine the layout of the QuickBooks program. If you have your own company file, you can use that for this chapter; however, your screen will not look exactly like the illustrations in this book.

FEATURE	QUICKBOOKS SIMPLE START	QUICKBOOKS PRO 2007	QUICKBOOKS PREMIER
Price (current as of 2007)	$99.95	$199.95 / $699.95	$399.95 / $1,399.95
Purchase Options	Single User	Single User/ Five-User Pack	Single User/ Five-User Pack
Number of simultaneous users	One	Up to five	Up to five
Integrated Customer Center with customer lists, transactions, and contact information		√	√
Integrated Vendor Center with vendor lists, transactions, and contact information		√	√
Ability to print packing slips and labels for FedEx and UPS		√	√
Ability to e-mail and save forms and reports as PDFs		√	√
Form customization and designs		√	√
Extended detail area on forms and statements		√	√
Ability to track inventory, including purchase order creation		√	√
Price-level customization for customer types (up to 100 price levels)		√	√
Individual item price levels		√	√
Job-costing reports		√	√
Time-tracking capability		√	√
Budget creation capability		√	√
Project cash flow capability		√	√
Ability to track vehicle mileage		√	√
Ability to manage loans		√	√
Ability to track fixed assets		√	√
Employee Center to manage payroll, direct deposit, and payroll taxes		√	√
Remote data access			√
Business plan creator			√
Forecast creation			√
Expert analysis of company performance			√
Ability to create inventory assemblies (for manufacturers of finished goods)			√
Ability to create purchase orders from sales orders			√

Table 1-1: Comparison of the Three Most Popular QuickBooks Editions

TIP

If you don't have QuickBooks installed yet, simply insert the CD and follow the steps. Single-user installation is clear and straightforward. See Chapter 8 for more details on Network Installation.

NOTE

"Default" is the setting that is automatically used if you haven't selected another setting.

NOTE

QuickBooks can have many levels of passwords. If you are working with an existing file, check with the owner to see what level of access you have.

Use the Start Menu to Open QuickBooks

A typical installation of QuickBooks includes a listing on the Start menu and a shortcut icon on the desktop. You can double-click the shortcut icon on the desktop to open QuickBooks or use the Start menu. To open QuickBooks using the Start menu:

1. Start your computer, if it is not already running, and log in to Windows if necessary.
2. Click **Start**. The Start menu is displayed.
3. Click **All Programs**, click **QuickBooks**, and then click **QuickBooks Premier 2007**.

QuickBooks now opens with the last company file used displayed, or, if no company file is open, you will see the screen shown in Figure 1-1. From here, you can view a tutorial video about QuickBooks, explore QuickBooks by opening one of the two sample files included, create a new company file, or open an existing company file.

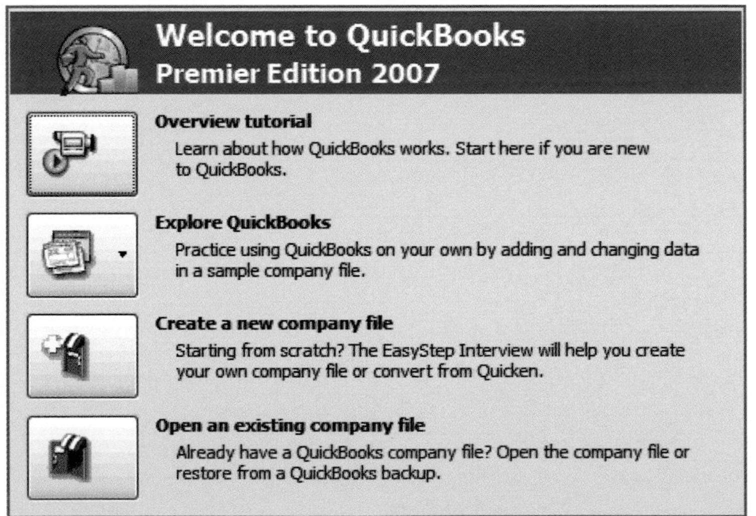

Figure 1-1: The QuickBooks 2007 Welcome screen presents you with four items to choose from.

If you have a QuickBooks company file from another computer or from a coworker, you can choose the option to open or restore an existing company file. If QuickBooks was installed for you and a company file was set up, QuickBooks will open that file by default (you may be prompted for a password).

> **NOTE**
>
> You can update your file to a newer version unless you need to share data with people who must use older versions of QuickBooks.

Open a Sample Company File

QuickBooks comes with a minimum of two sample (.qbw) files for you to explore and practice with before setting up your own files. You may have additional sample files, depending on your version of QuickBooks. Rock Castle Construction is a sample file for a product-based company. To open a sample company file:

1. Click the **Explore QuickBooks** button. A drop-down menu is displayed, listing the available sample company files.
2. Click **Sample Product-Based Business**. One of two dialog boxes appears, either notifying you that you are opening a sample file or prompting you to update this file to a newer version. If you are prompted to update, you will only have to do this once. See QuickSteps "Updating Older Company Files to Work with QuickBooks 2007" for more information.

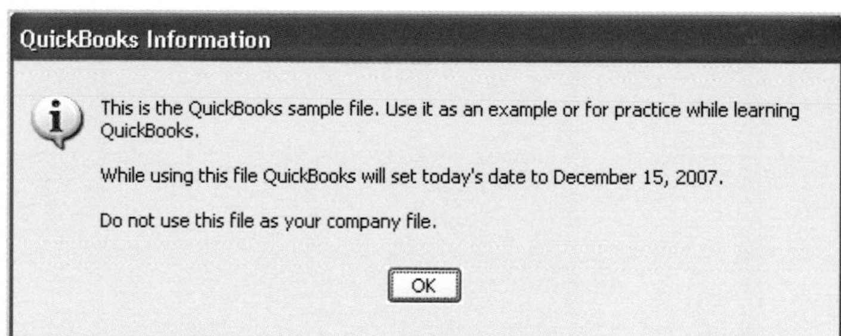

3. Click **OK** to acknowledge that this is a practice file. You will see either the registration screen or the QuickBooks Welcome screen with the QuickBooks Learning Center displayed, as shown in Figure 1-2. The QuickBooks Learning Center is available at any time on the Help menu.
4. Click **Begin Using QuickBooks**.

> **CAUTION**
>
> If the registration screen is displayed, you will have to register QuickBooks within thirty days. See QuickSteps "Registering QuickBooks" for more information on the registration process.

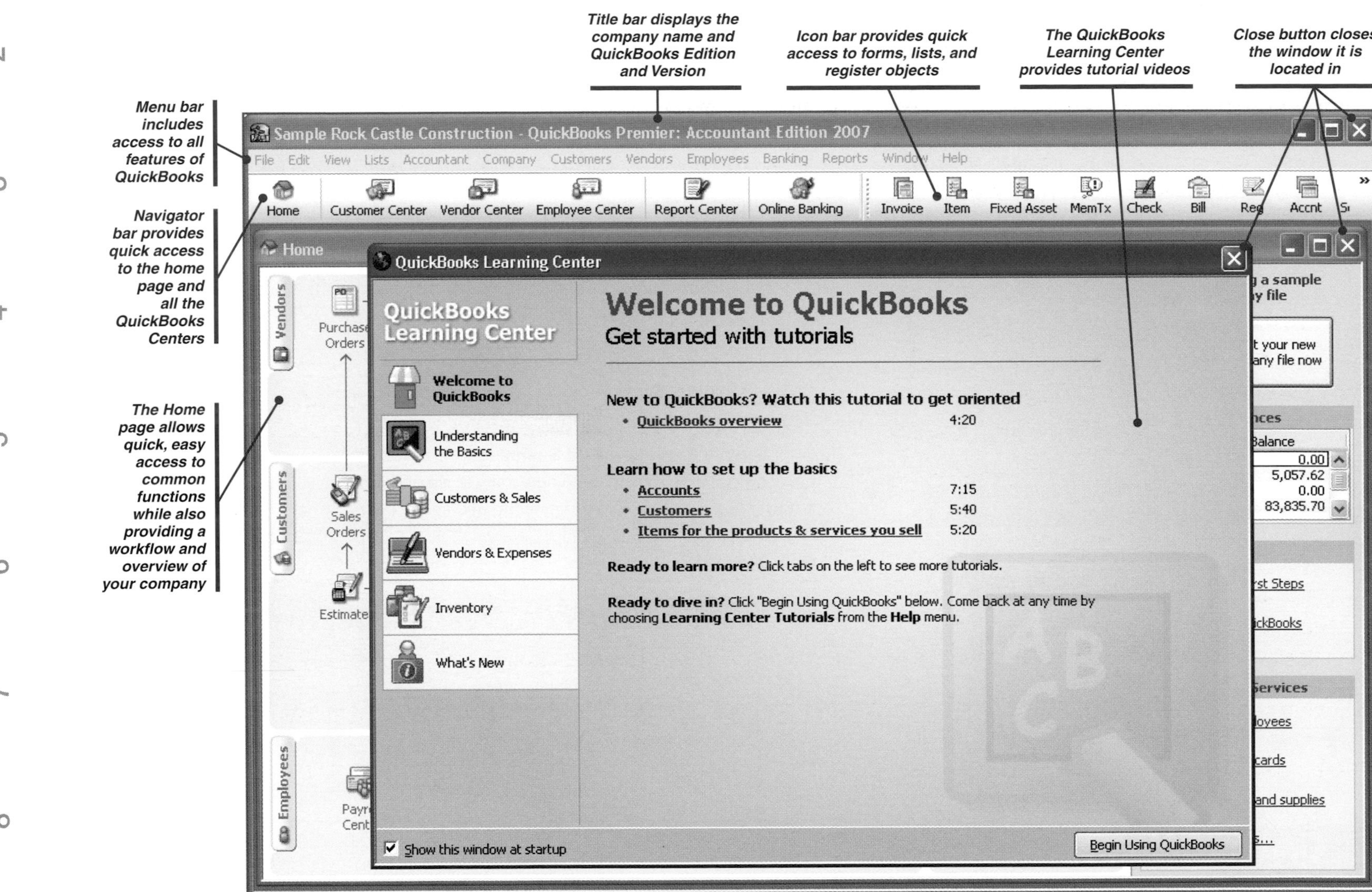

Figure 1-2: The QuickBooks Learning Center contains a collection of videos to help you learn how to use QuickBooks.

QUICKSTEPS

UPDATING OLDER COMPANY FILES TO WORK WITH QUICKBOOKS 2007

If you have an older QuickBooks company file, you can easily update it to work with the latest version of QuickBooks. The only reason you would *not* want to upgrade is if you have not yet upgraded all computers on which the file is used. QuickBooks is *not* backward-compatible; while any file can be upgraded, once you make entries in the current version, you cannot open that version using an older copy of QuickBooks. To update an older company file:

1. Open the company file you want to update.
2. If QuickBooks asks you to update your file to a newer version, type Yes in the white box, and click **OK**.
3. Click **OK** to back up the file. The QuickBooks Backup dialog box appears (see Figure 1-3). Review the filename and location, and change these items if necessary.
4. Click **OK**. A dialog box appears with information on backing up files to a local drive and prompting you to verify that you want to back up your data to your hard drive.
5. Click **Yes**. A dialog box appears, notifying you that once you update, you won't be able to access this file from older versions of QuickBooks. If multiple users are using this file, they cannot access it until they update their QuickBooks program. You are asked if you want to continue with the update process.
6. Click **Yes**. The backup and file update process takes place in less than two minutes for most files.

Tour the QuickBooks Window

When you first start QuickBooks, the home page and QuickBooks Learning Center windows are open (see Figure 1-2). The title bar displays the name of the currently open company file and the program—in this case, Sample Rock Castle Construction – QuickBooks Premier Edition 2007. Below the title bar are the menu bar and the icon bar.

The *menu bar* contains menus familiar to most Windows users, such as File, Edit, View, Window, and Help, and menus specific to QuickBooks, such as Lists, Company, Customers, Vendors, Employees, Banking, and Reports.

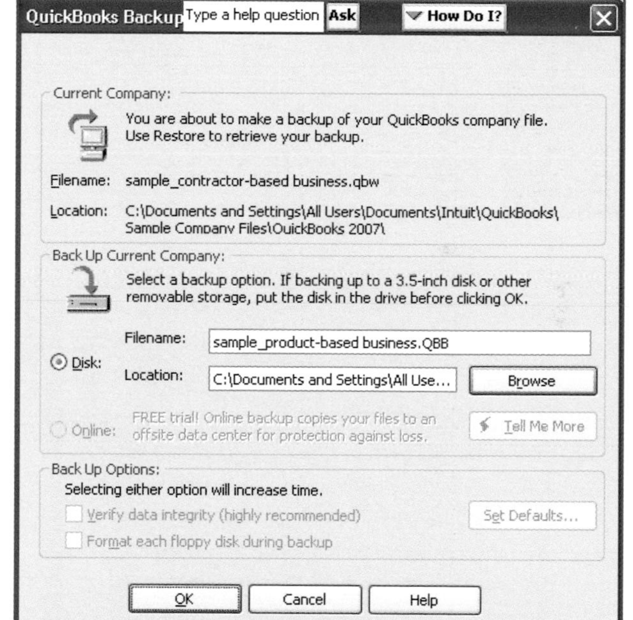
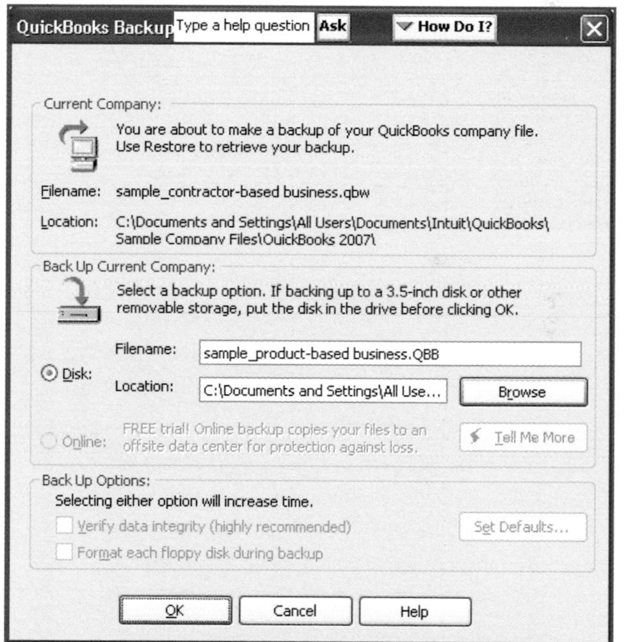

Figure 1-3: Back up files to your hard disk when upgrading. When backing up your data for security purposes, use a CD, thumb drive, or other removable media, and store them offsite to prevent data loss.

QUICKSTEPS

REGISTERING QUICKBOOKS

You are required to register QuickBooks within 30 days in order to continue to use the product. If you do not register within this time, you will not be able to proceed past the registration screen without registering. To register QuickBooks:

Register QuickBooks Premier: Accountant Edition 2007

You have 30 Day(s) remaining - please register now!

By registering, you become eligible for:

- Free callback support for 30 days from registration*
- Software Updates to QuickBooks

QuickBooks will go online to check your registration status

Learn more about QuickBooks registration.

*** 30 consecutive days of QuickBooks 2006 support included from first-time registration. Offer valid 90 days from software purchase; U.S. only. Callback support; Internet access required. Terms and conditions, features, pricing, and service availability subject to change at any time.**

Begin Registration > | Remind Me Later

1. Click **Begin Registration**. A screen appears with a series of registration questions. Providing this information is optional.
2. Click **Next**. A dialog box appears, notifying you that QuickBooks needs to start your web browser, which may be useful to see each time if you need to connect to a dial-up line. Select the **Do Not Display This Message In Future** check box if you don't want to see this message again.

Continued . . .

The *navigation bar* includes shortcuts to the integrated Customer Center, Vendor Center, Employee Center, and Report Center, as well as the home page and Online Banking.

The *icon bar* contains shortcuts to frequently used objects, such as forms, lists, registers, and reports. As you move your cursor over the icon bar, you will see yellow ToolTips for each button. This icon bar can be completely customized to streamline your business according to your company's needs.

The home page shows a flow of typical business tasks. You can access the most commonly used tasks by clicking the related icon.

You can use any of the following methods to accomplish a task in QuickBooks:

- Click the corresponding icon on the appropriate Center or home page.
- Click the corresponding menu and select the desired option.
- Click the corresponding button on the icon bar.
- Use a keyboard shortcut to quickly open a window.

Use the Home Page

The home page in QuickBooks 2007 (see Figure 1-4) shows a typical company structure, with tasks separated into logical groups and workflow arrows indicating the "typical" business flow. This page can be customized to your needs, and you can click any icon to open the related window for that task.

To return to the home page at any time, click the **Home** button on the Navigation bar.

QuickBooks Centers are intended to help you get a clear view of the major areas in QuickBooks, such as Customers, Vendors, Employees, Reports, and Learning. Click each of the Centers in the Navigation bar (or on the Help menu) to see the resources available to you.

QUICKSTEPS

REGISTERING QUICKBOOKS *(Continued)*

3. Click **OK** and wait for your computer to connect to the Internet. If you cannot connect to the Internet, you will be notified to call a toll-free number to register your product. If your computer connects successfully, you will see a registration page. Enter information in any field that has an asterisk.
4. Click **Next**. The Thank You page is displayed.
5. Click **Next**. A page appears with advertisements for other Intuit products.
6. Click **Finish Registration** and then click **Yes** in response to the dialog box that appears, notifying you that the web page you are viewing is trying to close this window. Your registration is now complete.

CAUTION

Clicking the uppermost X in the QuickBooks title bar will close the program. If you click this by accident, simply open QuickBooks again. The last company file you used is automatically opened.

TIP

You can easily add and remove icons to customize the icon bar for your business needs.

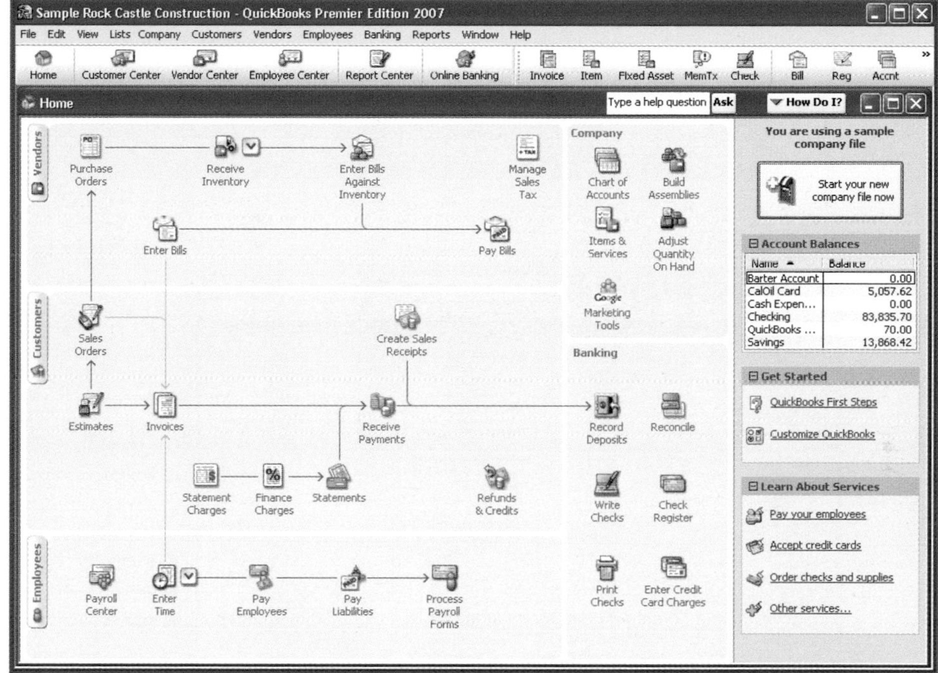

***Figure 1-4:** The home page shows a summary of your business and common company-related actions you can perform.*

Use the Icon Bar

QuickBooks is easy to use because there is a consistent interface among forms, lists, and registers. Once you learn to navigate in one of these types of objects, you'll be able to transfer your skills to similar objects:

- Examples of forms: Checks, Deposits, and Receive Payments
- Examples of lists: Chart of Accounts, Item List, and Reminders List
- Examples of registers: Checking Account, Accounts Receivable, and Accounts Payable
- Examples of centers: Customer Center, Vendor Center, and Employee Center

To open any of these objects, simply click the one you want on the icon bar, such as the Item List, shown in Figure 1-5, or click the corresponding menu and click the desired option.

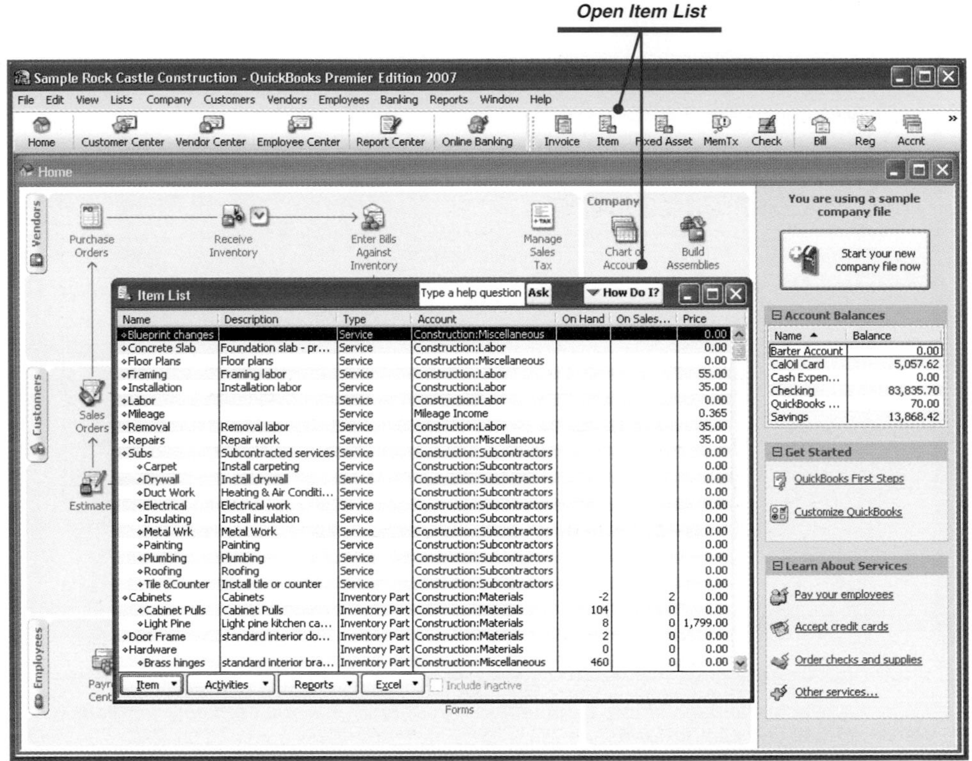

Figure 1-5: Item List shows the standard information for items your company sells.

The Item List contains all the items you can use on Invoices and other sales forms, including Service, Discount, Payment, Subtotal, Sales Tax, Group, Inventory and Non-Inventory. It will be covered in Chapters 3, 6, and 7.

Explore the Menu Bar

QuickBooks has menus similar to most Windows programs, for example, File, Edit, and Help. If you are new to QuickBooks, focus on those aspects that are similar to Windows programs, such as how to open and close a program and get help, and then focus on what you need to know for your business, such as daily data entry and report generation. Don't worry or get overwhelmed by features you don't yet know. You can add skills as you need them.

Click **File** and move your cursor along the menu bar to view each menu. An arrow indicates that a submenu is available. Move your mouse over that menu topic to see the next menu level, as shown in Figure 1-6.

Customize QuickBooks

You have many ways to customize QuickBooks to meet your needs. You can customize the desktop, Icon bar, and Open Window List; turn features on and off; and edit invoice, statement, and estimate templates. This chapter will cover customizing the desktop and Icon bar.

TIP

Use keyboard shortcuts listed on menus to quickly open a window. To the right of many menu items are the corresponding shortcuts, such as Chart of Accounts **CTRL+A**, which indicates you should hold down the **CTRL** key while pressing A to quickly open this window.

TIP

If you are sharing a file on a network, be sure to map your network drive for the most stable environment (see Chapter 8 for more information). If you are in a multiuser environment, select the Open File In Multi-User Mode check box in the Open A Company dialog box.

NOTE

The Set Number Of Previous Companies option is available only when a company is open.

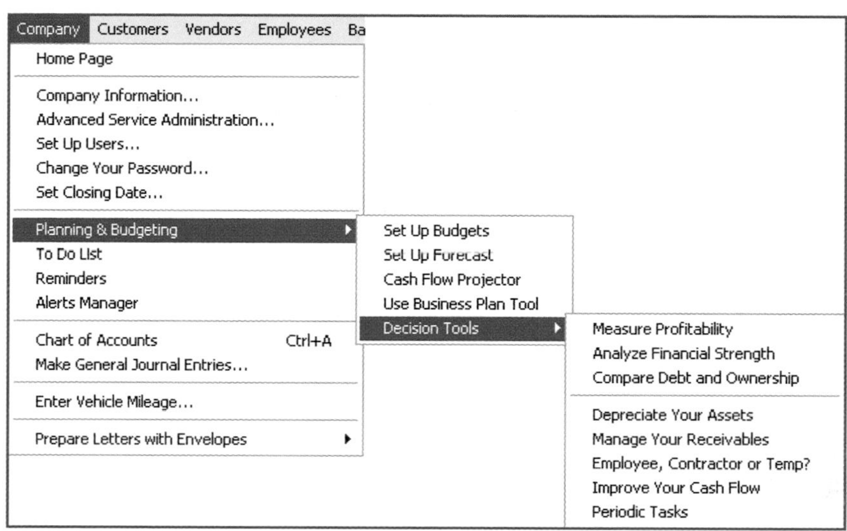

Figure 1-6: The arrows indicate that a submenu is available for a menu item.

Use the View Menu to Customize Your Desktop

The View menu contains a number of options to customize your QuickBooks company file, including a number of toggle items. A *toggle item* is an object that can be clicked once to turn it on. Clicking the item again turns it off. A check mark or dot next to a toggle item indicates that it is turned on.

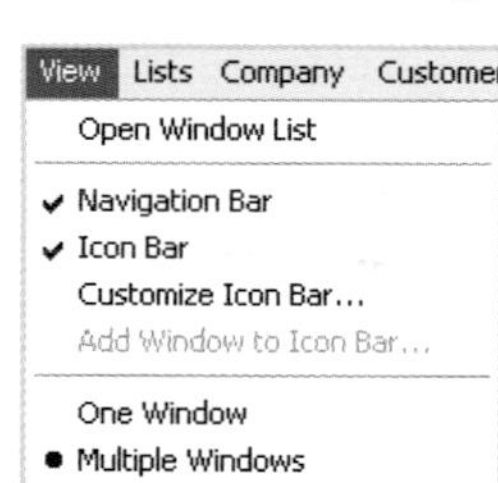

TOGGLE THE OPEN WINDOW LIST ON AND OFF

Click the **View** menu, and then click **Open Window List** to toggle the Open Window List on (off is the default). The Open Window List appears on the left side of the screen. Repeat this step to turn it off.

TOGGLE THE NAVIGATION BAR ON AND OFF

Click the **View** menu, and then click **Navigation Bar** to toggle the Icon bar off (on is the default). Repeat this step to turn it back on.

QUICKSTEPS

OPENING OTHER COMPANY FILES (.QBW)

You can open a different company file at any time. You may have multiple companies or simply want to practice something in the sample file before trying it in your real file. When you open a new company file, the currently open company file automatically closes. Two methods exist by which you can open a company file.

USE A DIALOG BOX TO OPEN A COMPANY FILE

1. Click the **File** menu and click **Open Company**. The Open Company: Type dialog box will appear with Open A Company File (.QBW) selected by default

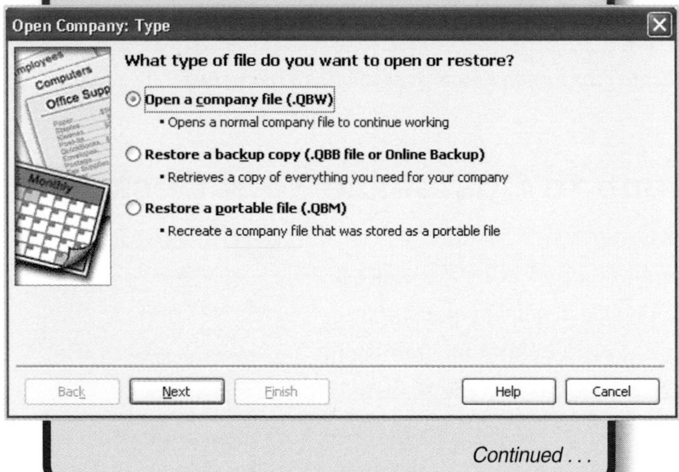
Open Company: Type
What type of file do you want to open or restore?
Open a company file (.QBW)
• Opens a normal company file to continue working
Restore a backup copy (.QBB file or Online Backup)
• Retrieves a copy of everything you need for your company
Restore a portable file (.QBM)
• Recreate a company file that was stored as a portable file
Back
Next
Finish
Help
Cancel

Continued . . .

NOTE

Each time you open a window, it will open to the same size you previously set it to.

TOGGLE THE ICON BAR ON AND OFF

Click the **View** menu, and then click **Icon Bar** to toggle the Icon bar off (on is the default). Repeat this step to turn it back on.

VIEW ONE WINDOW OR MULTIPLE WINDOWS

By default, QuickBooks displays multiple open windows at the same time. If you only want one window displayed at a time, click the **View** menu, and click **One Window**. In this mode, you can't resize or move the window. Each new window you open fills the screen; to switch between windows, click the **Window** menu and click any of the open windows listed.

You can return to having multiple windows displayed at once by clicking the **View** menu again and clicking **Multiple Windows**. In this mode, windows in QuickBooks can be maximized, minimized, or closed using the standard Windows symbols in the upper-right corner. Resize a window by moving your mouse pointer to the edge of a window until the mouse pointer changes to a double-headed arrow, and then clicking and dragging the window where you want it. Move a window by clicking and dragging its title bar.

USE THE WINDOW MENU

When multiple windows are open, you can switch from one window to another by clicking the **Window** menu and choosing the desired window from the list. A check mark next to a window name indicates that this is the currently active window. Close any window by clicking the X in the upper-right corner of the window. You also have the following choices available on the Windows menu bar.

- Click the **Window** menu and click **Cascade**, **Tile Vertically**, or **Tile Horizontally** to change how multiple windows are displayed.
- Click the **Window** menu and click **Arrange Icons** if you have all your windows minimized to group the minimized window icons. You won't see anything happen if windows are not already minimized.
- Click the **Window** menu and then click **Close All** to close all open windows.

Window
Help
Arrange Icons
Close All
Tile Vertically
Tile Horizontally
Cascade
1 Item List
2 Home

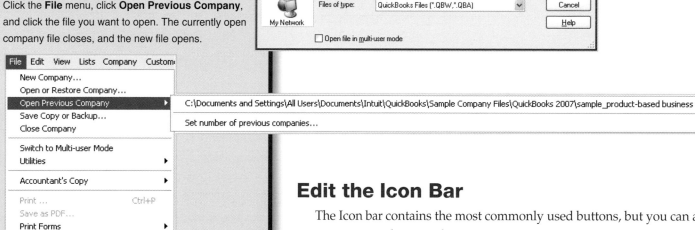

QUICKSTEPS

OPENING OTHER COMPANY FILES (.QBW) *(Continued)*

2. Click **Next**. The currently open company file will close and the Open A Company dialog box will appear.
3. Click the **Look In** list down arrow, or click any of the buttons on the left (for example, **My Recent Documents**) and browse to the company file you want.
4. When you have located the file you want to open, double-click the file to open it.

USE OPEN PREVIOUS COMPANY TO OPEN A COMPANY FILE

Click the **File** menu, click **Open Previous Company**, and click the file you want to open. The currently open company file closes, and the new file opens.

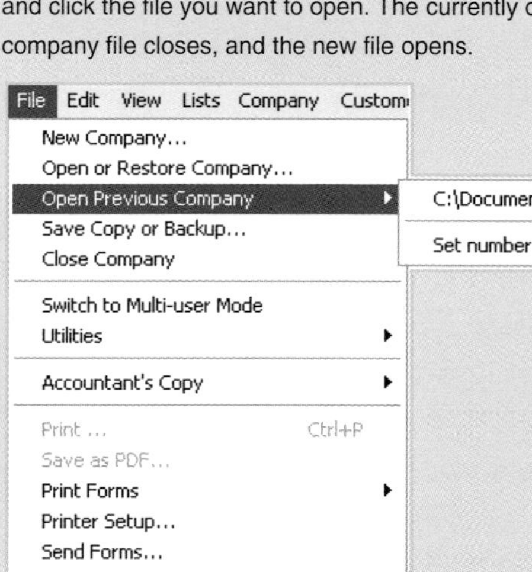

To set the number of previously open company files displayed in the list, click the **File** menu, click **Open Previous Company**, and click **Set Number Of Previous Companies**. Enter a number from 1 to 20.

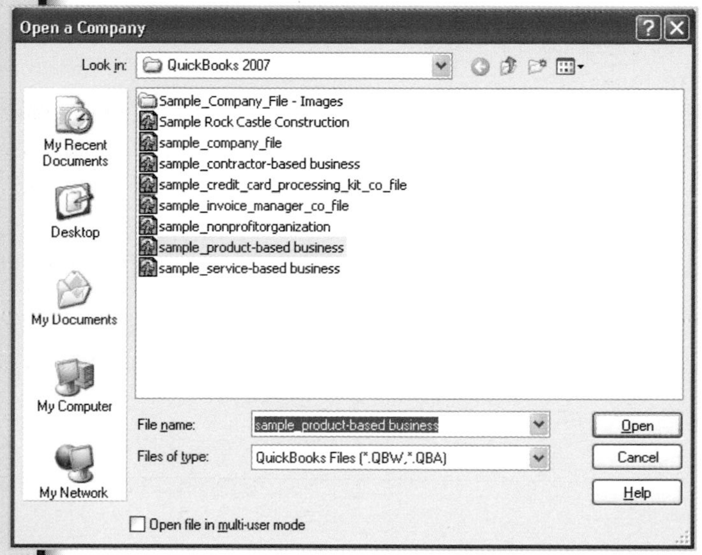

Edit the Icon Bar

The Icon bar contains the most commonly used buttons, but you can add, delete, rearrange, and rename buttons to customize the Icon bar to meet your company's specific needs. While most daily work flow is now located on the Home page, there are some additional items you may like to have on your icon bar, such as the Calculator, Fixed Asset List, Memorized Transactions, or custom reports.

> **NOTE**
>
> The Add "Window" to Icon Bar text will change to reflect whichever window is currently active.

ADD A WINDOW TO THE ICON BAR

Almost any open window can be added to the Icon bar at any time.

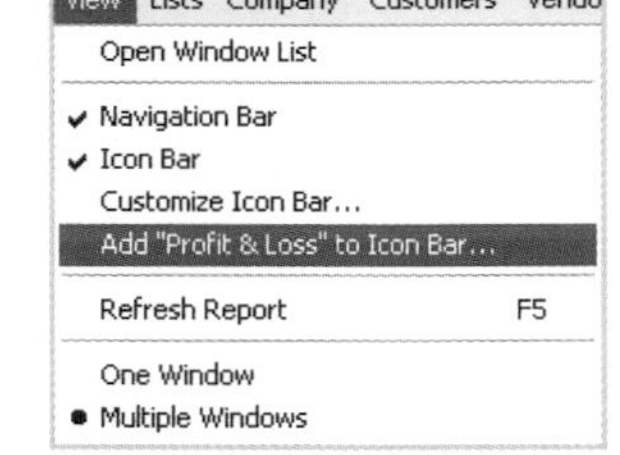

1. On the Menu bar, click the **Reports** menu, click **Company & Financial**, and click **Profit & Loss Standard**. The Profit & Loss Report will open.
2. Click the **View** menu and click **Add "Profit & Loss" To Icon Bar**. The Add Window To Icon Bar dialog box appears.
3. Scroll through the list on the left, and click the image you want to represent the new icon.
4. Edit the **Label** and **Description** fields, if necessary. The label is what you will see on the Icon bar. The description is what pops up in a ToolTip when you hover your mouse over the icon.
5. Click **OK** when finished. The new icon is added to the right end of the Icon bar.
6. Close the **Profit & Loss Report** window.

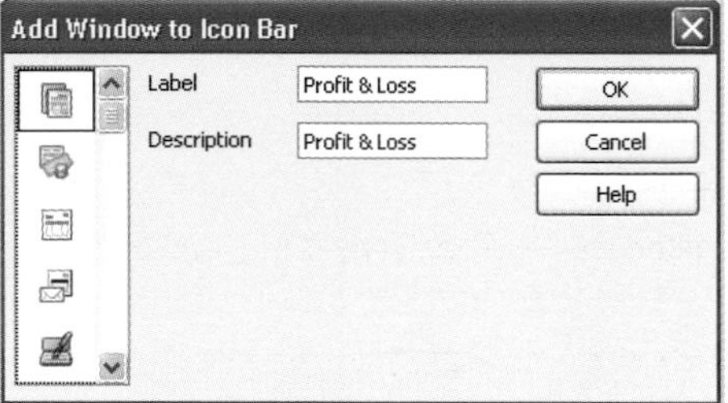

Delete, Edit, and Rearrange Icons

After you have used QuickBooks for a while and become familiar with it, you may find that you need to delete, edit, or rearrange icons to better reflect the tasks you perform.

Delete an Icon

To delete an icon from the Icon bar (in this case, the Register icon):

1. Click the **View** menu and click **Customize Icon Bar**. The Customize Icon Bar dialog box appears.
2. In the Icon Bar Content pane on the left, click **Reg**.
3. Click the **Delete** button on the right. The Register icon is immediately deleted from view.
4. Click the **OK** button to save your changes, or click **Cancel** to return the icon to the Icon bar.

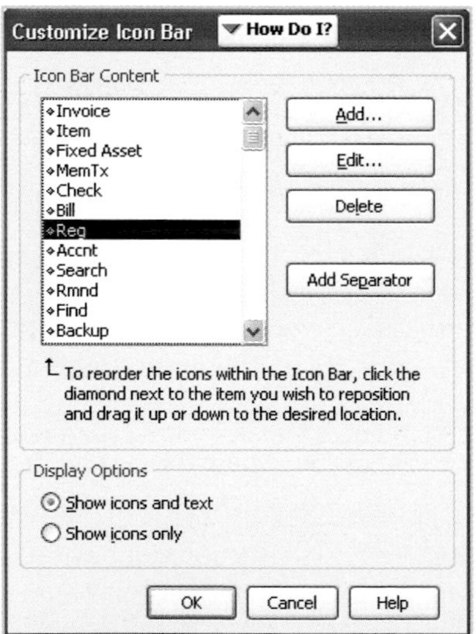

> **TIP**
>
> In the Customize Icon Bar window, click the **Show Icons And Text** option or the **Show Icons Only** option, and you will immediately see the change.

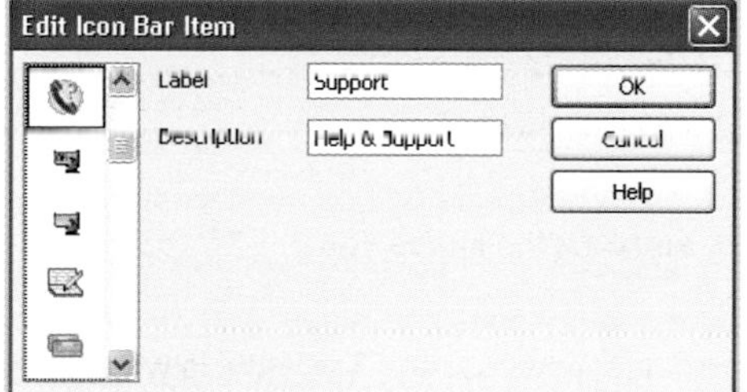

> **TIP**
>
> Consider adding budget, cash flow, and other tools to your Icon bar to help in daily business management.

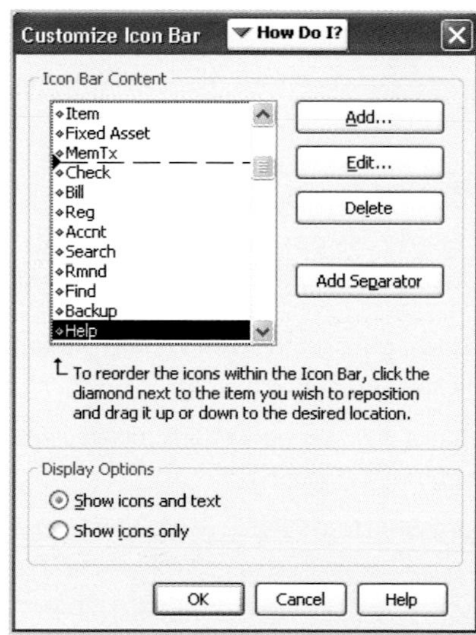

Edit an Icon

To edit an icon (in this case, the Support icon):

1. Click the **View** menu and click **Customize Icon Bar**. The Customize Icon Bar dialog box appears.
2. In the Icon Bar Content pane on the left, click **Support**.
3. Click the **Edit** button on the right. The Edit Icon Bar Item dialog box appears.
4. Scroll through the list on the left, and click the new image you want to represent the icon.
5. Click in the **Label** field.
6. Delete the word "Support," and type Help.
7. Edit the **Description** field, if desired.
8. Click **OK** when finished. The edited icon is displayed on the Icon bar.

Rearrange the Order of Icons

To rearrange the order in which icons appear on the Icon bar:

1. Click the **View** menu and click **Customize Icon Bar**. The Customize Icon Bar dialog box appears.
2. Click the diamond to the left of the icon you want to move, and drag up or down to the new location for the icon. A dashed line and arrow indicate where the icon will be placed.
3. Release the mouse button, and the icon is now present in its new place.
4. Click **OK** when finished.

Add a Separator Between Icon Buttons

To group your icons into meaningful sections, you can add separators between any two icons.

1. Click the **View** menu and click **Customize Icon Bar**. The Customize Icon Bar dialog box appears.
2. In the Icon Bar Content pane on the left, click the icon to which you would like to add a space.
3. Click the **Add Separator** button. A space (and a line) is created below (and to the right of) the selected icon.

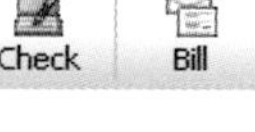

4. Click **OK** when finished.

TIP

Not all items are listed in the Add Icon Bar Item list, which is why you can also add icons using the procedure described in the section "Add an Icon to the Icon Bar."

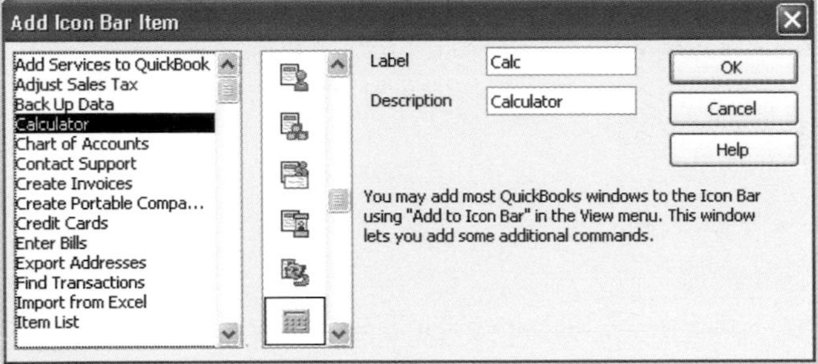

Add an Icon to the Icon Bar

You can add icons to the Icon bar beyond the standard ones already included in the Customize Icon Bar window. To add an icon to the Icon bar:

1. Click the **View** menu and click **Customize Icon Bar**. The Customize Icon Bar dialog box appears.
2. In the Icon Bar Content pane on the left, click the icon above (and to the left of) where you would like the new icon to be added.
3. Click the **Add** button. The Add Icon Bar Item dialog box appears.
4. Scroll through the list on the left, and click the task for which you want to make an icon. QuickBooks will recommend a suggested icon, label, and description. If you don't want to use QuickBooks's recommendation, select a different icon, and edit the Label and Description fields.
5. Click **OK** when finished. The new icon is added to the Icon bar.

Find Help Within QuickBooks

Help is available in three places within QuickBooks:

- Type a question in the **Type A Help Question** field, and click the **Ask** button.
- Click the **How Do I?** drop-down menu to find the relevant topic.
- Click the **Help** menu located on the Menu bar.

CAUTION

Many Help topics will take you online for the latest information. If you have a dial-up connection, you may need to connect to the Internet before accessing some Help topics.

Ask a Help Question

All windows in QuickBooks include "Type a help question" text box in their title bar. Enter keywords in this box to quickly search the help files.

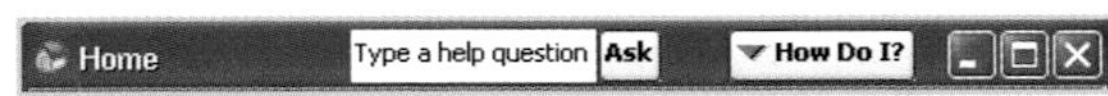

1. On the home page (or any window), click in the **Type A Help Question** text box, and type keyboard shortcuts (or any key phrase).
2. Click the **Ask** button. A QuickBooks Help window opens, displaying the Help topics that relate to your question, as shown in Figure 1-7.
3. Click the **QuickBooks Keyboard Shortcuts** topic. Detailed information is displayed in the pane on the right.
4. Review the Help information and close the window when finished.

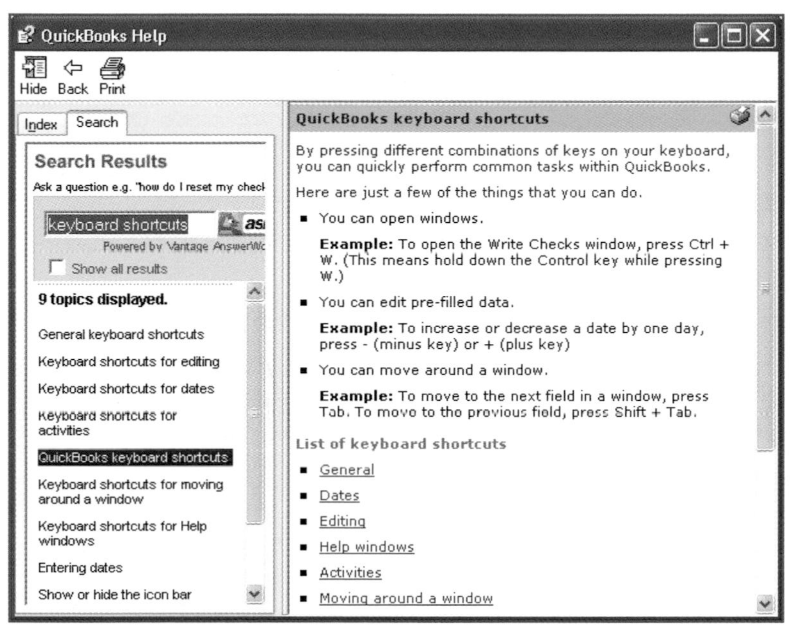

***Figure 1-7:* QuickBooks Help can quickly provide you with answers to your questions.**

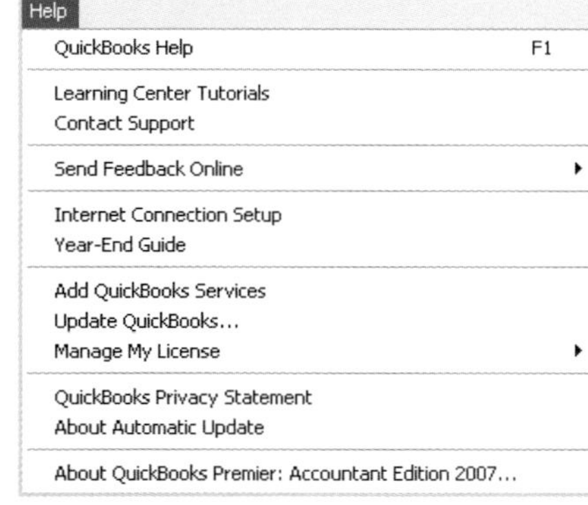

TIP

Click the **How Do I?** down arrow whenever you first use a new section of QuickBooks to learn what you can do in that area.

Use the How Do I? Drop-Down Menu

The How Do I? drop-down menu contains helpful information pertaining only to the currently active window—in this case, the home page.

1. Click the **How Do I?** down arrow, and click **Customize The Home Page For My Business**. A window similar to the QuickBooks Help window shown in Figure 1-7 opens, displaying instructions on how to customize your home page.

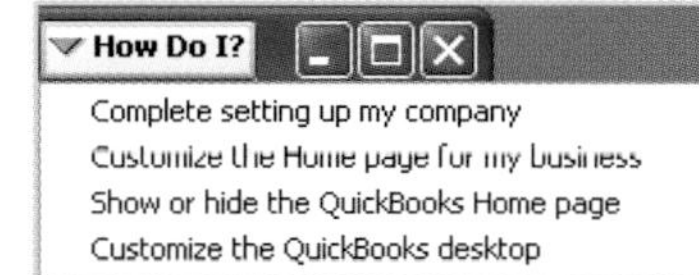

2. Review the Help information and close the window when finished.

Use the Help Menu

The Help menu—which is located on the Menu bar—provides you with a variety of ways to access additional help when using QuickBooks. Click the **Help** menu and then click one of the following options:

- Click **QuickBooks Help** to access the general Help files. These are the same files accessed when using the Type A Help Question text box and the How Do I? drop-down menu.
- Click **Learning Center Tutorials** to access a collection of tutorial videos, such as "Welcome to QuickBooks," "Understanding the Basics," "Customers and Sales," and "What's New."
- Click **Contact Support** for online reference and links to support options.
- Click **Send Feedback Online** to communicate with Intuit about product suggestions or problems.
- Click **Internet Connection Setup** to change your Internet settings.
- Click **New Business Checklist** for online reference and links to new business advice.
- Click **Year-End Guide** to see a list of typical end-of-year activities for most businesses.

TIP

Press the **F1** key to access the Help system from anywhere in QuickBooks.

- Click **Add QuickBooks Services** to activate options such as accepting credit cards.
- Click **Register QuickBooks** if you wish to register your software before being reminded.
- Click **Update QuickBooks** if you wish to manually download an update. QuickBooks has an automatic update activated by default.
- Click **Manage My License** to synchronize your information with Intuit's.
- Click **QuickBooks Privacy Statement** for information pertaining to your QuickBooks information safety.
- Click **About Automatic Update** for information pertaining to your QuickBooks update process and keeping up to date.
- Click **About QuickBooks Premier Edition 2007** for information pertaining to your QuickBooks installation, such as license and product number.

Use Keyboard Shortcuts

Since QuickBooks is an accounting program, it involves a lot of data entry using the keyboard. *Keyboard shortcuts*—combinations of keystrokes that can be used to perform tasks that would otherwise require the use of the mouse—will save you time in the long run. Some shortcuts are easy and intuitive, while others require regular use before being committed to memory. Table 1-2 lists the most common data-entry keyboard shortcuts used in QuickBooks.

CAUTION

When you press **CTRL+DEL** to delete the current line, you will not see a dialog box confirming this action, nor can you undo this action. If you accidentally press **CTRL+DEL**, you will need to retype whatever you deleted.

KEYBOARD SHORTCUT	ACTION PERFORMED
TAB	Move through fields in a form
SHIFT+TAB	Move backwards through fields in a form
CTRL+INS	Insert a new line (for example, in an invoice)
CTRL+DEL	Delete the current line

Table 1-2: Data Entry Keyboard Shortcuts

Table 1-3 lists the most common keyboard shortcuts used to perform general commands in QuickBooks.

Table 1-4 lists the most common keyboard shortcuts used when working with lists in QuickBooks.

You can also use keyboard shortcuts to access menus. Just as with most Windows programs, the menu items in QuickBooks give an easy clue as to their keyboard shortcuts. Press **ALT** and look for the underlined letter in each menu item name. While holding down the **ALT** key, press the key corresponding to that letter, and you can open any menu you want. Table 1-5 lists the most common keyboard shortcuts used in QuickBooks to access menus.

File Edit View Lists Company Customers Vendors Employees Banking Reports Window Help

KEYBOARD SHORTCUT	ACTION PERFORMED
ALT+F4	Exit QuickBooks
F1	Open a Help window
F2	Show QuickBooks software product information
CTRL+I	Open a Create Invoice form
CTRL+W	Open a Write Checks form
CTRL+D	Delete the current transaction (invoice, check, and so on)
CTRL+F	Open a context-sensitive Find window
CTRL+A	Open the Chart of Accounts
CTRL+J	Open the Customer Center
CTRL+M	Memorize the current transaction or report
CTRL+P	Open a Print window
CTRL+T	Open the Memorized Transactions List
ESC	Close the currently open window

Table 1-3: General Keyboard Shortcuts

CAUTION

Always confirm that your entries have the correct date. QuickBooks default is to use today's date when you first open your file, but if you change your date to enter old transactions, that date becomes the new default until the file is closed or until the date is changed, even if you switch to other windows. This default can be changed under General preferences.

KEYBOARD SHORTCUT	ACTION PERFORMED
CTRL+N	Open an Enter New Item window
CTRL+E	Edit a list item
CTRL+D	Delete the current item
CTRL+Q	View a QuickReport of a current item

Table 1-4: Keyboard Shortcuts for Lists

QuickBooks also gives you the ability to use shortcuts when entering dates, which can be useful when entering lists of past transactions. Table 1-6 lists the most common keyboard shortcuts used in QuickBooks for entering dates.

Exit QuickBooks

It's a good idea to exit QuickBooks every night to protect your company file from corruption should a power failure occur and to prevent others from viewing or changing your data.

Close the Company File

When you exit QuickBooks, the company file automatically closes. The next time you open QuickBooks, the same company file will open. For most users, this is convenient and preferred. If you have multiple companies, however, you might not want a company file to open by default. In this case, close the company file before exiting QuickBooks.

- Click the **File menu** and click **Close Company**. The No Company Open screen will be displayed. You can then open a different file or exit QuickBooks.

How to Exit QuickBooks

To exit QuickBooks, click the **Close** button (the X in the upper-right corner) in the QuickBooks window, or click the **File** menu and click **Exit** or press **ALT+F4**. QuickBooks saves all of your transactions as you make them, so you don't need to worry about saving information before you exit. If you

KEYBOARD SHORTCUT	CORRESPONDING MENU
ALT+F	File
ALT+E	Edit
ALT+V	View
ALT+L	Lists
ALT+C	Company
ALT+U	Customers
ALT+O	Vendors
ALT+Y	Employees
ALT+B	Banking
ALT+R	Reports
ALT+W	Window
ALT+H	Help

Table 1-5: Keyboard Shortcuts for Menus

have an incomplete transaction, you will see a dialog box notifying you of such and prompting you to record the transaction. If you click **Yes**, QuickBooks will save the current transaction and close. If you click **No**, QuickBooks will not save the transaction but will close. If you click **Cancel**, QuickBooks will not close but will display the transaction in question.

KEYBOARD SHORTCUT	DATE ENTERED
T	Today's date.
+	The next day's date. The date will continue to increase by one day each time this key is pressed.
–	The previous day's date. The date will continue to decrease by one day each time this key is pressed.
W	The date of the first day of the currently displayed week. This will be Sunday's date unless you have changed your preferences. The date will change to that of the previous Sunday each time this key is pressed. See Chapter 8 for more information on changing your preferences.
K	The date of the last day of the currently displayed week. This will be Saturday's date unless you have changed your preferences. The date will change to that of the next Saturday each time this key is pressed. See Chapter 8 for more information on changing your preferences.
M	The date of the first day of the currently displayed month. The date will change to that of the first day of the previous month each time this key is pressed.
H	The date of the last day of the currently displayed month. The date will change to that of the last day of the next month each time this key is pressed.
Y	The date of the first day of the currently displayed year. The date will change to that of the first day of the previous year each time this key is pressed.
R	The date of the last day of the currently displayed year. The date will change to that of the last day of the next year each time this key is pressed.

Table 1-6: Keyboard Shortcuts for Date Fields

How to...

- *Use an Existing Company File*
- *Migrate to QuickBooks*
- *Convert to QuickBooks*
- *Gather Information and Choose a Start Date*
- *Gathering Data for a New Company File*
- *Understand the EasyStep Interview*
- *Create your QuickBooks Company File*
- *Customize QuickBooks for Your Business*
- *Receiving Payments*
- *Using Accrual- vs. Cash-Based Accounting*
- *Review Income and Expense Accounts (Chart of Accounts)*
- *Review the QuickBooks Learning Center*
- *Set Up Multiple Users*

Chapter 2
Creating a Company File

If you already have a company file set up, this chapter will help you review and fine-tune it further. If you are new to QuickBooks, this chapter will show you how to use the EasyStep Interview to set up your company and follow up with manual adjustments. Later chapters will cover how to customize additional settings.

Use a Company File

You have four options regarding company files in QuickBooks:

- You can use an existing file, if one exists, including a file from an older version of QuickBooks.
- You can migrate manually from another accounting system to QuickBooks.
- You can convert a PeachTree or Quicken file to QuickBooks.
- You can create a new company file.

TIP

If there are multiple users of QuickBooks in your company, you may see a dialog box warning you that the file you want to open is already open on another system. If this happens, you need to ask that person to click the File menu and click Switch To Multi-User so that you can also open the file.

CAUTION

Make sure that all QuickBooks users in your company have the latest version installed before you update a company file.

CAUTION

If you are converting to QuickBooks from another accounting system, make sure to choose your start date carefully and match your balance sheets between systems. You may want to have an accountant or bookkeeper help you with the transfer and/or reconciliation of accounts.

Use an Existing Company File

If your company is already using QuickBooks, open the existing company file as shown in Chapter 1. If the existing company file was created using the same version of QuickBooks, it will open.

If the company file you are attempting to open was created using an earlier version of QuickBooks, the program will automatically update your file to the current version, but it will ask you to make a backup and confirm that all users have the same QuickBooks version. See Chapter 1 for update instructions.

Migrate to QuickBooks

When migrating to QuickBooks from an accounting system other than PeachTree or Quicken, you will need to manually enter the information from the old system. You may follow the steps in the next section to do this, but make sure you have gathered the following information from your old system first:

- Balance sheet
- Customer list with balances owed
- Vendor list with balances owed
- Employee list with all payroll information
- Reconciled statements for all bank and credit card accounts with statement dates on or just before the start date.
- Most current tax returns, including:
  - Federal
  - State
  - Payroll
- Current inventory list with costs and quantities

How much information you enter into QuickBooks is up to you. If your old system is less than a year old, you should enter all information in QuickBooks so that your entire business history is available for reports. If you've used an alternative accounting system for 15 or more years, find a logical point in time

CAUTION

If you have been using Quicken for home and business accounts, you can migrate your accounts to QuickBooks, but EasyPayroll will not work and you will lose the ability to track stock-related items other than in a general way. QuickBooks does not update stock prices or track shares. Your Quicken data will still be accessible after converting to QuickBooks.

CAUTION

If you are converting from Peachtree Data, you will need to go online to download the conversion tool, so make sure you are connected to the Internet.

NOTE

The start date you pick for QuickBooks does not have to be the start of your fiscal year or calendar year. If your company has been in business for a while, you already have year-end and year-start dates, which are not easy to change. So, unless you are near those dates, pick another start date for QuickBooks.

NOTE

The start date is key to all balances in the EasyStep Interview. For example, if you have a checking account with $4,000 in it but it was opened after the starting date, then in the EasyStep Interview, the opening balance would be zero. You will add transactions later.

from which all data will be entered in the new QuickBooks system. You can refer to the old system if historical data is needed prior to that point.

Convert to QuickBooks

QuickBooks has the capability to convert data from PeachTree or Quicken. To convert from either, you will see the choices under the section "Create Your QuickBooks Company File" in this chapter. Be sure to click **View Help** when offered in those windows to understand the conversion before proceeding.

Create a New Company File

The rest of this book will use the sample company Butterfly Books and Bytes to demonstrate procedures. Concerns for other businesses will be pointed out using Tips and Notes.

Butterfly Books and Bytes is a retail shop selling computer-related books, coffee, and snacks. Inventory will need to be maintained, and ISBN numbers will be used to identify the books; coffee, coffee supplies, and snack items will be identified by descriptions or vendor IDs.

Four employees run the shop, and the owner has a single business checking account. The shop was started with $50,000: $20,000 from a capital investment and $30,000 from a private loan.

Gather Information and Choose a Start Date

It's important to choose an appropriate start date when setting up a new company file. If you are starting a new company with no current accounting system in place, use the first day of your fiscal year in the year you start your business. If you have no reason to choose a different date, use the calendar year (January 1–December 31) as your fiscal year. It will make your tax returns and other paperwork easier to do.

GATHERING DATA FOR A NEW COMPANY FILE

Before creating a new company file, gather as much of the following information as you can.

- Company name, address, phone number, fax number, and e-mail and web addresses
- Company EIN (employer identification number), fiscal year, tax structure/income tax form, and type of business
- Number of QuickBooks users and their names
- Employee names (see Chapter 9 for payroll)
- All bank statements for account numbers, types, entries, and balances back to your start date
- Balance sheet from current accounting system (if existing)
- List of customer names and balances owed as of the company start date (this will be zero if your start date is also the actual start date of your company)
- List of vendor names and balances due as of the company start date (this will be zero if your start date is also the actual start date of your company)
- List of credit cards, lines of credit, loans, notes, and other debts and amounts owed as of the company start date (this will be zero if your start date is also the actual start date of your company)
- List of assets and their value as of the company start date
- All transactions made since your start date
- Sales tax number, rate, and agencies' names
- List of items you sell, including services, inventory, and non-inventory items
- Whether your company will report on a cash or accrual basis

If you are migrating to QuickBooks from another system, choose an easy-to-remember date, such as the beginning of a quarter: January 1, April 1, July 1, or October 1. Once you've set up your new file, you can run identical reports from each system to make sure everything is set up correctly.

Butterfly Books and Bytes opened its doors on April 1, 2007, but business transactions started before that, so the QuickBooks start date will be January 1, 2007, so that the business's financial reporting dates will line up with the traditional calendar year. The farther back your start date is, the more historical information you will have to enter; however, this will give you more accurate reporting and control in the long run.

Understand the EasyStep Interview

The EasyStep Interview process listed next steps you through entering your company's information and answering questions about what you will do in your company. Based on the information that you enter in the following sections, QuickBooks will create a file set with your preferences:

- **Get Started** After reviewing information regarding other options such as conversion or quick entry, QuickBooks EasyStep Interview walks you through entering your Company Information, selecting your Administrator Password, and creating and saving your Company File.
- **Customizing QuickBooks for Your Business** This section asks you questions regarding your company, including selecting your industry, the products you sell, how you sell them, how you track orders, your accounting practices, and whether you have employees.
- **Using Accounts in QuickBooks** This section creates and allows you to review your Chart of Accounts based on the industry you chose and then asks you for your Start Date and allows you to enter your Bank Account Information.

After completing those sections and clicking Finish, QuickBooks EasyStep Interview will congratulate you and display your new company file and the Learning Center.

Create Your QuickBooks Company File

1. Open QuickBooks.
2. Click the **File** menu and click **New Company**. If a company file is currently open, QuickBooks closes it and the EasyStep Interview starts. If no company file is open, you may click the **Create A New Company** button as seen in Figure 2-1. The EasyStep Interview starts, as shown in Figure 2-2.

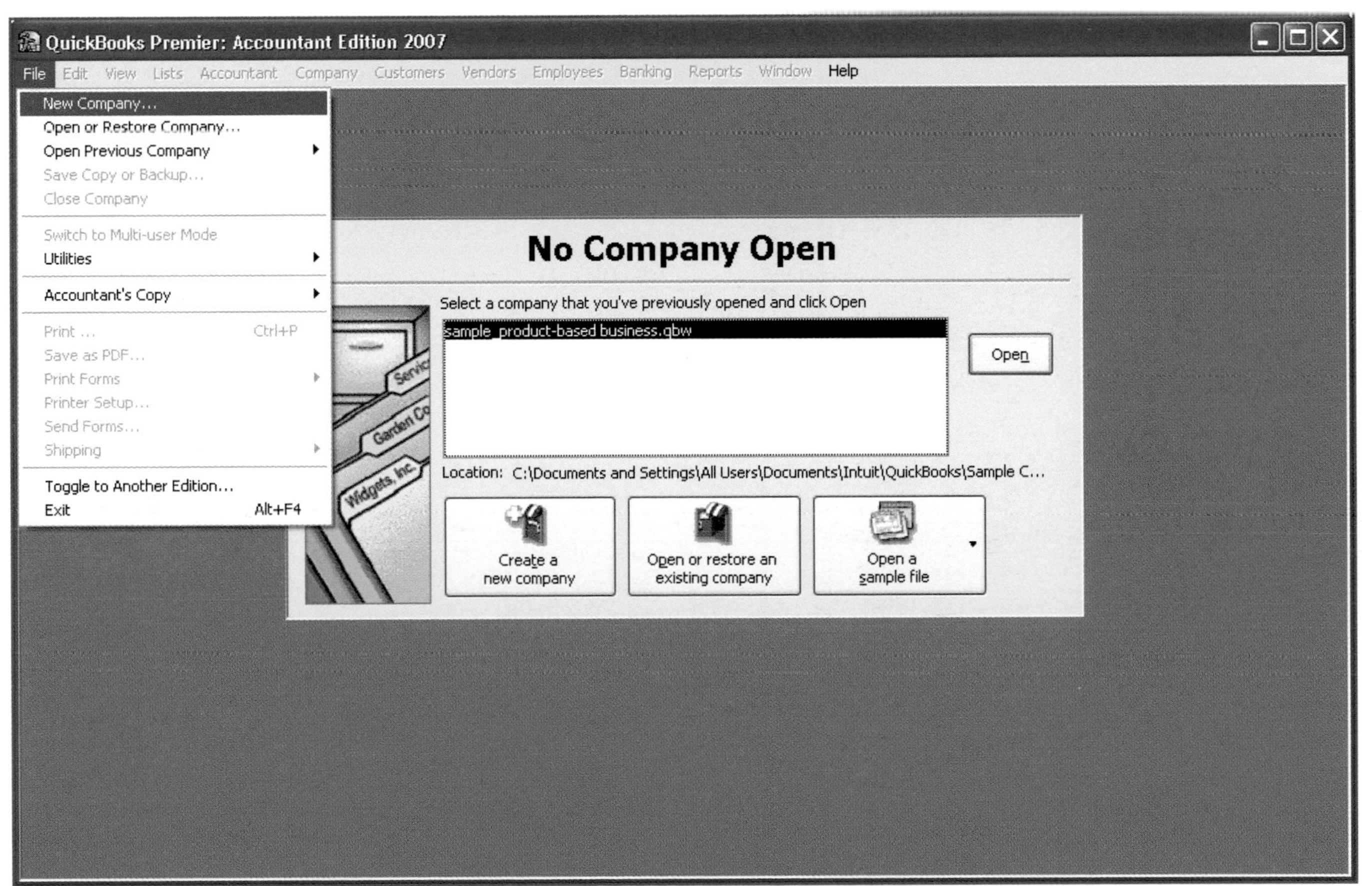

Figure 2-1: You can start a new company using the File menu or the Create A New Company button.

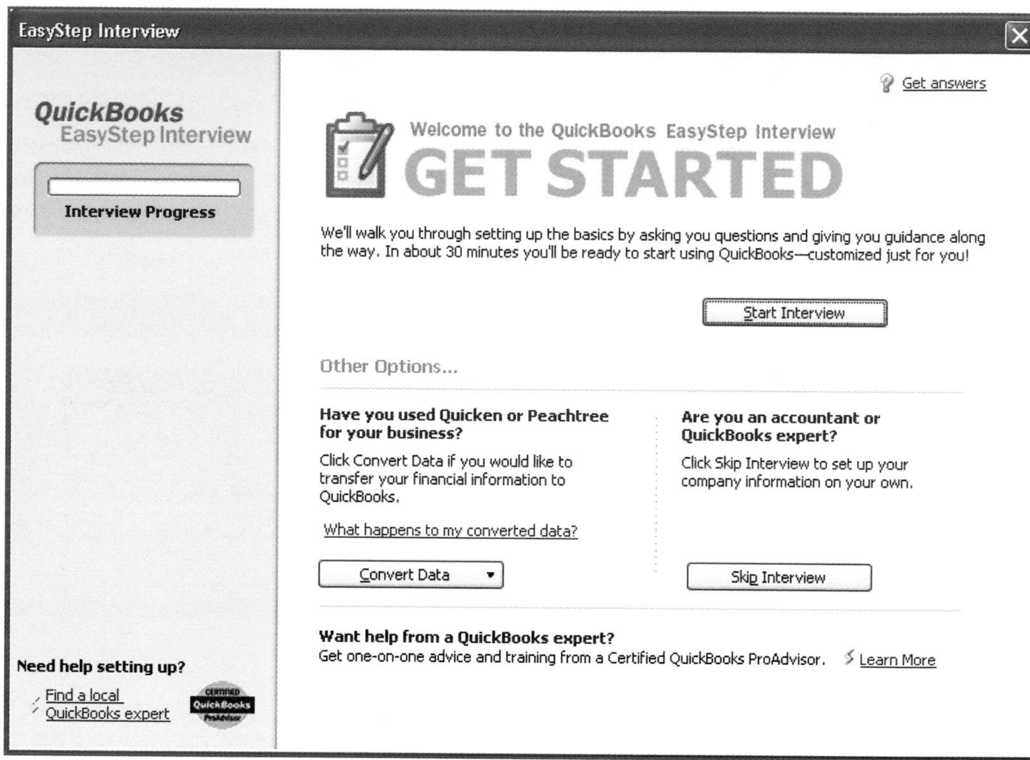

Figure 2-2: The EasyStep Interview simplifies the process of creating a new company file.

TIP

You can't change your company type, but you can create and delete the Chart of Accounts QuickBooks creates based on this selection. If you have an established business with a Chart of Accounts, you will be able to edit your Chart of Accounts to reflect your business after you complete the EasyStep Interview (see Chapter 3).

TIP

Click underlined blue words (such as Get Answers or What if I have more than one business?) to open the related Help File on any EasyStep Interview window.

In the Get Started window seen in Figure 2-2, you have the following choices:

- Click **Start Interview** to continue on in this chapter and the EasyStep Interview.
- Click **Convert Data** and select Quicken or Peachtree if you wish to convert your data from one of those programs.
- Click **Skip Interview** to enter only your company name, type, and filename. QuickBooks will then create a new company file, leaving the preference setting up to you.
- Click **X** in the upper-right area to exit the EasyStep Interview.

3. Click **Start Interview**.

TIP

If you own several companies, set up each one with its own QuickBooks file for accurate record keeping.

ENTER YOUR COMPANY INFORMATION

The next page of the EasyStep Interview asks for your company's information as seen in Figure 2-3. Note the three buttons at the bottom of the window.

- Click **Leave** to exit the EasyStep Interview. If you've not yet saved your file, QuickBooks will warn you and you will need to enter all this information again later; otherwise, you can leave once you've saved your file if you need to find out information.
- Click **Back** throughout the EasyStep Interview to return to an earlier page and correct or review an entry.
- Click **Next** after you complete each section to continue on to the next section.

EasyStep Interview

QuickBooks EasyStep Interview

Interview Progress

Get answers

Enter your company information

QuickBooks uses this information on your tax forms and forms you use to communicate with your customers and vendors.

* Company name: Butterfly Books and Bytes

Legal name: Butterfly Books and Bytes

The name you use on your tax and legal forms. Unless you use a DBA name, this will probably be the same as the company name. Explain

Tax ID: 20-1234567

Your Federal Employer Identification Number (EIN) or Social Security Number. Used only on tax forms.

Street address: 123 East Main Street

City: Mesa State: AZ Zip: 85201

Country: U.S.

Phone: 480-507-1234 Fax: 480-507-5678

Use the format you would like displayed on your forms, e.g. (555) 555-1212

E-mail address: info@butterflybooks.org

Web site: www.butterflybooks.org

* required field What if I have more than one business?

Need help setting up? Find a local QuickBooks expert

Leave... < Back Next >

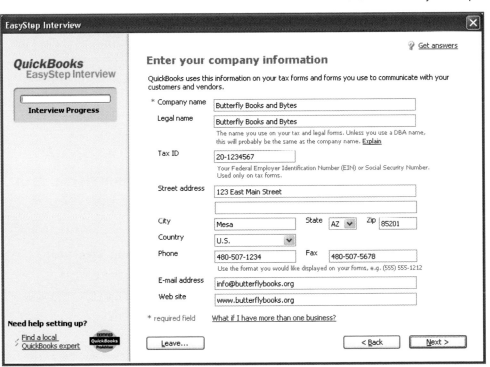

Figure 2-3: Company Information is used throughout QuickBooks, in invoices, reports, and e-mails.

1. Enter as much of the following information as you can, although only Company Name is required:
   - **Company Name** This name will appear on invoices, reports, and other correspondence you create using QuickBooks.
   - **Company's Legal Name** This name will appear on Tax and Government forms.
   - **Company's Tax ID** This is usually an EIN (Employer Identification Number) or your social security number (SSN) if you are a sole proprietor. You may leave the EIN or SSN fields blank if you do not have this information yet. You can obtain an EIN from the IRS (www.irs.gov) and will need it if you will be running payroll.
   - **Company's Street Address, City, State, Zip, Country, Phone and Fax** These are to be used on invoices for receiving payment from customers.
   - **E-mail address** This is used for sending online invoices. Can also be added to invoices and other forms.
   - **Web site** This can be added to invoices and other forms for client information.
2. Click **Next** to continue.

SELECT YOUR INDUSTRY

The QuickBooks EasyStep Interview includes a variety of industries that have customized settings and an initial list of income and expense accounts for your Chart of Accounts. You can change any customized settings in your QuickBooks file at a later time.

1. Click the listed industry as seen in Figure 2-4 that matches your company type most closely. Don't worry if your exact business type is not present. Choose whatever is closest to it or select Other/None.
2. Click **Next** to continue.

SELECT YOUR COMPANY ORGANIZATION

To create tax forms or export information correctly to a tax program, select the correct company structure for your company. If you've not set up a specific structure, your company will be a Sole Proprietorship. Verify this with your accountant.

1. Click the correct business entity type as seen in Figure 2-5.
2. Click **Next** to continue.

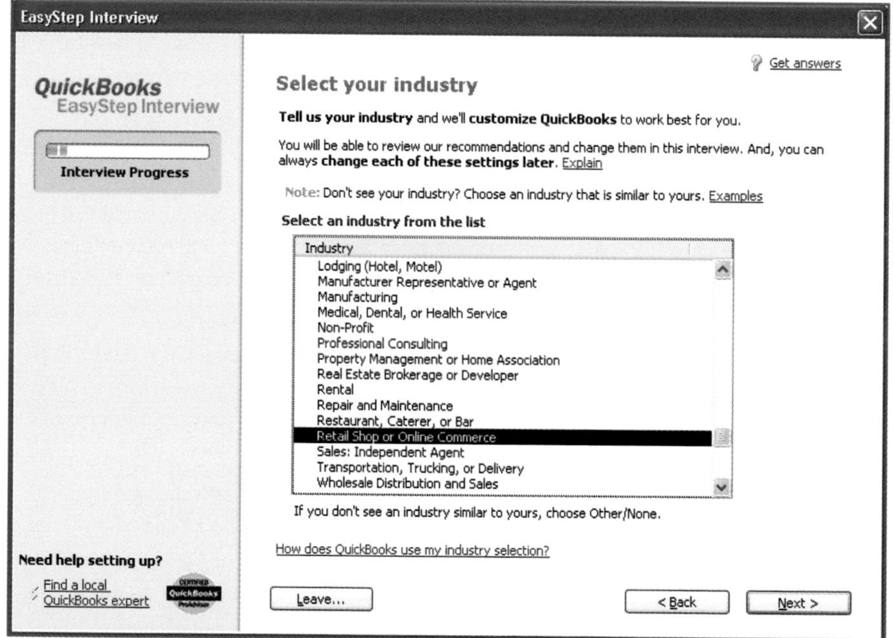

Figure 2-4: Select your industry. Retail Shop is selected for the sample company.

SELECT THE FIRST MONTH OF YOUR FISCAL YEAR

Most businesses use a calendar year of January to December.

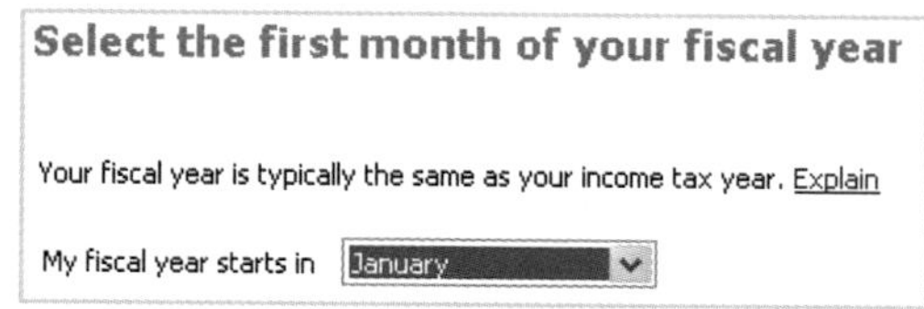

1. Click the down arrow and select your month if different from January.
2. Click **Next** to continue.

Figure 2-5: *Select your business entity type. Sole Proprietorship is being selected for the sample company.*

SET UP YOUR ADMINISTRATOR PASSWORD

The Administrator is the QuickBooks user who will have full power to make changes and set passwords for other users. Although you can leave the password field blank, it is not recommended as anyone can then open your financial records. Instructions for setting up additional users (employees) are at the end of this chapter.

1. Type your administrator password in the Administrator password field.
2. Type your password again in the Retype password field.
3. Record this password in a safe location, including upper- and lowercase, if used.
4. Click **Next** to continue.

CAUTION

User names and passwords must be typed exactly, as these fields are case-sensitive.

CAUTION

Once you enter the administrator password, if you forget it, you won't be able to get into your file, so make sure to note it correctly and store it securely.

CREATE YOUR COMPANY FILE

Now that you have entered basic company information, QuickBooks will create an actual data file. Be sure you know where it will be stored and back it up on a regular basis. If you are sharing the file with others, see Chapter 8 for networking information.

1. Click **Next**. The Filename for new Company (Save As) Window opens as in Figure 2-6.
2. Select a new location if you wish or leave your file in the default location.

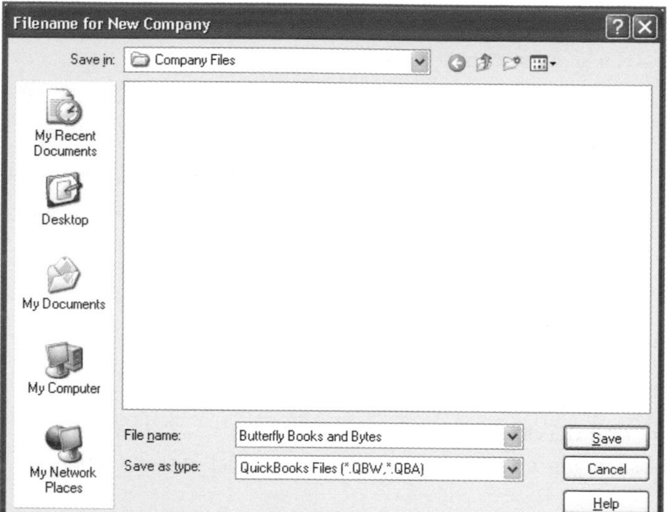

Figure 2-6: When saving a new company file, the default name is your company name.

NOTE

When you create a backup, you will create a file with the same name but with a QBB extension, such as Butterfly Books and Bytes.QBB, which you may then save on a floppy disk, CD, or other media.

CAUTION

Be sure you know where this file will be stored on your computer and what its name is. All of your financial data is stored in this file. Write down the location and name you choose, and keep it in a safe place.

3. Change the filename if you wish or leave it as is. There is an extension of ".qbw," but this may be hidden on your computer.
4. Click **Save** to create your new QuickBooks company file. A small progress bar will appear as the file is saved, and then the next section of the EasyStep Interview will appear.

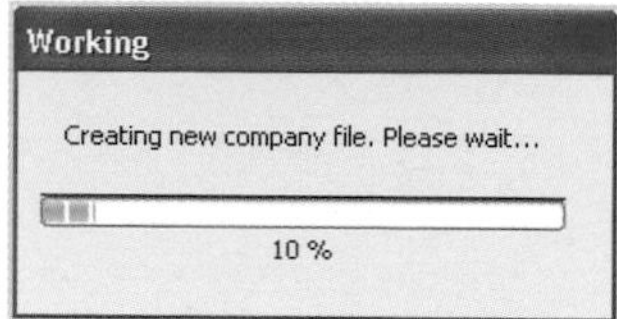

Customize QuickBooks for Your Business

The next section, as seen in Figure 2-7, involves the customization of your business in its current state. When your business changes, you'll be able to change your preferences in your QuickBooks file.

1. Read the information.
2. Click **Next** to continue.

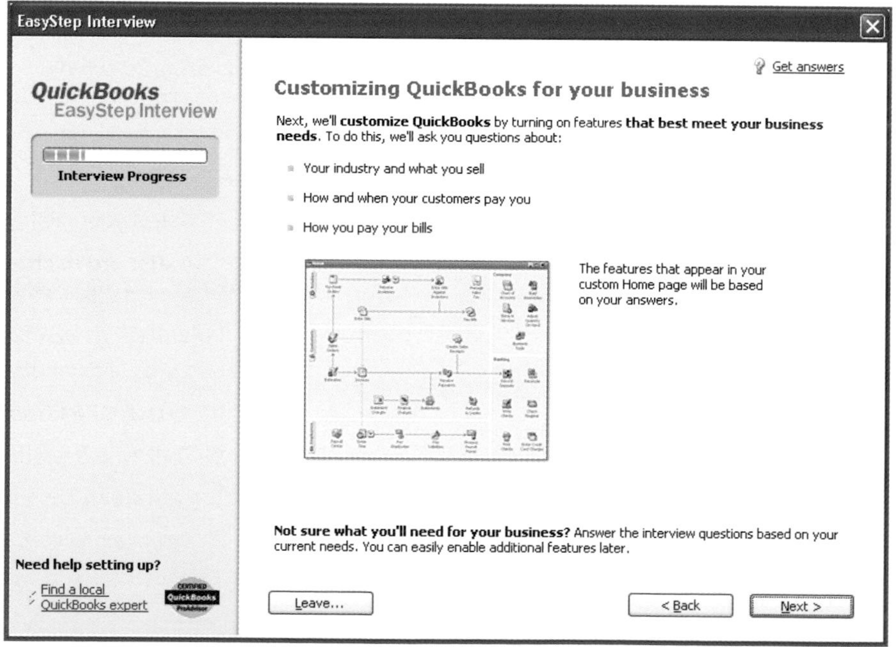

Figure 2-7: The Customization section allows you to set preferences for your company.

TIP

Once you've saved your file, you can choose to leave the interview at any time by clicking the **Leave** button at the lower-left corner. A small window will appear informing you that you may return. Click **OK** to leave the interview or click **Cancel** to return to the interview. Another window will welcome you back the next time you open that company file.

NOTE

The Interview progress bar on the left side of the EasyStep Interview tells you how far you are through the process.

IDENTIFY WHAT YOU SELL

Some companies are strictly service oriented, while others may only sell products, but most companies sell both. QuickBooks uses an Item List to identify what you sell, regardless of whether it is a service or a product. Research, coffee, and books are all items, but they can be different item types, including Service, Non-Inventory, Other Charges, and Inventory. Chapter 3 will cover item types in more detail.

1. Select the type of items you sell:
   - **Services Only**, such as such as massage, accounting, or airline tickets.
   - **Products Only**, such as a snacks, books, or clothing.
   - **Both Products And Services**, such as haircuts and hair products, massage and massage oils, or (as with our example company) books, snacks, and research.
2. Click **Next** to continue.

What do you sell?

○ **Services only**
Such as consulting, rentals, gym memberships, hair styling services, event services, construction and labor.

○ **Products only**
Such as lamps, fertilizer, books, hardware, tickets, insurance policies. Manufacturers and distributors should also select this option.

◉ **Both services and products**
Such as a bicycle repair shop that sells bikes, a carpet installation company that sells carpet.

IDENTIFY HOW YOU RECORD YOUR SALES

Consider your business. Do you use specialty software to manage daily business? Some companies, like printing, delivery-oriented, or other specialty services, do. Do you use cash registers or have salespeople out in the field recording sales by other methods? In any of those cases, you may only be entering the daily totals from that software or your registers.

1. Select your method of recording sales:
   - **Record each sale individually** if you will be using QuickBooks to create your invoices, sales receipts, and sales orders.
   - **Record only a summary of your daily or weekly sales** if you are using cash registers or other software as just described.
   - **Use QuickBooks Point of Sale** if you have installed or will be installing QBPOS.
2. Click **Next** to continue.

How will you enter your sales in QuickBooks?

◉ **Record each sale individually**
You can also print sales receipts to give customers.

○ **Record only a summary of your daily or weekly sales**
If you use a cash register to ring up individual sales, you can enter the sales totals (for the day, week, etc.) into QuickBooks.

○ **Use QuickBooks Point of Sale**
You can send the details of each individual sale into QuickBooks—with just one click.

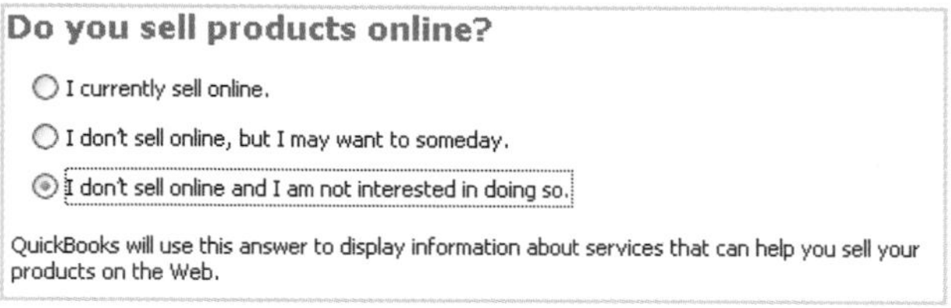

1 2 3 4 5 6 7 8 9 10

Do you sell products online?

- I currently sell online.
- I don't sell online, but I may want to someday.
- I don't sell online and I am not interested in doing so.

QuickBooks will use this answer to display information about services that can help you sell your products on the Web.

TIP

If you're not sure if you need to collect sales tax, you can select **No** now and turn on Sales Tax options at a later time.

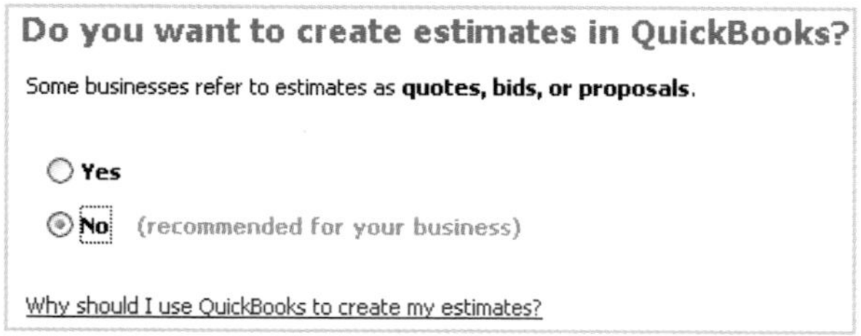

Do you want to create estimates in QuickBooks?

Some businesses refer to estimates as **quotes, bids, or proposals**.

- **Yes**
- **No** (recommended for your business)

Why should I use QuickBooks to create my estimates?

QUICKFACTS

RECEIVING PAYMENTS

Do you receive full payment from your customers when you provide services or sell a product? If so, you can generate *sales receipts*, which itemize the sale and have a place to enter payment information, including check number and payment type, but partial payments cannot be entered. *Invoices* itemize the sale but do not have a place to enter payments.

Continued . . .

INDICATE IF YOU SELL PRODUCTS ONLINE

More and more businesses these days are selling their products online.

1. Select one of the following options, depending upon your situation and level of interest:
   - I currently sell online.
   - I don't sell online, but I may want to someday. QuickBooks will provide you with more information about selling online.
   - I don't sell online and I am not interested in doing so.
2. Click **Next** to continue.

INDICATE IF YOU CHARGE SALES TAX

Do you charge sales tax?

- **Yes** (recommended for your business)
- **No**

If you sell products, you normally need to charge sales tax.

1. Select either **Yes** or **No**, depending on whether you need to charge sales tax.
2. Click **Next** to continue.

INDICATE IF YOU WANT TO CREATE ESTIMATES IN QUICKBOOKS

If you regularly create invoices from estimates, QuickBooks can assist you by creating single or progressive invoices based on your estimates. If you create estimates in another fashion, such as on the job, you may or may not want to use QuickBooks estimates. You can turn this feature on or off at any time.

1. Select either **Yes** or **No**, depending on whether you want to use estimates.
2. Click **Next** to continue.

TRACK CUSTOMER ORDERS IN QUICKBOOKS

Sales orders are only available in the Premier versions of QuickBooks and are used for back orders or for services not yet completed; these are later converted into invoices once sales are complete. If you will use QuickBooks to manage your inventory or you will allow customers to order items that you need to create or may not currently have in stock, you should choose to use Sales Orders.

Do you want to track sales orders before you invoice your customers?

- **Yes** (recommended for your business)
- **No**

RECEIVING PAYMENTS *(Continued)*

When choosing whether to use sales receipts and invoices in the EasyStep Interview, keep the following in mind:

- **Sale receipts only** A business such as a sunglasses kiosk or an ice cream truck will always receive full payment at the time a service or item is purchased. In this case, you would use sales receipts, both so that customers have proof of their purchase and so that you can track sales. If you have another system whereby you track sales receipts, such as a cash register, another computer program, or a handwritten accounting system, you might want to enter the day's receipts into QuickBooks as a single sales receipt to better track your item sales or income accounts. This will be explained further in Chapter 6.
- **Both sales receipts and invoices** Many businesses receive some full payments at the time a service or item is produced, in which case a sales receipt is used, but may receive partial payment or extend credit to some customers, which means that payment is received at a later date. In this case, generate an invoice and collect payment at a later date.
- **Invoices only** Some businesses, such as a consulting service, only use invoices to collect on accounts. Such a business might also operate using only statements. Note that with monthly (or weekly or daily) statements, you cannot add sales tax, so you will need to create an invoice if you need to apply tax to the amount of a sale.

1. Select either **Yes** or **No**, depending on whether you want to use sales orders.
2. Click **Next** to continue.

USE SALES RECEIPTS IN QUICKBOOKS

There are two ways to generate sales in QuickBooks. Sales receipts are used when the customer pays in full at the time of purchase. If you sell items only at your store location and receive payments right away upon the completion of a sale, you may choose to use sales receipts rather than invoices. If you sell some items via phone orders, for example, and receive payment later, you should use invoices as well as receipts.

Do you want to use sales receipts in QuickBooks?
Yes (recommended for your business)
No

1. Select either **Yes** or **No**, depending on whether you want to use sales receipts.
2. Click **Next** to continue.

USE STATEMENTS IN QUICKBOOKS

Statements are useful for recurring lists of debts your customers owe. If you have simply a monthly recurring charge, you can also use an invoice.

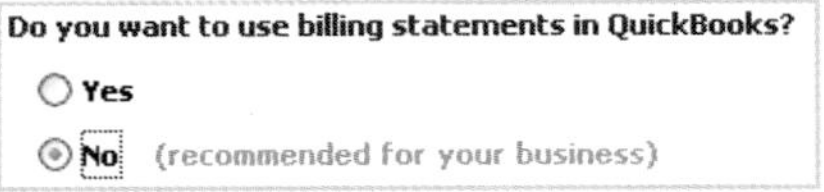

1. Select either **Yes** or **No**, depending on whether you want to use billing statements.
2. Click **Next** to continue.

USE INVOICES IN QUICKBOOKS

Invoices are used when customers are billed for their sales and can pay at a later date. You can choose to generate all sales using invoices, but then an extra step is required to apply payment. You can choose to generate all sales using sales receipts, but then you would have no way to track unpaid transactions.

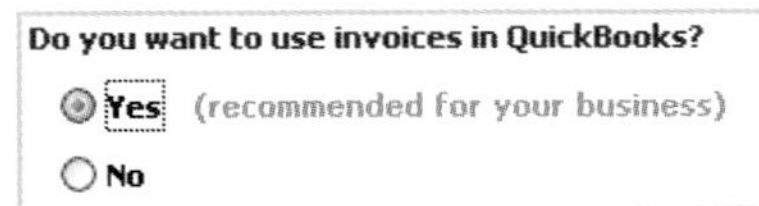

1. Select either **Yes** or **No**, depending on whether you want to use invoices.
2. Click **Next** to continue.

> **TIP**
>
> You may use several types of invoices within your business as well as set up custom invoices. Invoices are covered in more detail in Chapter 6.

USE PROGRESS INVOICING IN QUICKBOOKS

If you use estimates and want to invoice the customer during the project, you will want to use progress invoicing. This feature will allow you to selectively bill for a large project based on percentages, amounts, or specific line-by-line charges. This feature is extremely helpful for those who want to ensure accuracy in their estimates. This is not typical for a retail store, but helpful for contractors (see Chapter 6).

1. Select either **Yes** or **No**, depending on whether you want to use progress invoicing.
2. Click **Next** to continue.

MANAGE BILLS YOU OWE

There are two ways to pay bills. You can write a check for each bill as it comes in, or you can enter the bills and then pay the bills later. Entering checks directly is easier and usually preferred by small companies. Entering bills and paying them is often preferred in larger companies, in any situation where one person enters the bills and another person pays them or in any company that desires to have a true accrual system. See Chapter 5 for bill payment and see Using Accrual- vs. Cash-based Accounting QuickFacts.

1. Select either **Yes** or **No**, depending on whether you want to enter bills separately from payment.
2. Click **Next** to continue.

USING ACCRUAL- VS. CASH-BASED ACCOUNTING

The difference between accrual-based accounting and cash-based accounting is best demonstrated by way of example. In this example, the current date is June 25. On this day, you charge $20 worth of supplies on your business credit card and make a sale to a customer over the phone worth $50, billed to the customer's account. On July 15 you pay the credit card bill, and on July 1 you receive the money from your customer.

ACCRUAL-BASED ACCOUNTING METHOD

Under the *accrual-based* accounting method, on June 25, your business has a net income of $30 (the $50 sale—your revenue—minus the $20 you spent in supplies—your expense). Your balance sheet reflects these transactions as having taken place in June.

CASH-BASED ACCOUNTING METHOD

Under the *cash-based* accounting method, transactions are reflected as occurring when money actually changes hands. Thus, in this example, your income statement shows July 15 as the date the $20 expense was incurred and July 1 as the day the income was earned—the day the client's check arrives in the mail. Thus, these two transactions look like they happened in July, rather than June.

The accrual-based method provides a more accurate day-to-day picture of your finances, and to do true accrual reports, be sure to also select Yes in keeping track of the bills you owe in order to have a record of the date of the bill separate from the date of the check. In QuickBooks, all transactions are always entered on the date they actually occurred; only the reports are affected when you choose accrual- or cashed-basis on your report.

PRINT CHECKS

There are three ways to use checks in QuickBooks. You can handwrite them and enter the transactions into QuickBooks, create the checks in QuickBooks and print on your printer, or create the checks in QuickBooks and send online if you use Online Banking (see Chapter 4).

Do you print checks?

- (•) I print checks.
- ( ) I don't currently print checks, but I would like to.
- ( ) I don't currently print checks and I don't plan to.

1. Select one of the following options, depending upon your situation and level of interest:
   - I print checks.
   - I don't currently print checks, but I would like to. QuickBooks will provide you with more information about buying and printing checks.
   - I don't currently print checks and I don't plan to.
2. Click **Next** to continue.

TRACK INVENTORY IN QUICKBOOKS

Inventory consists of items you purchase to hold for resale, such as in a retail store. If you are primarily a service company and use parts for repair, you might want to talk with your accountant to determine if you are better off holding inventory or purchasing items as you need them. You may choose to use QuickBooks for this function or have a specialized program depending on your needs. Inventory will be covered in more detail in Chapter 7.

Do you want to track inventory in QuickBooks?

- ( ) Yes
- (•) No

1. Select either **Yes** or **No**, depending on whether you want to track your inventory.
2. Click **Next** to continue.

1 2 3 4 5 6 7 8 9 10

TIP

If you make a mistake at any point, simply click the **Back** button to return to the previous screen.

ACCEPT CREDIT CARDS

If you accept credit cards, you can track the payment method as well as record credit card numbers and approval numbers.

Do you accept credit cards?

- ◉ I accept credit cards and debit cards. Examples
- ○ I don't currently accept credit cards, but I would like to.
- ○ I don't currently accept credit cards and I don't plan to.

1. Select one of the following options, depending upon your situation and level of interest:
   - I accept credit cards and debit cards
   - I don't currently accept credit cards, but I would like to. QuickBooks will provide you with more information about accepting credit cards.
   - I don't currently accept credit cards and I don't plan to.
2. Click **Next** to continue.

TRACK TIME IN QUICKBOOKS

Do you want to track time in QuickBooks?

- ○ Yes
- ◉ No (recommended for your business)

If you are a consultant, time tracking is useful in your billing. If you have employees, time tracking is useful when entering payroll data. You can enter time on single projects or as a weekly timesheet. See Chapter 9 for more information on time tracking and payroll.

1. Select either **Yes** or **No**, depending on whether you want to track time.
2. Click **Next** to continue.

TIP

Contractors are treated differently than employees, as they are considered vendors. See Chapter 6 for vendors and Chapter 9 for employees.

TRACK EMPLOYEES IN QUICKBOOKS

Some companies use QuickBooks to pay employees, while others may use outside services or do not have employees.

Do you have employees?
Yes
We have W-2 employees.
We have 1099 contractors.
No

1. Select either **Yes** or **No**, depending on whether you want to track employees and/or contractors.
2. If you chose Yes, select one or both of **W-2 employees** and/or **1099 contactors**.
3. Click **Next** to continue.

Using accounts in QuickBooks

Next, we'll help you set up your **Chart of Accounts**, which are categories of income, expenses and more that you'll use to track your business.

Why is the chart of accounts important?

To set up your chart of accounts, you'll need to:

- Decide on a date to use as the starting point to track your business finances in QuickBooks (e.g., beginning of fiscal year, first of this month, etc.)
- Understand how you want to categorize your business' income and expenses. (You may want to discuss this with your accountant, if you have one.)

CHOOSE COMPANY TYPE IN QUICKBOOKS

Your chart of accounts includes income, expense, asset, liability, and bank accounts. Depending on which Company Type you chose, you will have a Chart of Accounts set up for you, but you may change them after you've completed the interview. Chapter 3 explains how to add, delete, and edit the Chart of Accounts.

1. Read the information.
2. Click **Next** to continue.

Select a date to start tracking your finances

The date you select will be your **start date** in QuickBooks.

◉ **Beginning of this fiscal year: 01/01/2007**

- In order to complete this year's tax returns, you'll need to enter transactions from the beginning of this fiscal year to today.

○ **Use today's date or the first day of the quarter or month.**

- You'll need to enter transactions from this date forward.

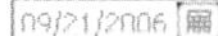

ENTER YOUR START DATE

It is highly recommended that you use the beginning of a year, beginning of your company's existence, or beginning of a quarter if you are moving from another system in the middle of the year.

1. Select one of the following options, depending upon your situation:
   - Beginning of this fiscal year
   - Use today's date or the first day of the quarter or month
2. Click **Next** to continue.

Add your bank account

You should add one bank account to the QuickBooks chart of accounts for **each checking, savings, or money market account** your company has. We recommend you add at least one bank account now. You can always add more accounts in QuickBooks later.

Would you like to add an existing bank account?

◉ **Yes.**

○ **No,** I'll add a bank account later.

ADD YOUR BANK ACCOUNT

Bank accounts include money market, savings, and checking accounts. You will have at least one bank account. You can modify your banking account information at any time. You can add basic bank account information at this time or select No to skip the next section. Banking is covered in Chapter 4.

1. Click **Yes** to enter a bank account now. Click **No** to skip this section.
2. Click **Next** to continue.

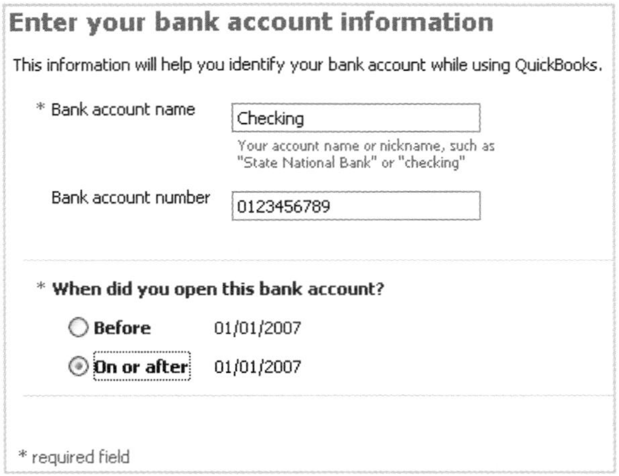

Enter your bank account information

This information will help you identify your bank account while using QuickBooks.

* Bank account name: Checking

Your account name or nickname, such as "State National Bank" or "checking"

Bank account number: 0123456789

* **When did you open this bank account?**

- **Before** 01/01/2007
- **On or after** 01/01/2007

* required field

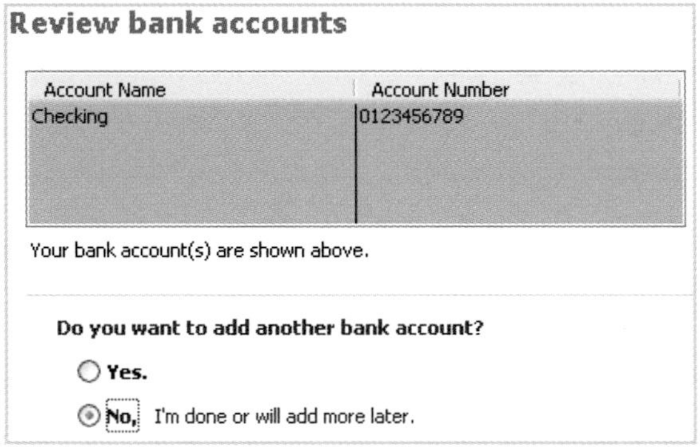

Review bank accounts

Account Name	Account Number
Checking	0123456789

Your bank account(s) are shown above.

Do you want to add another bank account?

- **Yes.**
- **No,** I'm done or will add more later.

SET UP BANK ACCOUNT

Enter the name and date of your account as required. The account number can be added later.

1. Type your account name. Use a descriptive name, such as "Checking" or "Business Checking."
2. Type your bank account number in the Bank account number field if you wish. This step is optional, but if you want to use online banking, you will need to provide this information before you can access your online accounts. It can be entered at any time.
3. Click the date range in which you opened your account. If you choose a date before your company starting date, you will be prompted to enter your balance at the company start date.
4. Click **Next** to continue.
5. Read the information about your account balance, or enter your starting balance and date, depending on which choice you selected.
6. Click **Next** to continue.
7. Review your bank account information and click **Next**. If you choose to add more bank accounts here, repeat Steps 1–7 or refer to Chapter 3 for adding additional accounts later.

Review Income and Expense Accounts (Chart of Accounts)

Based on the industry you chose earlier in the EasyStep Interview, you will see a list of suggested Income and Expense Accounts such as in Figure 2-8. Butterfly Books and Bytes is a retail store, so if you chose a different type of business, your screen will look different. If you have a specific, very different set of accounts, simply deselect anything not pertinent to your company and then add new accounts later. Chapter 3 will explain how to change, add, and delete your starting list of accounts.

Within your Chart of Accounts are two categories: Balance Sheet Accounts and Income and Expense Accounts.

Income and Expense Accounts track the flow of your income and expenses, but the actual money will be added to or subtracted from Balance Sheet Accounts.

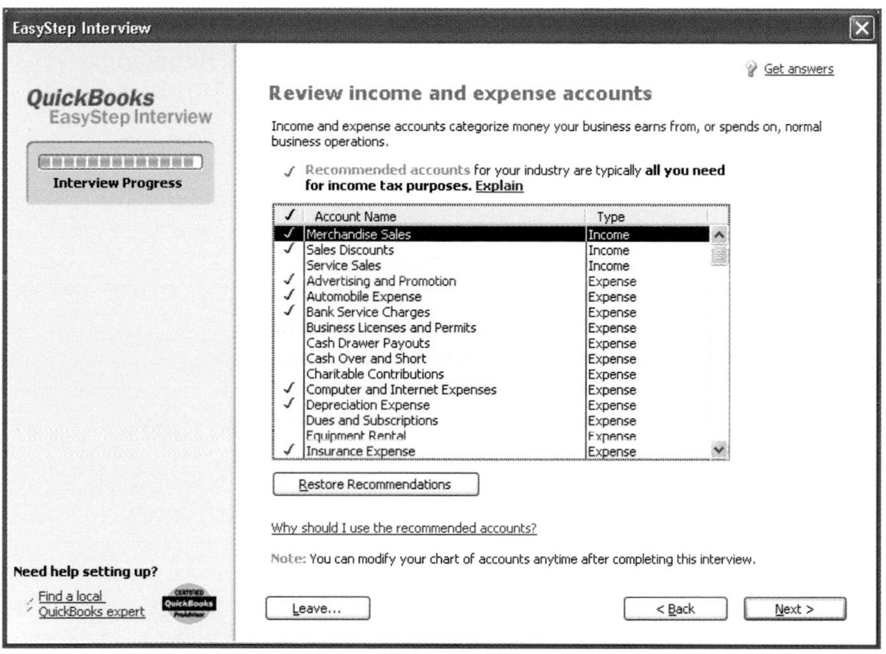

Figure 2-8: See Chapter 3 for more explanation on Cost of Goods vs. Expenses.

Balance Sheet Accounts include your bank accounts, Accounts Payable (money you owe people), and Accounts Receivable (money people owe you). They track the actual value of your business at any given point in time.

Thus, the two most important reports you will later generate will be the Profit and Loss report, based on Income and Expense Accounts, and the Balance Sheet report, based on the Balance Sheet Accounts.

REVIEW INCOME ACCOUNTS

Income accounts are the categories by which you choose to track your income. Although it is possible to have only one income account, simply called Sales, most companies want to break down their sales (and expenses) into the various types so that they can quickly see what is most profitable and what is most costly in their business. Butterfly Books and Bytes will be tracking merchandise sales and service sales. Using these two income accounts will give a quick view on the profit and loss statement of the income these two areas are producing.

To see sales details, various sales reports may be used to provide individual item-level detail.

REVIEW COST OF GOODS ACCOUNTS

Cost of Goods accounts track expenses directly related to your sales. These are costs that you wouldn't have if you didn't sell any products or services, for example, books, coffee, cups, bags, and so on. Some business—for example, service-related businesses—may have little to no cost of goods.

TIP

Click the check box to uncheck the option for the QuickBooks Learning Center to continue to appear each time you open your file. You can open it from the Help menu when you need it.

REVIEW EXPENSE ACCOUNTS

Expense accounts track expenses related to your business overhead, for example, rent, utilities, computer supplies, paper, and so on. These are items you need to pay for whether or not a customer walks in your door.

1. Scroll through the list to review the recommended accounts.
2. Click in the leftmost column to toggle the check mark on or off to select or deselect an account.
3. Click **Next** to continue. You have finished the EasyStep Interview!
4. Read the information and click **Finish**.

Review the QuickBooks Learning Center

The QuickBooks Learning Center opens after you've completed the EasyStep Interview as in Figure 2-9. The following tutorials are available for you to learn more about QuickBooks.

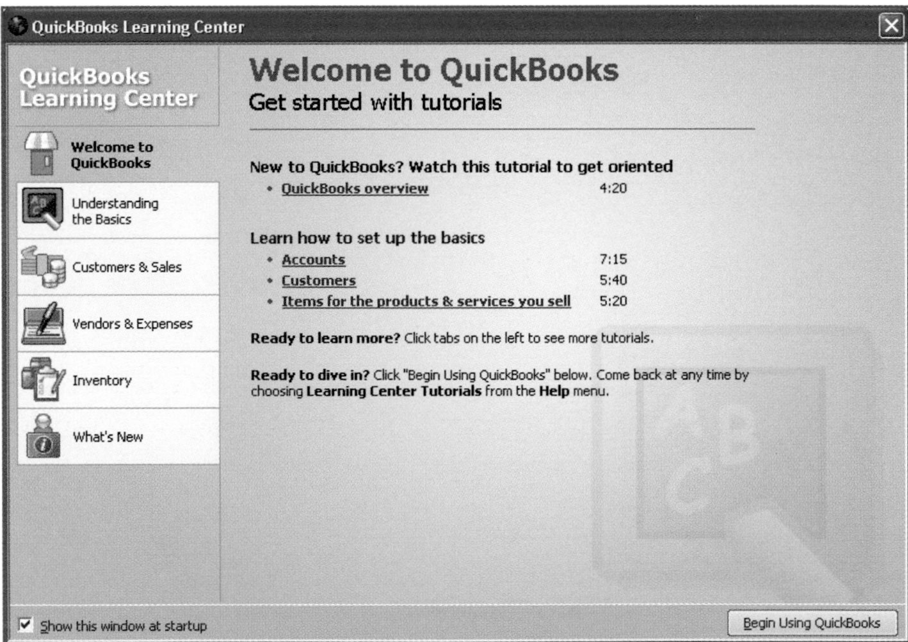

Figure 2-9: The QuickBooks Learning Center is always available by clicking the Help menu.

Chapter numbers indicate where these topics will be covered in this book:

- Welcome to QuickBooks
  - QuickBooks Overview (Chapter 1)
  - Accounts (Chapter 3)
  - Customers (Chapter 6)
  - Items for the products & services you sell (Chapter 7)
- Understanding the basics
  - Understanding QuickBooks accounts (Chapter 3)
  - Using items (Chapter 3)
  - Overview of reports (Chapter 10)
- Customers & Sales
  - Using the Customer Center (Chapter 6)
  - How to create an invoice (Chapter 6)
  - How to generate a sales receipt (Chapter 6)
  - How to create a statement (Chapter 6)
  - How to enter and deposit customer payments (Chapter 6)
  - Customizing sales forms for your business (Chapter 8)
  - Preparing estimates (Chapter 6)
  - Handling upfront deposits and retainers (Chapter 6)
- Vendors & Expenses
  - Using the Vendor Center (Chapter 5)
  - How to write checks and enter expenses (Chapter 4)
  - How to enter bills (Chapter 5)
  - How to pay bills (Chapter 5)
  - Tracking and paying sales tax (Chapters 6 and 9)
- Inventory
  - Inventory overview (Chapter 7)
  - Set up inventory (Chapter 7)
  - Buying and selling inventory (Chapter 7)
  - Using reports to manage inventory (Chapters 7 and 10)
- What's New
  - What's new in QuickBooks 2007 (tips throughout)
  - Use the Home page (Chapter 1)
  - Use the Customer Center (Chapter 6)
  - Use the Vendor Center (Chapter 5)
  - Use the Employee Center (Chapter 9)
  - Use the Payroll Center (Chapter 9)
  - New QuickBooks inventory capabilities (Chapter 7)
  - Learn about Audit Tracking (Chapter 8)

Additional concerns include the following. Again, chapter numbers indicate where these topics will be covered in this book:

- Backing up your data (Chapter 2)
- Entering historical transactions (Chapters 5 and 6)
- Setting up users and passwords (see "Set Up Multiple Users and Passwords" later in this chapter)
- Customizing forms (Chapter 6)
- Setting up 1099 tracking (Chapter 5)
- Signing up for payroll services (Chapter 9)
- Signing up for online banking (Chapter 4)
- Networking QuickBooks (Chapter 8)

Click the **Begin Using QuickBooks** button when ready. You have finished the EasyStep Interview, and your new company file is open and ready for you to work in, as shown in Figure 2-10.

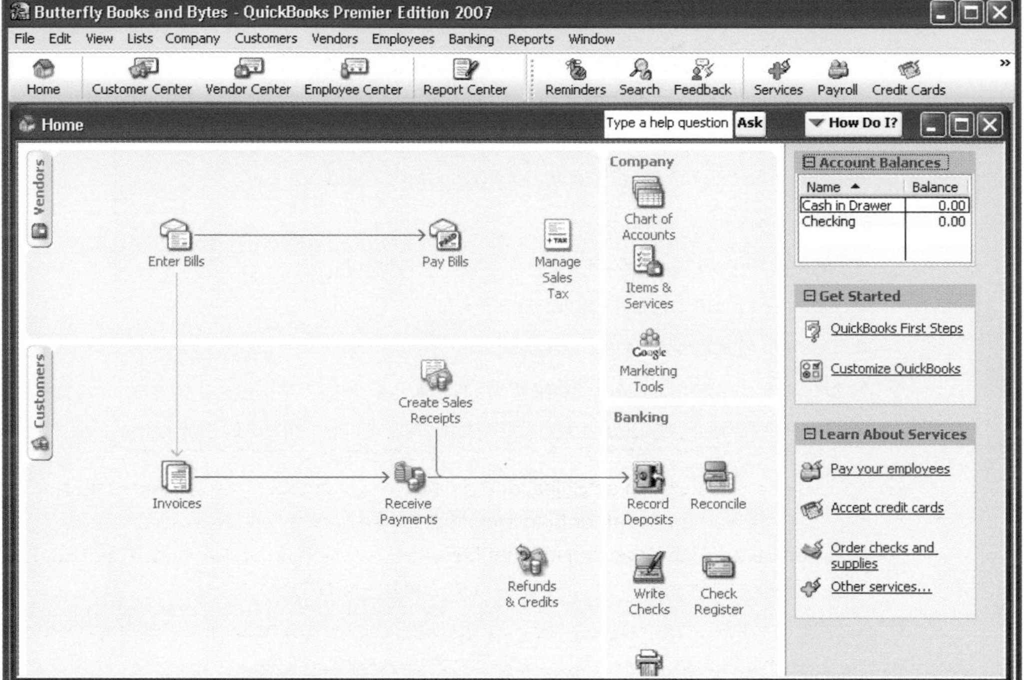

Figure 2-10: When you complete the EasyStep Interview, you can then begin working in your new company file.

Set Up Multiple Users

If you are the sole employee of your business, you don't need to worry about multiple users. If you have employees, there are three ways of handling multiple users on QuickBooks.

- Let everyone use the same computer and same user name—not recommended, since you will have no tracking of who changes what, nor will you have any limit to what each person can do.
- Let everyone use the same computer and assign user names to everyone who needs to use QuickBooks. Set up individual user accounts and restrict access to areas and privileges so that some people can only enter data while others can make changes to data.
- Use multiple computers that all access one QuickBooks file. See Chapter 8 for details on how to set up this configuration. You will need a copy of QuickBooks for each computer it will be used on and the computer hosting the QuickBooks file.

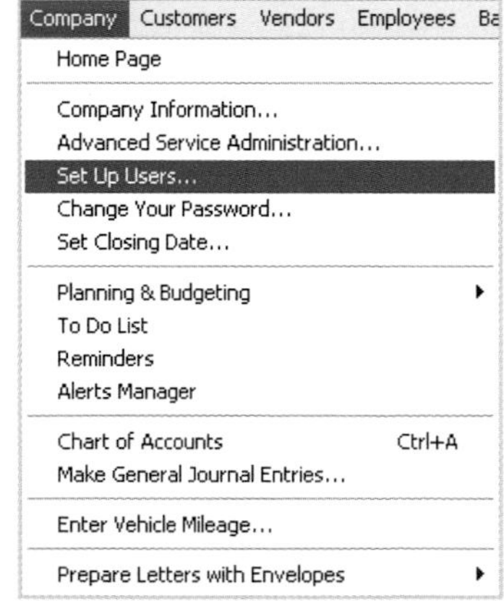

If you choose to set up individual users, you can restrict users from "seeing" information as well as restricting what they can change. For instance, on the Home page, the account balances on the right will not show for users without that permission.

To set up user accounts:

1. Click the **Company** menu and click **Set Up Users**.
2. If you chose to use a password during your company setup, the QuickBooks Login dialog box appears. Type the password in the Password field and click **OK**. The User List appears displaying the Admin User.

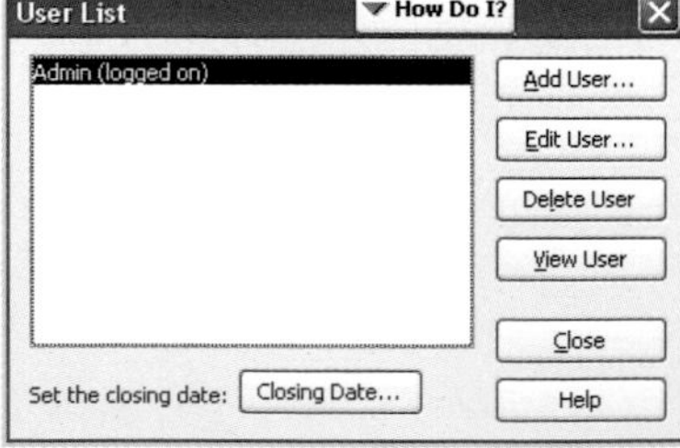

CAUTION

You *cannot* merge separate QuickBooks files. It is imperative that all users share a single file, or you will be missing data. That file can be accessed by multiple computers at the same time, but each user must have the same version of QuickBooks installed.

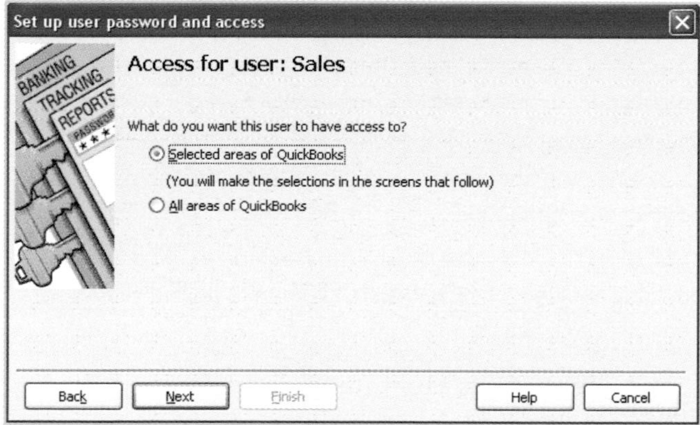

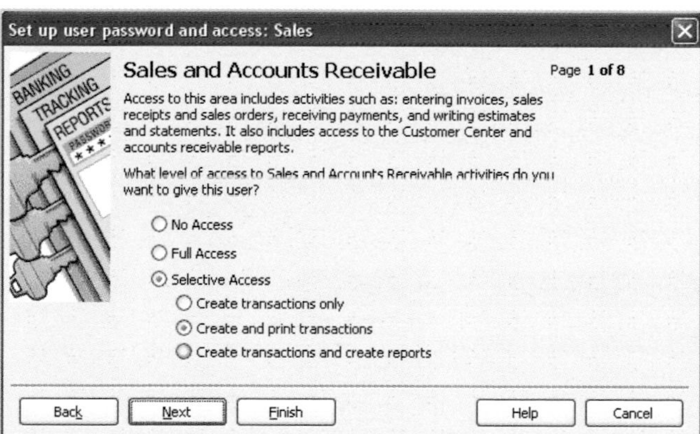

3. Click the **Add User** button. The Set Up User Password And Access screen is displayed.

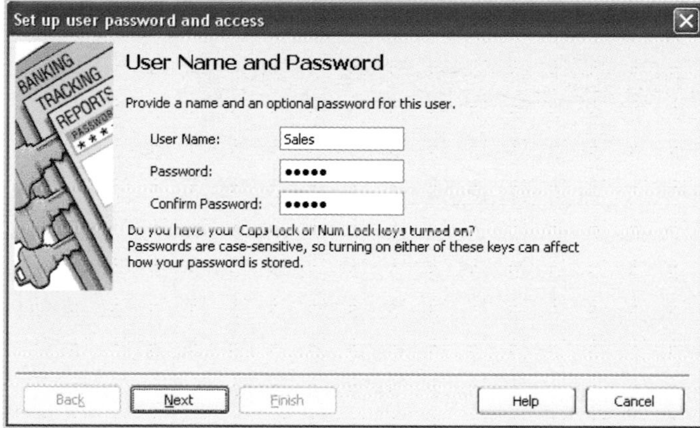

4. Type a user name, such as Sales, and a password that you will easily remember. Use descriptive names rather than employees' personal names to ease employee turnover transitions. Keep in mind that both the User Name and Password fields are case sensitive and must be typed *exactly* as they are entered here.
5. Click **Next**. Select the level of access you want this user to have. For the purposes of our example, we will give this user a selective level of access.
6. Click **Selected Areas of QuickBooks**, and click **Next**. In each of the following areas, choose the level of access you want this user to have, clicking **Next** after each selection:
   - **Sales and Accounts Receivable** Create and print transactions has been selected for this account because the Sales user will be creating invoices and cash sales and printing them for customers. The Sales user will not have any other access.
   - **Purchases and Accounts Payable** You may want to give a manager this type of access, but not someone who just performs Sales functions unless he or she must order items as well.
   - **Checking and Credit Cards** Indicates whether you will allow this user to write checks or enter credit card charges (for a company card, not accepting from customer).
   - **Inventory** These activities should be reserved to a few people responsible for inventory (if a company uses the inventory features). This will not show up if you did not turn on Inventory.

NOTE

A closing date is the date you chose—usually the end of the previous year—at which point transactions prior to the closing date are locked. This protects sensitive tax information from being changed by accident.

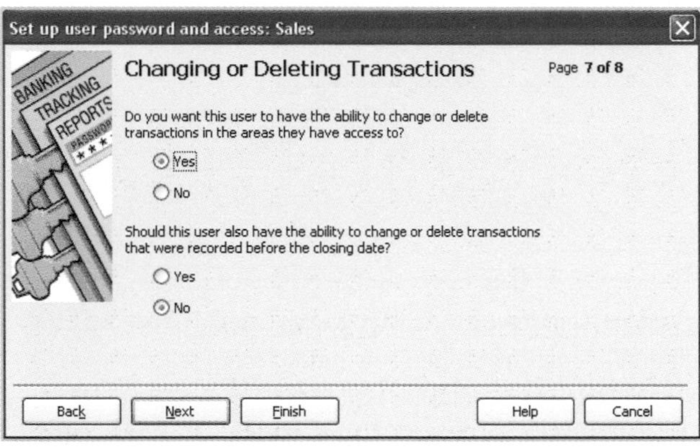

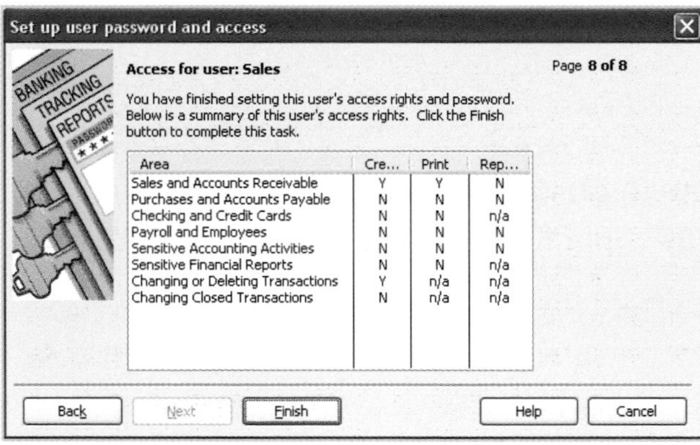

Area	Cre...	Print	Rep...
Sales and Accounts Receivable	Y	Y	N
Purchases and Accounts Payable	N	N	N
Checking and Credit Cards	N	N	n/a
Payroll and Employees	N	N	N
Sensitive Accounting Activities	N	N	N
Sensitive Financial Reports	N	N	n/a
Changing or Deleting Transactions	Y	n/a	n/a
Changing Closed Transactions	N	n/a	n/a

- **Payroll and Employees** Should be limited to the owner and accountant or bookkeeper.
- **Sensitive Accounting Activities** Includes transfer funds, online banking, and general journal entries. This should also be limited to the owner and accounting staff.
- **Sensitive Financial Reporting** Includes *all* reports in QuickBooks. Otherwise, reports can be chosen in specific areas.
- **Changing or Deleting Transactions** Most employees will need this access unless you have a manager always on staff to override. This is not advisable, since they would have to log out as the employee, log in as the manager, and then make the change. The default is to allow them to change transactions in their area. You can use the Audit Trail Report or Voided/Deleted Transaction Report to review user activities rather than restricting them in this area.
- **Changing Transactions That Were Recorded Before the Closing Date** Once you've filed tax forms, a closing date should be set in QuickBooks and no previous transactions prior to the filing date changed.

7. Review the summary of access rights for this user. Click the **Back** button to go back and change any of your previous choices, or click **Finish** if you are satisfied with access rights you have created for this user.
8. The user account is created and displayed in the User List window. From the User List window you can perform the following actions:
   - Click **Add User** to continue to add users.
   - Click **Edit User** to return to previous screens and change access levels for this user.
   - Click **Delete User** to remove this user from the User List.
   - Click **View User** to see the summary of the user's access levels.
   - Set the **Closing Date** to prevent anyone from making changes before a specific date.
9. Click **Close** to exit the User List window.

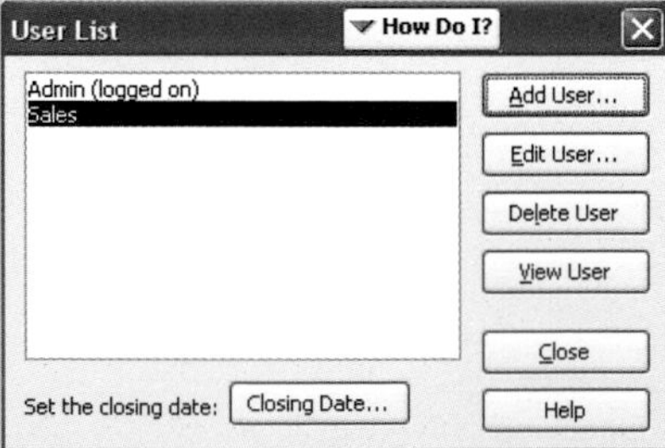

How to...

- *Use Lists*
- *Examine List Similarities*
- *Understand Balance Sheet Accounts*
- *Understand Income and Expense Accounts*
- *Use Menu Buttons for Activities and Reports*
- *Understanding Cost of Goods Sold Accounts*
- *Move and Sort Accounts and Subaccounts*
- *Customize Columns*
- *Add Accounts and Subaccounts*
- *Delete Accounts and Subaccounts*
- *Make an Account Inactive*
- *Editing an Account*
- *Rename and Merge Accounts*
- *Print Lists of Accounts*
- *Use the Item List*
- *Use the Other Names List*
- *Setting Tax Forms and Tax Lines*

Chapter 3
Working with Lists

One of the major advantages in learning QuickBooks is the consistency found throughout the forms, lists, registers, centers, and reports. Once you learn how to work with one type of object, you'll find your skills easily transfer to other objects as well. Lists are at the heart of QuickBooks and help you to easily manage your business. In this chapter, you'll look at the lists in QuickBooks and then learn to edit, add, and delete items in the Chart of Accounts. Other lists use the same steps, although in each list, different entry forms are displayed. Registers will be covered in the Chapter 4, and forms will be covered in more detail in their related chapters.

TIP

Take each step slowly. Focus on accuracy, and speed will follow.

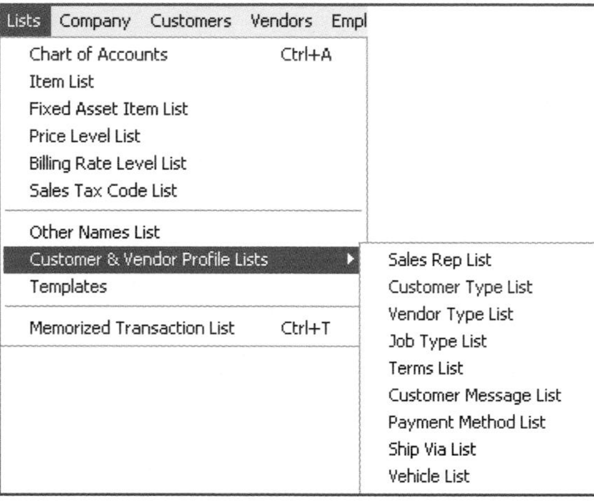

Figure 3-1: The Lists menu provides a quick way to access almost any list.

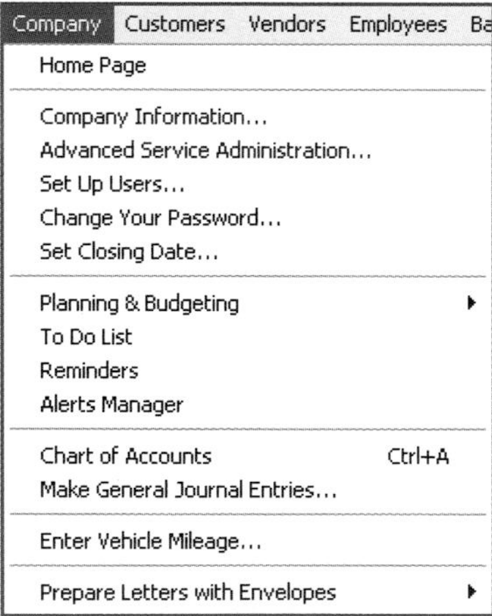

Figure 3-2: The Company menu includes a number of tools to make company management easier.

Understand Lists

You can access most lists from the Lists menu, as shown in Figure 3-1. Some lists also appear on related menus, and a few are found only on other menus and not on the Lists menu at all. The list items you see are dependent, to a degree, on the choices you made when setting up your company file, so you may not see all of the same items pictured in this chapter. Explore what is listed on your menus.

Use Lists

When you determine the lists that you use most often, you can add them to your icon bar for quick access, as you learned in Chapter 1. Until then, or at any time, you can access lists through the following menus.

THE LISTS MENU

The Lists menu contains almost all of the lists included in QuickBooks. Table 3-1 describes each of the choices on the Lists menu, and Table 3-2 describes the choices available on the Customer & Vendor Profile Lists submenu (which can be accessed from the Lists menu).

THE COMPANY MENU

The Company menu shown in Figure 3-2 includes three special company lists that are not available on the Lists menu:

- **User List** allows you to assign passwords and rights to multiple users in QuickBooks Pro and QuickBooks Premier editions. Click the **Company** menu and then click **Set Up Users**. Once you have entered the first user, the User List is displayed, from which you can add, delete, and edit users (see Chapter 2 for more information).
- **To Do List** contains notes that you enter that will appear on dates you set.
- **Reminders** allows you to monitor transactions that need to be entered, printed, or sent. This includes online banking transactions, to-do notes, deposits, unpaid bills, overdue invoices, checks, invoices, purchase orders, receipts, inventory, assembly items (in Premier editions), and other business alerts. You can double-click any entry to open the actual transaction (see Chapter 8 for more information).

LIST NAME	DESCRIPTION
Chart of Accounts	Lists balance sheet and income and expense accounts. (Also on the Company menu.)
Item List	Tracks items and services you sell on a detailed level, as well as payment items and discounts. Each item is linked to one or more accounts in the Chart of Accounts, but by using the Item List, you can view more detailed reports for use in job costing. (Also on the Customers and Vendors menus.)
Fixed Asset Item List	Tracks furniture, vehicles, equipment, and other assets used over a longer period of time (more than a year), and provides a means to manage depreciation.
Price Level List	Provides flexibility in designating prices, discounts, or surcharges for specific customers and items.
Billing Rate Level List	Allows you to bill your customers at different rates for each employee or vendor, depending on their experience level, skill, or labor burden costs. (Also on the Employees menu.) Available only in the Contractor, Professional Services, and Accountant Editions.
Sales Tax Code List	Lists different types of taxes that you might need to track. (Also on the Sales Tax submenu of the Vendors menu.)
Payroll Item List	Includes items that may appear on a paycheck, including salaries, hourly wages, additions (such as bonuses and reimbursements), and deductions (such as taxes, direct deposits, and insurance). (Also on the Manage Payroll Items submenu of the Employees menu.)
Class List	Classes add a third layer of accuracy to your data. For example, if you want to track an expense by department, location, or other non-customer, non-item-related topic, you will benefit from classes. Classes are also beneficial to non-profit organizations and companies with multiple locations.
Workers Comp List	Works with QuickBooks Enhanced and Assisted Payroll to track and report the Workers Compensation premiums. (Also on the Workers Compensation submenu of the Employees menu.)
Other Names List	Tracks information for anyone who doesn't fit into the Customer, Vendor, or Employee categories. This is a limited category, but the advantage is the ability to later move an entry from this list to any of the other three (Customer, Vendor, Employee), so someone just hired can be entered as an "other" name if you are unsure whether he or she will have a 1099 (vendor) or employee status. (Also on the Banking menu.)
Templates	Lists all form templates in one location to easily manage the look of invoices, credit memos, sales receipts, purchase orders, statements, estimates, and sales orders. Editing templates will be covered in Chapter 6.
Memorized Transactions List	Tracks recurring transactions. Once a transaction is entered, you can configure it so that it is automatically entered on a regular basis or so that QuickBooks reminds you to manually enter the transaction.

Table 3-1: Lists Accessible from the Lists Menu

LIST NAME	DESCRIPTION
Sales Rep List	Keeps a reference of salespeople's names, type, and initials for use on invoices and other sales forms. You can use this list to identify names on the Vendors, Employees, or Other Names Lists to indicate who is responsible for a sale.
Customer Type List	Allows you to categorize your customers by industry, location, source, or any other way your business is structured.
Vendor Type List	Allows you to categorize your vendors by industry, location, source, and so on.
Job Type List	Allows you to categorize your jobs by industry, location, source, and so on.
Terms List	Allows you to indicate payment terms for clients and vendors, including discounts and deadlines used in billing. Standard terms are included, but you can add others.
Customer Message List	Allows custom messages to be added to the bottom of invoices and estimates. These can also be easily added on the fly.
Payment Method List	Includes commonly used payment methods, such as cash, check, and credit cards, but you can easily add new methods, such as store credit or PayPal.
Ship Via List	Contains a simple list of shipping methods, such as FedEx, USPS, and UPS. You can add custom items, such as pick up or delivery, either in this list or the first time you need it, using the Quick Add feature.
Vehicle List	Tracks all company vehicle mileage for tax, billing, and depreciation purposes.

Table 3-2: Lists Accessible from the Customer & Vendor Profile Lists Submenu

1 2  4 5 6 7 8 9 10

NOTE

Throughout QuickBooks, if you enter a name, item, or message that is not already on a list, you will see a dialog box prompting you to add the item to the list, set up item information, or cancel this item. If you believe you made a mistake, click **Cancel**; otherwise, click **Quick Add** to add the name or item to the list, or click **Set Up** to display a detailed entry form.

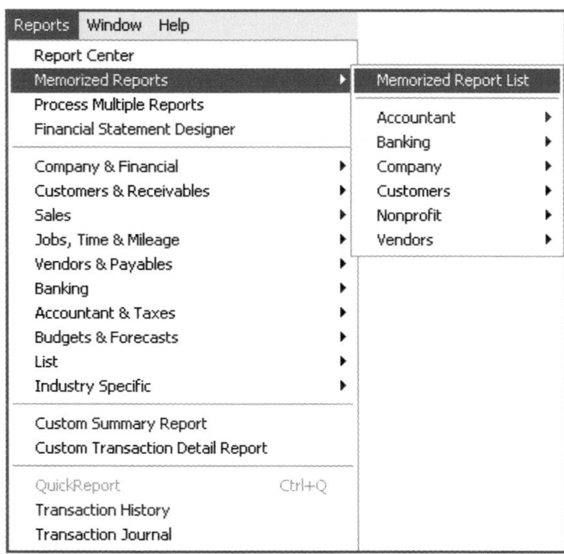

Figure 3-3: The Memorized Report List allows you to organize your custom reports.

TIP

Consider naming your users according to their function rather than by name to easily identify the level of access.

THE REPORTS MENU

The Reports menu includes one additional list, the Memorized Report List (see Figure 3-3), which tracks customized reports, allowing you to manage memorized (custom) reports. Process Multiple Reports, seen also in Figure 3-3, allows you to run a group of reports at the same time.

OTHER LISTS

Three other lists in QuickBooks are integrated into their related Centers. The Customer & Job List, located on the left of the Customer Center, tracks information on your customers; individual jobs (or projects) you set up for them; and their current balances, notes, and job status. The Vendor List, located on the left of the Vendor Center, tracks information on your vendors (including 1099s), such as their current balances and notes. The Employee List, located on the left of the Employee Center, tracks information on your employees, including their tax status and any custom fields you care to add, such as licensing, spouse's name, or birthday, as well as social security number and notes.

Examine List Similarities

Although this chapter focuses primarily on the Chart of Accounts, if you substitute the word "item" instead, almost everything that will be covered in this chapter using the Chart of Accounts as an example applies to every other list within QuickBooks as well.

LIST TYPES

These are the three major groups of lists in QuickBooks:

- **Main lists** are the lists that are critical to QuickBooks, such as Chart of Accounts, Item List, and Memorized Transaction List.
- **Name lists** include the Other Names List. Previous versions of QuickBooks used Customer:Job, Vendor, and Employee Lists, but those have all been integrated into Centers in QuickBooks 2006 and later.
- **Sublists** include drop-down lists on forms, such as the Payment Method List or Sales Rep List. These lists typically have no detail level other than their name, unlike the other lists, which include detailed fields for each item.

The closer you get to any software's maximum capabilities, the larger and slower your data file will be. If you approach these limits, consider switching to QuickBooks Enterprise Solutions Edition, which will double your list capacities.

NOTE

The Class Tracking List is used to monitor items such as multiple locations or departments. It only appears on the List menu if it has been enabled in Preferences (see Chapter 8).

TIP

Ask your accountant about cost levels at which you can write off an item as an expense or set it up as a fixed asset. Fixed assets are not expended in the course of doing business. Typically, items that cost less than $500 are considered expenses, while any expense larger than that amount may be capitalized (written off over a number of years) and is thus considered a fixed asset.

LIST CAPACITY

The lists in QuickBooks can hold a large number of entries. The combined total of the Item, Customers, Vendors, and Other Names Lists is 14,500 entries. The Chart of Accounts, Class, Terms, Payment Methods, Customer Type, Vendor Type, Job Type, and Customer Message Lists can hold 10,000 entries each. The Memorized Transaction List can hold 14,500 entries, and the Price Levels List is a special list that links other lists and can hold up to 20 entries.

Understand Accounts

The most important list of all is your Chart of Accounts. It lists your balance sheet accounts, such as bank and loan accounts, and your income and expense accounts, such as sales and rent.

1. Open QuickBooks, and your last used file will open—either your new company file or the sample file. Use whichever you prefer. This example uses the new file created in Chapter 2.
2. Click the **Lists** menu.
3. Click **Chart of Accounts**.
4. You will see a list of accounts for your company similar to that shown in Figure 3-4. The sample company file will show a more comprehensive list of accounts.

The four basic types of accounts in QuickBooks are:

- Balance sheet accounts
- Income and expense accounts
- Cost of goods sold accounts
- Other income and expense accounts

Understand Balance Sheet Accounts

Balance sheet accounts list what your company owns and what it owes. These accounts are easily identified in the Chart of Accounts—just look for an account with an amount (even zero) in the Balance Total column, as seen in Figure 3-4.

The title bar shows the list name on the left, as well as the standard resizing buttons on the right

Get help on any list in QuickBooks

Balance sheet accounts; double-clicking them opens a register

Click a column header to sort your list by this field

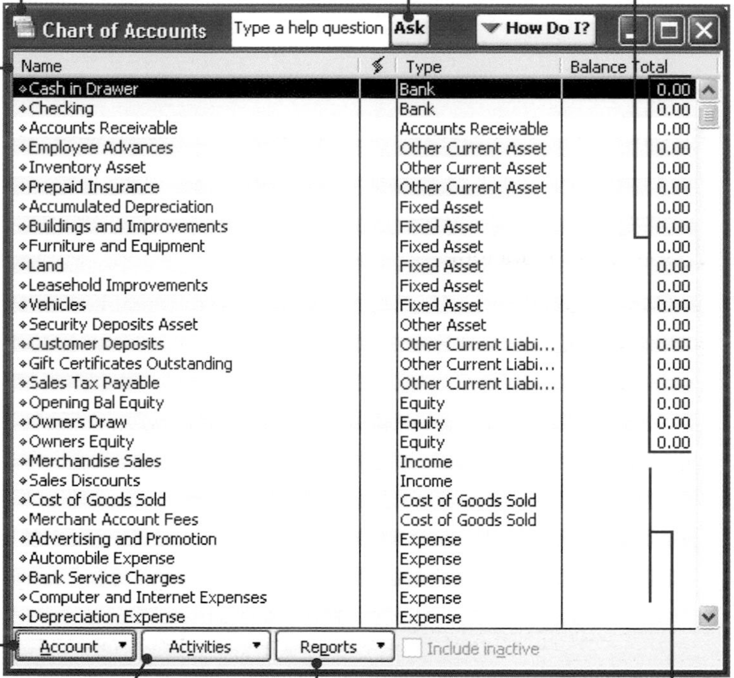

Click to perform various list actions

Click to open forms, registers, and reports related to the list's area

Click to access QuickReports on any selected account (or item) in a list, as well as reports related to the list's area

Income and expense accounts; double-clicking them displays a QuickReport of transactions that have used that account

Figure 3-4: The Chart of Accounts contains a comprehensive list of your company's accounts.

These accounts each have an associated register that will be displayed if you double-click the account name in the Chart of Accounts.

The Balance Sheet report is one of a number of preset reports included in QuickBooks (see Chapter 10). It shows your company's current position in terms of your assets, liabilities, and equity (the difference between assets and liabilities), an example of which is shown in Figure 3-5. Equity, also called net worth, tells you how much the business is actually worth. A balance sheet is called such because the total of all liabilities and equities combined equals (or balances with) the total assets.

Three types of accounts are present on a balance sheet:

- Assets
- Liabilities
- Equity

ASSETS

Assets include:

- Bank accounts, such as checking and savings accounts
- Accounts receivable (A/R), which are the current outstanding balances of your clients
- Other current assets, such as advances made to employees
- Fixed assets, such as furniture, buildings, and cars
- Other assets, such as investments and loans made to others

LIABILITIES

Liability accounts track what your business owes and include:

- Accounts payable (A/P), which are often unpaid bills from vendors
- Credit cards, which reflect balances owed on company credit cards and not the credit cards customers use (these are a part of A/R)

- Other current liabilities, such as sales tax and payroll tax to be paid to the government
- Long-term liabilities, such as loans and mortgages

EQUITY

Equity accounts show a company's net worth and reflect the difference between assets and liabilities. Equity changes in two ways:

- Money invested in or removed from the company (usually in the form of owner investment or draws)
- Profits and losses in the business

Equity accounts can include:

- Opening balance
- Retained earnings
- Owner's equity
- Owner's draws
- Capital investment
- Capital stock

Understand Income and Expense Accounts

Income and expense accounts do not have a register where you can enter information, as do balance sheet accounts; however, most transactions you enter in QuickBooks require an income or expense account to be specified. This allows you to run reports, such as the Profit and Loss (P & L) statement, shown in Figure 3-6, which shows where your money is coming from and where it is going. An even more accurate way to track this information (and which is required for job costing) is to use items. This method will be introduced in this chapter and covered in more detail in Chapters 6, 7, and 10.

INCOME ACCOUNTS

Income accounts can be lumped into one category, such as sales, or set up as separate or subaccounts, such as book sales, coffee sales, and other sales,

8:45 PM — Larry's Landscaping & Garden Supply
12/15/07 — **Balance Sheet**
Accrual Basis — As of December 15, 2007

		Dec 15, 07
ASSETS		
Current Assets		
Checking/Savings		
Checking		102,893.52
Cash Expenditures		225.23
Savings		5,887.50
Total Checking/Savings		109,006.25
Accounts Receivable		
Accounts Receivable		35,810.02
Total Accounts Receivable		35,810.02
Other Current Assets		
Prepaid Insurance		500.00
Employee advances		100.00
Inventory Asset		6,937.08
Undeposited Funds		110.00
Total Other Current Assets		7,647.08
Total Current Assets		152,463.35
Fixed Assets		
Truck		
Accumulated Depreciation	-1,725.00	
Original Purchase	13,750.00	
Total Truck		12,025.00
Total Fixed Assets		12,025.00
TOTAL ASSETS		**164,488.35**
LIABILITIES & EQUITY		
Liabilities		
Current Liabilities		
Accounts Payable		
Accounts Payable		2,554.57
Total Accounts Payable		2,554.57
Credit Cards		
CalOil Card		1,403.99
QuickBooks Credit Card		
QBCC Field Office	45.00	
QBCC Home Office	25.00	
Total QuickBooks Credit Card		70.00
Total Credit Cards		1,473.99
Other Current Liabilities		
Payroll Liabilities		4,090.70
Payments on Account		-1,520.00
Sales Tax Payable		2,086.50
Total Other Current Liabilities		4,657.20
Total Current Liabilities		8,685.76
Long Term Liabilities		
Bank of Anycity Loan		19,932.65
Equipment Loan		3,911.32
Bank Loan		6,013.06
Total Long Term Liabilities		29,857.03
Total Liabilities		38,542.79
Equity		
Opening Bal Equity		151,970.07
Owner's Equity		
Owner's Draw	-5,000.00	
Total Owner's Equity		-5,000.00
Retained Earnings		-40,198.24
Net Income		19,173.73
Total Equity		125,945.56
TOTAL LIABILITIES & EQUITY		**164,488.35**

Figure 3-5: The Balance Sheet report provides you with a picture of your company's health at any given point in time.

1 2 3 4 5 6 7 8 9 10

8:48 PM	Rock Castle Construction	
12/15/07	**Profit & Loss**	
Accrual Basis	December 1, 2007	
		Dec 1, 07
Ordinary Income/Expense		
Income		
Construction		
Labor	3,757.00	
Materials	8,187.80	
Miscellaneous	762.58	
Subcontractors	627.38	
Total Construction		13,334.76
Total Income		13,334.76
Cost of Goods Sold		
Cost of Goods Sold		1,509.54
Total COGS		1,509.54
Gross Profit		11,825.22
Expense		
Insurance		
Disability Insurance	50.00	
Liability Insurance	350.00	
Work Comp	275.00	
Total Insurance		675.00
Job Expenses		
Job Materials	80.50	
Subcontractors	500.00	
Total Job Expenses		580.50
Payroll Expenses		4,874.50
Professional Fees		
Accounting	250.00	
Total Professional Fees		250.00
Rent		1,200.00
Total Expense		7,580.00
Net Ordinary Income		4,245.22
Net Income		**4,245.22**

Figure 3-6: A Profit and Loss statement shows you the source and outflow of your company's money.

depending on the level of detail you want. Three to five categories of income accounts are usually sufficient, since reports run using items can give more-detailed sales information.

EXPENSE ACCOUNTS

While income accounts tend to be few, expense accounts can be numerous and detailed. For example, a utilities account might include subaccounts for water, electricity, and phone. Exactly how they are arranged depends on the level of information needed by the company owner or investors.

When you begin using QuickBooks, it is actually better to have too many accounts as opposed to too few; it's easier to merge accounts than it is to go through a list of combined transactions and accurately move transactions into new accounts.

OTHER INCOME AND EXPENSE ACCOUNTS

Other income and expense accounts are used for any income or expense not generated by your primary business. Many businesses will never use these types of accounts, but some may use them for such things as interest or losses on investments, since these are things that affect you but that are not generated by your primary business.

Review and Edit Your Chart of Accounts

In looking at the Chart of Accounts (see Figure 3-4), you will see certain features that are common to most lists in QuickBooks, including the How Do I? and Ask A Help Question areas at the top and the Account, Activities, and Reports menu buttons at the bottom.

Use Menu Buttons for Activities and Reports

At the bottom of every list are one to four menu buttons; the most common are:

- <List Name>

TIP

Keep your business and personal records in separate files. Also keep a separate file for each business you run.

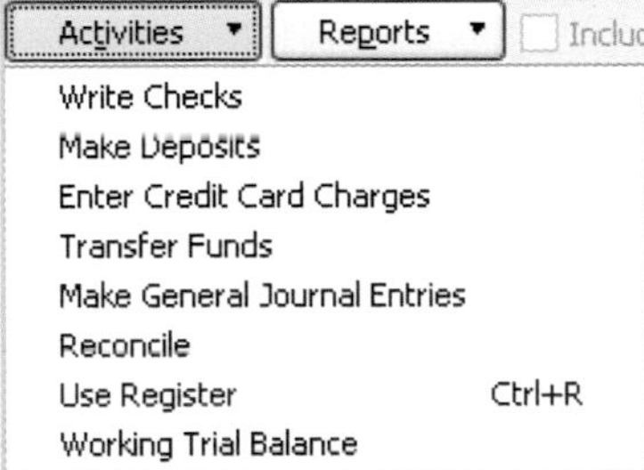

QUICKFACTS

UNDERSTANDING COST OF GOODS SOLD ACCOUNTS

Cost of Goods Sold accounts are similar to expense accounts but hold a different place on the profit and loss report, as seen in Figure 3-6.

They are subtracted from the total income to give a gross profit. Expenses are then subtracted to give a net profit or loss for the time period of the report.

The difference between Cost of Goods Sold and expense accounts can be easily determined by asking yourself if you would need to pay for something whether or not a sale had occurred. For example, your telephone bill, electric bill, and rent are considered expenses and need to be paid regardless if you've made any sales. Cost of Goods, however, are items you purchase for resale, for example, books, coffee, and snacks. Items used as an ancillary to the main products, such as milk and sugar, can be considered a supply item, which may be considered an expense.

- Activities
- Reports

Every standard list has a menu button corresponding to the list name on the left, which allows you to perform common activities, such as create a new account, edit an account, or delete an account.

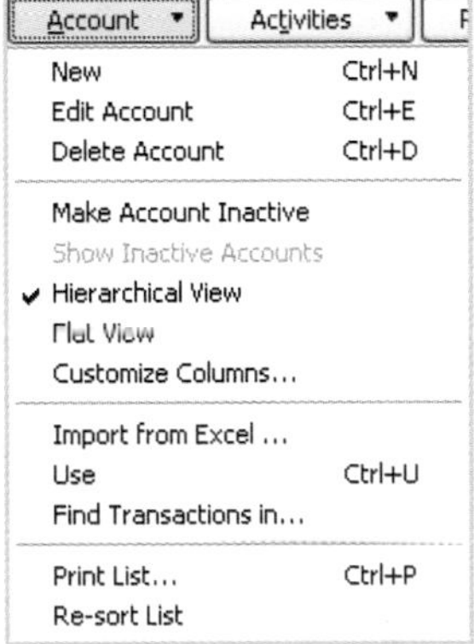

The name of this menu button generally reflects the name of the list. For example:

- Account menu button on the Chart of Accounts List
- Item menu button on the Fixed Asset Items and Items Lists
- Shipping Method menu button on the Ship Via List
- Vendor Type menu button on the Vendor Type List
- Payment Method menu button on the Payment Method List

Some lists also have an Activities menu button in the middle, allowing you to quickly access related activities, such as Change Item Prices and Build Assemblies on the Item List and Write Checks or Make Deposits on the Chart of Accounts.

Most lists also have a Reports menu button on the right, listing commonly used reports for the area to which the list relates. This is a quick way to access reports that are also on the Reports menu. The exception is the QuickReport, which gives you a list of transactions for the currently selected account.

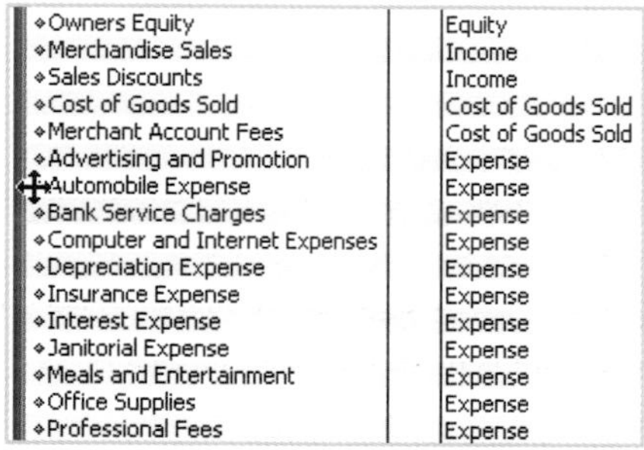

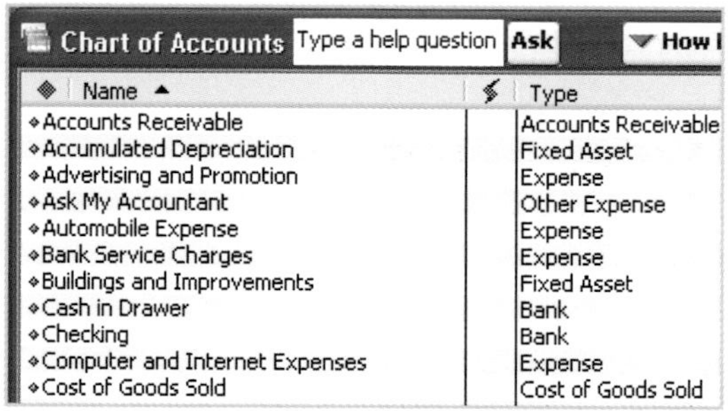

Move and Sort Accounts and Subaccounts

The Chart of Accounts is normally sorted first by account type and then alphabetically by name. Other lists are normally sorted just by name. You can change the list's sort order or move any account within its account type. Although some companies use account numbers in the Chart of Accounts, in which case the accounts are sorted numerically, we will use the default of names in our examples. The advantage of using names is that it's an easy-to-remember system and account names will automatically appear as you type entries throughout QuickBooks, as you will see later.

Name	Type
◆Owners Equity	Equity
◆Merchandise Sales	Income
◆Sales Discounts	Income
◆Cost of Goods Sold	Cost of Goods Sold
◆Merchant Account Fees	Cost of Goods Sold
◆Advertising and Promotion	Expense
◆Automobile Expense	Expense
◆Bank Service Charges	Expense
◆Computer and Internet Expenses	Expense
◆Depreciation Expense	Expense
◆Insurance Expense	Expense
◆Interest Expense	Expense
◆Janitorial Expense	Expense
◆Meals and Entertainment	Expense
◆Office Supplies	Expense
◆Professional Fees	Expense

MOVE ACCOUNTS WITHIN LISTS

This section applies primarily to the Chart of Accounts, Item List, and Fixed Assets List. To move accounts within lists:

1. Pause your mouse cursor over one of the small diamonds next to any list item, for example, to the left of Automobile Expense. The cursor changes to a four-headed arrow.
2. Drag the account up or down the list.
3. When you are at the desired location, release your mouse button.

You can only move an account within the group to which it belongs and when the list is in its original order. If you move an account too far above or below the group it was part of, you will see an error message when you release it and it will remain where it was.

SORT LISTS

You can sort a list according to a column heading by clicking it. For example, clicking the **Name** column sorts your list by name in ascending order (as indicated by the up arrow next to the column name). Click the **Name** column again to sort the list in descending order (as indicated by the down arrow next to the column name).

Chart of Accounts | Type a help question | Ask | How I

◆ Name ▲	Type
◆Accounts Receivable	Accounts Receivable
◆Accumulated Depreciation	Fixed Asset
◆Advertising and Promotion	Expense
◆Ask My Accountant	Other Expense
◆Automobile Expense	Expense
◆Bank Service Charges	Expense
◆Buildings and Improvements	Fixed Asset
◆Cash in Drawer	Bank
◆Checking	Bank
◆Computer and Internet Expenses	Expense
◆Cost of Goods Sold	Cost of Goods Sold

RETURN A LIST TO THE DEFAULT ORDER

When you have sorted the list by clicking a column heading, you will see a diamond to the left of the Name column. Click the diamond to return the list to being grouped by account type.

NOTE

The first two columns in the Chosen Columns pane (normally Active Status and Name) cannot be moved or deleted.

TIP

You can return to the default column headings by clicking the **Default** button at any time.

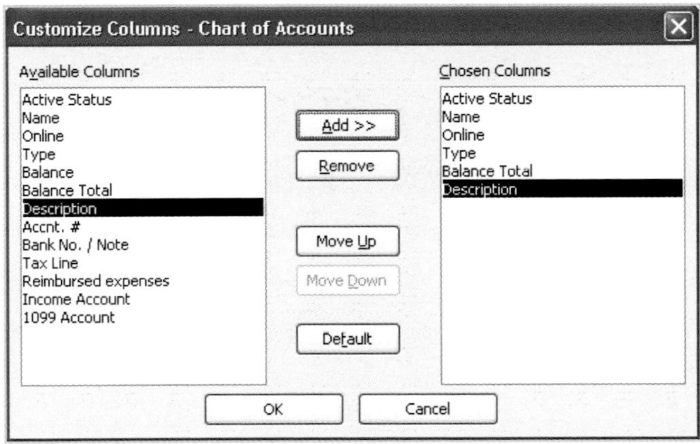

If you have moved items on the list manually and want to return your list to its default original order, which is by account type and then by name:

1. Click the **Account** button.
2. Click **Re-Sort List**.
3. Click **OK** when prompted to confirm this action.

Customize Columns

Most column headings at the top of any list can be customized to better meet your needs.

1. Click the **<List Name>** button (for example, **Account**).
2. Click **Customize Columns**. A window opens with the available column headings on the left and the currently active column headings on the right.
3. Double-click a column name (for example, **Description**) in the Available Columns pane to move it to the Chosen Columns pane (or click the item in the Available Columns pane, and click **Add**).
4. Click a column name (for example, **Description**) in the Chosen Columns pane, and click the **Move Up** or **Move Down** button to move it left or right across the top of the column headings.
5. Click **OK** when you are finished. Click **Cancel** if you decide not to make these changes.

You will see the new column heading in your Chart of Accounts.

Add Accounts and Subaccounts

You will probably add new accounts to QuickBooks as your business grows and changes, for example, when you add a new product line, incur a new expense, open a new bank account or credit card, or purchase a new piece of equipment. You can also create subaccounts in the Chart of Accounts, Item List, and Fixed Assets Item List, for example, if you want to refine your Auto Expenses category to track spending on gas, insurance, and repairs.

1 2 3 4 5 6 7 8 9 10

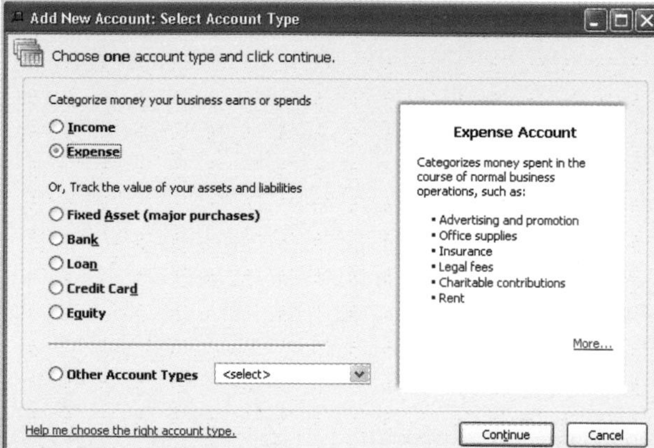

To create a new account:

1. Click the **Account** button.
2. Click **New**. The Select Account Type window opens.
3. Select **Expense**. A description of the account type will appear and click **continue**.
4. In the **Account Name** field type Auto Expense. You can fill in the Description or Note fields also, if you want, but it isn't necessary.
5. Click **Save & Close**. The Auto Expense account is created.

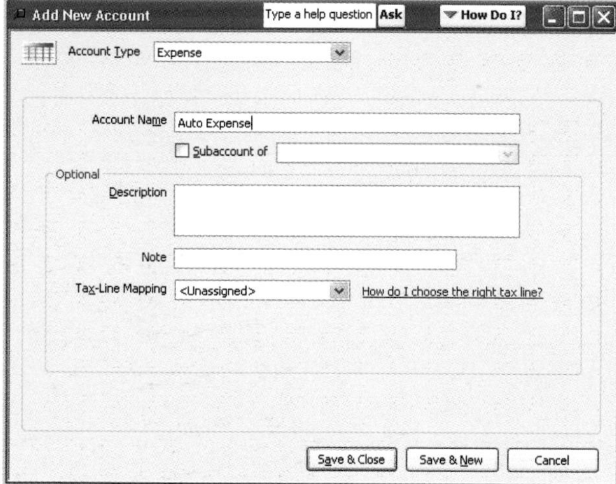

ADD A SUBACCOUNT

To create a subaccount for this account:

1. Click the **Account** button.
2. Click **New**.
3. Select **Expense** and click **continue**.
4. In the **Account Name** field type Gas.
5. Click the **Subaccount of** check box, click the down arrow, and click **Auto Expense**.

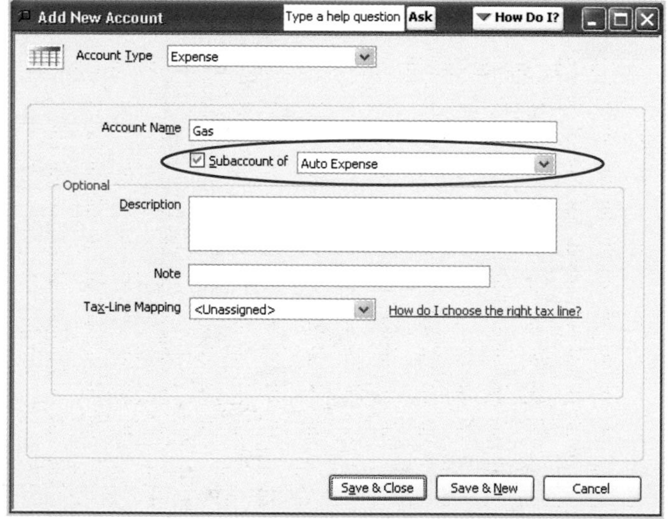

6. Click **Save & Close**.
7. Repeat Steps 1–6 to add the Insurance and Repairs subaccounts (see the Tip).

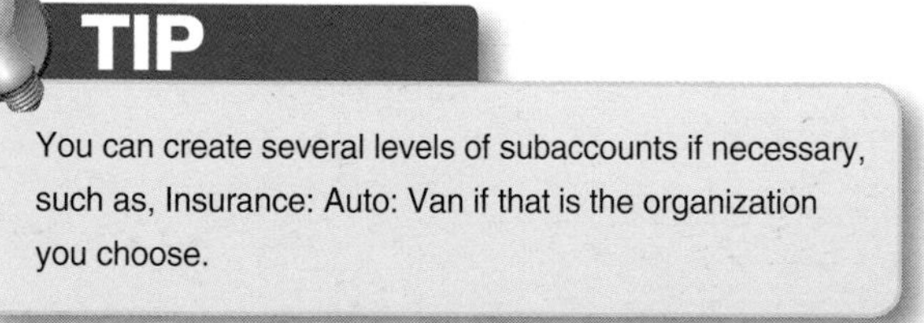

TIP

You can create several levels of subaccounts if necessary, such as, Insurance: Auto: Van if that is the organization you choose.

If you are entering multiple accounts, click **Save & New** instead of **Save & Close** in step 6.

Delete Accounts and Subaccounts

You can delete an account at any time, with the exception of the Payroll Liabilities and Payroll Expenses accounts. However, if you have entered transactions into an account, you cannot delete it unless you first delete or change the transactions within the account. In that case, you can choose to make the account inactive or merge it with another account. You must also delete or move any subaccounts before you delete a parent account.

To delete an account:

1. Click the account name you want to delete (for example, **Uniforms**).
2. Click the **Account** button and then click **Delete Account**. If you have subaccounts, items, or transactions within this account, you will see a message that the account cannot be deleted; otherwise, the Delete Account dialog box appears, asking if you are sure you want to delete this account.
3. Click **OK**.

Make an Account Inactive

In some cases, you may no longer need to use an account, but QuickBooks will not allow you to delete it because it has transactions in it. As your business grows and changes, you won't want to see old items in the list and on your reports. In a situation like this, you can make the account inactive.

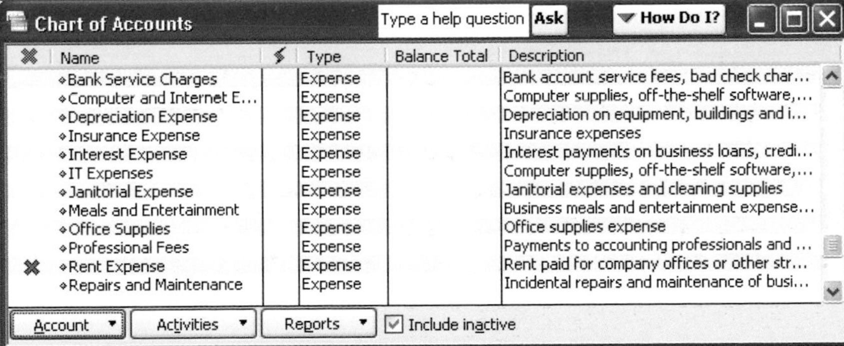

Figure 3-7: You can view or hide your inactive accounts by selecting or clearing, respectively, the Include Inactive check box.

1. Click the account name you want to make inactive (for example, **Rent Expense**).
2. Click the **Account** button and then click **Make Account Inactive**. If you have subitems or transactions in this account, QuickBooks will automatically make those accounts inactive as well.

To review your inactive accounts, click the **Include Inactive** check box at the bottom of the list window and you will see all your list items, with an X next to the inactive accounts, as shown in Figure 3-7.

EDITING AN ACCOUNT

You can edit any account, changing the name, type, description, account number, tax line, and online information.

To edit an account:

1. Click the account name you want to edit (for example, **Computer and Internet Expenses**).
2. Click the **Account** button and click **Edit Account**.

   –Or–

   Right-click the account name and click **Edit Account**.
3. Type the new account name or make any other desired changes, and click **Save & Close**.

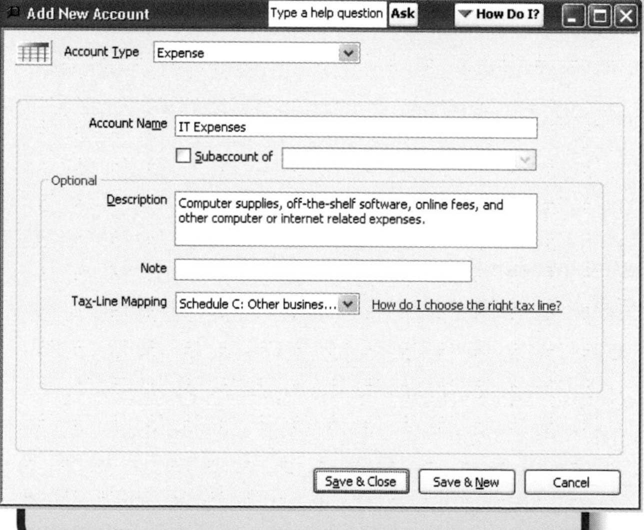

Rename and Merge Accounts

A common mistake among QuickBooks users is misnaming or creating duplicate accounts. Fortunately, QuickBooks makes it easy to correct these mistakes. You can rename an account, or if you have duplicate accounts with different names, such as Auto Expense and Automobile Expense, you can merge the accounts by renaming one account to the other account.

To rename or merge an account:

1. Click the account name you want to rename (for example, **Automobile Expense**).
2. Click the **Account** button and click **Edit Account**.

   –Or–

   Right-click the account name and click **Edit Account**.
3. Make your desired changes (for example, type Auto Expense), and click **Save & Close**. If the account name is not currently in use, your changes will take effect immediately. If it is, a confirmation dialog box appears.

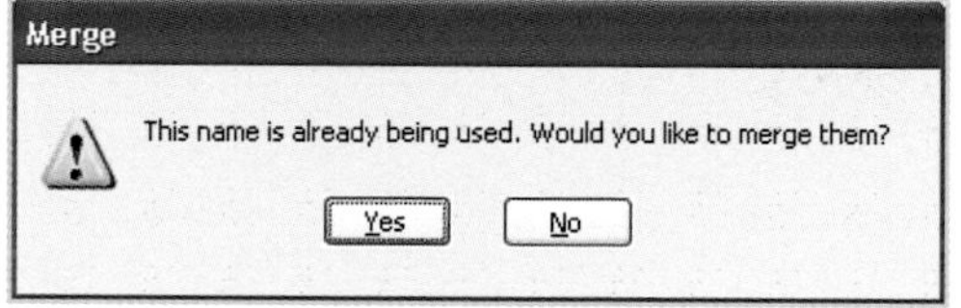

4. Click **Yes** if you want to merge these two accounts.

Print Lists of Accounts

The Reports menu is the best means by which you can print a list of your accounts or items. In addition to simple lists, you can print phone and contact lists for customers, employees, vendors, and others. Although reports will be covered in Chapter 10, explore the related reports in each section to see what is available to you:

- Click the **Reports** menu and then click **List** to see a list of available reports you can print.
- Click **Account Listing** to see a report on your accounts, an example of which is shown in Figure 3-8.

- Click the **Print** button at the top of the screen to send the report to your printer.
- Click the **Close** button (the X) in the upper-right corner of the report window to close it.

Advantages of printing from the Reports menu include added detail and the ability to customize the printout and save reports. However, not all lists can be printed from the Reports menu. You can print any list by clicking the **File** menu and clicking **Print List** or by clicking the **Account** menu and clicking **Print List**. This will give just a basic report, listing the account name and account type.

Use the Item List

While the Chart of Accounts tracks your accounts, the Item List tracks specific things that you sell, including products, services, shipping and handling, discounts, and sales tax. Of the 12 item types provided by QuickBooks, some are directly related to items you sell, such as Service, Inventory Item, and Non-Inventory Item; while others, such as Subtotal, Discount, and Sales Tax, allow you to perform calculations in your sales form (see Chapter 7 for more information).

The Item List works similar to the Chart of Accounts. To open the Item List:

Click the **Lists** menu and click **Item List**.

Figure 3-9 shows the Item List with items displayed based on your choices in the EasyStep Interview.

As you can see in Figure 3-9, in addition to the Item, Activities, and Reports buttons, the Item List includes a fourth button, called Excel, which gives you the ability to import or export items from Microsoft Excel.

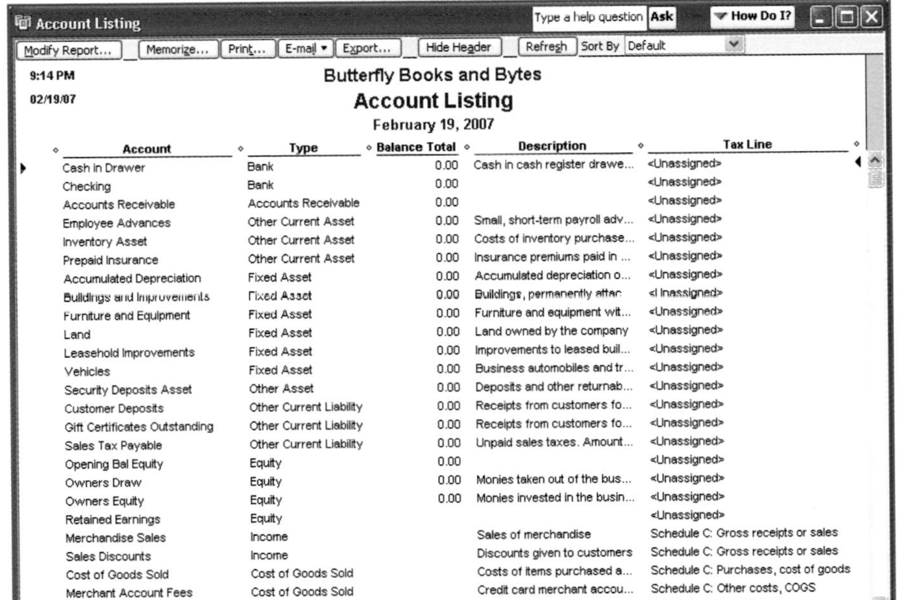

Account Listing — Type a help question Ask — How Do I?
Modify Report... Memorize... Print... E-mail Export... Hide Header Refresh Sort By Default

9:14 PM
02/19/07

Butterfly Books and Bytes
Account Listing
February 19, 2007

Account	Type	Balance Total	Description	Tax Line
Cash in Drawer	Bank	0.00	Cash in cash register drawe...	<Unassigned>
Checking	Bank	0.00		<Unassigned>
Accounts Receivable	Accounts Receivable	0.00		<Unassigned>
Employee Advances	Other Current Asset	0.00	Small, short-term payroll adv...	<Unassigned>
Inventory Asset	Other Current Asset	0.00	Costs of inventory purchase...	<Unassigned>
Prepaid Insurance	Other Current Asset	0.00	Insurance premiums paid in ...	<Unassigned>
Accumulated Depreciation	Fixed Asset	0.00	Accumulated depreciation o...	<Unassigned>
Buildings and Improvements	Fixed Asset	0.00	Buildings, permanently attac	<Unassigned>
Furniture and Equipment	Fixed Asset	0.00	Furniture and equipment wit...	<Unassigned>
Land	Fixed Asset	0.00	Land owned by the company	<Unassigned>
Leasehold Improvements	Fixed Asset	0.00	Improvements to leased buil...	<Unassigned>
Vehicles	Fixed Asset	0.00	Business automobiles and tr...	<Unassigned>
Security Deposits Asset	Other Asset	0.00	Deposits and other returnab...	<Unassigned>
Customer Deposits	Other Current Liability	0.00	Receipts from customers fo...	<Unassigned>
Gift Certificates Outstanding	Other Current Liability	0.00	Receipts from customers fo...	<Unassigned>
Sales Tax Payable	Other Current Liability	0.00	Unpaid sales taxes. Amount...	<Unassigned>
Opening Bal Equity	Equity	0.00		<Unassigned>
Owners Draw	Equity	0.00	Monies taken out of the bus...	<Unassigned>
Owners Equity	Equity	0.00	Monies invested in the busin...	<Unassigned>
Retained Earnings	Equity			<Unassigned>
Merchandise Sales	Income		Sales of merchandise	Schedule C: Gross receipts or sales
Sales Discounts	Income		Discounts given to customers	Schedule C: Gross receipts or sales
Cost of Goods Sold	Cost of Goods Sold		Costs of items purchased a...	Schedule C: Purchases, cost of goods
Merchant Account Fees	Cost of Goods Sold		Credit card merchant accou...	Schedule C: Other costs, COGS
Advertising and Promotion	Expense		Advertising, marketing, grap...	Schedule C: Advertising

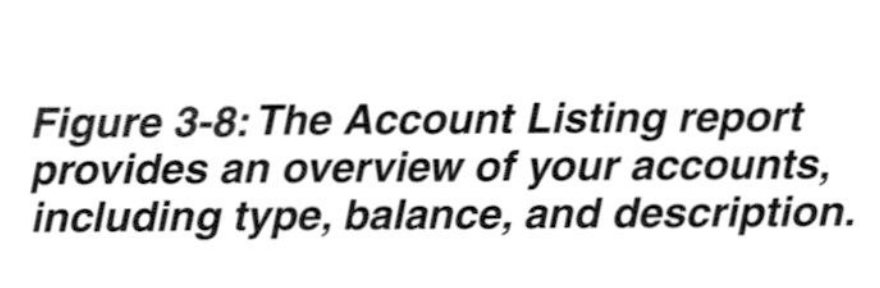

***Figure 3-8:* The Account Listing report provides an overview of your accounts, including type, balance, and description.**

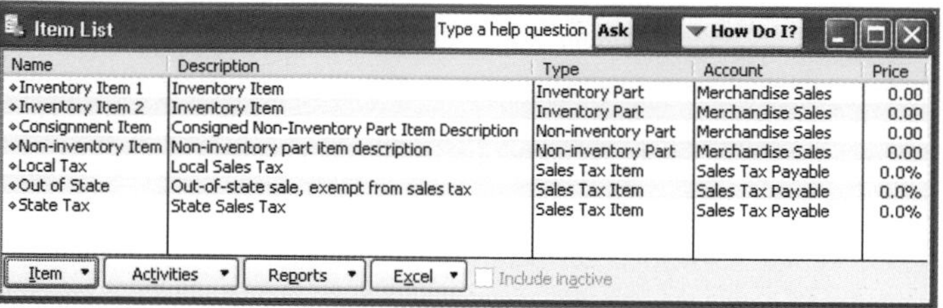

Figure 3-9: From the Item List, you can add, edit, and manage items.

You can create a new item or edit, delete, rename/merge, or make inactive any item on the Item List in the same manner as with accounts in the Chart of Accounts. You also can have subitems in the Item List, just as in the Chart of Accounts.

TIP

The Item List is important to both accounts receivable and accounts payable, since the items are used for job-costing purposes and can be linked to income and expense accounts.

EDIT AN ITEM

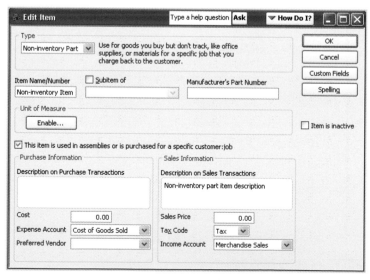

To edit an item on the Item List:

1. Double-click the desired item, such as **Non-Inventory Item**. The Edit Item window opens.
2. Click the **This Item Is Used In Assemblies Or Is Purchased For A Specific Customer:Job** check box. You will now see space to enter purchase information, which will allow you to track expenses by item.
3. Click the Expense Account down arrow, and click **Cost of Goods Sold**.
4. Click **OK** to close the Edit Item window. A dialog box appears, notifying you that you have changed the account associated with this item and asking if you want to apply this change to past transactions.
5. Click **Yes**.

When you use this item on purchase transactions, such as purchase orders, bills, or checks, the expenses will post to the Cost of Goods account; when you use this item on sales transactions, such as invoices or sales receipts, the income will post to the Merchandise Sales account.

Use the Other Names List

QuickBooks contains four name lists, three of which are integrated directly into their related centers (Customer, Vendor, and Employee). The Other Names List works similar to the Chart of Accounts. To open the Other Names List:

Click the **Lists** menu and click **Other Names List**.

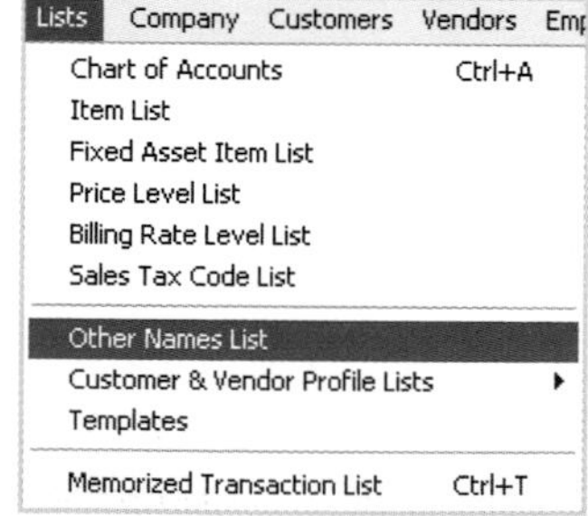

QUICKSTEPS

SETTING TAX FORMS AND TAX LINES

To help aid in tax preparation, each of the accounts in your Chart of Accounts can be associated with a specific line on your tax form. This is useful if you or your accountant will export QuickBooks information to a compatible tax-preparation program. To set the tax form:

1. Click the **Company** menu and click **Company Information**. The Company Information window opens, as shown in Figure 3-10.
2. Click the **Income Tax Form Used** down arrow (in the lower-left corner), and select your company's filing type.
3. Select the correct beginning month in the **Fiscal Year** and **Tax Year** drop-down lists if your company does not use the calendar year.
4. Click **OK** to save your changes and close the window.

Each Edit Account window has a drop-down list with default choices displayed when a tax form is set. To set the tax lines for your accounts:

1. Open your Chart of Accounts (click the **Lists** menu and click **Chart Of Accounts**).
2. Right-click an account, such as **Meals and Entertainment**, and click **Edit Account**. The Edit Account window opens, with the Tax Line drop-down list included.
3. Click the drop-down to see your choices. Review the selection in this list, and change it if necessary.
4. Repeat these steps for all of your accounts.

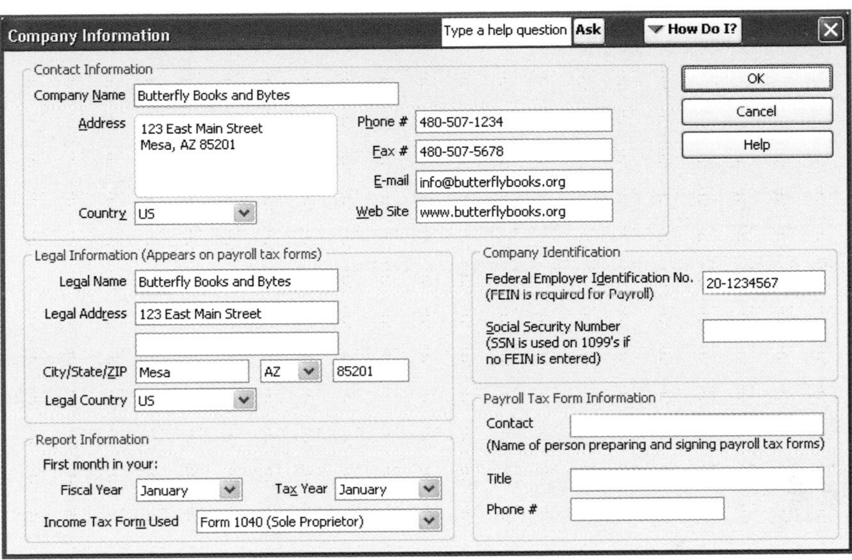

Figure 3-10: Company information should be kept accurate because it is used throughout QuickBooks.

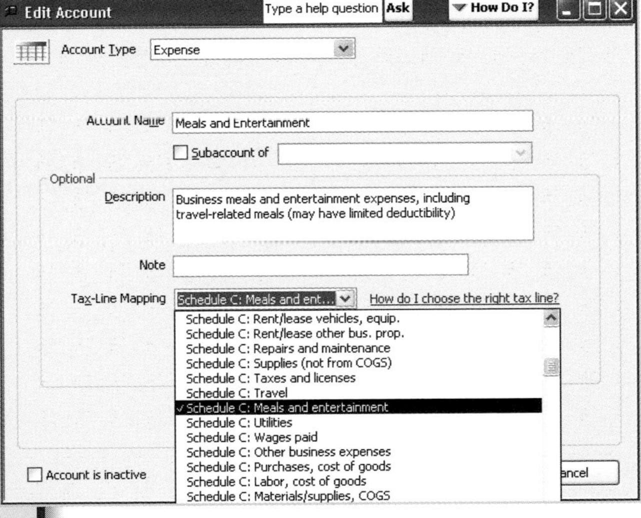

TIP

Names on the Other Names List are the only Name Types that you can change to another type (such as Customer, Vendor, or Employee), so if you are unsure what list to use, consider using Other Names until you determine the appropriate list for a person or company.

NOTE

You can't re-order the Other Names List as you can the Chart of Accounts List. It will always appear in alphabetical order; however, you can rename items on the Other Names List so that they appear in a specific order.

Figure 3-11 shows the Other Names List containing the name Owner. This name doesn't fall into any of the other three name types (Customer, Vendor, or Employee). An Other Name entry can consist only of the name (which is required), or it can include additional information, such as address, phone number, contacts, and so on. Since all the name lists are related to each other, you must use unique names throughout the list. If you try to add a name that already exists, you will receive a warning message.

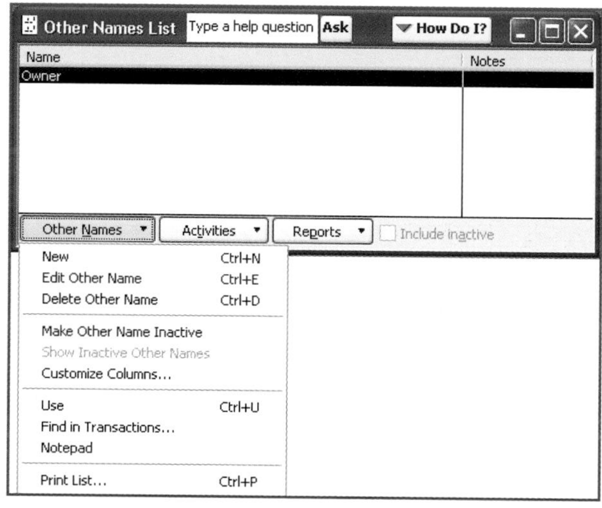

Figure 3-11: From the Other Names List, you can add, edit, and manage other names.

How to...

- Choosing a Bank
- Create a New Account
- Activate Online Banking
- Order Checks
- Sending and Receiving Online Transactions
- Write Checks
- Edit, Void, or Delete Checks
- Make Deposits
- View and Edit Bank Account Registers
- Transferring Funds Between Accounts
- Manage Business Credit Cards
- Set Up a Credit Card Account
- Enter Credit Card Transactions
- Receive and Enter Online Business Credit Card Transactions
- Reconcile Credit Card Accounts
- Reconcile Bank Accounts

Chapter 4
Setting Up and Using Your Bank Accounts

Maintaining a good cash flow, knowing where you stand on a daily basis, and reviewing and revising your collections and bill payment methods are all integral to your business's success. In QuickBooks, you can use online banking to further automate tasks or to simply record manual transactions in forms that look similar to their real-life counterparts, such as checks, deposits, and credit card transactions.

Use Banking Functions

The home page (seen in Figure 4-1) represents common banking activities, including:

- Record Deposits
- Reconcile
- Write Checks
- Check Register
- Print Checks
- Enter Credit Card Charges

The Account Balances List contains all of your current bank accounts, including credit cards

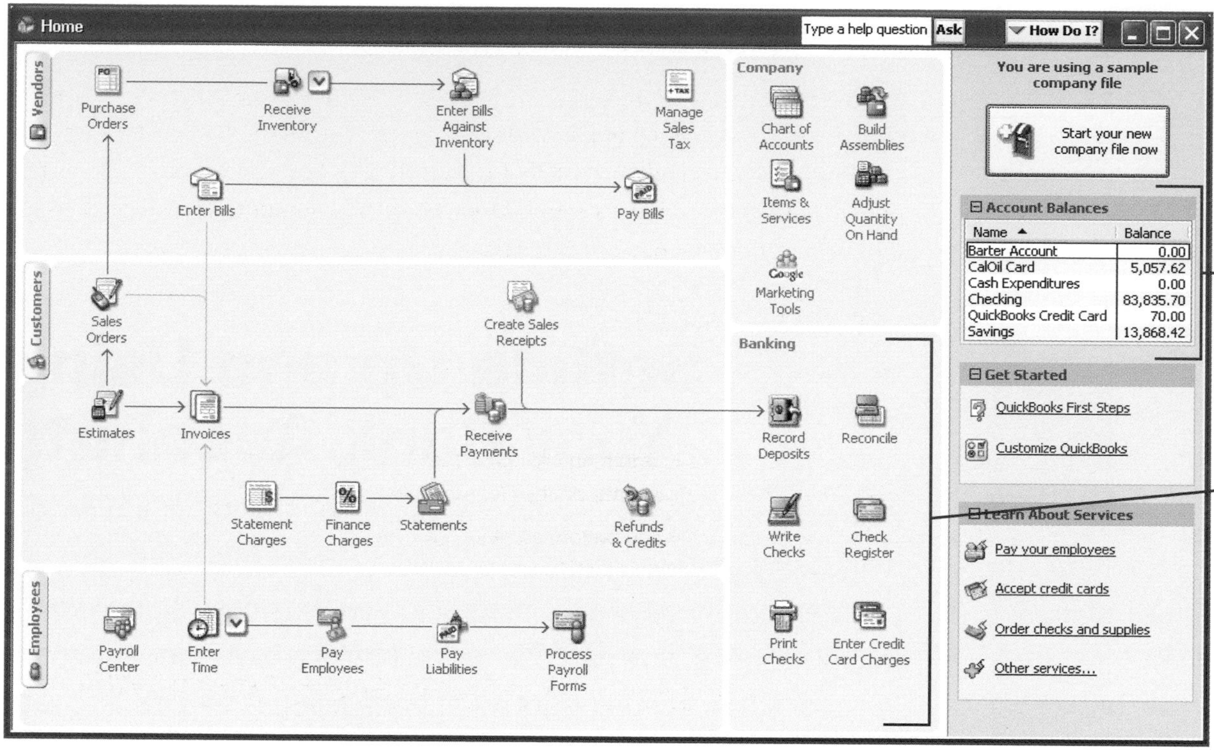

Common banking functions are easily accessible; click any icon to open a corresponding window

Figure 4-1: This sample company home page includes common banking activities, including credit card charges.

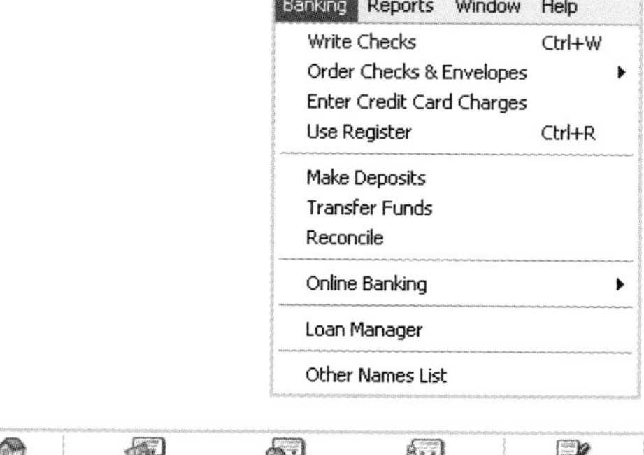

Other banking functions are available on the Banking menu, including:

- Transfer Funds
- Enter Credit Card Charges

You can access banking functions by one of three ways:

- Click the **Banking** menu and then click the desired function.
- From the home page, click the desired function.
- On the Navigation or Icon bar, click the desired function.

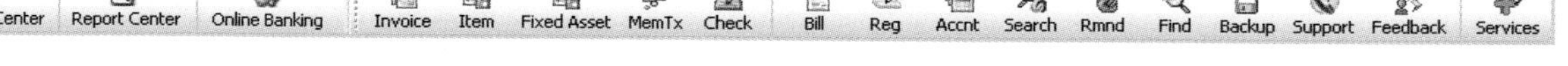

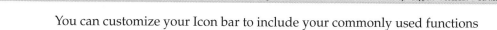

You can customize your Icon bar to include your commonly used functions (see Chapter 1).

NOTE

All of the examples in this chapter reflect the default settings in QuickBooks preferences. If your file does not exactly match the examples, refer to Chapter 8 for details on setting your preferences.

QUICKFACTS

CHOOSING A BANK

You may already have a bank, but your bank may not support the features that are important to you in your business; for example, online banking is a convenient feature that you'll want in a bank that serves your business. When comparing banks, use the following checklist as a guide to determine what features are important to you, and see if they are supported by the bank you are considering:

- Online banking through QuickBooks.
- Online viewing of checks.
- Debit card.
- Sweep accounts (moves money in excess of preset limits from a checking to a savings account automatically).
- Employee direct deposit (some banks offer this as a free benefit).
- No minimum balance (or compare minimums).
- No monthly fees (or compare fees). Don't forget to compare check fees, deposit fees, overage fees, stop-payment fees, telephone transfer fees, and any other fees that might apply to your business.

Set Up Bank Accounts

If you set up a new company file in Chapter 2, you may have already set up a checking account. Many businesses use two checking accounts: one for deposits and bill payments, and one strictly for payroll. Some businesses may also use a money market or savings account if they hold large amounts of cash, such as in the construction business, so that they may receive interest on that cash.

Create a New Account

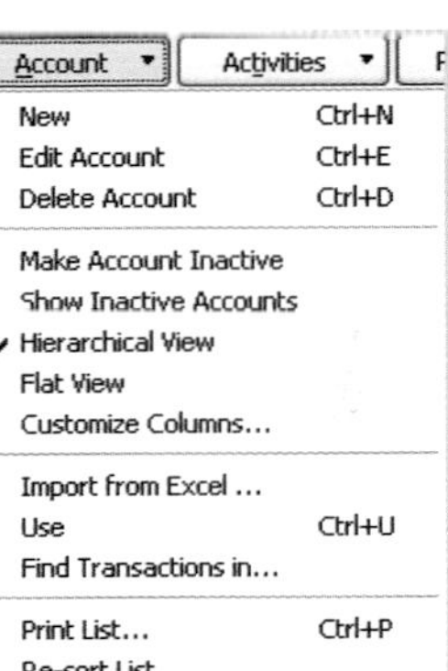

Creating a new account in QuickBooks is a simple process.

1. Click the **Lists** menu and then click **Chart of Accounts** (or click **Chart of Accounts** on the Home page).
2. Click the **Account** menu button, and then click **New**. The Add New Account:Select Account Type window opens.
3. Select Bank as the account type and click **Continue**.

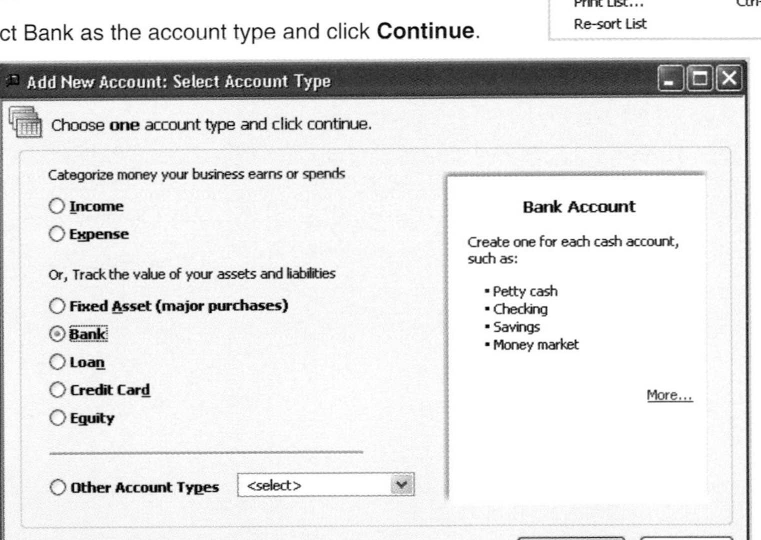

4. Type the account name in the Name field (for example, Payroll Checking).

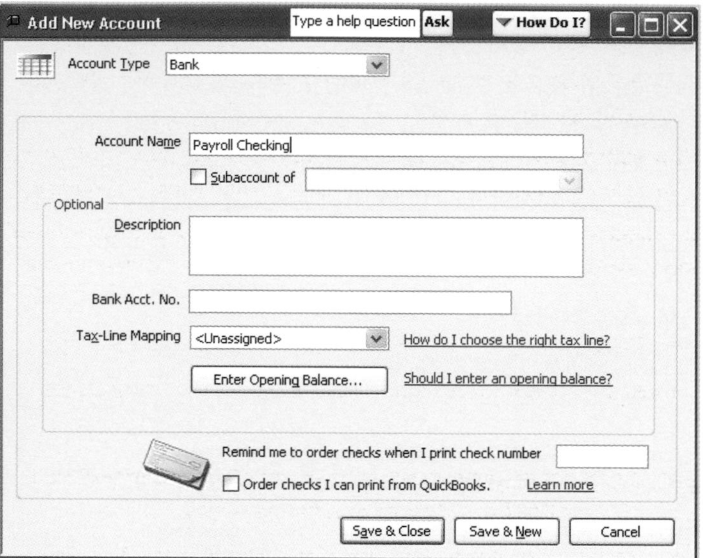

5. Click **Save & Close**. The account is created and will appear in the Chart of Accounts List.

All of the other fields are optional. It is best not to use the opening balance, but instead enter a deposit after you create the account in order to make sure the funds are credited to the correct accounts.

Activate Online Banking

Online banking is convenient and safe. It pays for itself in time and cost savings, since you no longer have to print, stamp, and mail payments to vendors. Many banks support online banking; however, you need to clarify that they support online banking *through* QuickBooks. If you are not sure if your current bank does, the simplest way to find out is to try to set up an account online and see if they are listed.

To set up an online banking account, you first need your bank to set up the account for online banking, and then you need to activate that account within QuickBooks for use with online banking.

TIP

Online access can be used for more than just bank accounts. Many credit card companies also allow you to download transactions, thus saving you time when doing data entry.

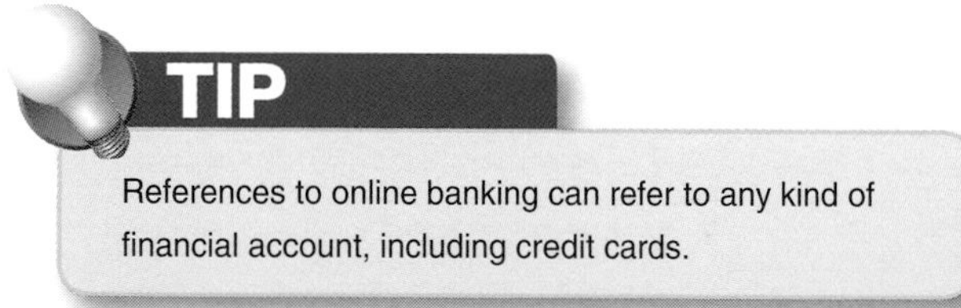

TIP

References to online banking can refer to any kind of financial account, including credit cards.

APPLY FOR ONLINE BANKING

1. Click the **Banking** menu, select **Online Banking**, and click **Available Financial Institutions**. Click **OK** if you see a dialog box notifying you that QuickBooks must connect to the Internet to continue. The Financial Institutions Directory window opens.

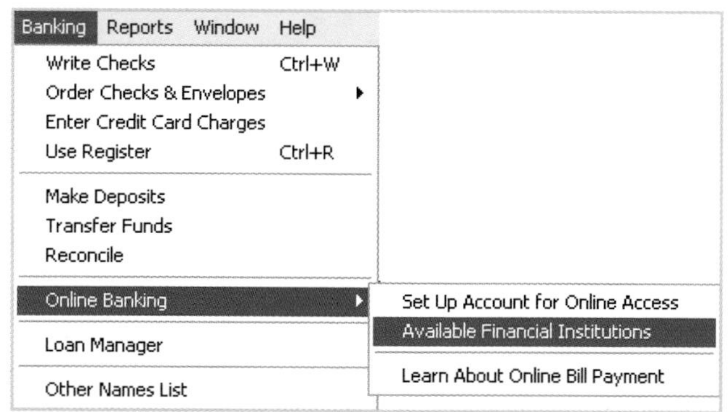

2. Click one of the four buttons in the upper-left area of the screen to indicate the type of account you want to access, and then click your bank from the list located underneath,

TIP

When asking your bank about online banking, be sure to emphasize that you need it through QuickBooks. Some banks combine support for QuickBooks and Quicken (a home financial program). "Online banking" often refers to accessing information through a bank's web site, which, while useful, will not give you all the benefits of online banking through QuickBooks.

as shown in Figure 4-2. You may have to scroll down to find your bank. The middle of the page displays a summary of what that bank offers in the way of online banking. Look for the word "Direct" under Supported Download Method, which indicates that your bank can link up directly with QuickBooks.

3. Click the **Apply Now** button to find out exactly how to activate online banking. You may be able to apply directly online, or you may need to call or go into your local branch.
4. Once you have chosen a bank, click the **Close** button (the X in the upper-right corner) to close the window. QuickBooks will note which institution you selected and update your list of banks.

ENABLE QUICKBOOKS BANK ACCOUNT FOR USE WITH ONLINE BANKING

Once you have received confirmation from your bank that online banking is activated:

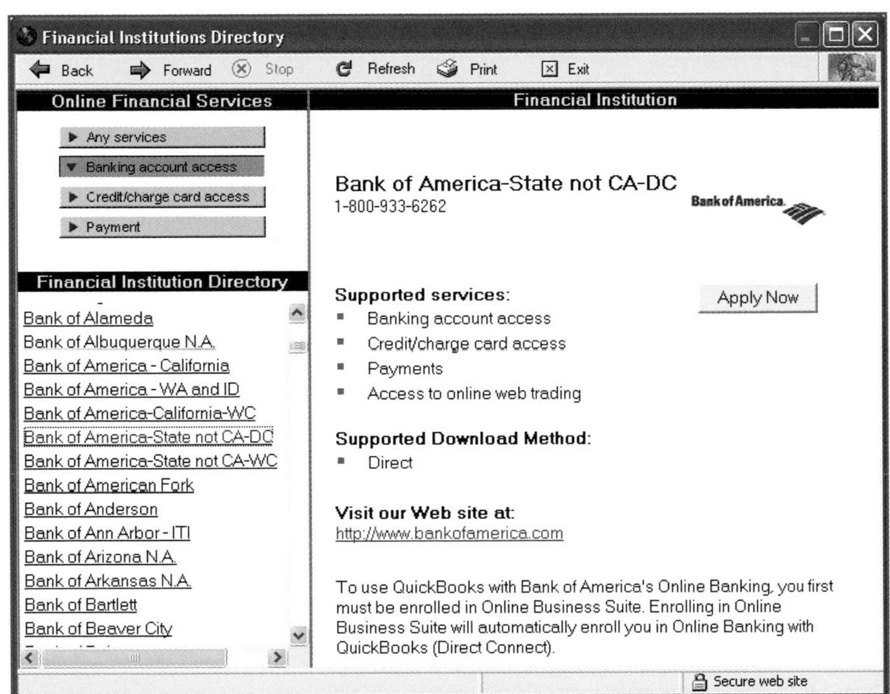

Figure 4-2: The first step in setting up an online banking account in QuickBooks is to select your bank from the list.

1. Click the **Banking** menu, click **Online Banking**, and then click **Set Up Account For Online Access**.
2. Click **Yes** if you see a dialog box notifying you that QuickBooks needs to close all open windows. The Online Banking Setup Interview Wizard starts.

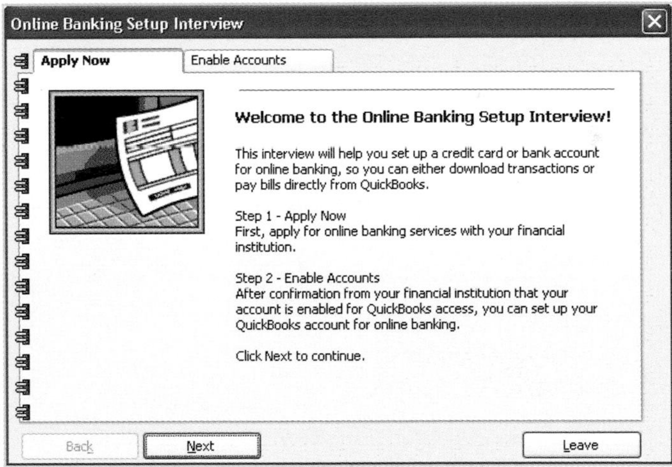

3. Click **Next**.
4. Select **Bank account ar QuickBooks Bill Pay service** and click **Next**.

TIP

You can verify that your account is active by looking at your Chart of Accounts. Notice the lightning bolt icon next to the checking account, which denotes that it is now an active online account.

5. Select **I have already completed an application with my institution**.
6. Click the **Enable Accounts** tab at the top of the window and click **Next**.
7. Select your bank from the drop-down list, and click **Next**. If your bank is not on the list, click **Leave** and repeat the steps in the preceding section, "Apply for Online Banking."
8. Click **Yes. I've Received My Confirmation Letter From <*Your Bank*>**. Click **Next**.
9. Type your routing number in the Routing Number field, and type your customer ID in the Customer ID field. These numbers should be in the letter you received from your bank. Click **Next**.
10. Select the relevant account name (such as **Checking**) from the drop-down list. Click **Next**.

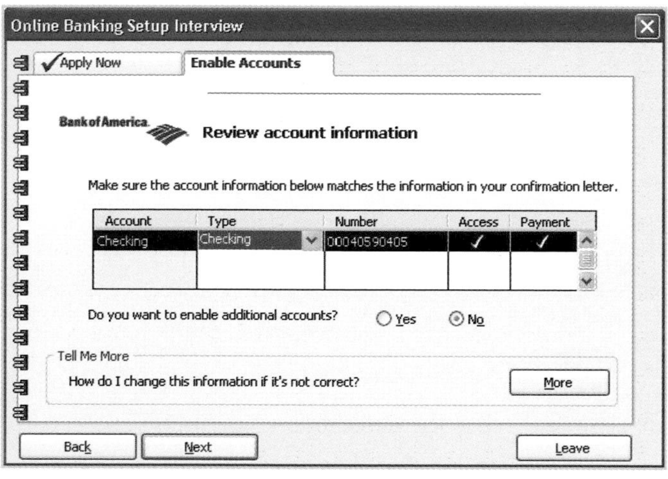

11. Select your account type from the drop-down list, and type your account number in the Account Number field. Click the **Online Account Access** and **Online Payment** options. (Do not click the Online Payment option if your bank doesn't offer this service.) Click **Next**.
12. Review your information, confirm that **No** is selected (unless you want to configure additional accounts), and click **Next**.
13. Click **OK** in response to the dialog box that appears, asking you to acknowledge that these services are provided by your banking institution and not by Intuit.
14. Click **No** in response to the dialog box that appears, asking if you want to set up accounts at another institution, and click **Next**.
15. Read the congratulations message and click **Leave**. The Online Banking Center will open, similar to that shown in Figure 4-3. You can close it by clicking the **X** in the upper-right corner. See "Sending and Receiving Online Transactions" in this chapter for more information.

NOTE

QuickStatements are a great way to find out if a check has cleared or a transaction has occurred, but they don't take the place of your monthly paper statement. It's always a good idea to periodically review transactions during reconciliation.

Order Checks

When writing checks in QuickBooks, you have three choices:

- Use the Online Bill Payment method, which does not require you to purchase any forms.
- Print checks on bank-approved, QuickBooks-style checks.
- Handwrite checks, and then enter the information into QuickBooks.

Deposit slips can also be printed or handwritten, although not completed online, since you need to physically deliver your deposit to the bank.

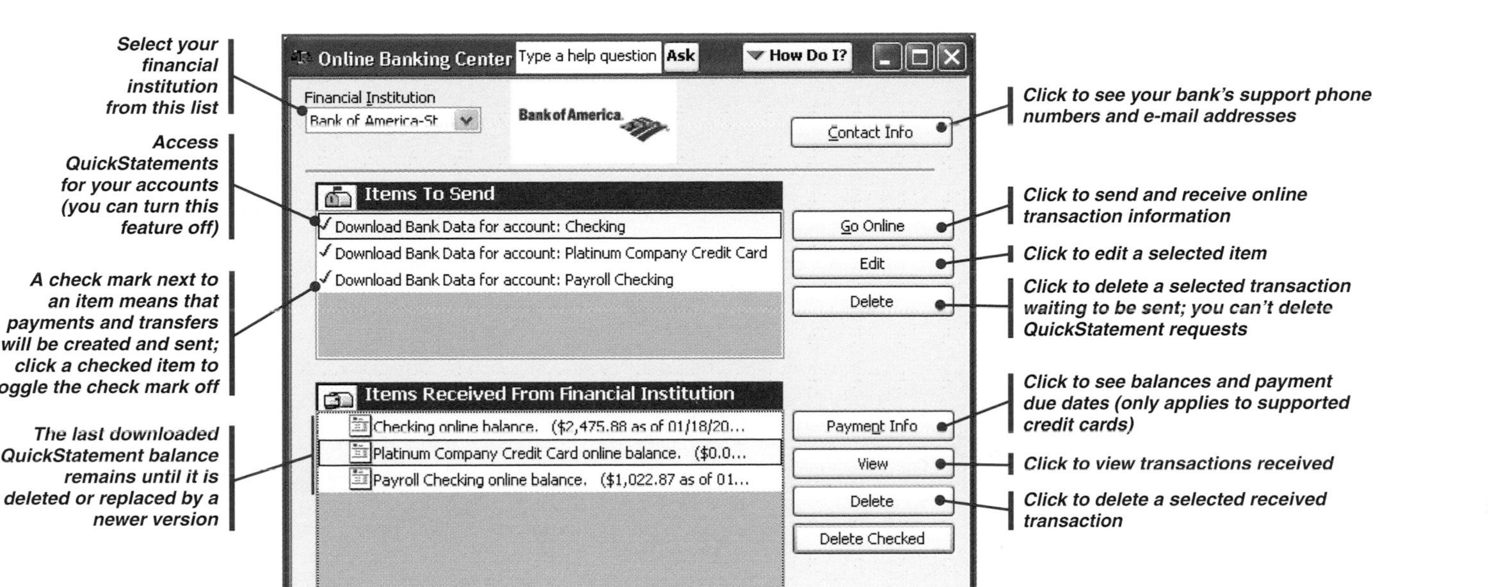

***Figure 4-3:** Use the Online Banking Center in QuickBooks to manage your accounts, financial institution information, and transaction types.*

NOTE

Your QuickBooks online banking account uses a different password from your QuickBooks user account, so keep this password private to prevent unauthorized persons from sending electronic checks.

If you currently have manual (handwritten) checks, you can continue to use those and enter the checks in QuickBooks; however, if you process a large number of checks each month, consider online banking with a bank that supports online payment or getting checks that will fit in your printer.

To order checks directly from Inuit, click the **Banking** menu, select **Order Checks & Envelopes**, and click **Order Checks**. The Order Supplies window opens. Follow the directions on the screen.

You can also choose to order from your bank or other check companies. Be sure to clarify that you need QuickBooks compatible checks.

Manage Your Accounts on a Daily Basis

The following sections will show you how to accomplish daily tasks, such as writing checks, making deposits, transferring funds, and reviewing transactions.

SENDING AND RECEIVING ONLINE TRANSACTIONS

To send and receive online transactions, use the Online Banking Center, shown in Figure 4-3 with two checking accounts and a credit card activated for online banking.

To send and receive online transactions at any time:

1. Click the **Banking** menu, select **Online Banking**, and click **Online Banking Center**. The Online Banking Center is displayed.
2. Click the **Go Online** button (on the right side of the screen). You are prompted for your PIN number (which was provided to you by your bank).
3. Type your PIN number and click **OK**. QuickBooks contacts your bank, downloads the latest transaction information to your computer, and uploads the latest information from your QuickBooks company file to the bank, including checks to send online. When finished, you will see either a summary of the transaction-information exchange or a message notifying you that no new transactions exist.
4. Click **OK** or **Close**. You are returned to the Online Banking Center and have a QuickStatement record from the bank in the Items Received From Financial Institution area, as shown in Figure 4-3.
5. Double-click the QuickStatement to review it. Understanding the QuickStatement and reconciling your account will be covered in later sections.

TIP

Be sure to verify your routing number and account number, as well as your name, address, and other data both during your order and after receiving your checks.

Write Checks

QuickBooks makes it easy to write checks. Whether you are handwriting checks and then entering the information into QuickBooks for bookkeeping, entering checks to be printed on check forms, or entering checks to be sent online, the process is basically the same.

1. Click the **Banking** menu and click **Write Checks** (or click the **Write Checks** icon on the home page). The Write Checks window opens, as shown in Figure 4-4. Confirm that you are in the correct bank account from which to write a check. If not, click the Bank Account down arrow and select the correct account.
2. Press the **TAB** key to move to the Date field. Click the **Calendar** icon to select the date from a drop-down calendar, or type the date in the field.
3. Press the **TAB** key again to move to the Pay to the Order of line.
4. Type the payee's name, for example, <u>Desert Breeze Phone Company</u>.

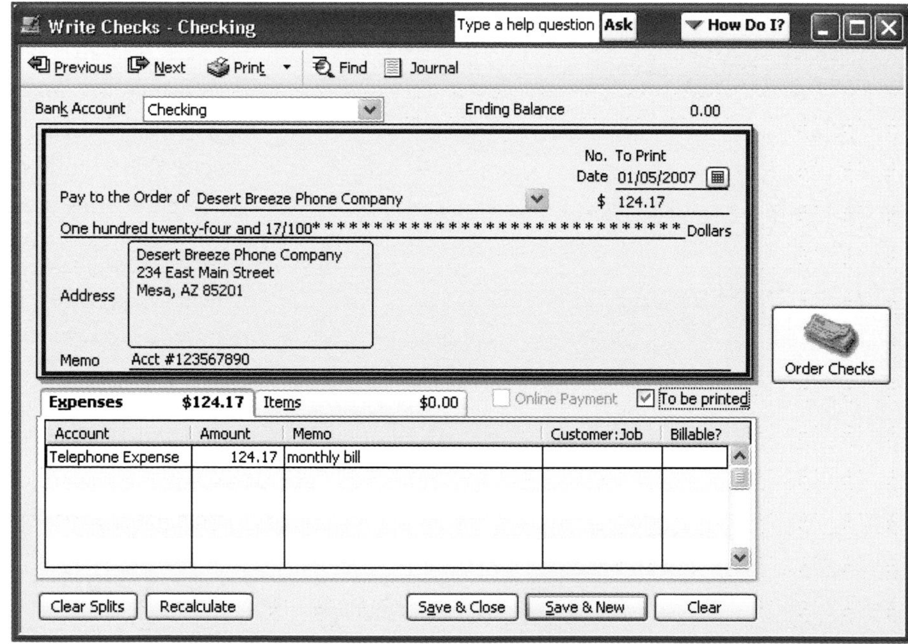

Figure 4-4: The Write Checks feature in QuickBooks makes writing checks a breeze.

Name Not Found

Desert Breeze Phone Company is not in the Name list.

To automatically add Desert Breeze Phone Company to the Name list, click QuickAdd. You can enter more detailed information later.

To enter the detailed information now, click Set Up (usually not required).

Quick Add | Set Up | Cancel

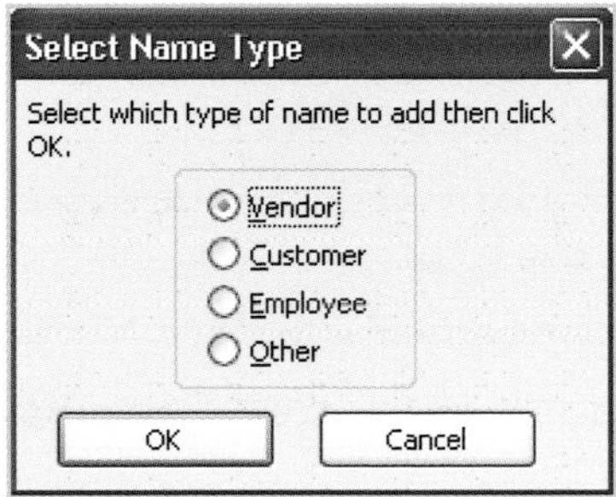

5. Press the **TAB** key again to move to the Amount line. If the payee's name is not in the Name List, the Name Not Found dialog box appears.
6. Click the **Quick Add** button. The Select Name Type dialog box appears. The Vendor option is chosen by default, since you are writing a check.
7. Click **OK**. The payee (in this case, Desert Breeze Phone Company) is added to the Vendor Name List, and the cursor moves to the Amount line.
8. Type the amount of the check (in this case, 124.17).
9. Press the **TAB** key again. QuickBooks automatically fills in the Dollars field with the correct wording based on the Amount field.
10. Press the **TAB** key to move to the Address area, where the Payee's name has already been filled in by QuickBooks.
11. Press the **ENTER** key to move to the next line, and type the payee's address.
12. Press the **ENTER** key to move to the next line, and type the payee's city, state, and ZIP code.
13. Press the **TAB** key to move to the Memo field.
14. Type a relevant memo, for example, Business Phone.
15. Choose one of the following:
    - To print the check, confirm that the **To Be Printed** check box is selected. The words "To Print" will appear in the No. line.
    - To send the payment online, click the **Online Payment** check box if you have online banking enabled (you may need to clear the To Be Printed Box to select Online Payment). When you select this feature, QuickBooks may notify you that you need more information. All online payments must include an account number and telephone number in addition to the address.
    - To handwrite the check, make sure that both these check boxes are clear, and type the check number that appears on the physical check you are writing in the No. field (located above the date).
16. Click in the first line under Account (in the bottom portion of the screen), and type Telephone Expense. (Typing T will cause Telephone Expense to appear automatically in this field if it is already in your Chart of Accounts.)
17. Press the **TAB** key twice to move to the Memo column. What you type here will serve as a memo for you and will not be printed on the check sent to the payee.

TIP

You can request your checks be **Reverse Numbered** if you place checks in your printer facedown.

TIP

You can also use QuickBooks-compatible checks for handwritten checks rather than ordering standard checks.

CAUTION

Do not use the Write Checks feature to create paychecks (see Chapter 9 for more information on payroll).

TIP

You can use the plus (+) and minus (–) keys to increase the date forward or backward by one day per keystroke.

TIP

To track expenses for customers (for more accurate profitability reports), enter the customer name for related expenses in the Customer:Job field.

TIP

You can click **Save & New** to continue entering checks.

NOTE

You can split any check, bill, or credit card charge into multiple expense accounts. See Chapter 5 for more information.

TIP

QuickBooks uses the most recently used date by default, but you can configure QuickBooks so that it always uses today's date by default instead (Click **Edit**, click **Preferences**, click **General**, click the **My Preferences** tab, and then click **Use Today's Date As Default**). To prevent mistakes, be sure to confirm that the date is correct during every transaction.

18. Click the **Save & Close** button. If the address for the payee doesn't match the one QuickBooks has on file, a dialog box will appear, asking you to confirm the new address. Click **Yes** if you want to use this address when writing future checks to this payee.

Edit, Void, or Delete Checks

If you make a mistake when writing a check, you can edit, void, or delete the check. Once a check has been sent, however, you should not change the check itself, just the items in the bottom portion of the Write Checks window.

1. Click the **Banking** menu and then click **Write Checks**.
2. Click **Previous** until you see the check you wish to change. To edit the check, simply make the desired changes to the check.
3. Click the **Edit** menu. You will see a list of options to use on this check.
4. To void or delete the check, choose one of the following:
   - To void the check, click **Void Check**. The check amount is changed to $0, and the Memo line on the check reads VOID.
   - To delete the check, click **Delete Check**. A dialog box will appear, confirming the action. If you click **Yes**, QuickBooks immediately carries out this action.
5. Click the **Save & Close** button. If you made changes to the check, including voiding the check, a dialog box appears, asking if you want to save your changes.
6. Click **Yes** to save the changes.

Make Deposits

Often, beginning QuickBooks users enter their checks but not their deposits. As a result, their bank accounts look like negative holes. To keep accurate records, you need to track your deposits in QuickBooks, as well as your checks.

> **TIP**
>
> The Edit menu changes throughout QuickBooks, depending on what area you are in. Click it to see what options you have throughout your QuickBooks user session.

> **TIP**
>
> See Chapter 8 to learn how to find transactions quickly.

> **CAUTION**
>
> Only delete checks when there is an actual error, such as two identical checks being entered into QuickBooks when only one check was actually written. Otherwise, void checks whenever possible.

> **TIP**
>
> If you have already sent the check to the recipient, don't change anything on the face of the check in the Write Checks window. Change only the information below the check, such as accounts, items, memo, or classes.

When you receive payments from customers, always use the Sales Receipt form or Receive Payments form to match customer payment with correct Sales Receipt or Invoice in order to keep accurate customer accounts. This process will be covered in Chapter 6.

You can use the Make Deposits form for compiling Received Payments from customers as well as any non-customer payments you have received, such as rebates or loans.

THE MAKE DEPOSITS WINDOW

1. Click the **Banking** menu and click **Make Deposits** (or click **Record Deposits** on the Home page). The Make Deposits window opens, as shown in Figure 4-5. If the default account in the Deposit To drop-down list is not the one you want to use, click the down arrow and select the correct account.
2. Press the TAB key to move to the Date field. Click the **Calendar** icon to select the date from a drop-down calendar, or type the date in the field.
3. Press the TAB key to move to the Memo field. The word "Deposit" may be changed.

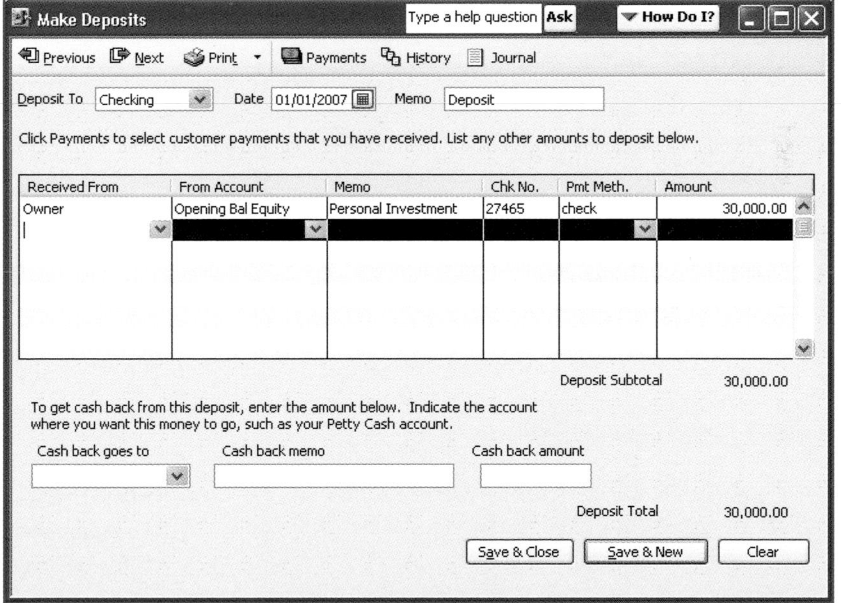

Figure 4-5: QuickBooks gives you the ability to easily record and track your deposits using the Make Deposits window.

TIP

If you use another system for tracking sales but use QuickBooks for tracking expenses, enter a single daily sales receipt so that you can more readily identify income areas. See Chapter 6 for more information.

NOTE

If you have received funds from customers, a Payments To Deposit window will open before the Make Deposits window, listing those items waiting for deposit. Select items from this list that will be included on your deposit, and then click **OK**. This method is covered in Chapter 6.

TIP

Name drop-down lists (Customer:Job, Vendors, Employee, and Other) are used throughout QuickBooks, and you often only need to type the first few letters to see the correct name appear. Alternatively, you can click the down arrow to view all names. If the name you want to use is not on the list, type it in the relevant field, and indicate what type of name it is when prompted by QuickBooks.

TIP

You can use the Quick Add button to add payment methods, as well as names and accounts. This applies to most lists throughout QuickBooks.

4. Press the TAB key to move to the Received From column. Click the down arrow and select the relevant name, or type the first few letters of the name to cause the correct name to appear. If this is a new name (for example, Owner), type it in the field.
5. Press the TAB key to move to the From Account column. If it's a new name, QuickBooks will ask if you want to add the name. Click **QuickAdd**. When QuickBooks asks you to select a name type, click **Other**, for this example, and click **OK**.
6. In the From Account column, click the down arrow and select the relevant account. If you type the first few letters of the name in that field, the correct account will automatically appear in the drop-down list. For example, typing Op causes "Opening Bal Equity" to automatically appear.
7. Press the TAB key to move to the Memo column, and type a memo pertaining to the deposit, for example, Personal Investment.
8. Press the TAB key to move to the Check Number column, and type the check number, for example, 27465.
9. Press the TAB key to move to the Payment Method column. Click the down arrow and select the relevant payment method. If you type the first few letters of the payment method, the correct name will automatically appear in the drop-down list. For example, typing Ch causes "Check" to automatically appear.
10. Press the TAB key to move to the Amount column, and type the check amount, for example, 30000.
11. Press the TAB key again. The cursor moves to the beginning of the next line and updates the Deposit Subtotal and Deposit Total amounts. If you want to continue entering checks and cash received to this deposit, repeat Steps 4–10.
12. If you are finished entering this deposit, click the **Save & Close** button.

PRINT A DEPOSIT SLIP

If you have QuickBooks-compatible deposit slips for your printer, you can print a deposit slip. If not, you will need to handwrite a deposit slip.

To print a deposit slip for use with your actual bank deposit:

1. Click the **Banking** menu and click **Make Deposits** (or click **Record Deposits** on the Home page). The Make Deposits window opens. If the default account in the Deposit To drop-down list is not the one you want to use, click the down arrow and select the correct account.

TIP

If you want a deposit summary or to see how the deposit slip will print before using a preprinted deposit slip, print your deposit on a blank sheet of paper as a test.

2. Enter the Deposit as directed in the section above, or click the **Previous** button to return to the last deposit you made. Make sure the actual amounts match the QuickBooks entry.
3. Load your preprinted deposit slip into your printer.
4. Click the **Print** button. The Print Deposit dialog box appears.
5. Click **Deposit Slip And Deposit Summary** if you have QuickBooks-compatible deposit slips. Otherwise, click **Deposit Summary Only** and use this to prepare a handwritten deposit slip or for reporting purposes and recordkeeping. Click **OK**. The Print Deposit Slips window opens, as shown in Figure 4-6.

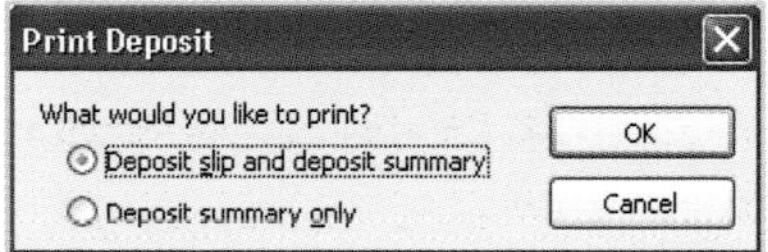

6. Make sure you have your deposit slip in the printer the correct way (you may want to test it with a blank sheet first), and then click the **Print** button.
7. Close the **Make Deposit** window.

NOTE

You can edit or delete deposits just as you can checks. Simply return to the deposit and make the necessary changes. While the Make Deposits window is open, if you want to delete or void the deposit, click the **Edit** menu and click **Delete Deposit** or **Void Deposit**.

View and Edit Bank Account Registers

QuickBooks is driven by forms, such as those found in the Write Checks, Make Deposits, and Transfer Funds windows, but all transactions are kept in a register,

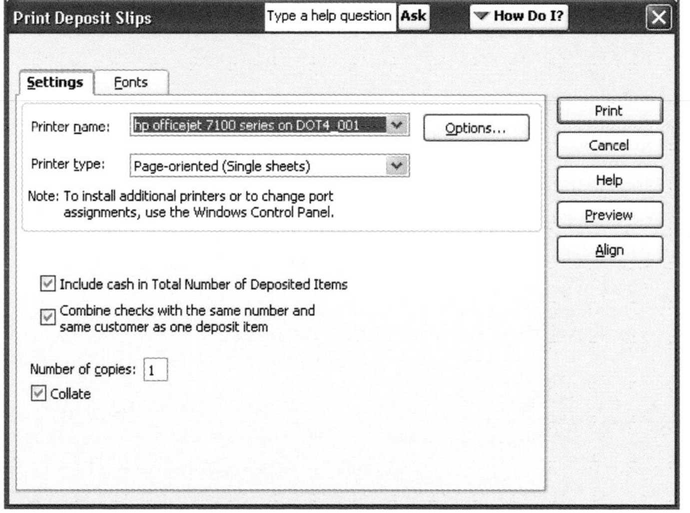

Figure 4-6: The Print Deposit Slips window enables you to include cash in your deposits and combine deposits from the same customer.

TIP

You can double-click the bank accounts in your Home page to open the register.

which you can view and edit. The easiest way to view your register is through the Chart of Accounts.

1. Click the **Lists** menu and click **Chart of Accounts** (or click **Chart of Accounts** on the Home page).
2. Double-click the **Checking** account. The check register is displayed, as shown in Figure 4-7. You can edit directly in this register, or click a transaction and click the **Edit Transaction** button to open the form the transaction refers to (for example, Make Deposit, Write Checks, or Transfer Funds). Follow the steps in previous sections, such as "Edit, Void, and Delete Checks," for specific information on editing a given transaction.

Manage Business Credit Cards

This section refers to credit cards you use to buy things for your business as opposed to merchant accounts—credit cards that you accept as payment from

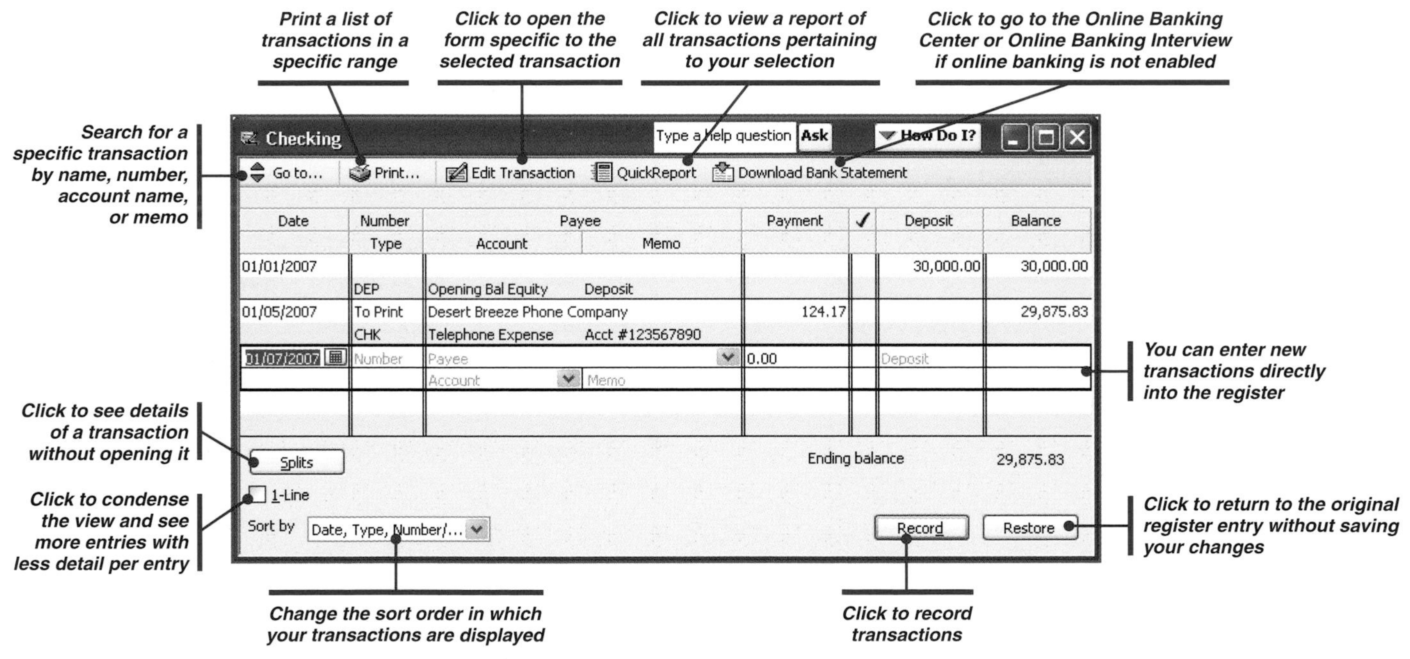

Figure 4-7: Registers, such as the check register shown here, help you monitor your transactions and, as a result, your company's financial health.

QUICKSTEPS

TRANSFERRING FUNDS BETWEEN ACCOUNTS

You can transfer funds between two bank accounts or between any liability or equity accounts, either online or manually, and enter these transactions into QuickBooks to keep your balances accurate.

1. Click the **Banking** menu and click **Transfer Funds**. The Transfer Funds Between Accounts window opens.
2. Click in the **Date** field, and type the date. Alternatively, you can click the **Calendar** icon to select the date from a drop-down list. Our example will use the date 1/2/2007.
3. Press the TAB key to move to the Transfer Funds From field. Click the down arrow and select the relevant account (in this case, the **Checking** account). Notice that all your bank accounts and asset, liability, and equity accounts are listed.
4. Press the TAB key to move to the Transfer Funds To field. Click the down arrow and select the relevant account (in this case, **Payroll Checking**). Alternatively, you can type the first few letters of the account name (for example, Pa), and the correct name should automatically appear in the drop-down list.
5. Click in the **Transfer Amount** line. If the account you are transferring money from and the account you are transferring money to are both online, you will have the option to click the **Online Funds Transfer** check box.
6. Type the transfer amount (such as 5,000).
7. Press the TAB key to move to the Memo field, and type a note reminding you of the reason for the transfer, for example, Weekly Payroll Transfer.
8. Click the **Save & Close** button.

your clients. If you use a business credit card, it's important to keep it separate from your personal credit card account. In rare cases, for example, if your business uses a credit card only occasionally, it may be more convenient to put your business expenses on a personal credit card and reimburse yourself with a check from your business account. This procedure is not advised, however, and you should check with your accountant as to the best course of action to take.

Set Up a Credit Card Account

To set up a credit card account:

1. Click the **Lists** menu and click **Chart of Accounts** (or click **Chart of Accounts** on the Home page).
2. Click the **Account** menu and click **New**. The Add New Account: Select Account Type window opens.
3. Select **Credit Card** and click **Continue**.
4. In the **Account Name** field, as seen in Figure 4-8, type your credit card name, for example, Platinum MasterCard. This is the only required field in this form. Enter other information if desired.
5. Click **Save & Close**.

Enter Credit Card Transactions

Entering credit card transactions in QuickBooks is similar to entering checks. You enter the vendor, date, and amount at the top of the form, and then fill in the account and memo information at the bottom of the form.

1. Click the **Banking** menu and click **Enter Credit Card Charges** (or click **Enter Credit Card Charges** on the Home page). The Enter Credit Card Charges window opens, as shown in Figure 4-9.
2. If the default account in the Credit Card drop-down list is not the one you want to use, click the down arrow and select the correct account.
3. Press the TAB key to move to the Purchased From field, and type the vendor name, for example, Texaco. If you have used this vendor before, typing the first few letters of the name will cause the correct name to appear in the field automatically; otherwise, QuickBooks will prompt you to add this name to the Vendor List. Choose QuickAdd and Vendor, if prompted.

1 2 3 4 5 6 7 8 9 10

TIP

Entering credit card charges in QuickBooks is easy, but it can get repetitive if you have a lot of entries to make. Refer to the section "Apply for Online Banking" and follow the same steps to see if your credit card company will support the downloading of online transactions.

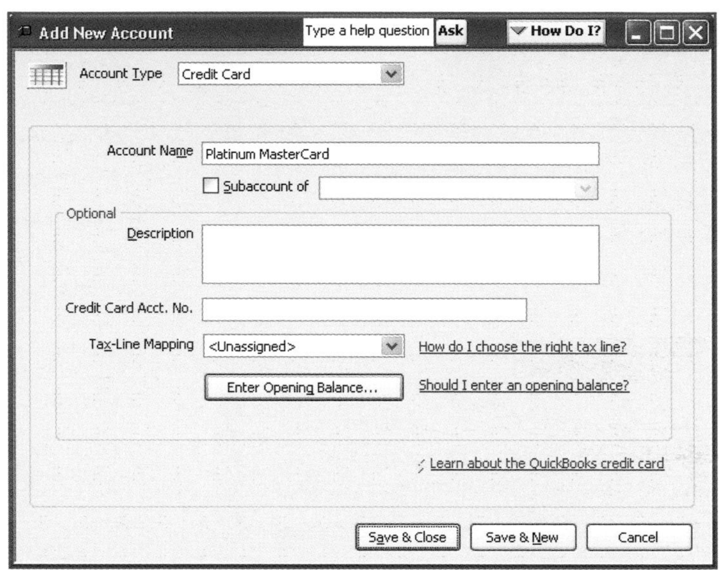

***Figure 4-8:** Fill in the fields for a complete record of your new credit card account. Entering your credit card number is optional but can be a useful reference when contacting the bank.*

TIP

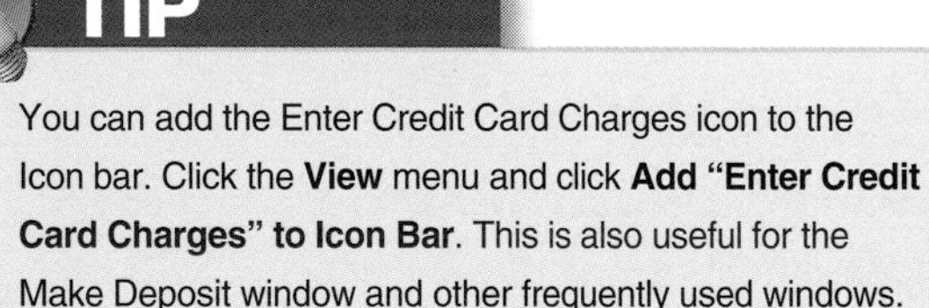

You can add the Enter Credit Card Charges icon to the Icon bar. Click the **View** menu and click **Add "Enter Credit Card Charges" to Icon Bar**. This is also useful for the Make Deposit window and other frequently used windows.

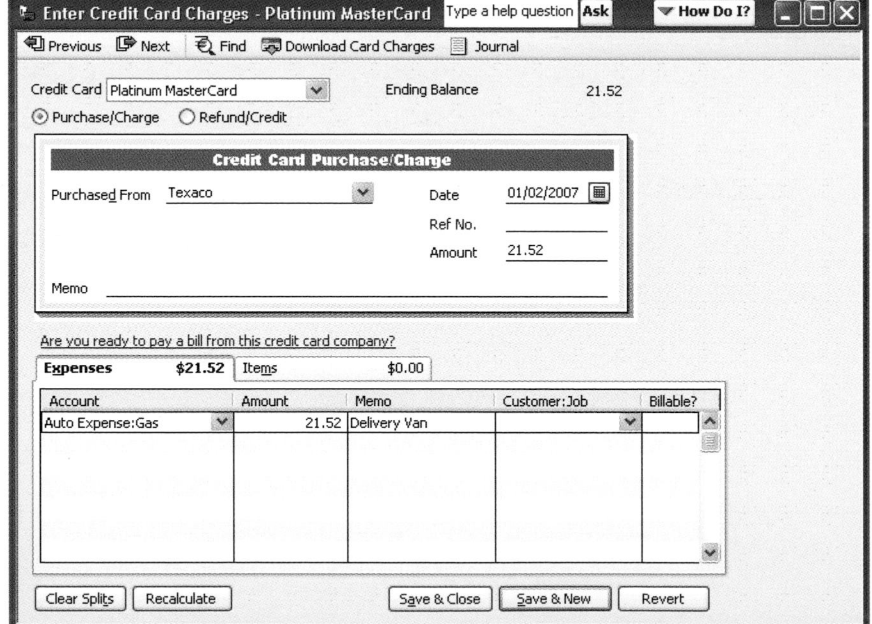

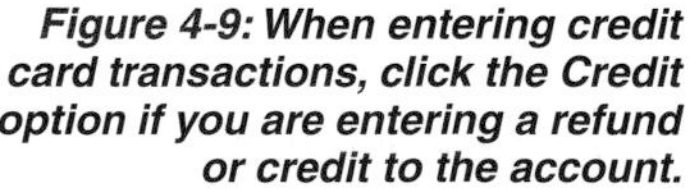

***Figure 4-9:** When entering credit card transactions, click the Credit option if you are entering a refund or credit to the account.*

CAUTION

Most of the time you will be entering charges. If you need to enter a credit, click the Refund/Credit option just under the Credit Card name.

NOTE

When you type G in the account column, "Gas" may appear because you have few accounts listed. Experiment with your names. Change them if typing the same few letters is liable to bring up different accounts. For example, typing the letters GA might cause both "Gas" and "Garbage" to appear, so you might change "Garbage" to "Trash."

4. Click in the **Date** field, and type the date of the charge. Alternatively, you can click the **calendar** icon to select the date from a drop-down list.
5. Press the **TAB** key twice to move to the Amount field. Type the amount of the charge, in this case, 21.52.
6. Press the **TAB** key twice to move to the Account column at the bottom.
7. Type the account name, in this case Auto Expense. If this is an account you have used before, typing A may cause this name to appear automatically in the field. If not, click **Add New** to add it to the Account List.
8. Type a colon (:) to accept the Auto Expense category and enter a subcategory.
9. Type G, and "Gas" appears if you are following the examples in this chapter using the sample company. Otherwise, you can add this account to the list or use a different one.
10. Press the **TAB** key to move to the Amount column. The amount—21.52—should have appeared automatically.
11. Press the **TAB** key to move to the Memo column. If you need a reminder as to why this charge was incurred, type it here, such as Delivery Van.
12. Press the **TAB** key to move to the Customer:Job column. This column is used to track expenses that are reimbursable from clients or to track for whom you bought supplies. If you enter a customer, you can click in the last column to identify whether this charge is billable to the client.
13. When finished, click **Save & Close**.

Receive and Enter Online Business Credit Card Transactions

Receiving online credit card transactions is just like receiving online banking transactions, except you can use a different account. If your account is not yet set up for online transactions, refer back to the Activate Online Banking section of this chapter.

1. Click the **Banking** menu, select **Online Banking**, and click **Online Banking Center**. The Online Banking Center is displayed.
2. If the default account in the Financial Institution drop-down list is not the one you want to use, click the down arrow and select the correct account.
3. Click **Go Online**. You are prompted for your PIN.

1 2 3 4 5 6 7 8 9 10

1 2 3 4 5 6 7 8 9 10

4. Type your PIN (or password), and click **OK**. QuickBooks connects to your bank and downloads any new transactions. When finished, a summary is displayed.
5. Click **Close** after reviewing the new transactions (click **OK** if you are notified that there are no new transactions). You are returned to the Online Banking Center, and the new downloaded transactions are listed in the Items Received From Financial Institution area in the bottom portion of the screen.

> **TIP**
>
> Many large, national vendors have a unique identifier for each store and each register within the store. To avoid having a long list of vendors that actually refer to one company, the Alias feature of QuickBooks allows you to assign multiple names to one vendor.

VIEW AND ENTER TRANSACTIONS

Once your transactions are downloaded, you can view them and match them to entries already in your credit card register or add them to your register, either one at a time or all at once.

1. Double-click the relevant QuickStatement in the bottom portion of the Online Banking Center. The Match Transactions window opens (see Figure 4-10), with your register displayed in the top and the current downloaded transactions displayed in the bottom. QuickBooks will automatically match items when possible.

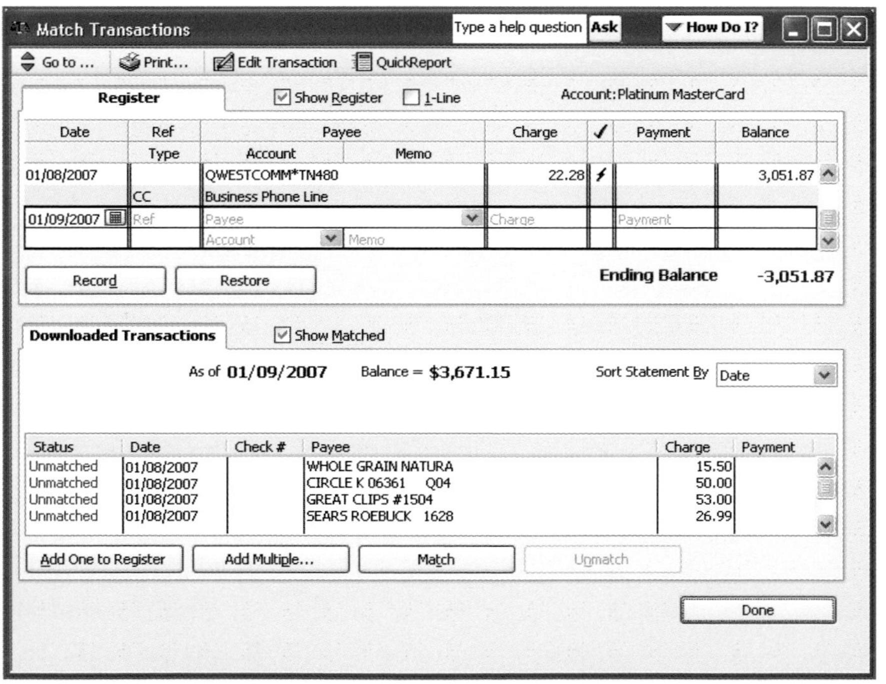

Figure 4-10: Compare your downloaded transactions to your register in order to reconcile an account.

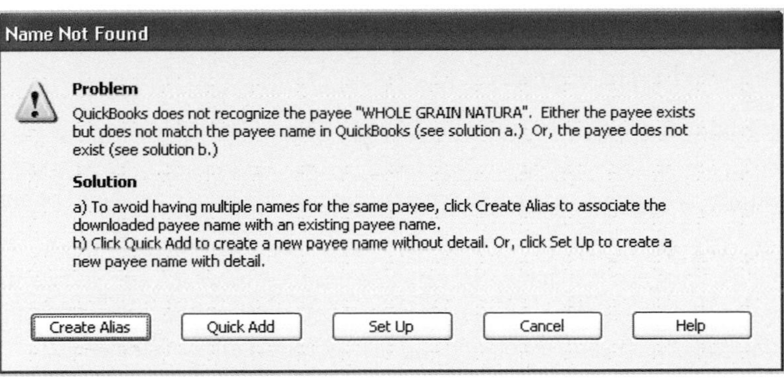

Name Not Found
Problem
QuickBooks does not recognize the payee "WHOLE GRAIN NATURA". Either the payee exists but does not match the payee name in QuickBooks (see solution a.) Or, the payee does not exist (see solution b.)
Solution
a) To avoid having multiple names for the same payee, click Create Alias to associate the downloaded payee name with an existing payee name.
b) Click Quick Add to create a new payee name without detail. Or, click Set Up to create a new payee name with detail.
Create Alias
Quick Add
Set Up
Cancel
Help

2. On the **Downloaded Transactions** tab, click an unmatched item.
3. Click the **Add One to Register** button to add the transaction to your account. If the Vendor name is not recognized, the Name Not Found window will appear. Click the **QuickAdd** button to add the name to the list, or click the **Create Alias** button if the payee name refers to a current name but with slight differences, such as a register identifier for stores, and then choose the vendor to associate it with. The transaction is then added to your register.
4. Click **Record**. The item is recorded. Repeat for other transactions.
5. Click **Done** when finished.

ADD MULTIPLE TRANSACTIONS AT ONCE

You can use the Add Multiple feature to add multiple transactions at one time.

Add Multiple Transactions to the Register

Transactions with recognized payees: (45)

All transactions must have an account selected.

✓	Date	Payee	Account	Charge	Payment
✓	01/08/2007	STREETS OF NEW YORK 21	Meals and Entertainment	108.60	
✓	01/08/2007	ARCO AM-PM GILBERT	Auto:gas	5.43	
✓	01/08/2007	DOLRTREE 2617 00026179	Office Supplies	10.81	
✓	01/08/2007	ARCO AM-PM GILBERT	Auto:gas	8.34	
✓	01/08/2007	ARCO AM-PM GILBERT	Auto:gas	50.00	
✓	01/08/2007	ALBERTSONS #957 S9H	Office Snacks	185.22	
✓	01/08/2007	INTERLAND INC/WEB.COM	IT Expenses	69.95	
✓	01/08/2007	WALGREEN 00040188	Office Supplies	4.05	
✓	01/08/2007	ANZIO LANDING	Meals and Entertainment	70.00	
✓	01/08/2007	HEALTHNET OF AZ IFP P	Medical:Insurance, Health	197.00	

Select All | Select None | Record | Cancel | Help

Transactions with unrecognized payees: (30)

These transactions must be added to the Register individually after clicking Record.

Date	Unknown Payee	Charge	Paym...
01/08/2007	FRANK'S ECONO LUBE N TUN	74.05	
01/08/2007	SADIES	97.21	
01/08/2007	WALGREEN 00039974	32.02	
01/08/2007	WENDYS 1238 Q25 Q25	19.82	
01/08/2007	COLDSTN CREAM #259 Q24	17.35	
01/08/2007	SKYRIVER COMMUNICATIONS	5.00	
01/08/2007	FARR'S SERVICE	43.46	

Figure 4-11: After payees (normally Vendors) are entered into QuickBooks the first time, all subsequent transactions from that payee can be automatically entered.

1. In the Match Transactions window, click the **Add Multiple** button. The Add Multiple Transactions to the Register window opens, as shown in Figure 4-11. Transactions with recognized vendors are shown at the top, while transactions with new vendors are shown at the bottom of the window.
2. Select the correct account in the Account column for each transaction.
3. Click the **Record** button. The transactions with recognized vendors are recorded, and you are returned to the Match Transactions window. You can now enter transactions with new vendors individually.
4. Click **Done**.

Manage Your Accounts on a Monthly Basis

When you receive your monthly bank or credit card statement, reconciliation is simply a matter of clicking each transaction in QuickBooks to place a check mark next to it. After your reconciliation is complete, you will have the option to write a check for the credit card balance or enter a bill.

Reconcile Credit Card Accounts

To reconcile your credit card accounts:

1. Click the **Banking** menu and click **Reconcile** (or click **Reconcile** in the Home page). The Begin Reconciliation window opens (see Figure 4-12). If your beginning balance doesn't match your statement, click the **Locate Discrepancies** button to view changes made since the last reconciliation.

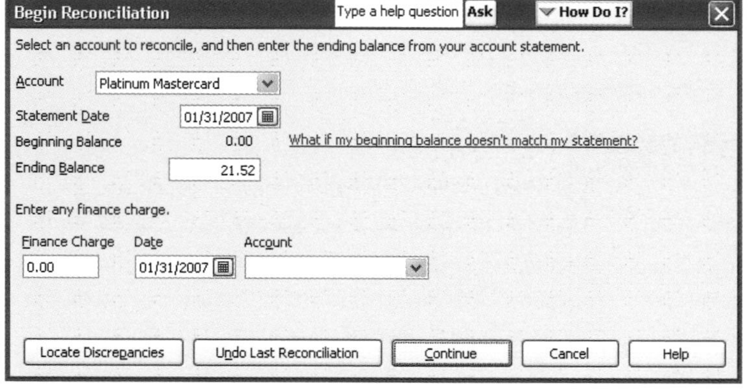

Figure 4-12: The Begin Reconciliation window is the starting place for reconciling bank accounts, credit card accounts, and equity accounts.

2. If the default account in the Account drop-down list is not the one you want to use, click the **Account** down arrow, and select the correct account. Note that bank, credit card, asset, and liabilities accounts are all listed.
3. Press **TAB** to move to the Statement Date field, and type the statement ending date, or click the **Calendar** icon and select the statement ending date.
4. Press **TAB** to move to the Ending Balance field, and type the ending balance that is listed on your statement, for example, 21.52.
5. If this account has finance charges, type it in the **Finance Charge** field, and confirm the date (type the date, or click the **calendar** icon and select the date from a drop-down list).
6. Click the **Account** down arrow located to the right of the Date field, and click the relevant account, for example, **Bank Service Charges**.
7. Click **Continue**. The Reconcile Credit Card window opens, as seen in Figure 4-13.

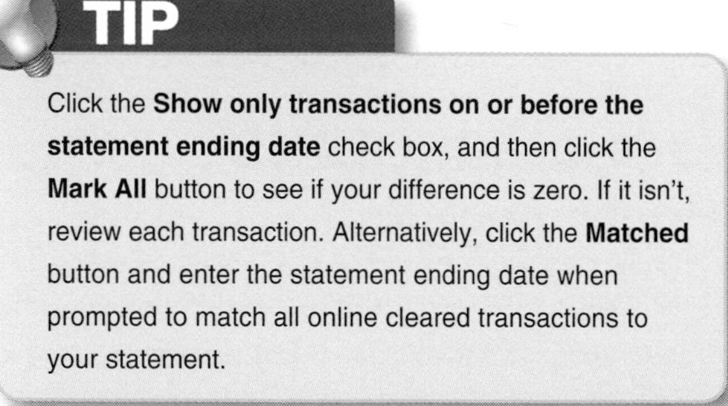

TIP

Click the **Show only transactions on or before the statement ending date** check box, and then click the **Mark All** button to see if your difference is zero. If it isn't, review each transaction. Alternatively, click the **Matched** button and enter the statement ending date when prompted to match all online cleared transactions to your statement.

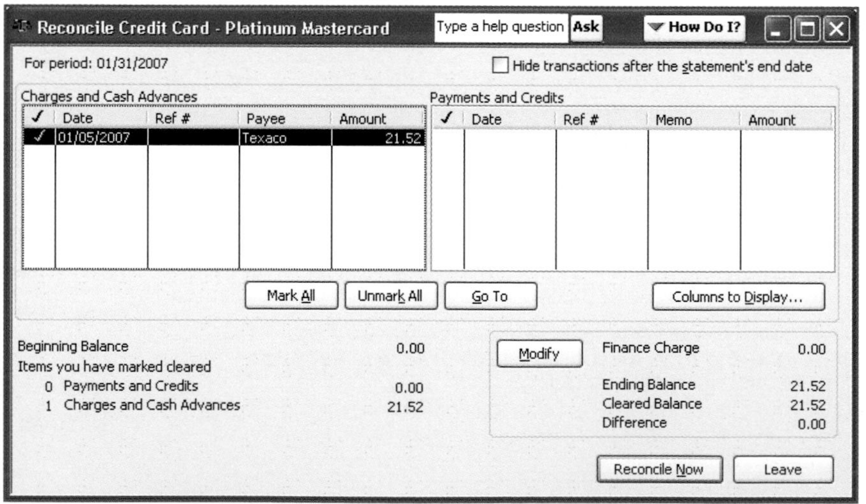

Figure 4-13: The Reconcile Credit Card window makes it easy to ensure that your credit card entries are accurate and up-to-date.

TIP

If an item entered in QuickBooks doesn't match your statement, double-click any transaction to review it, and make changes as needed. Save the edited transaction and click the **Save & Close** button to return to the Reconcile Credit Card window.

NOTE

Although you may use Enter Bill for paying credit card bills if your business prefers that process, Enter Bill does not change report information, since the actual transactions have already been recorded on their date of the credit card transaction.

8. Click individual items to mark them as cleared (a check mark is placed in the left column), or click **Mark All**. In the lower area of the screen, you can watch your balances change as you click each item.
9. Click the **Reconcile Now** button when your difference is zero. The Make Payment dialog box appears. The **Write A Check For Payment Now** option is selected by default.
10. Click **OK**. The Write Checks window opens, and the Select Reconciliation Report dialog box appears. You can choose to view and print reports if you would like to file a copy for your records.
11. Click **Close** and review the check entered in the Write Checks window. You may want to edit the amount to pay a portion less than the full balance. Edit the check information if needed, and identify it as a check that will be printed or a check sent in the form of an online payment. The first time you write a check to your credit card company, QuickBooks will prompt you to add its information to your Vendor List (see the section "Write Checks" for more information).

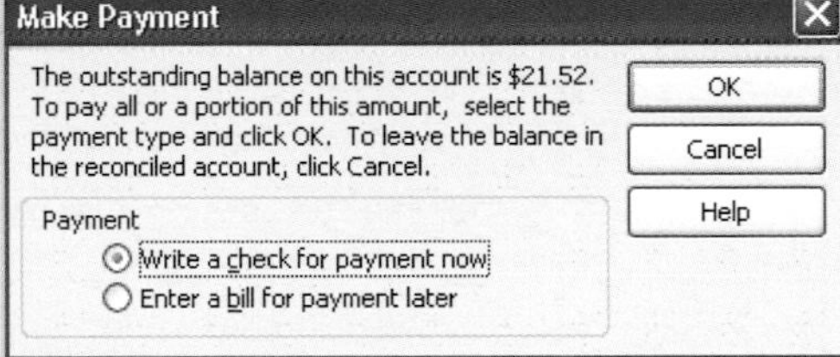

12. Click **Save & Close**.

Reconcile Bank Accounts

Reconciling bank accounts is similar to reconciling credit card accounts.

1. Click the **Banking** menu and click **Reconcile**. The Begin Reconciliation window opens, as shown in Figure 4-14.
2. If the default account in the Account drop-down list is not the one you want to use, click the down arrow and select the correct account.
3. Press **TAB** to move to the Statement Date field, and type the date, or click the **Calendar** icon and select the date from a drop-down list.
4. Press **TAB** to move to the Ending Balance field, and type your ending balance as listed in your bank account statement (for example, 24,875.83).
5. Press **TAB** to move to the Service Charge field, and type the service charge amount, for example, 9.95.
6. Press **TAB** to move to the Date field, and type the date, or click the **Calendar** icon and select the date from a drop-down list.

Begin Reconciliation | Type a help question | Ask | How Do I?

Select an account to reconcile, and then enter the ending balance from your account statement.

Account: Checking — last reconciled on 01/31/2007.

Statement Date: 01/31/2007

Beginning Balance: 0.00 — What if my beginning balance doesn't match my statement?

Ending Balance: 24,875.83

Enter any service charge or interest earned.

Service Charge: 0.00 | Date: 01/31/2007 | Account:

Interest Earned: 0.00 | Date: 01/31/2007 | Account:

Locate Discrepancies | Undo Last Reconciliation | Continue | Cancel | Help

Figure 4-14: Make sure that service charges are entered into an expense account and that interest accrued is entered into an income account.

1 2 3 4 5 6 7 8 9 10

1 2 3 4 5 6 7 8 9 10

TIP

If you make a mistake entering your dates or amounts in the Begin Reconciliation window, click the **Modify** button in the Reconciliation window to change your entries.

Select Reconciliation Report

Congratulations! Your account is balanced. All marked items have been cleared in the account register.

Select the type of reconciliation report you'd like to see.

- Summary
- Detail
- Both

To view this report at a later time, select the Report menu, display Banking and then Previous Reconciliation.

Display | Print... | Close

7. Click the second **Account** down arrow, and click the relevant account, for example, **Bank Service Charges**.
8. If you earn interest on this account, click in the **Interest Earned** field, and type that amount.
9. Press **TAB** to move to the second Date field, and type the date, or click the **Calendar** icon and select the date from a drop-down list.
10. Click the third **Account** down arrow, and click the relevant account.
11. Click **Continue**. The Reconcile window opens, as seen in Figure 4-15.
12. Click individual items to mark them as cleared. In the lower area of the screen, you can watch your balances change as you click each item.
13. Click the **Reconcile Now** button when your difference is zero. The Select Reconciliation Report window opens. Click the type of report you want to see: **Summary**, **Detail**, or **Both**.
14. Click **Display** to see the reports. Click **Print** to create a hard copy of the reconciliation report. Close the reports when finished.

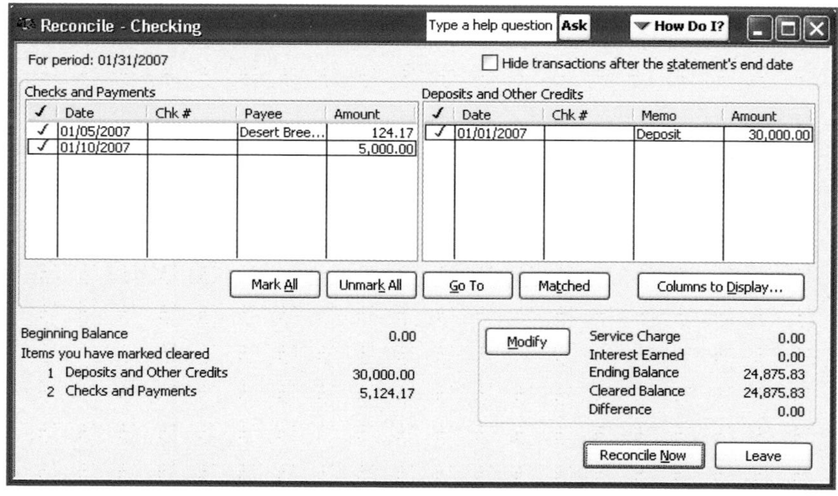

Figure 4-15: Use the Reconcile window to make sure your bank account information is accurate and up to date.

How to...

- *Use the Vendor Center*
- *Add a Vendor*
- *Merge, Delete, or Make Vendors Inactive*
- *Set Up and Print 1099s*
- *Adding Custom Fields to Your Name Lists*
- *Enter and Pay Bills*
- *Use Items on a Bill*
- *Memorize Reminder Transactions*
- *Memorize Automatic Transactions*
- *Manage Memorized Transactions*

Chapter 5
Entering and Paying Bills

Managing your accounts payable (A/P) and vendors is a large part of staying in business. You have to pay bills, and QuickBooks makes it easy to do. With accurate vendor reports, you may be able to negotiate better discounts or deferred-payment terms. Entering all your expenses is important in knowing how profitable your business is. In addition, if you charge items directly to your clients, you can use QuickBooks to track billable expenses and items so that you don't miss out on any potential chargebacks.

Manage Vendors

Vendors are anyone from whom you purchase items or services. This includes contractors, some of which are considered 1099 vendors. The IRS requires that a Form 1099 be issued at the end of the year to any unincorporated contractor paid more than a certain amount during the course of the year (currently $600).

> **CAUTION**
>
> QuickBooks does not allow duplicate names among lists, so if you have a customer, for example, that is also a vendor, when adding this name to the Vendor List, include a "-v" at the end of the name.

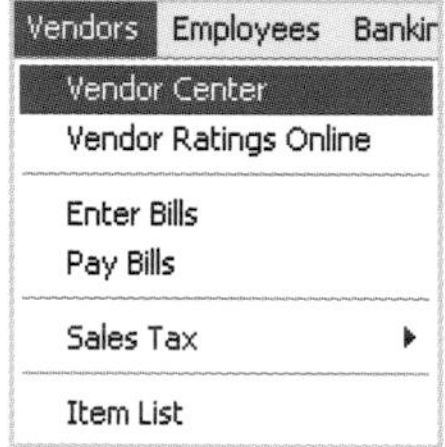

> **NOTE**
>
> Use a consistent naming policy. SRP is a good example of an easy-to-mistype vendor name. SRP; S.R.P; SRP Electric; and Salt River Project are all completely different to QuickBooks, although they represent the same company.

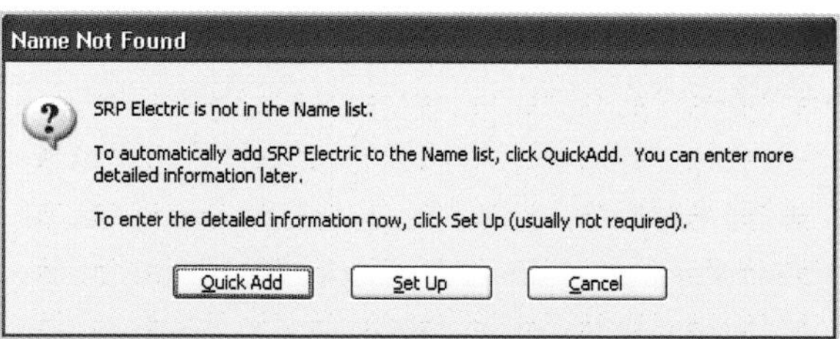

Name Not Found
SRP Electric is not in the Name list.
To automatically add SRP Electric to the Name list, click QuickAdd. You can enter more detailed information later.
To enter the detailed information now, click Set Up (usually not required).
Quick Add
Set Up
Cancel

Use the Vendor Center

The Vendor Center is one of the three centers in QuickBooks, the others being Customer Center and Employee Center. The Vendor Center is simple to use and includes a Vendor List on the left side and details of the selected vendor on the right side (in this example, Desert Breeze Phone Company). Use any of the following methods to open the Vendor Center:

Click the Vendor Center icon on the Navigation bar.

–Or–

Click the **Vendors** menu and click **Vendor Center**.

–Or–

Click **Vendors** on the home page.

Figure 5-1 shows the Vendor Center with three vendors: Desert Breeze Phone Company, Platinum MasterCard, and Texaco. Each vendor was entered using the Quick Add feature when writing a check (see Chapter 4). Some vendor entries only consist of the name (which is required), whereas other vendor entries include additional information, such as address, phone number, contacts, and so on. The level of detail you require in your reports will dictate how you create your vendor entries.

Click the **Close** button (the X in the upper-right corner) to close the Vendor Center.

Add a Vendor

QuickBooks offers three ways to add vendors:

- Use the Quick Add feature
- Use the Set Up feature
- Use the Vendor Center

Anytime you use a name in any part of QuickBooks (such as Write Checks) that is not already in QuickBooks' records, the Name Not Found dialog box appears:

- Click **Quick Add** to add just the vendor name to the Vendor List.

Open the New Vendor window

Open the selected transaction with the currently highlighted vendor entered

Print Vendor List, vendor information, or Vendor Transaction List

Import from or export to a Microsoft Excel spreadsheet

Create vendor letters or modify templates using Microsoft Word

Open Edit Vendor window

Open QuickBooks Notepad window

Show Vendor Transaction List (not showing)

Show Vendor List (showing)

Filter vendors according to criteria

Vendors List

Show or hide vendor details (on the right side)

Select transaction types and transaction date range to display

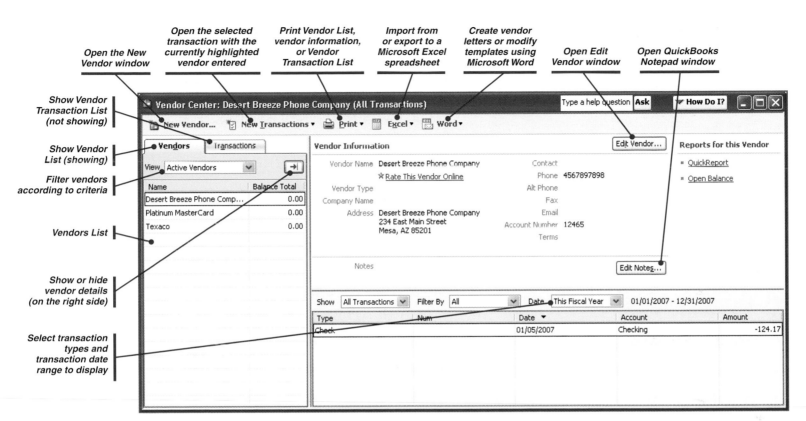

Figure 5-1: ***The Vendor Center enables you to quickly access features and information pertaining to your vendors.***

TIP

You can correct any errors in Name lists by editing an incorrect name to the correct one. If the correct name already exists, QuickBooks will ask if you want to merge these names. Say Yes and all the data from both names are now contained in one name. This works on all lists, including Customers, Vendors, and Employees.

- Click **Set Up** to open a New Vendor window. From here, you can enter as much or as little information as you want.
- Click **Cancel** to return to the Name field in whatever window you were in previously (for example, Write Checks). This is extremely useful in the event that you mistyped the name.

If the Name Not Found dialog box appears and the vendor is one your company has used before, click **Cancel** to return to the previous window, click the **Name** down arrow, and look up the correct entry.

ADD A VENDOR FROM THE VENDOR CENTER

The Quick Add and Set Up features are useful when you need to add a new name to any list. You can also directly add vendors in the Vendor Center,

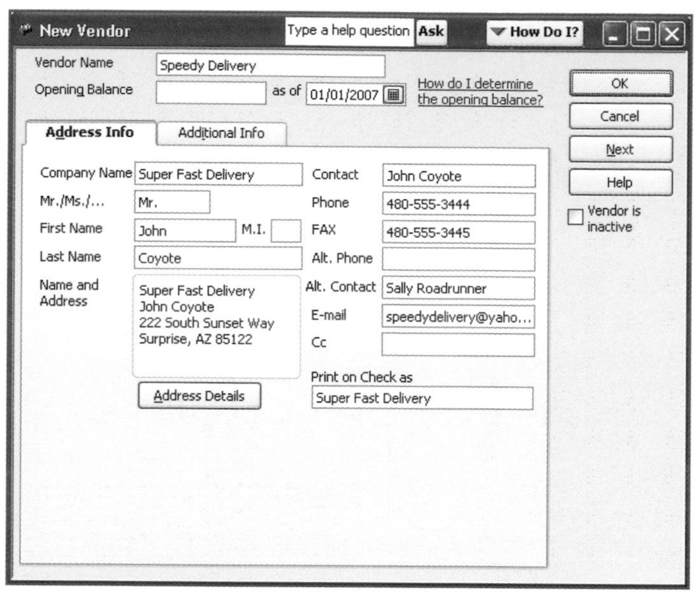

Figure 5-2: ***The New Vendor window gives you the ability to store detailed information for a vendor, including an e-mail address or alternate contact information.***

TIP

The name you type in the Vendor Name field should be whatever is easiest for you to remember, such as the company name, phone number, or contact. The name in the Company Name field should be the name you will use to communicate with the vendor.

TIP

If you use online banking, the account number is a required field. If a vendor doesn't use account numbers and you want to pay online, simply type your name or company name in the Account No. field.

such as when you establish a new account with a vendor or if you are transferring information from another system. To add a vendor directly from the Vendor Center:

1. Click the **Vendors** menu and click **Vendor Center**.
2. Click the **New Vendor** button (located at the top). The New Vendor window opens (see Figure 5-2).
3. Type your vendor name in the **Vendor Name** field, for example, Speedy Delivery. If you have an outstanding balance owed to this vendor, type it in the Opening Balance and include the "as of" date; otherwise, the vendor name is the only required field.
4. Click in the **Company Name** field. Type Super Fast Delivery. (Speedy Delivery is the name the company does business as (DBA), but Super Fast Delivery is the legal name of the company, a common practice among companies.) The entry in the Company Name field automatically populates the Print on Check as field.
5. Press the **TAB** key to move to the Mr./Ms./... field. Type the correct prefix, such as, Mr.
6. Press the **TAB** key to move to the First Name field, and type the vendor's first name, for example, John.
7. Press the **TAB** key twice to move to the Last Name field, and type the vendor's last name, for example, Coyote.
8. Press the **TAB** key again. The cursor moves to the Name and Address field, which has been automatically populated with the company name and first and last names of your contact. The Contact field has also been updated with the first and last names of your contact.
9. Press the **ENTER** key and type the vendor's address.
10. Press the **ENTER** key again, and type the vendor's city, state, and ZIP code.
11. Click in the **Phone** field, and type the vendor's phone number.
12. Press the **TAB** key to move to the FAX field, and type the vendor's fax number.
13. Press the **TAB** key twice to move to the Alt. Contact field, and type a name, if necessary.
14. Press the **TAB** key to move to the E-Mail field, and type the vendor's e-mail address, for example, speedydelivery@yahoo.com. If you want to send a copy to another person at the company when you e-mail information, enter this address in the Cc field.

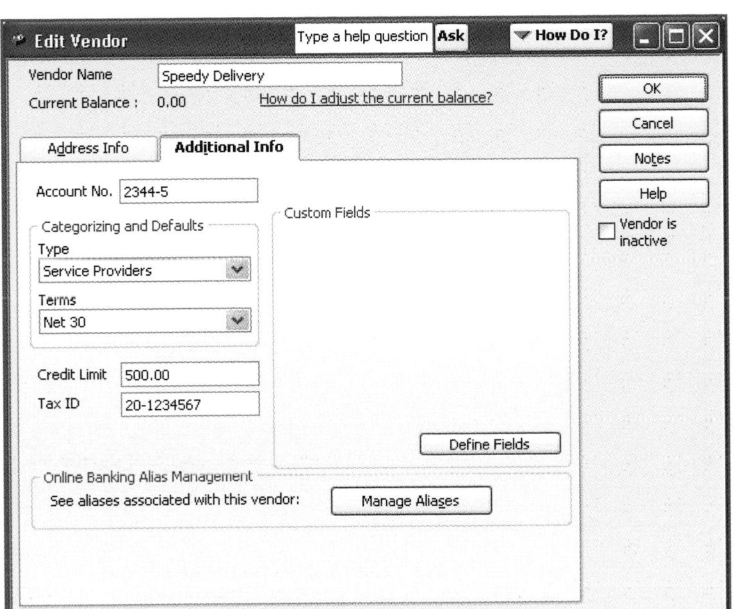

Figure 5-3: ***Use the fields on the Additional Info tab to record further information for a vendor.***

TIP

If this vendor is a subcontractor and you will be billing them out at an unusual rate, you can click the **Billing Rate Level** down arrow to select or add a specific rate.

TIP

You can add types, terms, and billing rate levels on the Additional Info tab of the New Vendor window by clicking **Add New** on the relevant drop-down list. This will open a dialog box where you enter the new type or term to identify groups of vendors. This option is common on drop-down lists throughout QuickBooks.

15. Click the **Additional Info** tab to enter more information, as shown in Figure 5-3.
16. Click in the **Account No.** field, and type the account number the vendor uses for you.
17. Press the **TAB** key to move to the Type field. Click the down arrow and click the vendor type, for example, **Service Providers**.

Type
Suppliers
< Add New >
Consultant
Service Providers
✓ Suppliers
Supplies
Tax agency

18. Press the **TAB** key to move to the Terms field. Click the down arrow and click the terms type, for example, **Net 30**.
19. Press the **TAB** key to move to the Credit Limit field. If you have a credit limit, you can enter it. It is only for your information.
20. Press the **TAB** key to move to the Tax ID field. Enter the Tax ID field for 1099 contractors.
21. Click **Next** to enter another vendor. You can continue to add vendors in this manner.
22. When you are finished adding new vendors, click **OK** and the window will close. The vendors appear on your Vendor List in the Vendor Center.
23. Click the **Close** button to close the Vendor Center.

EDIT A VENDOR

To edit a vendor:

1. Click the **Vendors** menu and click **Vendor Center**. The Vendor Center is displayed.
2. Click the vendor (such as **Desert Breeze Phone Company**) whose information you want to edit.
3. Click the **Edit Vendor** button. The Edit Vendor window opens, as shown in Figure 5-4. Make any changes as needed.
4. Click **OK** when you are finished making changes, and the window will close.

ADD NOTES OR REMINDERS TO A VENDOR

From the Vendor Center, you can add notes or reminders regarding a vendor.

1. With the Vendor Center open, select the vendor (such as **Speedy Delivery**) that you want to add a note to, and click the **Edit Notes** button. The Notepad window opens, as shown in Figure 5-5.
2. Click the **Date Stamp** button to automatically enter today's date within the note area.

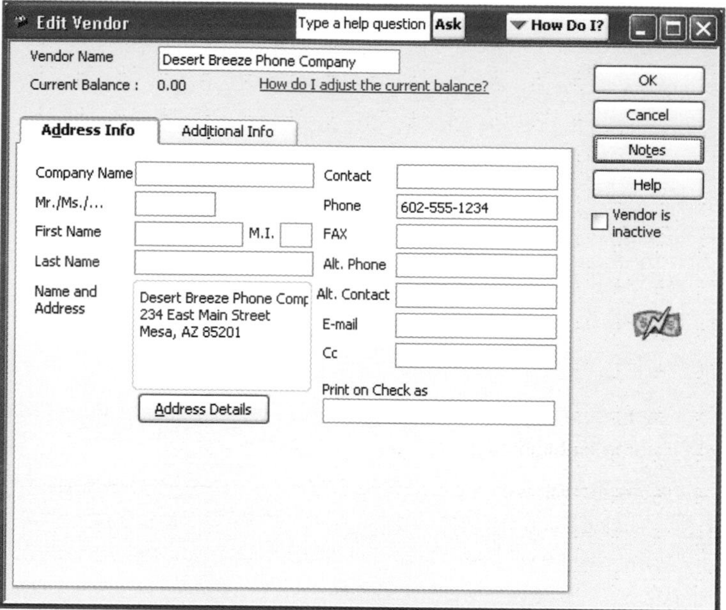

Figure 5-4: ***Easily change any vendor information by clicking in the desired field and editing.***

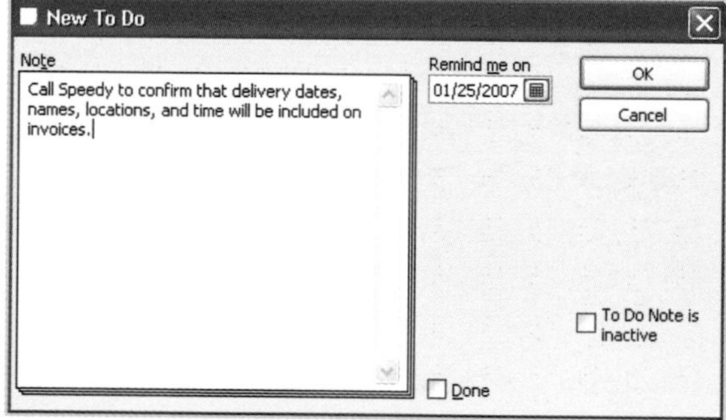

> **NOTE**
>
> See "Adding Custom Fields to Your Name Lists" later in this chapter to create Custom fields that work throughout Vendors, Customers, and Employees.

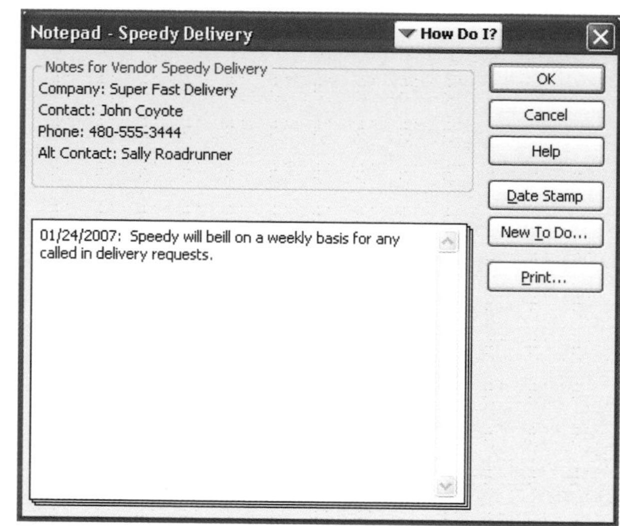

Figure 5-5: ***You can add notes regarding a vendor beyond what is included in the Vendor List, such as special offers or revised payment terms.***

3. Type your note. Click **OK** if you are finished. If you want to add a reminder, however, click the **New To Do** button. The New To Do window opens.
4. Type a reminder in the Note field.
5. Edit the reminder date. It will be today's date by default.
6. Click **OK** to close the New To Do window.
7. Click **OK** to close the Notepad window. In the Vendor Center, notice that the note appears in the vendor detail section. The To Do item will appear on your Reminders List (see Chapter 8 for information on setting preferences for reminders).

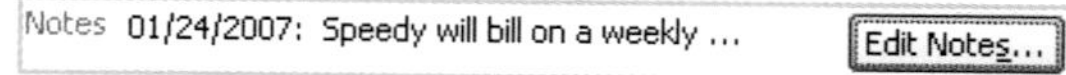

Merge, Delete, or Make Vendors Inactive

When a vendor is listed twice in QuickBooks with slightly different names, you can merge the two names so that you don't lose any transactions. If a vendor is entered in QuickBooks but has never been used, you can delete this vendor. If a vendor was once used but isn't any longer, QuickBooks will not allow you

TIP

You can use aliases for items like an identical vendor in different locations (for example, Texaco). You can also use "Unknown" if you can't recall a vendor, for example, due to a cash expenditure at an off-brand gas station.

to delete this vendor; however, you can make this vendor inactive so that the name no longer appears in your Vendor List. If you start to use the vendor again, you can easily change the status back to active.

MERGE VENDORS

If you change the name of a vendor to one that already exists, QuickBooks asks if you want to merge the information. This is useful if you have entered names incorrectly, such as SRP Electric and Salt River Electric.

To merge vendors:

1. Click the **Vendors** menu and click **Vendor Center**.
2. Double-click the vendor name you want to merge. The Edit Vendor window opens with the selected vendor name highlighted in blue.

Salt River Electric

3. Type the name of the vendor with whom you want to merge the first vendor, and click **OK**. A dialog box appears, asking if you would like to merge these two items. If you mistakenly type the name, the name change will take place immediately without confirmation.
4. Click **Yes** to complete the merge.

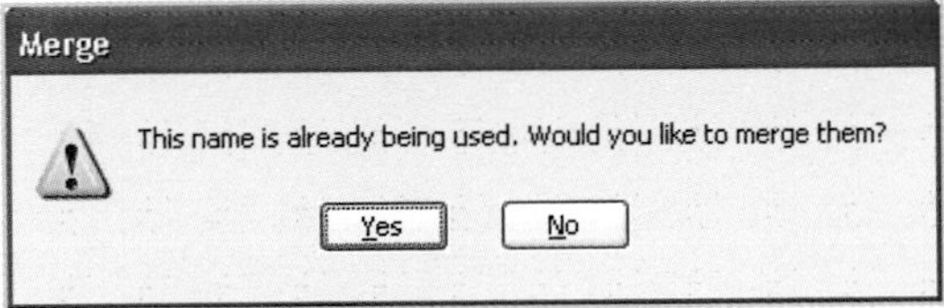

DELETE A VENDOR

You can only delete a vendor if no entries exist pertaining to it.

1. Click the **Vendors** menu and click **Vendor Center**. The Vendor Center is displayed.
2. Click the vendor name you want to delete.
3. Click the **Edit** menu. Click **Delete Vendor**. A dialog box appears, asking you to confirm this action.
4. Click **OK** to delete the vendor.

Edit View Lists Company Custo
Nothing to Undo Ctrl+Z
Revert
Cut Ctrl+X
Copy Ctrl+C
Paste Ctrl+V
Edit Vendor Ctrl+E
New Vendor Ctrl+N
Delete Vendor Ctrl+D
Make Vendor Inactive
Notepad
Use Register Ctrl+R
Use Calculator
Search...
Find... Ctrl+F
Preferences...

MAKE A VENDOR INACTIVE

If you've previously used a vendor but no longer plan to, you can mark it inactive, since QuickBooks will not allow you to delete this vendor.

1. Click the **Vendors** menu and click **Vendor Center**. The Vendor Center is displayed.
2. Click the vendor that you want to make inactive.

TIP

You can double-click a vendor on the Vendor List to open the Edit Vendor window.

TIP

QuickBooks displays reminders each time you open your company file.

TIP

You can press the **ESC** key to close any window instead of clicking the **Close** button.

CAUTION

When vendors (or any names) are merged, any existing transactions are linked to the new vendor, but information in the vendor form you are merging information from will be lost. If you have partial information in each of the two names you are merging, manually correct information in the vendor form you will be merging *to* before merging.

TIP

Remember, the Edit menu choices change, depending on where you are in QuickBooks, but certain options, like Preferences, will always be available.

Edit View Lists Company
Undo Ctrl+Z
Revert
Cut Ctrl+X
Copy Ctrl+C
Paste Ctrl+V
Use Register Ctrl+R
Use Calculator
Search...
Find... Ctrl+F
Preferences...

3. Click the **Edit** menu. Click **Make Vendor Inactive** (alternatively, you can right-click the vendor name, and click **Make Vendor Inactive**). There is no confirmation dialog box; the vendor immediately becomes inactive and disappears from the Vendor Center.

VIEW INACTIVE VENDORS

To view inactive vendors in your Vendor List:

Click the **View** down arrow, located at the top of the Vendor List in the Vendor Center, and select **All Vendors**.

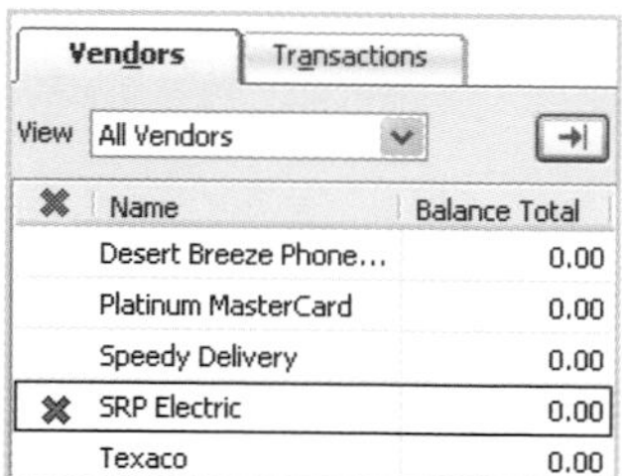

A new column is created to the left of the Name column, designated by an X. That same X is next to any vendor that you have made inactive, as you can see here. You can click in the X column to toggle the vendor's status to active or inactive.

Set Up and Print 1099s

As previously mentioned, contractors are considered 1099 vendors and need to be set up as such in QuickBooks. At the very least, you need to do this to track nonemployee compensation (Box 7 on the 1099 Form). If you're unsure whether you need to track any of the other 1099 categories, check with your accountant. Upon setting up a 1099 vendor, QuickBooks will track the amount you pay to that vendor so that you can print 1099 statements at the end of the year.

SET UP 1099 ACCOUNTS

The IRS tracks different categories under the 1099 form. Edit your QuickBooks preferences to identify accounts from your Chart of Accounts that should be associated with the categories that pertain to your company.

To set up a 1099 account:

1. Click the **Edit** menu and click **Preferences**. The Preferences window opens.
2. Click the **Tax: 1099** button, located on the left, and then click the **Company Preferences** tab to see the preferences, as shown in Figure 5-6.
3. Click the **Yes** option next to Do You File 1099-MISC Forms?

4. Click in the **Account** column next to Box 7: Nonemployee Compensation. Click the down arrow and click a single account for your business or click Multiple accounts as for this sample company. A Select Account window will open.
5. Click on the accounts you may use subcontractors for, such as **IT Expenses** (consultants), **Janitorial Expenses** (independent individuals), and **Repairs and Maintenance**. QuickBooks will now track expenses in these categories that are paid to 1099 vendors.
6. Click **OK** to close the window and save your account choices.
7. Click **OK** to close the window and save your preferences.

SET UP 1099 VENDORS

To set up a 1099 vendor so that QuickBooks can track the amounts paid in these selected categories:

1. Click the **Vendors** menu and click **Vendor Center**.
2. Click the **New Vendor** menu button. The New Vendor window opens.
3. Type your new vendor name, for example, Tom Sawyer – IT Guy. Fill in the relevant fields (see the section "Add a Vendor").
4. Click the **Additional Info** tab.
5. Click in the **Tax ID** field. Type the vendor's Tax ID number.
6. Click the **Vendor Eligible For 1099** check box. This option now appears, since you changed the preferences in the previous section.
7. Click **OK** to close and save this vendor setting.

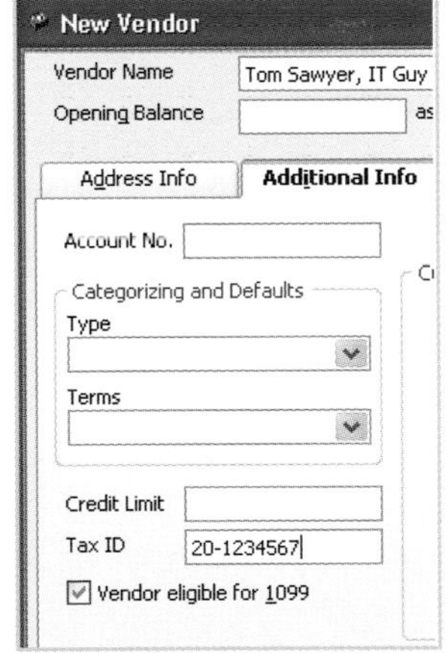

WRITE A CHECK TO VENDORS

Although you can write checks to anyone using the Write Checks feature, you can also use the shortcut menu on the Vendor List to write checks from the Vendor Center.

TIP

Vendor names can be entered in any manner that makes it easy for you to use. For example, rather than typing Tom Sawyer – IT Guy, if this is a vendor you use infrequently, you might want to type IT Guy – Tom Sawyer or Computers – Tom Sawyer so that you can look for a subject rather than a name.

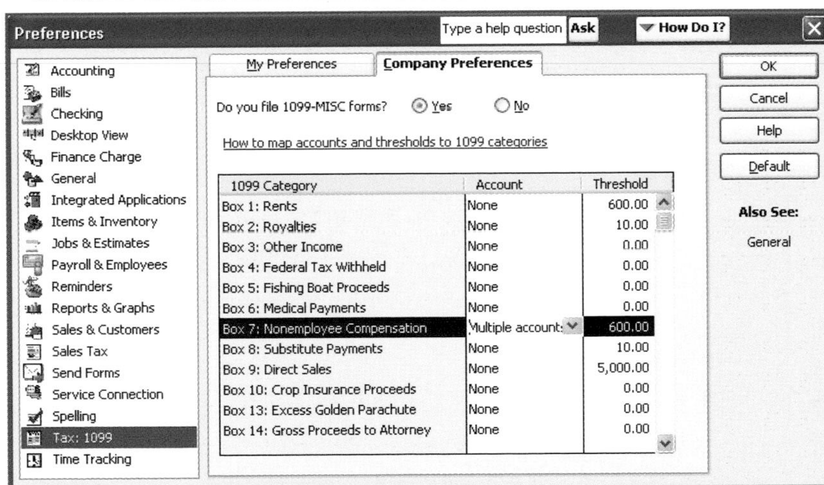

Figure 5-6: ***From the Preferences window, you can customize all facets of QuickBooks.***

1 2 3 4 5 6 7 8 9 10

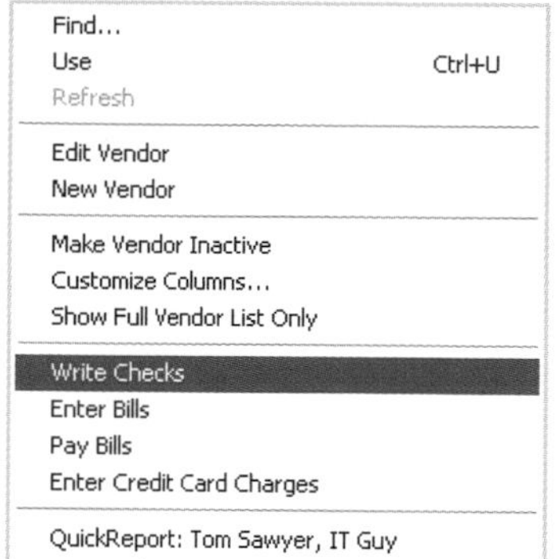

1. Right-click a vendor (like **Tom Sawyer, IT Guy**), and click **Write Checks** on the shortcut menu. The Write Checks window opens, as shown in Figure 5-7.
2. Provide the relevant information in the **Account**, **Amount**, and **Memo** columns, such as IT Expenses, $980, and "Set up network and install software," respectively.
3. Click **Save & Close**.

REVIEW AND PRINT 1099s

Each January, you must review and print your 1099 forms for the year before. If you've set up your accounts and marked your vendors as 1099 vendors in the previous sections, this is a simple annual task.

1. Click the **Vendors** menu and click **Print 1099s/1096**. The 1099 And 1096 Wizard opens. This wizard allows you to:
   - Run a status report of all your current vendors.
   - Map accounts (by taking you to the 1009-Tax Preferences window).
   - Preview a report of 1099 obligations.
   - Print your actual 1099 forms.

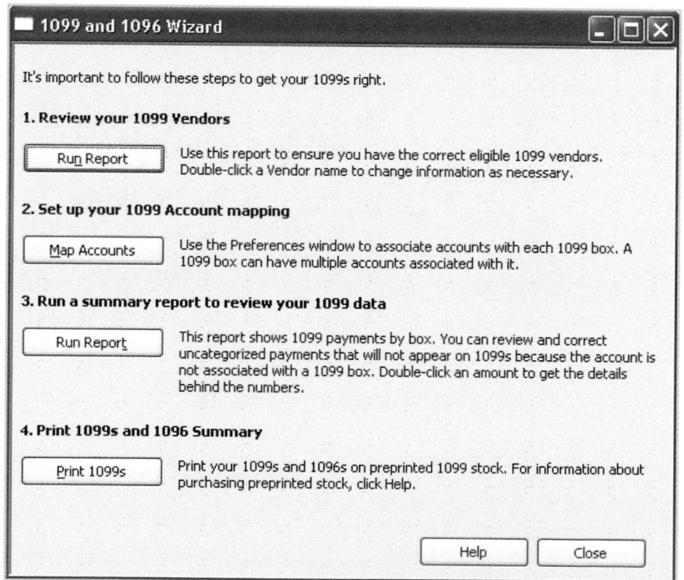

CAUTION

The Vendor must be set as Vendor Eligible for 1099 in order to show up on 1099 reports at the end of the year. Be sure to get SSN or EIN information from your vendors as soon as you first do business with them.

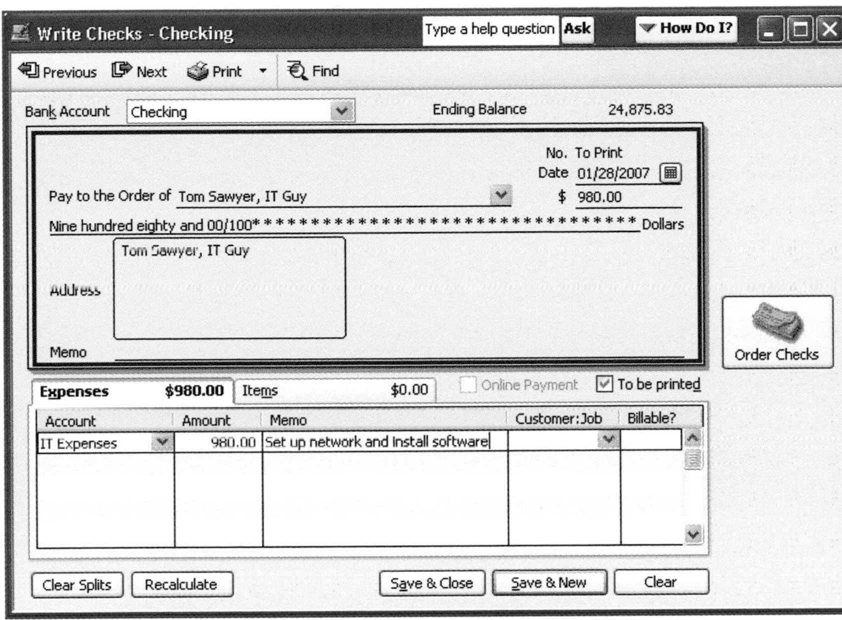

Figure 5-7: ***If the vendor is a 1099 vendor and the expense account is a 1099 account, this check will be tracked for 1099 reporting.***

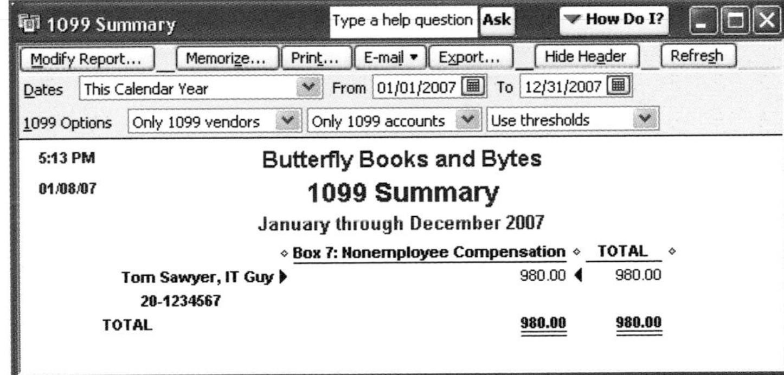

Figure 5-8: ***All 1099 reports are normally run in January to send 1099s to vendors that exceeded the previous year's thresholds.***

2. Click the **Run Report** button under 3. Run a summary report to review your 1099 data. A 1099 report is displayed, as shown in Figure 5-8. You can run this report at any time to view the previous year's data (the default), the current year's data, or any other date range you choose.

3. Click the **Close** button to close the report and return to the wizard.

4. Click **Print 1099s** in the 1099 And 1096 Wizard. The Printing 1099-MISC And 1096 Forms window opens. **Last Calendar Year** is selected by default. If you want to use a different range of dates, click the date range down arrow or change the **From** and **To** fields.

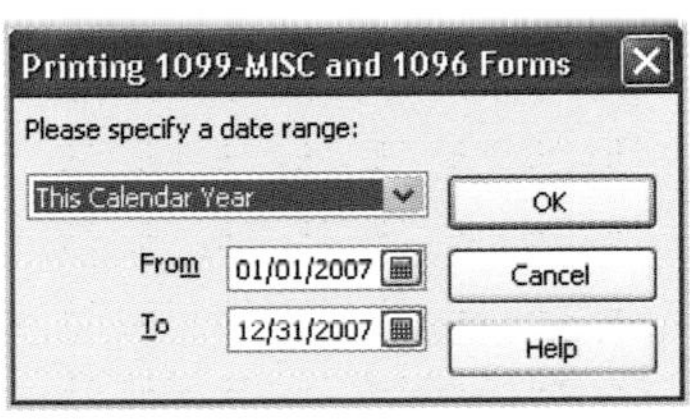

5. Click **OK**. Provided you have vendors who have been paid the minimum amount (as of this writing, $600), a list of 1099-eligible vendors is displayed. If you don't have vendors who have been paid the required amount, a message is displayed notifying you of that and no list is displayed. Figure 5-9 shows a sample list. Note the Valid ID and Valid Address columns. If either of these say No, you'll need to correct this information in the Edit Vendor window before you print a 1099.

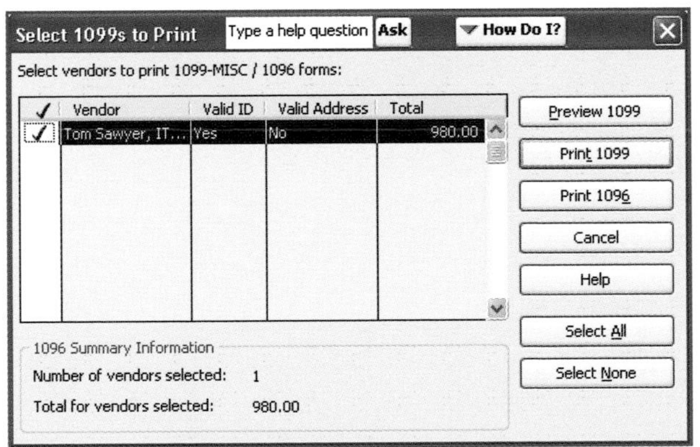

Figure 5-9: ***View 1099-related reports prior to printing 1099 forms.***

1 2 3 4 5 6 7 8 9 10

NOTE

The 1096 is a summary of all your 1099 vendors who have been paid. Print this after you are finished printing all 1099s.

QUICKSTEPS

ADDING CUSTOM FIELDS TO YOUR NAME LISTS

You might find that you need specific fields that are not included in QuickBooks, for example, a vendor's contractor number or license number. You may also want to track birthdays or special thank-you gifts for employees or customers. Customized fields can be added to all or some of the name lists.

To add customized fields:

1. Click the **Vendors** menu and click **Vendor Center**. The Vendor Center is displayed.
2. Double-click the vendor name you want to customize. The Edit Vendor window opens.
3. Click the **Additional Info** tab.
4. Click the **Define Fields** button. The Define Fields window opens.
5. In the first Label field, type the name of the custom field you want to create (for example, License Number). The name must be 30 characters or fewer. Click the **Vendors** and **Employees** check boxes so that this new field is displayed in these name lists. You can continue to add custom fields along with the sections in which you wish them to display. You can display any seven in each section.

Continued . . .

6. Click **Print 1099s**. The Print dialog box appears. Place your 1099 forms in your printer.
7. Click **Print**. If you have multiple 1099 vendors and a laser or inkjet printer that prints on individual sheets (as opposed to a dot matrix with carbon copies), load each page type individually, and print the set of 1099 vendors twice.
8. Click the **Close** button on each of the windows you have open when you are finished printing 1099s.

Pay Bills

With QuickBooks, you can pay your bills in one of two ways, depending on if you use the cash-based method of accounting or the accrual-based method of accounting (see Chapter 2). With the cash-based method, you receive a bill and write a check for it immediately in one step. With the accrual-based method of accounting, you receive a bill and then enter the bill and pay the bill in two steps.

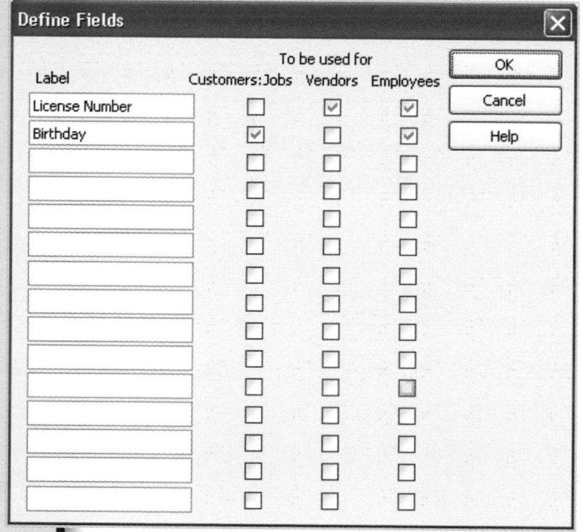

Butterfly Books is set up using the accrual-based method, because there are multiple employees and the owner wants to be the person who actually writes the checks and have a different person enter the bills.

When writing checks (see Chapter 4 for more information), you can set the To Be Printed date or Online Payment date for a future time—for example, five to seven business days before it is due—to allow for mail delivery and processing. If you handwrite checks, you can still use this process as a reminder to write checks by looking at the Checks To Be Printed List in the Reminders List (see Chapter 8 for more information).

QUICKSTEPS

ADDING CUSTOM FIELDS TO YOUR NAME LISTS *(Continued)*

6. Click **OK**. A dialog box appears, notifying you that custom fields can also be used on your forms. Click **OK**. You are returned to the Edit Vendor window, and custom fields you created will appear in the Custom Fields area.
7. Click in the field you have just created, and type the relevant information.
8. When finished, click **OK**.

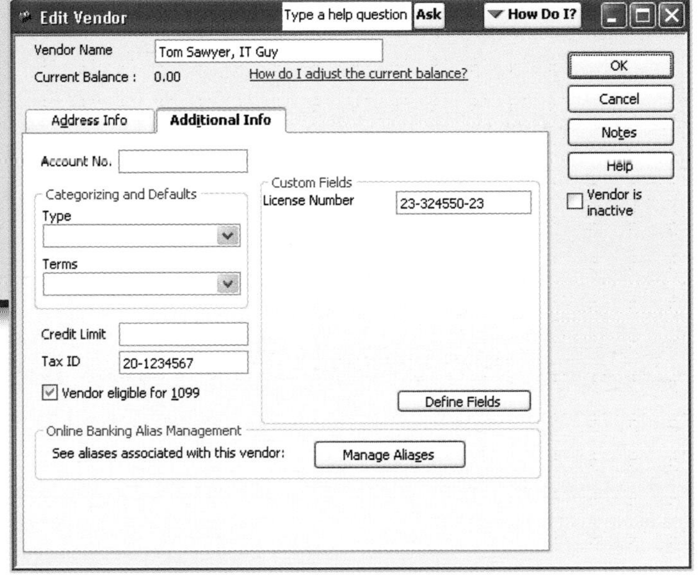

NOTE

The cash-based method should be used if you are running your business on a cash basis. If you enter and then pay your bills, use the accrual-based method.

TIP

The owner should be the only one to sign checks and the only one to know the online PIN number. That way, he or she can personally review all checks. Keep blank checks safely locked up to prevent theft or fraud.

Enter and Pay Bills

Although entering bills and then paying them in QuickBooks is a multistep process, it is the best way to accurately track your expenses. In addition to providing information on both the date the expense was incurred and the date the expense was paid, QuickBooks warns you if a bill for the same vendor and reference number has already been entered, which will help you avoid duplicate payments.

ENTER BILLS

To enter bills in QuickBooks:

1. Click the **Vendors** menu and click **Enter Bills**. The Enter Bills window opens (see Figure 5-10).
2. In the purple bill area, in the **Vendor** line, type the vendor's name, such as <u>Speedy Delivery</u>.

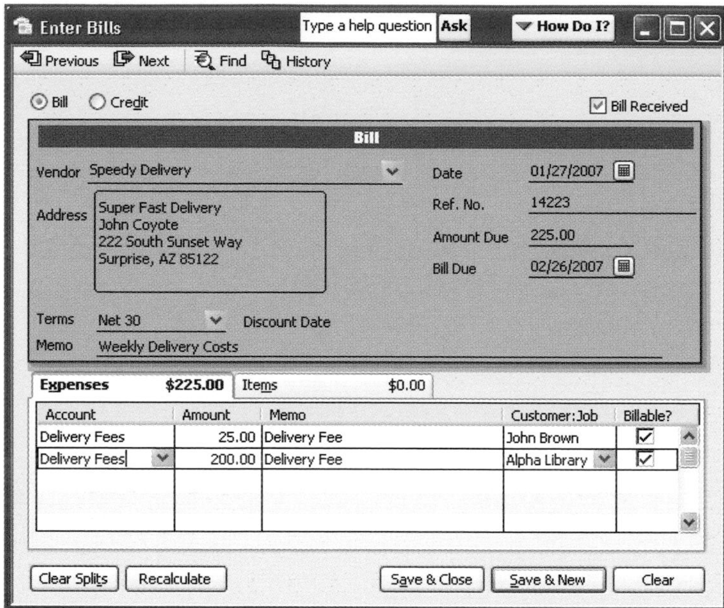

***Figure 5-10:* From the Enter Bills window, you can enter bills the day you receive them and pay them when due.**

Click the **Credit** option in the Enter Bills window to enter credits issued by vendors.

Try to negotiate early-payment discounts with your vendors. If you have a good cash flow, you'll make more money with an early-payment discount than with any savings account. Second best is to negotiate long payment terms, such as net 30 days, net 60 days, or longer. Long payment dates are like free loans.

3. Press the **TAB** key to move to the Date line. Type or select the date you received the bill.
4. Press the **TAB** key to move to the Ref. No. line, and type the invoice number on the billing statement you received (if applicable).
5. Press the **TAB** key to move to the Amount Due line, and type the amount.
6. Press the **TAB** key to move to the Bill Due line. QuickBooks automatically calculates the expected due date based on the vendor terms indicated when you added this vendor to your Vendor List. If you need a different date, type it, or click the **Calendar** icon and select a date.
7. Press the **TAB** key to move to the Terms line, which is automatically filled in for you based on the vendor terms indicated when you added this vendor to your Vendor List. If you change this line, your due date will change accordingly. When you are finished with this bill, QuickBooks asks you if you want to save any changes made to the Terms line.
8. Press the **TAB** key to move to the Memo field, and enter any comments if applicable.
9. Press the **TAB** key to move to the Account column, and type the name of the relevant expense account, such as Delivery Fees. If it does not exist, you can create the account at this time.
10. Press the **TAB** key to move to the Amount field, and confirm that the entire amount should be charged against this account (such as Delivery Fees) or enter the amount for this line.
11. Press the **TAB** key to move to the Memo field, and enter any comments if applicable.
12. Press the **TAB** key to move to the Customer:Job field, and enter the name of a Customer if this fee is directly associated with them. You can add them or use an existing customer.
13. Repeat Steps 10–12 for as many different accounts or customers as this bill pertains to. To use the Items tab at the bottom of the Enter Bills screen, see the Use Items on a Bill section, later in this chapter.
14. Click the **Save & Close** button.

PAY BILLS

To pay bills in QuickBooks:

1. Click the **Vendors** menu and click **Pay Bills**. The Pay Bills window opens, as shown in Figure 5-11.

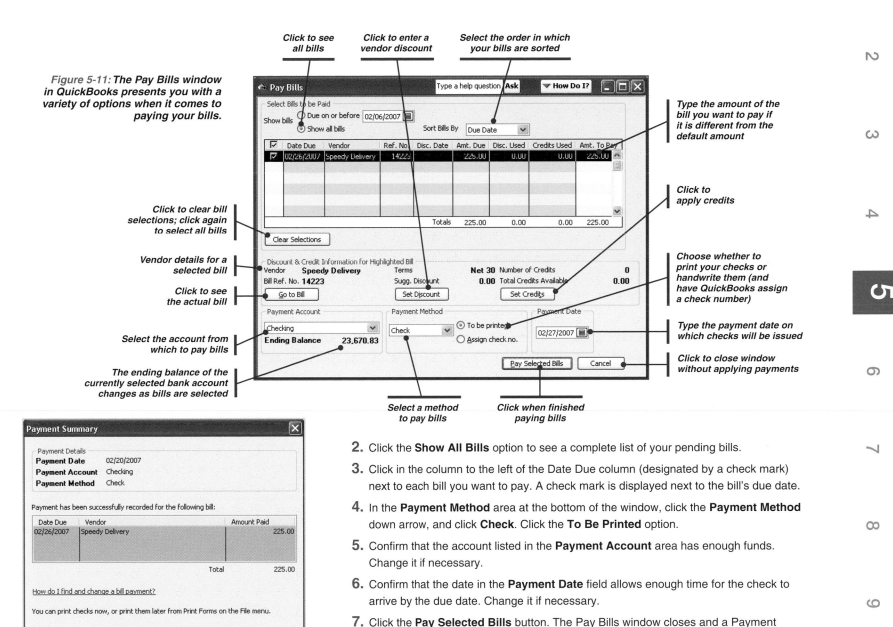

Figure 5-11: **The Pay Bills window in QuickBooks presents you with a variety of options when it comes to paying your bills.**

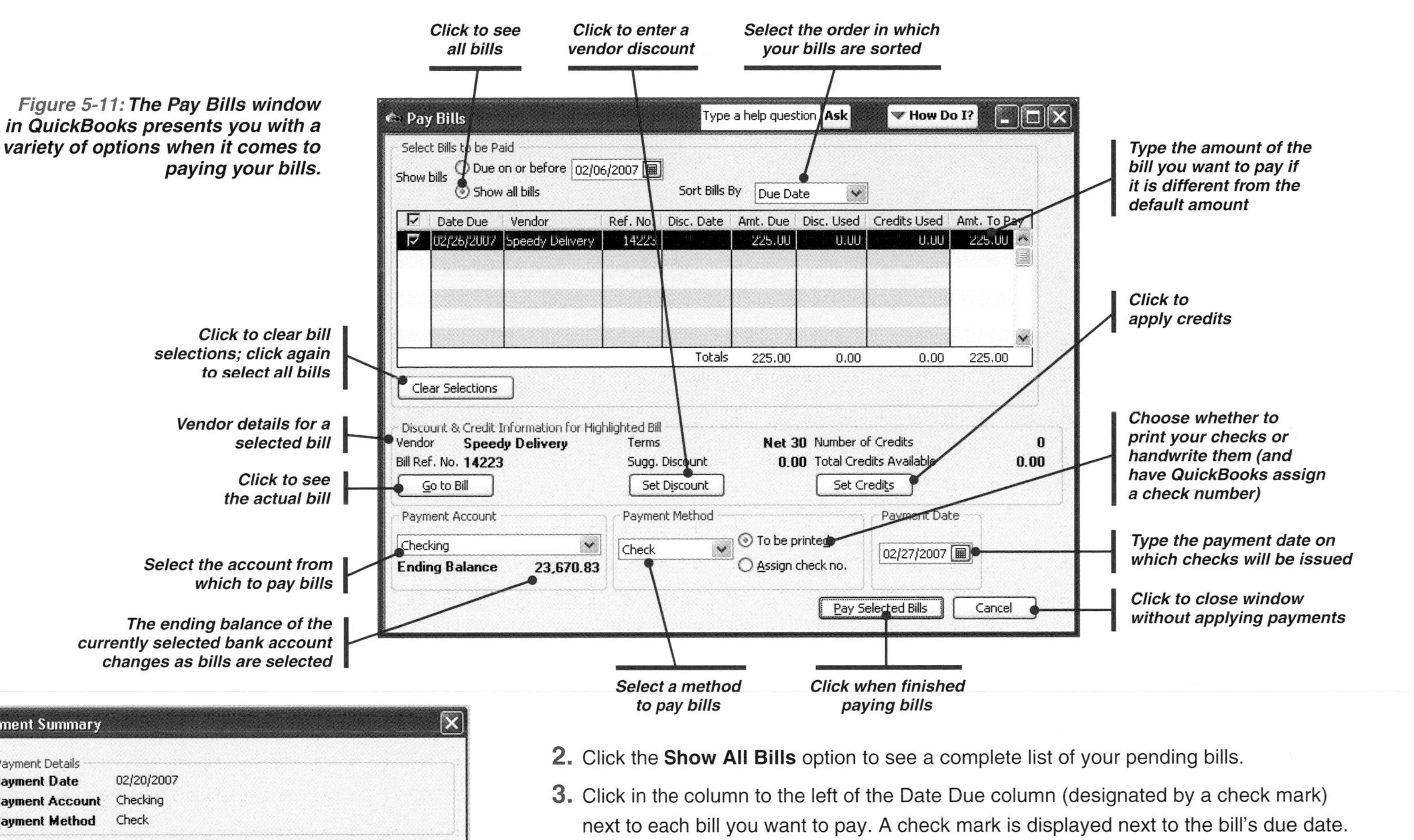

Payment Summary

Payment Details

Payment Date	02/20/2007
Payment Account	Checking
Payment Method	Check

Payment has been successfully recorded for the following bill:

Date Due	Vendor	Amount Paid
02/26/2007	Speedy Delivery	225.00
	Total	225.00

How do I find and change a bill payment?

You can print checks now, or print them later from Print Forms on the File menu.

Print Checks Done

2. Click the **Show All Bills** option to see a complete list of your pending bills.
3. Click in the column to the left of the Date Due column (designated by a check mark) next to each bill you want to pay. A check mark is displayed next to the bill's due date.
4. In the **Payment Method** area at the bottom of the window, click the **Payment Method** down arrow, and click **Check**. Click the **To Be Printed** option.
5. Confirm that the account listed in the **Payment Account** area has enough funds. Change it if necessary.
6. Confirm that the date in the **Payment Date** field allows enough time for the check to arrive by the due date. Change it if necessary.
7. Click the **Pay Selected Bills** button. The Pay Bills window closes and a Payment Summary window appears.

1 2 3 4 5 6 7 8 9 10

TIP

Pay attention to the dates you use when you enter transactions, as those dates will be used to determine when an expense is reflected in your reports. It's better to have a monthly bill of $50 for a recurring expense than to have one month with an expense of $100 and another month with an expense in the same category of $0.

TIP

You can add a Pay Bills icon to the Icon bar for easy access in the future (see Chapter 1).

TIP

Don't pay bills without first confirming their accuracy. File all bills after entering them so that they are available for periodic review.

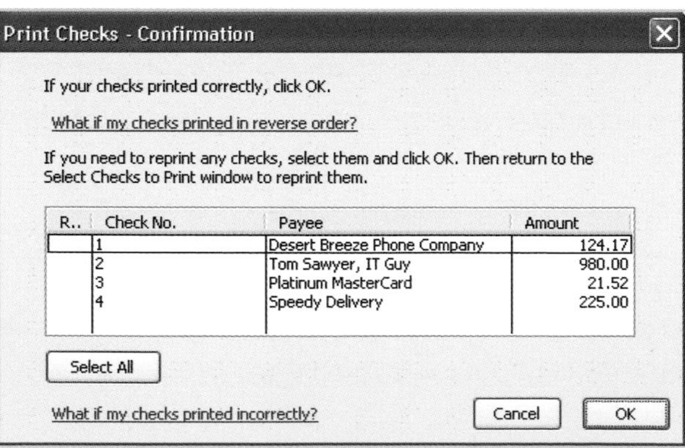

8. Click either **Print Checks** or **Done**. If you click Done, the window will close and you can print the checks later. If you click Print Checks, the Select Checks to Print window will appear with the option for you to select which checks to print.

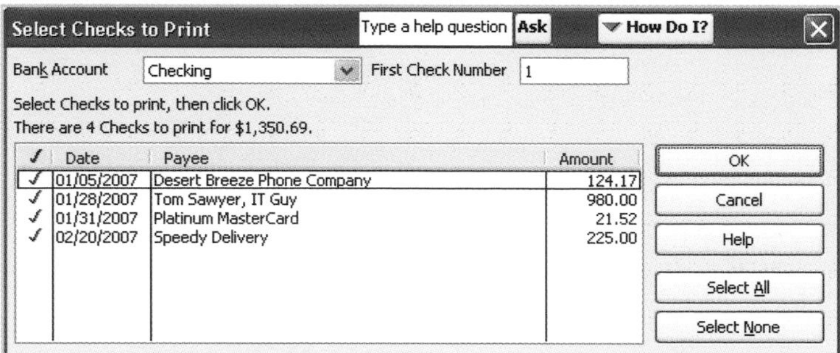

9. Click **OK** once you have confirmed your checks and check number, and the Print Checks window will open. Be sure to load checks into your printer and confirm the Check type before you print.

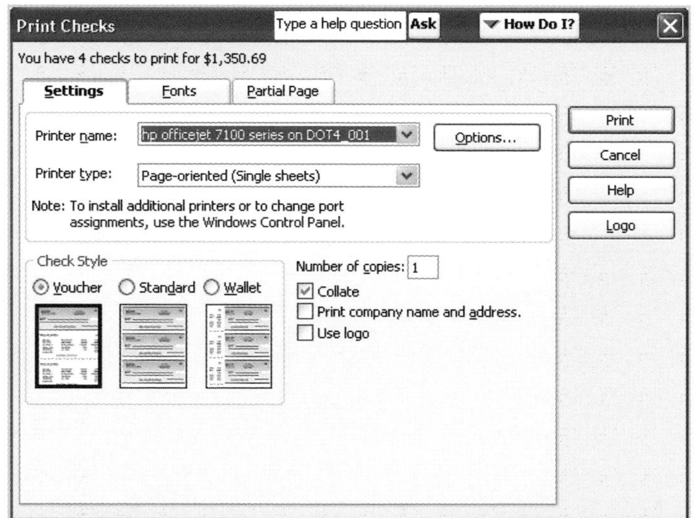

10. Click **Print** to complete the actual printing of checks. If you chose to pay online, you will need to go online to send your checks to the bank (see Chapter 4). Once your checks print, the Print Checks – Confirmation window will appear.

TIP

If QuickBooks prompts you to add the vendor name and item name to the relevant lists, do so by clicking **Quick Add**.

TIP

If you don't see the item you want to enter, make sure you are on the Items tab and not on the Expenses tab.

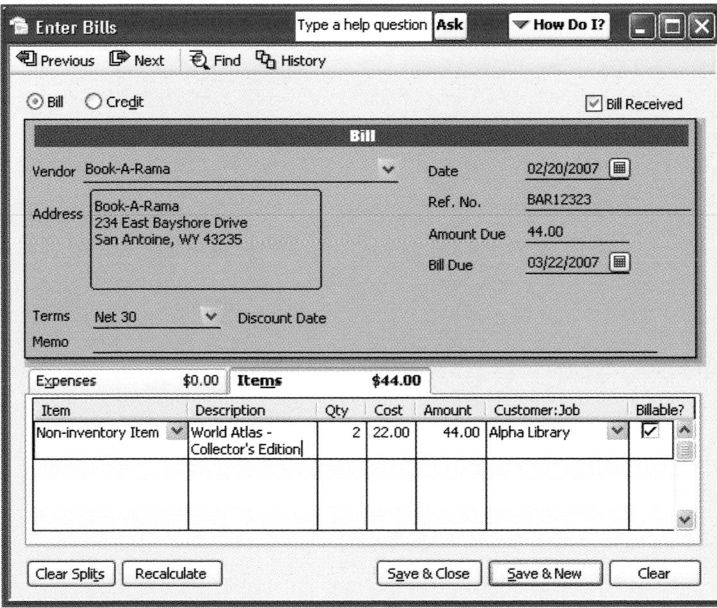

Figure 5-12: ***Be sure the Items tab is active if you want to enter items in the Enter Bills window.***

11. Click the **OK** button once you confirm that your checks printed correctly. If any check did not print correctly, click those checks in order to print them again. You will need to click File | Print Forms | Checks in order to return to the Select Checks to Print window.

Don't forget to sign your checks before mailing to vendors.

Use Items on a Bill

At the bottom of the Write Checks, Enter Bills and Enter Credit Card Charges windows are two tabs: Expenses and Items.

Earlier in this chapter, a bill was entered using the Expenses tab to directly associate the bill with a specific expense. When creating a chargeback for an item, you should use the Items tab to enter the item which is still associated with an account. This is especially important for companies that use job-costing reports, since the report will compare the cost of items to the sale price of items, but only if they are set up as items and used both in entering bills and creating invoices.

1. Click the **Vendors** menu and click **Enter Bills**. The Enter Bills window opens (see Figure 5-12).
2. In the **Vendor** field, type the vendor's name, for example, Book-A-Rama.
3. Click the **Items** tab, located at the bottom of the Enter Bills window.
4. Click in the **Item** column, click the down arrow, and click **Non-Inventory Item** from the drop-down list (see Chapter 3 for information on editing items for purchase information).
5. Press the **TAB** key to move to the **Description** column, and type a relevant note.
6. Press the **TAB** key to move to the Quantity column, and type the number of items.
7. Press the **TAB** key to move to the Cost column, and type the amount.
8. Press the **TAB** key to move to the Total column. A window may appear indicating that you have changed the cost for "Non-Inventory Item" and asking if you want to make this cost change permanent for this item. Since this is a generic item, you do not, but this is a useful feature of QuickBooks when prices change.

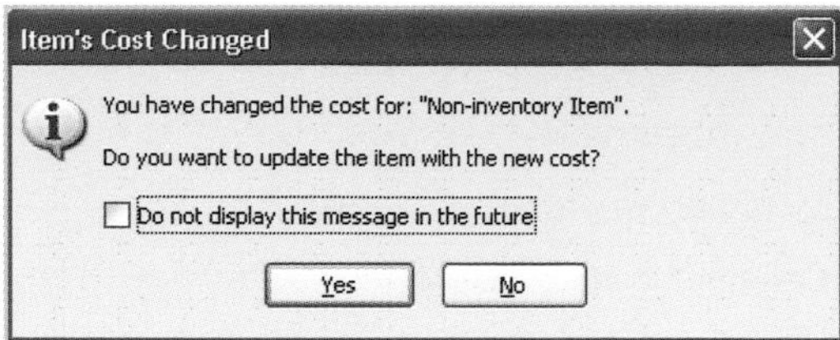

9. Click **No** to keep your Item List unchanged. QuickBooks calculates the amount due and populates the Amount column and the Amount Due line in the purple bill area.
10. Press the **TAB** key to move to the Customer:Job column. Type the customer's name. Note the Billable column. This check mark indicates this item is billable to this customer. Click the box to uncheck it if you are not going to charge the client for this item.
11. Verify the entries in the **Date, Bill Due, Ref. No., Terms,** and **Vendor Address** fields for this bill.
12. Click the **Save & Close** button when finished. The transaction is entered, and the window closes.

Memorize Transactions

Whenever you have a recurring transaction, such as a monthly bill or an invoice, you can have QuickBooks *memorize* it and give you a reminder regarding the transaction, make it available to you when needed, or automatically enter the transaction on a regular basis.

Each time you enter a bill or write a check, consider whether you will need to enter this transaction on a recurring basis. If so, memorize this transaction. If it's a fixed amount, such as a rental payment, you can have QuickBooks automatically enter the amount. If it's a variable amount, such as your electric or water bill, you can configure the memorized transaction so that QuickBooks reminds you of the transaction and you can enter the correct amount before recording the transaction.

Memorize Reminder Transactions

For transactions that occur regularly but with varying amounts, QuickBooks reminder transactions will appear in the Reminders window so that you can enter the transaction with the correct amount.

1. Click the **Vendors** menu and click **Enter Bills**. The Enter Bills window opens.
2. Enter the bill according to the steps outlined in the previous section "Enter and Pay Bills." The example used here will use a new vendor, SRP, for monthly electric bills.
3. Click the **Edit** menu and click **Memorize Bill**. The Memorize Transaction window opens with the vendor's name already in the Name field.

NOTE

Any expense from your bank account uses a check form for entry, so an ATM transaction, services charges, and so on, will appear as "checks" simply because they are expenditures from your bank account. Use "ATM" for your check number or leave that field blank.

TIP

When filling in the Days In Advance To Enter field for automatic transactions, consider whether you need to write and mail a check, if it is an online transaction, or if it is automatically deducted from your account.

4. Click the **Remind Me** option.
5. Click the **How Often** down arrow, and click the frequency with which you must pay this bill, such as **Monthly**.
6. Click in the **Next Date** field, and type the next date you want to be reminded of this bill. (Alternately, you can click the **Calendar** icon, and select the date from the drop-down calendar.)
7. Click **OK**. The Memorize Transaction window closes and QuickBooks memorizes your bill. You are returned to the Enter Bills window.
8. Click the **Save & Close** button in the Enter Bills window.

Memorize Automatic Transactions

For recurring transactions with consistent amounts, QuickBooks can automatically enter checks, bills, or invoices, but make sure the information makes sense for a recurring charge, such as saying "Monthly Fee" instead of "January Fee" to eliminate the work of changing every month.

1. Click the **Banking** menu and click **Write Checks**. The Write Checks window opens.
2. Write the check according to the steps outlined in Chapter 4. This example will use a monthly bank service charge.
3. Click the **Edit** menu and click **Memorize Check**. The Memorize Transaction window opens.
4. Type a name for this transaction in the Name field, for example, <u>Bank Service Charge</u>. The default name is the name of the bank (or whomever the check is written to), but you can edit any memorized transaction so that it is more explanatory.
5. Click the **Automatically Enter** option.
6. Click the **How Often** down arrow, and click **Monthly**.
7. Click in the **Next Date** field, and type a date that is a month away from the check's current due date. (Alternatively, you can click the **Calendar** icon, and select the date from the drop-down calendar.)
8. Leave the Number Remaining field blank, indicating to QuickBooks that this transaction cycle will never end. If this were a recurring loan payment, you could type the number of payments.
9. Leave the Days In Advance To Enter field at 0, since this is an automatic transaction. In other cases, you might choose to enter a number of days before a payment is due in order to have time to print and mail the payment.

TIP

When Memorizing a check, be sure that the Online Payment or To Be Printed box is selected if appropriate for future payments.

10. Click **OK** when finished. You are returned to the Write Checks window.
11. Click **Save & Close**.

Manage Memorized Transactions

Every time you memorize a transaction, it is added to the Memorized Transaction List. Review and manage your memorized transactions as often as needed. You can add the Memorized Transaction List to your Icon bar if you will be using it on a regular basis (see Chapter 1).

EDIT MEMORIZED TRANSACTIONS

To edit a memorized transaction:

1. Click the **Lists** menu and click **Memorized Transaction List**. The Memorized Transaction List is displayed (see Figure 5-13).

Memorized Transaction List

Transaction Name	Type	Source Account	Amount	Frequency	Auto	Next Date
Bank Service Fee	Check	Checking	9.95	Monthly	✓	03/01/2007
SRP	Bill	Accounts Payable	0.00	Monthly		03/05/2007

Memorized Transaction ▾ | Enter Transaction

Edit Memorized Transaction Ctrl+E
New Group
Delete Memorized Transaction Ctrl+D
Customize Columns...
Print List... Ctrl+P
Re-sort List

Figure 5-13: ***You can edit, group, enter, and delete your memorized transactions from the Memorized Transaction List.***

2. Click the memorized transaction you want to edit.
3. Click the **Memorized Transaction** menu button (located at the bottom of the window), and click **Edit Memorized Transaction**. The Schedule Memorized Transaction window opens.

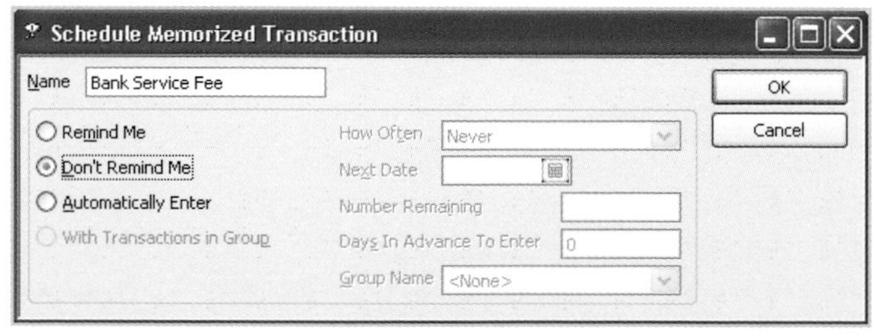

4. Make your desired changes. If you click the **Don't Remind Me** option, all other related choices become unavailable.
5. Click **OK**. The changes are saved and the Memorized Transaction List is updated.

GROUP MEMORIZED TRANSACTIONS

You can add groups to your Memorized Transaction List and then add memorized transactions to the groups (see "Move Memorized Transactions").

1. Click the **Lists** menu and click **Memorized Transaction List**. The Memorized Transaction List is displayed.
2. Click the **Memorized Transaction** menu button (located at the bottom of the window), and click **New Group**. The New Memorized Transaction Group window opens.

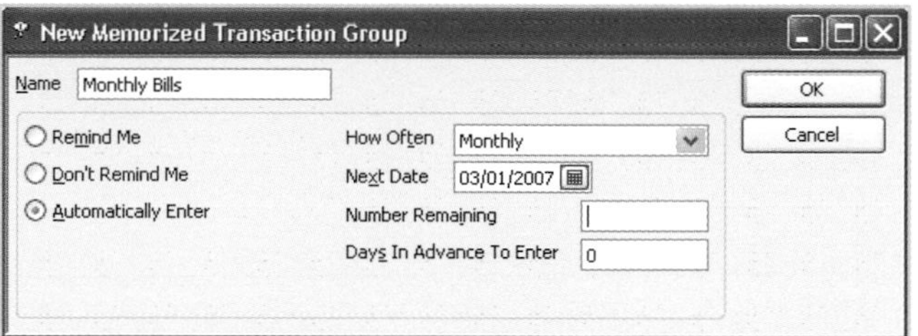

3. Click in the **Name** field, and type a name for the group, for example, Monthly Bills.
4. Click the **Automatically Enter** option.
5. Click the **How Often** down arrow, and click **Monthly**.
6. Click in the **Next Date** field, and type the date of the first day in the next month. (Alternatively, you can click the **Calendar** icon, and select the date from the drop-down calendar.)
7. Click **OK**. The group appears in the Memorized Transaction List; however, at this point the group doesn't contain any transactions. You need to move them to the relevant group.

MOVE MEMORIZED TRANSACTIONS

To move memorized transactions to a group:

1. Click the **Lists** menu and click **Memorized Transaction List**. The Memorized Transaction List is displayed.
2. Move your cursor over the **Diamond** icon located to the left of the transaction you want to move. The cursor changes to a four-headed arrow.

TIP

Once you have groups set up and are editing memorized transactions, you can click the **With Transactions In Group** option and then choose the group you want the transaction to be a part of, which will now control the date and frequency.

3. Click and drag the transaction directly under the group of which you want it to be a part, for example, **Monthly Bills**, and release.
4. Now, click and drag the transaction to the right so that it appears under the group of which you want it to be a part. This transaction, and any others you add to it, will now be entered every month as part of the Monthly Bills group.

5. Click the **Close** button to close the Memorized Transaction List.

How to...

- *Use the Customer Center*
- *Naming Customers*
- *Add and Edit Customers*
- *Merge, Delete, or Make Customers Inactive*
- *Set Up Service Items*
- *Set Up Non-Inventory Items*
- *Set Up Items with Purchase Information*
- *Set Up Sales Tax Items*
- *Changing Tax Preferences*
- *Create Invoices*
- *Edit Invoices*
- *Adding an Invoice to Memorized Transactions*
- *Send Statements to Customers*
- *Enter Sales Receipts*
- *Create Estimates*
- *Process Cash Payments and Checks*
- *Process Credit Card Payments*
- *Accepting Credit Cards from Customers*
- *Make Deposits*
- *Issue Credit Memos*
- *Review and Pay Sales Taxes*

Chapter 6
Selling Products and Services

The QuickBooks customer and accounts receivable (A/R) features include professional invoices and sales receipts, easy tracking of customer accounts, and customer letter templates (see Chapter 8). Items purchased for customers can be added directly to invoices, as can time tracked (see Chapter 9). Estimates created in QuickBooks can be turned into progressive invoices, standard invoices, or sales receipts. You can e-mail, fax, or mail estimates, invoices, and statements to customers, as well as check your business's health with accurate customer, sales, and job-costing reports. Payments can also be received against invoices and deposited. This chapter will cover managing customers, sending invoices, receiving payments, and collecting sales tax.

1 2 3 4 5 6 7 8 9 10

> **TIP**
>
> Always attempt to get customer information when a purchase is made—even when someone pays in cash—for use in future marketing campaigns, but keep in mind that some customers may choose not to share this information.

Manage Customers and Jobs

The Customer Center tracks information and records regarding your customers—anyone to whom you sell items or services. A *job* is a customer subcategory, and it can be used to track different departments, projects, or other business categories pertaining to a specific customer. This is particularly useful for contractors who use job costing. As with accounts and entries on other lists, you can make jobs inactive.

Use the Customer Center

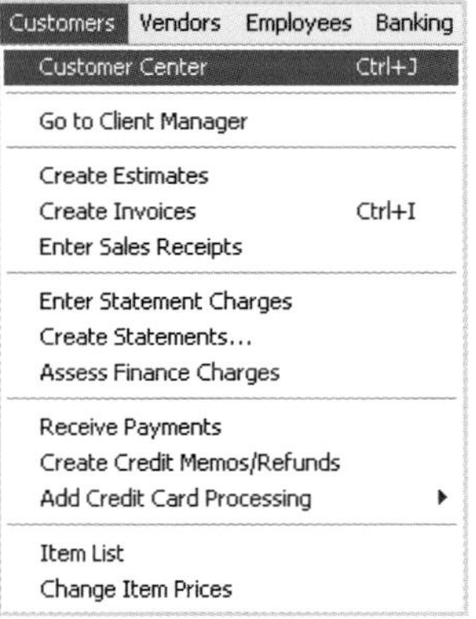

The Customer Center is one of the three centers in QuickBooks, the others being Vendor Center and Employee Center. The Customer Center, shown in Figure 6-1, is simple to use and includes the Customers & Jobs List on the left side and details of the selected customer (or job) on the right side (Bishop, Jeanne, in this example). This area gives you an overview of your customer's information, including all transactions, such as invoices and payments. You can add customers and jobs from the Customer Center or as you need them.

Use any of the following methods to open the Customer Center:

Click the **Customer Center** icon on the Navigation bar.

Customer Center

–Or–

Click the **Customers** menu and click **Customer Center**.

–Or–

Click **Customers** on the home page.

Figure 6-1 shows the Customer Center with three sample customers and a generic customer (Cash) with three jobs (In Store, Online, and Show). The Cash customer can be used for customers who don't want to give their names or who are likely to be one-time customers. Some customer entries only consist of the name (which is required), whereas other customer entries include additional information, such as address, phone number, contacts, and so on. If you use QuickBooks to send invoices, send letters, and otherwise manage your customers, you should create a higher level of detail. Close the **Close** button (the X in the upper-right corner) to close the Customer Center.

Opens the New Customer or New Job window

Show or hide customer details (right side)

Opens the selected transaction with the currently highlighted vendor entered

Prints Customers & Jobs List, Customer & Job Information or Customer & Job Transaction List

Import Customer List or transactions from or export to a Microsoft Excel spreadsheet

Create customer or collection letters or modify template using Microsoft Word

Show Transaction List (not showing)

Show Customers & Jobs List (showing)

Filters customers according to preselected or custom criteria

Customers & Jobs List

Opens Edit Customer (or Edit Job) window

Opens QuickBooks Notepad window

Select transaction types and transaction date range to display

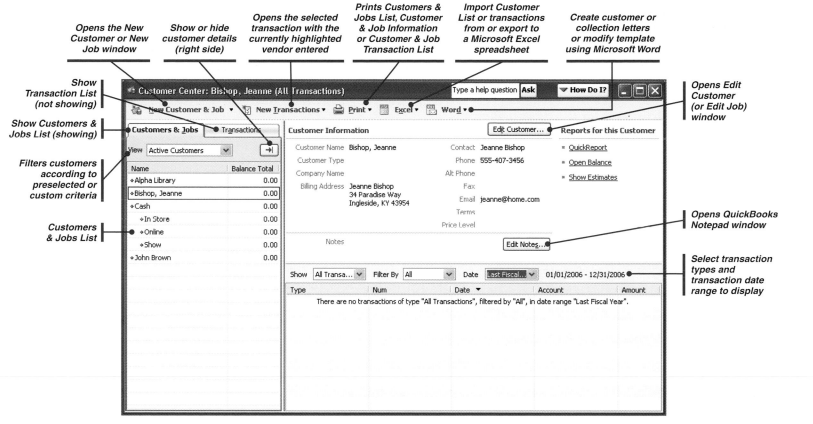

Figure 6-1: ***The Customer Center gives a complete view of your Customer List, details, and transactions—all on one page.***

TIP

Click on the Transaction tab in the Customer Center to see a list of transaction types for all customers.

You can use the Customer Center to manage your customers by quickly seeing their contact information above a list of all the transactions they have had with your company. For customers with a great many transactions, you can limit what transactions are shown by selecting the types, statuses, and dates of the transactions.

Create transactions for existing customers by clicking the **New Transactions** button. Some or all of the following options are displayed (depending on your edition and how your preferences are set):

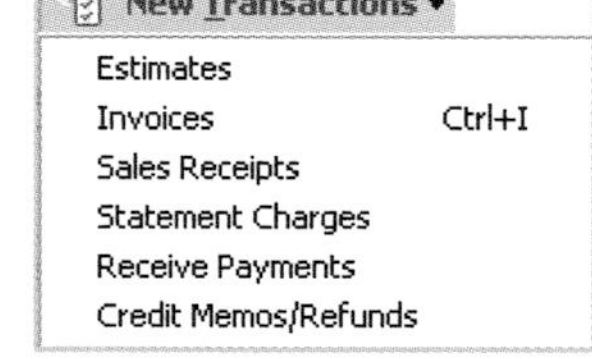

- **Estimates** can be created as needed and turned into invoices when accepted by the customer.

NAMING CUSTOMERS

The strategy whereby you name your customers is important. If you have a small client base and no employees, you can use client names, but you still need to decide the easiest method for looking up their information—by last name, first name, or company name, for example. If you have a small business, this might not be a significant issue. As your company grows, however, or if you have employees at a retail register, they cannot waste the customer's time looking up his or her information. In this case, you may choose to name your customers according to account number or phone number. This method can present difficulties, too—area codes change, and companies may have internal and external phone numbers or different locations. The point is to come up with a long-term method that will work for you and to be consistent with whichever method you choose.

TIP

When entering existing customers, don't enter an opening balance if you can enter outstanding invoices instead. Collection reports won't be accurate, since they don't include opening balances.

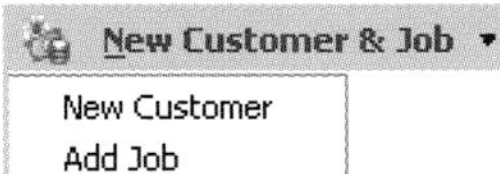

- **Sales Orders** (only in Premier and Enterprise Editions of QuickBooks) can be used to track out-of-stock items that customers have requested. They are turned into invoices or sales receipts upon delivery of the ordered items.
- **Invoices** are used when partial payment or no payment is received at the time of a sale or when services are performed. Invoices can have finance charges or early-payment discounts applied to them, as well as any refunds or credits the customer has outstanding.
- **Sales Receipts** are used only when payment is received in full at the time of purchase.
- **Statement Charges** can be entered for customers who receive a monthly statement.
- **Receive Payments** is used to apply funds (including credits and discounts) to outstanding invoices.
- **Credit Memos/Refunds** can be created and used by the customer for future purchases or to create a check for a refund.

The Customer Center includes options to print and send customer information to Excel or Word. Custom letters and mailing labels (see Chapter 8) are also included in QuickBooks.

Add and Edit Customers

This section will show you how to add a new customer and edit an existing customer.

ADD A CUSTOMER

Use the Quick Add feature to add customers at any time. The only required field is the customer name. If you are entering your Customer List into QuickBooks, you may want to use the Customer Center.

To add a customer:

1. Click the **Customers** menu and click **Customer Center**.
2. Click the **New Customer & Job** button, and click **New Customer**. The New Customer window opens (see Figure 6-2).
3. Type your customer name, for example, <u>Gardner, Stewart and Sarah</u>.
4. After you enter the address in the Bill To field, click the **Copy** button to copy it to the Ship To field. The Add Ship To Address Information window will open and prompt you

to confirm the information. In the Address Name field, change "Ship To 1" to something more descriptive, such as "Home." If you don't want this window to appear in the future, you can clear the **Show This Window Again When Address Is Incomplete Or Unclear** check box at the bottom. Click the **Default Shipping Address** check box if necessary.

5. Click **OK**. You are returned to the New Customer window.
6. Fill in any other customer information you want to store. Click **Next** to enter another customer, if desired.
7. When finished entering customers, click **OK**. The New Customer window closes, and your customer information is saved. Alternatively, you can click the **Next** button to continue entering customers.

EDIT A CUSTOMER IN THE CUSTOMER:JOB LIST

The Edit Customer window gives you the option of changing any Customer information as well as adding notes such as to store customer preferences or create a To Do item; for example, reminding you to place an order for a customer. Refer to Chapter 5 regarding adding a Note and To Do to Vendors, as it is the same throughout all the name lists.

To edit a customer:

1. Click the **Customers** menu. Click the **Customer Center**.
2. Double-click the customer you want to edit, for example, **John Brown**. The Edit Customer window opens with the Customer Name field highlighted, as shown in Figure 6-3. Type Brown, John in this field, replacing the previous entry of "John Brown."
3. Click **OK** when you are finished making changes.

CUSTOMER:JOB TABS

The Customer:Job window can hold a great deal of information. To view the Customer:Job tabs:

Right-click the customer or job you want to edit, and click **Edit Customer:Job**.

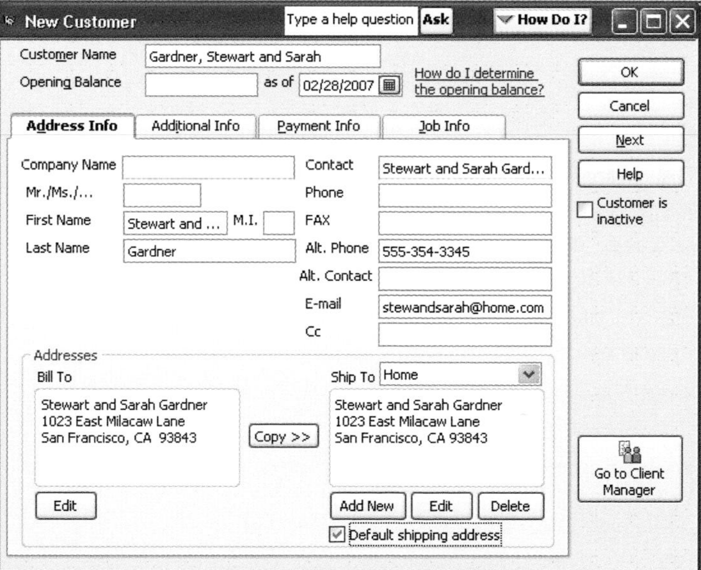

Figure 6-2: ***The New Customer window has four tabs for providing detailed information on your customers.***

TIP

Be consistent in naming your customers. Although you can use the format "First Name, Last Name," you will be better off using "Last Name, First Name," phone number, or whatever field is easiest to quickly look up in order to make finding customers quick and fast.

TIP

Press the **ESC** key instead of clicking the Close button (the X in the upper-right corner) and answer No when asked to save changes if you want to close any window *without* saving your changes.

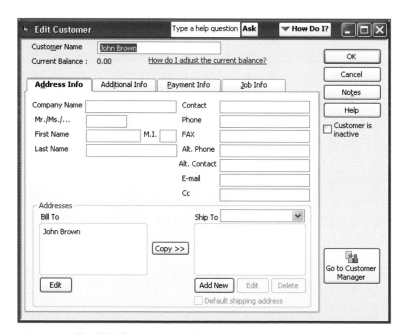

Figure 6-3: The Edit Customer window is similar to the New Customer window but includes a Notes button and a current balance.

Click each of the following four tabs to see the information they can contain:

- The **Address Info** tab includes standard contact information, as well as billing and shipping addresses and e-mail addresses, including carbon copy (Cc) addresses (used for e-mailing forms).
- The **Additional Info** tab includes the following fields and areas:

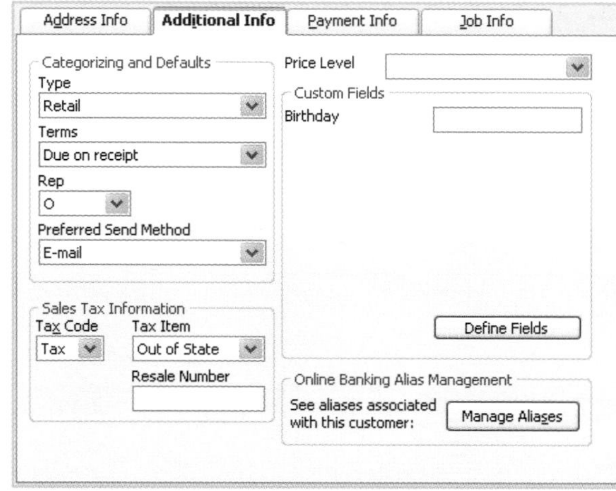

- **Type** allows you to create types, thereby classifying your customers in any way that is useful for you, such as Retail or Wholesale.
- **Terms** allows you to include payment terms. Standard terms, such as due on receipt, net 30, and net 60, are already set up, or you can create custom terms as needed.
- **Rep** assigns your company representative to a customer. This can be your employee or subcontractor.
- **Preferred Send Method** lets you keep track of whether a customer will accept e-mailed invoices or prefers them sent by regular mail.
- **Sales Tax Information** gives the option of identifying a customer as taxable or non-taxable, as well as what taxes to charge and a place to enter a reseller or nonprofit tax-exempt number.
- **Price Level** can be created to increase or decrease standard item prices, either on an individual basis or on a flat-percentage increase or decrease for all items.

Address Info | Additional Info | Payment Info | Job Info

Account No. Brown

Credit Limit 500.00

Preferred Payment Method

Cash

Credit Card No. Exp. Date /

Name on card

Address

Zip Code

CAUTION

If you collect credit card information for recurring charges, be extra cautious with your user name and password access in QuickBooks.

NOTE

The Job Info tab is displayed only if the customer has no jobs associated with him or her. If jobs exist, this tab will be displayed with the relevant jobs but not in the main Customer window.

- **Custom Fields** can be created here as well (see Chapter 5 for an example of how this is done).
- **Online Banking Alias Management** allows you to create an additional name by which a customer may be recognized (only applies to online banking services).

- The **Payment Info** tab includes such things as your customer's account number and credit limit, as well as his or her preferred payment method and credit card information.
- The **Job Info** tab includes such information as job status, start date, projected end date, actual end date, job description, and job type.

Address Info | Additional Info | Payment Info | Job Info

Job Status: None | Start Date | Projected End | End Date

Job Description | Job Type

Merge, Delete, or Make Customers Inactive

If a customer is listed twice with slightly different names, you can merge the two names so that you don't lose any transactions. If a customer is entered into QuickBooks but has no transactions associated with it, you can delete this customer. If a customer has past transactions and is simply no longer an active customer, QuickBooks will not allow you to delete this customer; however, you can make this customer inactive so that the name no longer appears in your Customer & Job List. If you start to use the Customer again, you can easily change the status back to active.

MERGE CUSTOMERS

If you change the name of a customer to one that already exists, QuickBooks asks if you want to merge the information. This is useful if you have entered names incorrectly, such as John Brown and Brown, John.

To merge customers:

1. Click the **Customers** menu and click **Customer Center**.
2. Double-click the customer name you want to merge. The Edit Customer window opens with the selected vendor name highlighted in blue.
3. Type the name of the customer with whom you want to merge the current customer.

CAUTION

When customers (or any names) are merged, any existing transactions are linked to the new customer, but information in the customer you are merging information from will be lost. If you have partial information in each of the two names you are merging, manually correct information in the customer you will be merging *to* before merging.

Edit | View | Lists | Accountant | Company

Nothing to Undo	Ctrl+Z
Revert	
Cut	Ctrl+X
Copy	Ctrl+C
Paste	Ctrl+V
Edit Customer:Job	Ctrl+E
New Customer:Job	Ctrl+N
Delete Customer:Job	Ctrl+D
Add Job	
Make Customer:Job Inactive	
Notepad	
Use Register	Ctrl+R
Use Calculator	
Search...	
Find...	Ctrl+F
Preferences...	

Customers & Jobs | Transactions

View: All Customers

✖	Name	Balance Total
	◆Alpha Library	0.00
	◆Bishop, Jeanne	0.00
	◆Cash	0.00
	◆In Store	0.00
	◆Online	0.00
	◆Show	0.00
✖	◆Gardner, Stewart a...	0.00
	◆John Brown	0.00

4. Click **OK**. A dialog box appears, asking if you would like to merge these two items. If you made an error in typing the name, the name change will take place immediately without confirmation.
5. Click **Yes** to complete the merge.

DELETE A CUSTOMER

You can only delete a customer if no entries exist pertaining to it. If a customer has transactions associated with it, you must make it inactive.

1. Click the **Customers** menu and click **Customer Center**. The Customer Center is displayed.
2. Click the customer name you want to delete.
3. Click the **Edit** menu. Click **Delete Customer:Job**. A dialog box appears, asking you to confirm this action.
4. Click **Yes** to delete the customer.

MAKE A CUSTOMER INACTIVE

If you've previously used a customer but no longer plan to, you must mark it inactive, since QuickBooks will not allow you to delete this customer.

1. Click the **Customers** menu and click **Customer Center**. The Customer Center is displayed.
2. Click the customer that you want to make inactive.
3. Click the **Edit** menu. Click **Make Customer:Job Inactive** (alternatively, you can right-click the customer name, and click **Make Customer:Job Inactive**). There is no confirmation dialog box; the customer immediately becomes inactive and disappears from the Customer List.

VIEW INACTIVE CUSTOMERS

To view your inactive vendors in your Customer List:

Click the **View** down arrow, located at the top of the Customer List in the Customer Center, and select **All Customers**.

A new column is created to the left of the Name column, designated by an X. That same X is next to any customer that you have made inactive, as can be seen in the illustration. You can click in the X column to toggle the customer's status to active or inactive.

Track Sales in QuickBooks

Sales are entered using invoices and sales receipts. In order to enter sales, you need to create items. Each item will have an internal name, description, and amount and be associated with the correct Income or Expense Account on the Chart of Accounts. Each time you use the item, it records the income or expense associated with that item in the appropriate account.

You can use the Quick Add feature to add items as you need them, but it's more accurate to set up items beforehand so that you can be consistent in your data entry. You will also need to set up tax items if you collect taxes. Inventory items will be covered in more detail in Chapter 7.

Set Up Service Items

If your company primarily provides services, you will want to create a number of service items to represent what you do. For example, a computer company might have service items for consulting, training, development, and maintenance; and a construction company will likely have a different service item for each trade. Butterfly Books and Bytes has only one service item; Research. To set up a service item:

1. Click the **Lists** menu and then click **Item List**.
2. Click the **List** menu button, and click **New** as shown in Figure 6-4. The New Item window opens with the Item Type drop-down list displaying **Service** as the default selection.
3. Press the **TAB** key to accept this default selection and move to the next field.
4. Type Research in the Item Name field. Your customers won't see this name. It is for your use only.
5. Click in the **Description** field, and type Research Services. Customers will see this name on invoices and sales receipts.
6. Press the **TAB** key to move to the next field, and type 50 for the hourly rate.
7. Press the **TAB** key to move to the next field, and type N for Non-Taxable Sales. As a rule of thumb, most services are not taxable, but contact your state and local agencies to determine your tax liability.

TIP

The description and rate will appear each time you use the item, but can be customized on the fly for each invoice or sales receipt to add detail to the description or raise or reduce the rate.

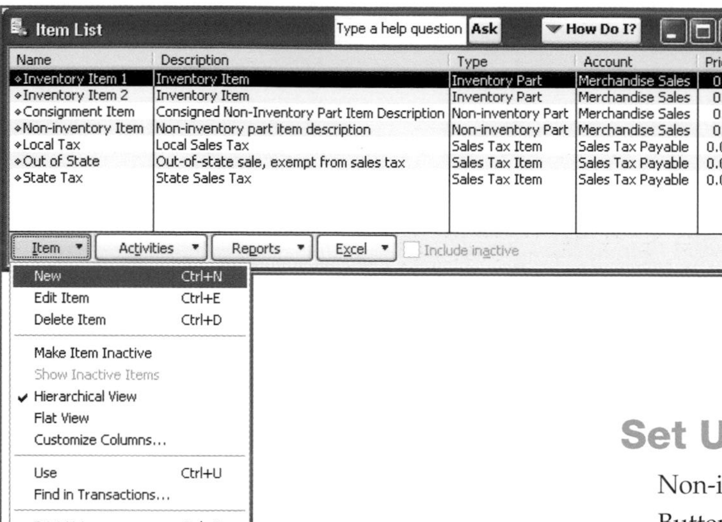

Figure 6-4: ***Items can have subitems just as the other lists do.***

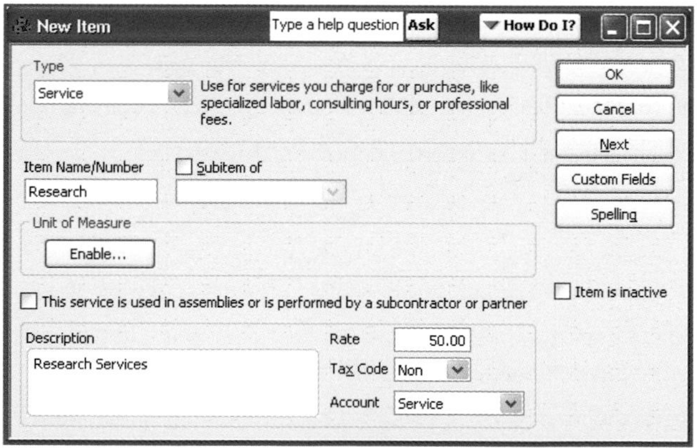

Figure 6-5: ***Each item (such as Research) is associated with a specific income account (such as Service).***

8. Press the **TAB** key to move to the next field, and type Service.
9. Press the **TAB** key and the Account Not Found box will appear.
10. Click **Set Up** and the Add New Account dialog box will appear.
11. Click **Save & Close** to create the new account and the window will close, returning you to the New Item window as in Figure 6-5.
12. Click **OK** to save the new item (or click **Next** if you will be setting up a number of items).

Account Not Found

Service is not in the Account list.

Set Up   Cancel

Set Up Non-Inventory Items

Non-inventory items are things you sell that you do not track. In the case of Butterfly Books and Bytes, this will include coffee, as a cup of coffee is not by itself an inventory item. Coffee beans and other items used to make coffee can be treated as supply expenses or cost of goods.

1. Click the **Lists** menu and then click **Item List**. The Item List opens.
2. Click the **List** menu button, and click **New** as seen in Figure 6-4. The New Item window opens.
3. Click **Non-Inventory Part** on the **Item Type** drop-down list.
4. Press the **TAB** key to move to the next field.
5. Type Coffee in the Item Name field.
6. Click in the **Description** field, and type Coffee.
7. Press the **TAB** key to move to the next field, and type 2.50 for the price.
8. Press the **TAB** key to move to the next field, and type N for Non-Taxable. While most items are taxable, food items often are not.
9. Press the **TAB** key to move to the next field, and click the Account down arrow. The Chart of Accounts Income list is displayed.
10. Click the **Merchandise Sales** account.
11. Click **OK** to save the new item (or click **Next** if you will be setting up a number of items).

NOTE

You can integrate QuickBooks with a POS (Point of Sale) system to better handle retail situations, using a register for high-volume sales, or enter information directly into a computer equipped with QuickBooks.

TIP

Items in the Item List are listed with their associated income accounts but may have an expense or Cost of Goods Sold account as well.

Set Up Items with Purchase Information

To track items that are bought and resold, create an item that has both income and Cost of Goods (or expense) accounts associated with it. By using items instead of directly using an account, you will be generating transactions that are tied both to the items and to the specific accounts with which they are associated. This produces reports on two levels: the account reports provide a high level of information, and the item reports provide a detailed level of information.

To enter items purchased for a specific job:

1. Click the **Items & Services** icon on the home page (or click **Lists | Item List**). The Item List is displayed, as shown in Figure 6-4.
2. From the Item List, click the **Item** menu and click **New**. The New Item window opens, as shown in Figure 6-6.
3. Click **Non-Inventory Part** on the **Item Type** drop-down list. You can also associate services or other charge items with a Cost of Goods or expense account.
4. Press the **TAB** key to move to the Item Name field. Type a name for the item, for example, Special Book Order.
5. Click the **This item is used in assemblies or is purchased for a specific customer:job** check box. The New Item window expands to include purchase information as well as sales information.
6. Click in the **Description On Purchase Transactions** field, and type a relevant description, for example, Special Order Book. This information will appear on purchase orders.
7. Press the **TAB** key to move to the Cost field. Whatever you typed in the Description On Purchase Transactions field will appear in the Description On Sales Transactions field (located to the right). This information will appear on sales orders and invoices. You can type a cost or leave it blank if you will be entering a different cost each time.
8. Press the **TAB** key to move to the Expense Account field. Click the down arrow and click **Cost of Goods Sold**. Completing the Preferred Vendor field is optional.

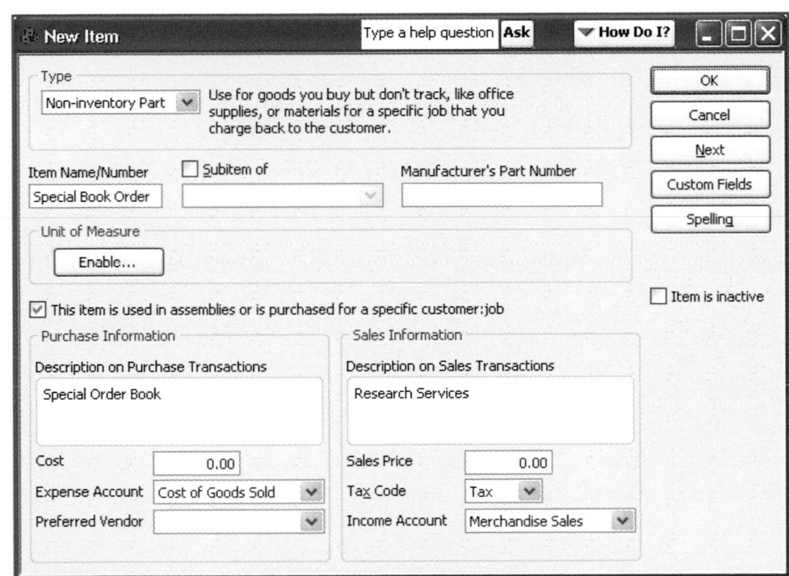

Figure 6-6: ***Use the New Item window to create an item that is often billed to clients.***

TIP

The Cost and Sales Price fields can be edited each time you use an item. If you have a standard cost, type it now. For special-order items, leave both amounts blank as a reminder that they need to be filled in.

CAUTION

QuickBooks requires all item entries to be associated with an account in the Chart of Accounts in order to have accurate accounting and reporting.

9. Click the **Income Account** down arrow, and click **Merchandise Sales**, or other appropriate Income Account.
10. Click **OK** to save the item and return to the Item List. Click the **Close** button (the X in the upper-right corner) to close the Item List.

Set Up Sales Tax Items

Selling items normally involves collecting taxes. You may need to collect a combination of different taxes that are payable to different tax entities. This section will show you how to set up individual sales tax items and then combine them into sales tax groups, which you will then apply to your invoices and sales receipts.

In our example, Butterfly Books and Bytes must collect a total tax rate of 7.8 percent, the combination of the following three taxes: the city of Mesa (1.5 percent), the state of Arizona (5.6 percent), and Maricopa County (0.7 percent). Research your location to understand what is taxable and to whom the taxes are payable. Make a list and then create the relevant tax items and groups in the Item List.

ACTIVATE SALES TAX IN PREFERENCES

Before you can create a sales tax item, you must activate this feature in QuickBooks.

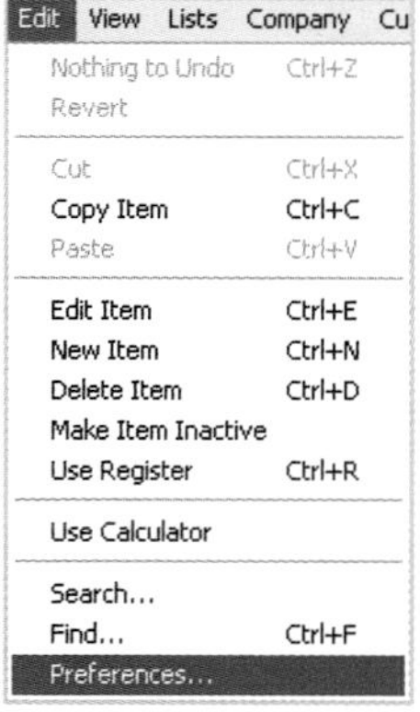

1. Click the **Edit** menu and click **Preferences**. The Preferences window opens (see Figure 6-7).
2. Click **Sales Tax** on the list on the left.
3. Click the **Company Preferences** tab.
4. Click **Yes** in the Do You Charge Sales Tax? area. All of the other items on this tab will become available. Identify the type, time, and frequency of your sales tax burden. See the following sections, "Create a Sales Tax Item" and "Create a Sales Tax Group," for more information.
5. Click **OK** to save your changes and close the Preferences window. The Updating Sales Tax dialog box may appear. If so, click **Make All Existing Customers Taxable**. Most of your customers will be taxable; you can mark items or customers as non-taxable on an individual basis.

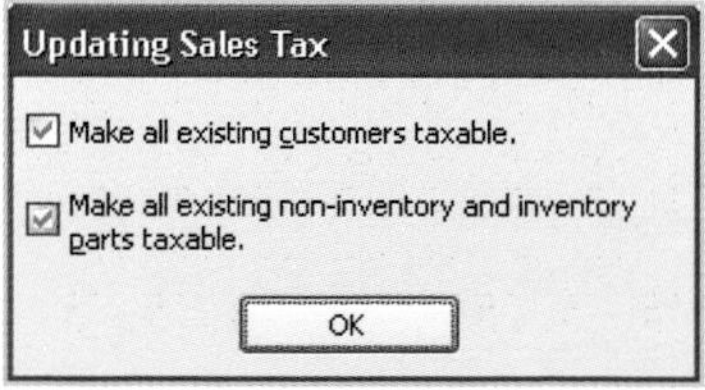

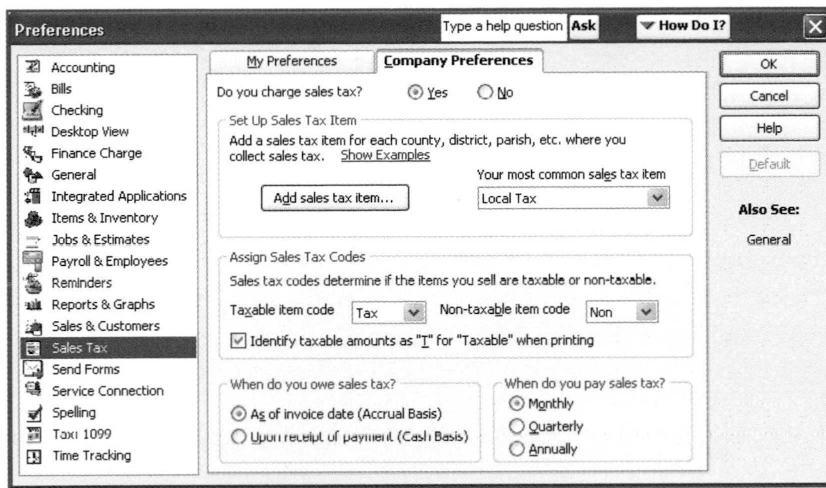

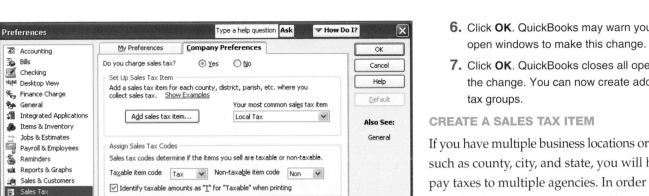

Figure 6-7: ***You can click different icons in the Preferences window to see more options.***

TIP

If you have multiple business locations in different taxable areas, create a tax item for each taxable area (like a city), and create a matching tax group for each taxable area.

NOTE

Some areas may have unusual rules; for example, a state may not charge sales tax for a specific category of items, but the county or city does, so a separate sales tax group will need to be set up for that situation.

NOTE

Tax groups allow the customer to see one tax total and allow the company to track tax amounts due to each agency separately.

6. Click **OK**. QuickBooks may warn you that it needs to close all open windows to make this change.
7. Click **OK**. QuickBooks closes all open windows and makes the change. You can now create additional tax items and tax groups.

CREATE A SALES TAX ITEM

If you have multiple business locations or multiple municipalities, such as county, city, and state, you will have to collect and pay taxes to multiple agencies. In order to collect multiple taxes (and ensure that you are collecting the correct amounts), you need to enter each of the tax items separately and then group them.

To create sales tax items:

1. Click the **Lists** menu and click **Item List**. The Item List is displayed.
2. Click the **Item** menu button (at the bottom of the screen), and click **New**. The New Item window opens, as seen in Figure 6-8.
3. Click the **Type** down arrow, and click **Sales Tax Item**. Press the TAB key to move to the Sales Tax Name field. Type the name of the tax, for example, State of Arizona.
4. Press the TAB key to move to the Description field. The words "Sales Tax" are there by default. This wording will appear on invoices and sales receipts. You can edit this if you want.
5. Press TAB to move to the Tax Rate field. Type the rate for this single tax, for example, 5.6.
6. Press TAB to move to the Tax Agency field. Type the agency name, for example, Arizona Department of Revenue.
7. Press TAB. If the Vendor Not Found dialog box appears, click **Quick Add**. You can edit this particular vendor and provide more specific information later if needed.
8. Click the **Next** button. This sales tax item is created and saved, and another New Item window opens.

1 2 3 4 5 6 7 8 9 10

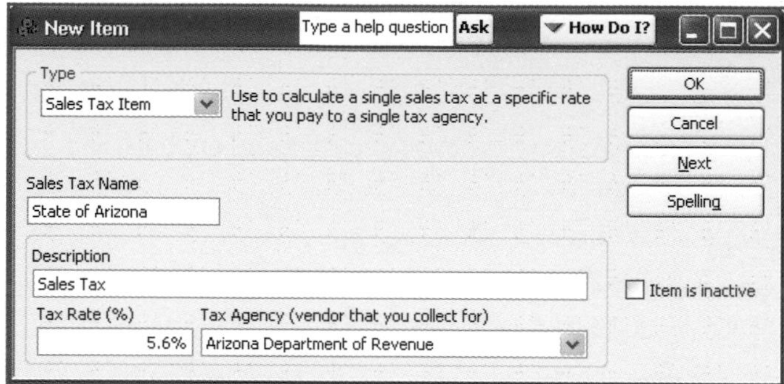

Figure 6-8: ***The New Item window changes options, depending on the type of item you are creating.***

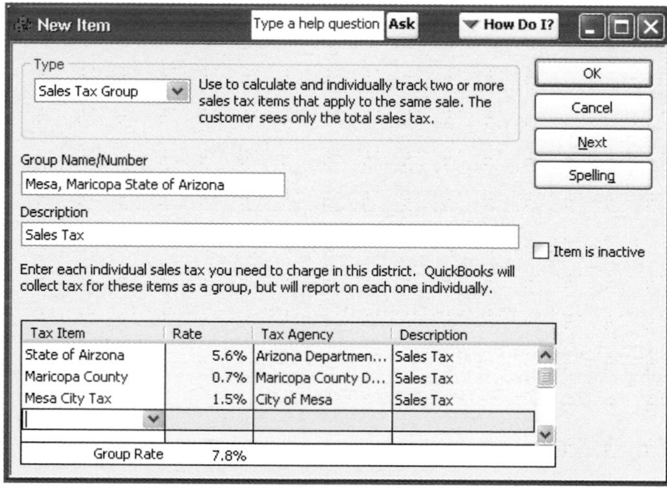

Figure 6-9: ***The Sales Tax Group allows you to use a combination of Sales Tax Items to show as one item on invoices and sales receipts, but track each tax obligation separately.***

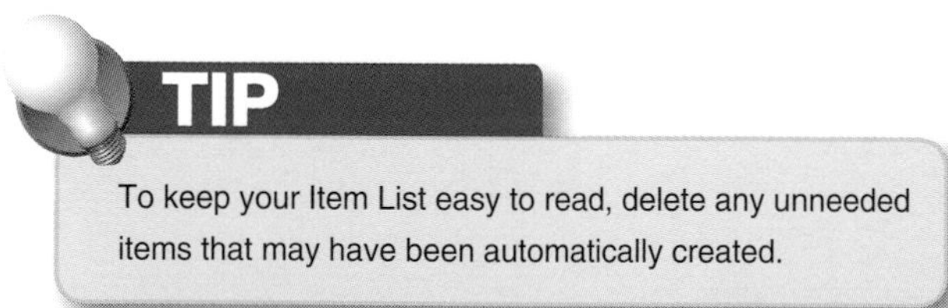

TIP

To keep your Item List easy to read, delete any unneeded items that may have been automatically created.

9. Repeat Steps 3–8 using Mesa City Tax at 1.5 percent payable to the City of Mesa and Maricopa County Tax at 0.7 percent payable to Maricopa County Department of Revenue.
10. Click **OK** when finished to save your new sales tax items.

CREATE A SALES TAX GROUP

Once you've created the individual tax items for your area, create a tax group to easily apply this group of taxes to each taxable item you sell. This will allow you to show a single tax line on your invoices and sales receipts but track and pay each tax in the tax group individually.

To create a sales tax group:

1. Click the **Lists** menu and click **Item List**. The Item List is displayed.
2. Click the **Item** menu button (located at the bottom of the screen), and click **New**. The New Item window opens as in Figure 6-9.
3. Click the **Type** down arrow, and click **Sales Tax Group**. Press the **TAB** key to move to the Group Name/Number field. Type the name of the tax group, for example, <u>Mesa, Maricopa, State Tax</u>.
4. Press **TAB** to move to the Description field. The words "Sales Tax" are there by default. This wording will appear on invoices and sales receipts. You can edit this if you prefer to have a specific tax listed.
5. Click in the **Tax Item** column, and a drop-down list will appear, displaying all the tax items you have entered.
6. Click the first tax you want to include, for example, **Maricopa County**.
7. Click in the next row, and click the next tax you want to include in the group, for example, **Mesa City Tax**. Repeat this step for each additional tax item you want to include in this tax group. The total tax will appear at the bottom of the window. Confirm that the total in the Item List is 7.8 percent for the tax group (or whatever the correct total for your tax group is).
8. Click **OK** to save the sales tax group. The New Item window closes, and you are returned to the Item List, where you will see your new tax group included, as shown in Figure 6-10.

QUICKSTEPS

CHANGING TAX PREFERENCES

Once your tax preferences are set, you may need to mark some items or customers as non-taxable.

MARK ITEMS AS NON-TAXABLE

Once you have activated the Sales Tax feature, tax items will contain a list box where you indicate whether an item should be marked taxable or non-taxable.

To change this setting:

1. Click the **Lists** menu and click **Item List**.
2. Double-click any item (in this example, **Research**), and the Tax Code drop-down list is displayed in the lower-right area.
3. Click the **Tax Code** down arrow, and click **Non-Taxable**.
4. Click **OK**.

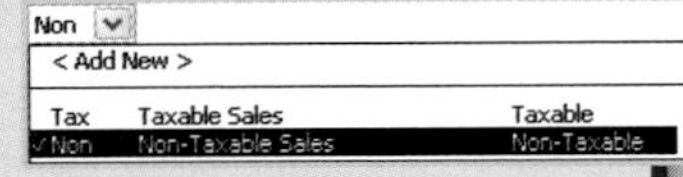

MARK CUSTOMERS AS NON-TAXABLE

You may have nonprofit customers or customers with a reseller number who are not required to pay sales tax. You can modify these customers individually.

1 Click the **Customer Center** button on the Navigation bar.
2. Double-click an existing customer, such as **Alpha Library**. The Edit Customer window opens.
3. Click the **Additional Info** tab. The Tax Code drop-down list is displayed in the lower-left corner in the Sales Tax Information area.
4. Click the **Tax Code** down arrow, and click **Non-Taxable**. The resale number is not required. Alternatively, you can use this section to assign a specific tax code to a customer, such as Out of State, Non-Profit, Governmental, or any code that would be useful for your business reporting.

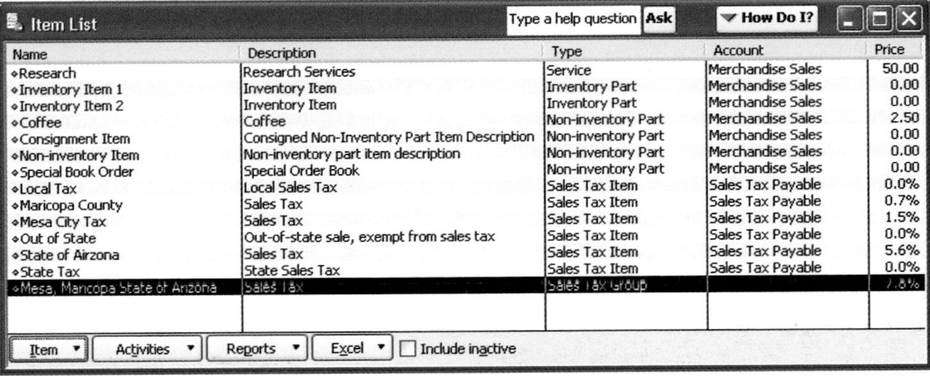

Figure 6-10: ***A sales tax group is displayed as one tax amount but puts separate amounts into the relevant accounts of the individual sales tax items of which it is comprised.***

CHANGE THE DEFAULT TAX

When you activated sales taxes in Preferences, you were required to establish a default tax for use as the most common sales tax. This tax will be applied to each item and each customer unless it is changed on an item or customer basis.

To change the default tax to the new tax group:

1. Click the **Edit** menu and click **Preferences**. The Preferences window opens.
2. Click **Sales Tax** on the left side, and click the **Company Preferences** tab.
3. Click the **Most Common Sales Tax** down arrow. You will see all the sales tax items and sales tax groups you have entered.

Mesa, Maricopa State of Ariz
< Add New >

Local Tax	Sales Tax Item	Local Sales Tax
Maricopa County	Sales Tax Item	Sales Tax
Mesa City Tax	Sales Tax Item	Sales Tax
Out of State	Sales Tax Item	Out-of-state sale, exempt from sales tax
State of Airzona	Sales Tax Item	Sales Tax
State Tax	Sales Tax Item	State Sales Tax
✓Mesa, Maricopa State of Ariz...	Sales Tax Group	Sales Tax

4. Click the new sales tax group you created (**Mesa, Maricopa, State Tax** in this example).
5. Click **OK**.

TIP

If you have a business such as roofing, where you perform work in different locations, you may need to apply the appropriate city tax to each customer. You can mark each customer with the appropriate tax in the Edit Customer window.

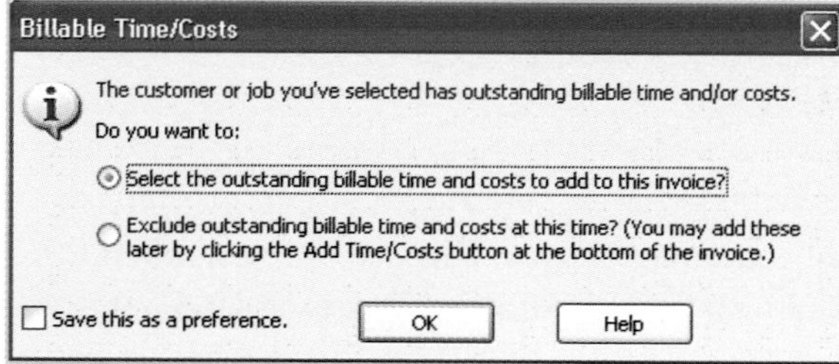

Billable Time/Costs
The customer or job you've selected has outstanding billable time and/or costs.
Do you want to:
Select the outstanding billable time and costs to add to this invoice?
Exclude outstanding billable time and costs at this time? (You may add these later by clicking the Add Time/Costs button at the bottom of the invoice.)
Save this as a preference.
OK
Help

TIP

Out-of-state customers are typically not taxable. Some companies create a tax item called Out of State with a zero-percent tax so that they can quickly change the tax item on the invoice instead of individually editing each customer.

TIP

Once you've viewed a dialog box, if you don't want to continue seeing the same reminder, click the **Do Not Display This Message In The Future** check box.

Create Invoices

Creating accurate invoices and sales receipts will help you track inventory, know what is selling, and collect your money from customers. Be sure to refer to "Receive Payments" later in this chapter in order to correctly apply customer payments to the correct invoices.

To create an invoice:

1. Click the **Customers** menu and click **Create Invoices**. The Create Invoices window opens (see Figure 6-11).
2. Click in the **Customer: Job** field, and type your customer's name, for example, Alpha Library. Since this is a customer you already created in QuickBooks, the name should automatically appear as soon as you type A. You can also select customers from the drop-down menu, or click the **Quick Add** button to add them if they are a new customer.
3. Press the TAB key. A reminder may appear if this customer has outstanding billable time or costs. After purchasing items for a specific customer and marking them as being for that customer, you need to charge the customer for these items on the invoice. If you were creating an invoice unrelated to those charges, you could click the option to Exclude. If so, skip Steps 4–7 in this section.
4. Click **OK**. The Choose Billable Time and Costs window opens (see Figure 6-12).
5. Click the **Items** tab to see the outstanding items.
6. Click in the **Checkmark** column to use an item in this list on the current invoice. A check mark will appear in this column.
7. Click **OK**. The Billable Time and Costs window closes. You are returned to the Create Invoices window.
8. Click in the **Description** field. Delete the existing description and type World Atlas.
9. Press the TAB key to move to the Price Each column. Type the price, for example, 45.
10. Press TAB to move to the Amount column. QuickBooks automatically calculates this for you. Since this item is for resale or use in the customer's business, it remains non-taxable. You will need to use your judgment or allow the customer to determine the tax liability for items purchased if the customer has a tax ID number.
11. Click the **Template** down arrow to choose a different invoice layout for your customer if desired.

TIP

You can return to a previous invoice and add an item if you have not yet sent it to the customer.

12. Click in the **Date** field to enter the correct date. You can also click the **Calendar** icon to choose a date.

13. Press **TAB** to move to the Invoice # field. If this is the first time you've used QuickBooks, your invoice number will be 1. Type 2001, or any number you prefer, to start at a higher number. This field will automatically increase by one each time you create a new invoice.

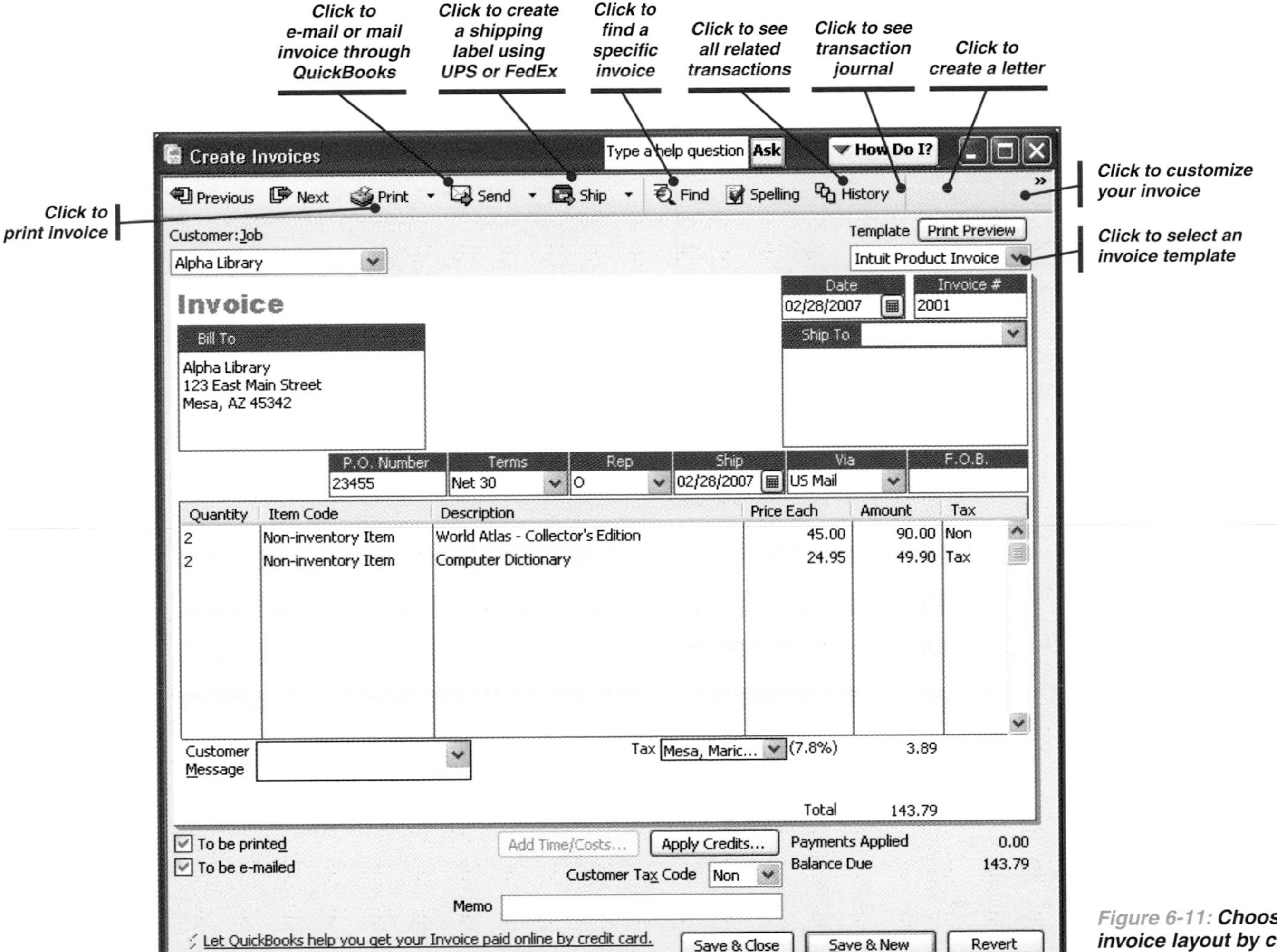

Figure 6-11: ***Choose your preferred invoice layout by clicking the template down arrow.***

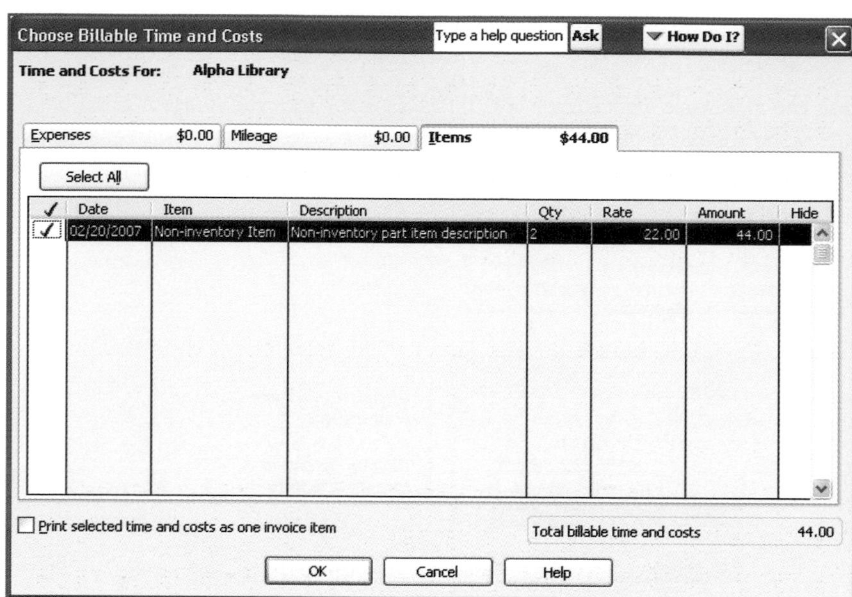

Figure 6-12: ***Use QuickBooks to track and charge items, expenses, time, or mileage back to your customers.***

14. Press the TAB key to move to the Bill To field. QuickBooks automatically fills in the customer name and any previously provided address information. You can edit or enter the customer's name, address, city, state, and ZIP code.
15. Press the TAB key to move to the Ship To field. This is an optional field, as are the PO Number, Terms, Rep, Ship, Via, and F.O.B. fields. If you are using these fields (perhaps because you are shipping your product), you can fill them in; however, if they do not apply to your business, you can remove them from your template (see Chapter 8).
16. Click in the **Quantity** field, either below the item already listed or in the first row, and type the number of items, for example, 2.
17. Press the TAB key to move to the Item Code field. Type N, and "Non-Inventory Item" may appear automatically, since it is a previously created item.
18. Press TAB to move to the Description field. You may see a dialog box regarding tax codes. Click **OK**. Notice that QuickBooks has automatically filled in the Description column, but this item was set up without a price, since each item will be unique.
19. Delete the existing description and type Computer Dictionary.
20. Press the TAB key to move to the Price Each column. Type the price for this item, for example, 24.95.
21. Press TAB to move to the Amount column. QuickBooks automatically calculates this value. A dialog box may appear regarding price levels. Click **OK**.
22. Press TAB to move to the Tax column, click the down arrow, and click **Taxable**. (This customer is non-taxable for resale items, but this is a personal item that is not for resale, so it can be marked taxable for this area.) The tax appears just above the total amount of the invoice.
23. Confirm that the **To Be Printed** check box is selected (located in the lower-left corner). Click the **Save & Close** button. (If you want to continue entering invoices, click the **Save & New** button.) If you edited the address, as in this example, a dialog box appears, prompting you to confirm the address change. This address will then be corrected in the customer's record and will appear in any future items using this customer.

TIP

If a customer has been marked as non-taxable, that setting supersedes the item tax code setting. However, you can always change the tax status of any item by clicking the Tax column down arrow and selecting a new tax status.

TIP

You can mark your invoices to be printed or e-mailed later by clicking the **To Be Printed** or **To Be E-Mailed** check box, respectively (see the lower-left area of Figure 6-11), or you can immediately print or e-mail them using the buttons at the top of the invoice.

24. Click **Yes**. The customer's information is updated, and the invoice is saved. You may have a spell check open. Click **Close** to cancel the spell check, or click **Ignore** or **Replace** for each possible error it finds. (To set spell check preferences, click **Edit**, click **Preferences**, and click **Spelling**.)

Be sure you accurately enter items and services. If you set up your items correctly and use them correctly on invoices and sales receipts, you will have accurate inventory and sales tracking.

SEND INVOICES TO CLIENTS

After you create your invoices, you can send them out right away, by clicking the Print or Send button at the top of the invoice or batch them for a group sending.

To print Invoices To Be Printed:

1. Click the **File** menu, click **Print Forms**, and click **Invoices**. The Select Invoices to Print window will open.

Select Invoices to Print

A/R Account: Accounts Receivable

Select Invoices to print, then click OK.
There is 1 Invoice to print for $143.79.

✓	Date	Type	No.	Customer	Template	Amount
✓	02/28/2007	INV	2001	Alpha Library	Intuit Product Invoice	143.79
	02/28/2007	INV	2005	Alpha Library	Intuit Product Invoice	0.00

OK | Cancel | Help | Select All | Select None | Print Labels

2. Click the Invoices you wish to print and click **OK**. The Print Invoices window appears. Confirm the printer and paper type.
3. Click **Print**. The invoices will be sent to the printer and the Print Invoices – Confirmation window will open. Confirm the invoices printed correctly. If not, click the invoices that need to be reprinted.
4. Click **OK**.

TIP

Accurate entry of items on bills, checks, credit cards, invoices, and sales receipts will ensure accurate job costing and other reports.

TIP

Invoices can be changed or deleted at any time, but it is inadvisable to "fix" an invoice that has already been given to the customer.

NOTE

You must use invoices or sales receipts in order to see accurate figures on sales reports.

TIP

Always ensure that the To Be Printed or To Be E-Mailed check box is selected if you are not sending the invoice immediately.

TIP

To edit the text of the e-mail message one time, click **Edit E-Mail** in the Select Forms to Send window. To permanently change the e-mail message, click **Edit Default Text** once editing the e-mail message.

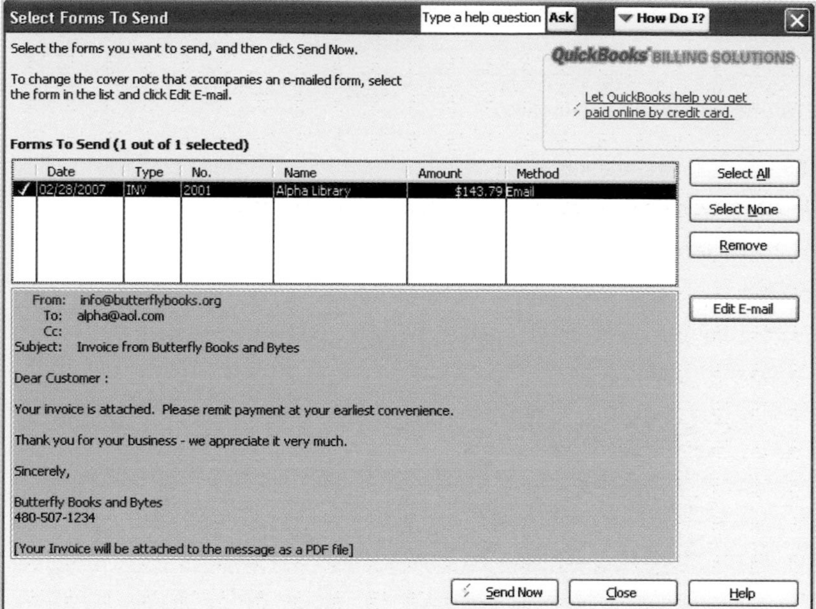

To e-mail Invoices To Be Sent:

1. Click the **File** menu and click **Send Forms**. The Select Forms to Send window will open.
2. Click **Send Now** if you are happy with the text. QuickBooks will connect to Intuit Business Services.
3. Enter your e-mail address and click **Next**. QuickBooks will initialize your free service and send your forms by e-mail.

Edit Invoices

Occasionally, you may need to edit an invoice. For example, if you create an invoice based on a customer's phone call and he or she then subsequently changes the order, you will have to correct the original invoice. To quickly find any customer transaction, open the Customer Center, click the desired customer and then double-click the specific transaction to open it.

EDIT A LINE

To edit a line, click in the line and make the changes you want. For example, in Invoice 2001:

1. Click after World Atlas. Type - Collector's Edition.
2. Click the **Save & New** button. A dialog box appears, asking if you want to save your changes.
3. Click **Yes**. If the spell check appears, click **Close**.

Edit View Lists Company Customers
Undo Typing Ctrl+Z
Clear
Cut Ctrl+X
Copy Ctrl+C
Paste Ctrl+V
Insert Line Ctrl+Ins
Delete Line Ctrl+Del
New Invoice Ctrl+N
Memorize Invoice Ctrl+M
Void Invoice
Go To Transfer Ctrl+G
Mark Invoice As Pending
Change Account Color...
Use Register Ctrl+R
Use Calculator
Search...
Find Invoices... Ctrl+F
Preferences...

INSERT A LINE

To insert a line (still using Invoice 2001 as an example):

1. Click in the line to insert a line above this one.
2. Click the **Edit** menu and click **Insert Line**. A new line appears above the currently selected line.

ADD A NEW ITEM

To add a new item while in an invoice (still using Invoice 2001 as an example):

1. Type the quantity for the new line item, for example, 4.

Item Not Found

QuickBooks did not find 'Book Covers' in your list of products and services.

Would you like to add it now? If not, go back and select an existing product or service.

Yes No

2. Press the **TAB** key to move to the Item Code column. Type Book Covers to enter a new item.
3. Press **TAB** to move to the Description column. QuickBooks asks if you want to add this new item.
4. Click **Yes**. A New Item window appears.
5. Click the **Item** type down arrow, and click **Non-Inventory Part**.
6. Click in the **Description** field, and type Clear Book Covers.
7. Press **TAB** to move to the Price field, and type 2.50.
8. Press **TAB** to move to the Tax field. Type T, and "Taxable" will be entered.
9. Press **TAB** to move to the Account field, and type Merchandise Sales.

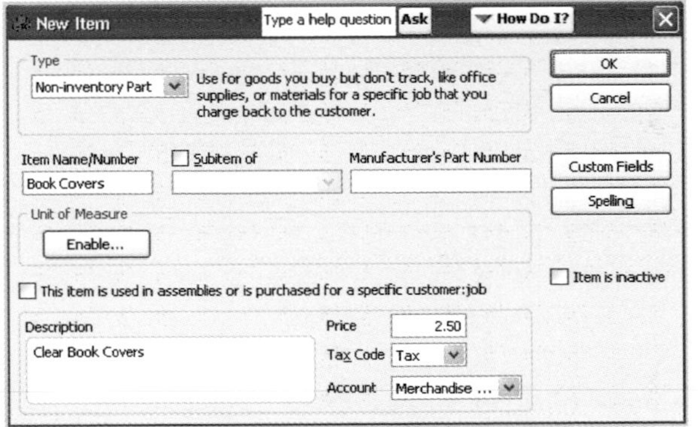

10. Click **OK**. The New Item window closes, and you are returned to the invoice.
11. Click **Save & New**. A dialog box appears, asking if you want to save your changes.
12. Click **Yes**. If the spell check appears, click **Close**.

TIP

If at any time before saving you make a mistake in an invoice, you can click the Revert button to remove all your changes.

TIP

Click **Options** while in the Check Spelling on Form window to turn off or set other spell check options.

NOTE

When your cursor is in the list of items, you have a different list of choices in your Edit menu than when your cursor is in any field in the header (such as the Address field).

DELETE A LINE

To delete a line (still using Invoice 2001 as an example):

1. Click the line you want to delete, such as **Clear Book Covers**.
2. Click the **Edit** menu and click **Delete Line**. The line is immediately deleted; you are not prompted to confirm this action. If you choose to delete the entire invoice, your choice will be confirmed.
3. Click **Save & Close**. A dialog box appears, asking if you want to save your changes.
4. Click **Yes**. If the spell check appears, click **Close**.

1 2 3 4 5 6 7 8 9 10

QUICKSTEPS

ADDING AN INVOICE TO MEMORIZED TRANSACTIONS

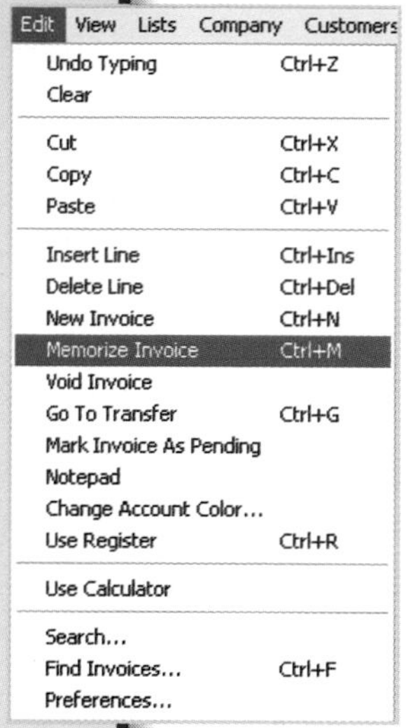

Monthly invoices can be set up in groups to be billed each month, such as a monthly fee or standing order. To add an invoice to your Memorized Transaction List:

1. Click the **Customer Center** on the Navigation bar, select a customer with invoices and double-click the invoice you wish to make recurring. Ensure that the **To be printed** or **To be e-mailed** check box is selected, as preferred.
2. Click the **Edit** menu and click **Memorize Invoice**. The Memorize Transaction window opens with the customer name, which can be edited to further identify the invoice.
3. Click the **Automatically Enter** option, since this is a standard monthly billing. (You can still review this invoice before printing it.)
4. Select **How Often** and choose your next date.

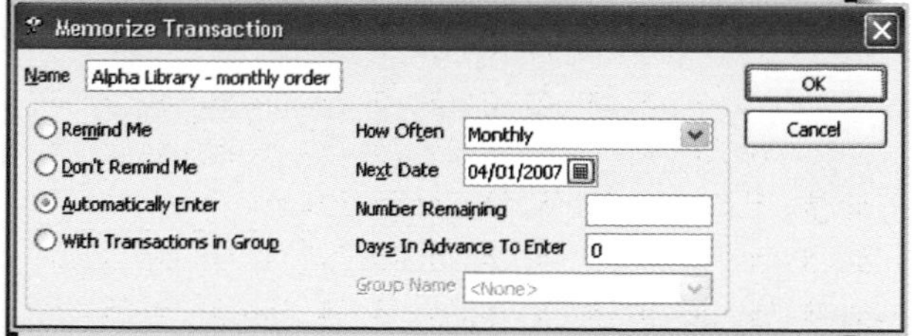

5. Click **OK**. The Memorize Transaction window closes, memorizing your transaction.

You can add this transaction to a monthly group. See Chapter 5 for more information on setting up memorized transactions.

Send Statements to Customers

If you extend credit to customers, chances are you'll need to send them statements. If you run a consulting firm, you may only send statements. Statements are simply a list of charges and payments with dates and descriptions, as well as an aging report at the bottom, listing how long an account has been outstanding.

To create a statement:

1. Click the **Customers** menu and click **Create Statements**. The Create Statements window opens, as shown in Figure 6-13.
2. Confirm the entry in the **Statement Date** field (by default, it is today's date).
3. Edit the statement's beginning and ending dates in the **Statement Period From** and **To** fields, respectively. Use monthly, quarterly, or annual ranges, as you prefer. Statements normally show all transactions. Alternately, you may click **All open transactions as of Statement Date** for emphasis of overdue invoices, but a full statement is more useful for customers to see how their payments were applied.

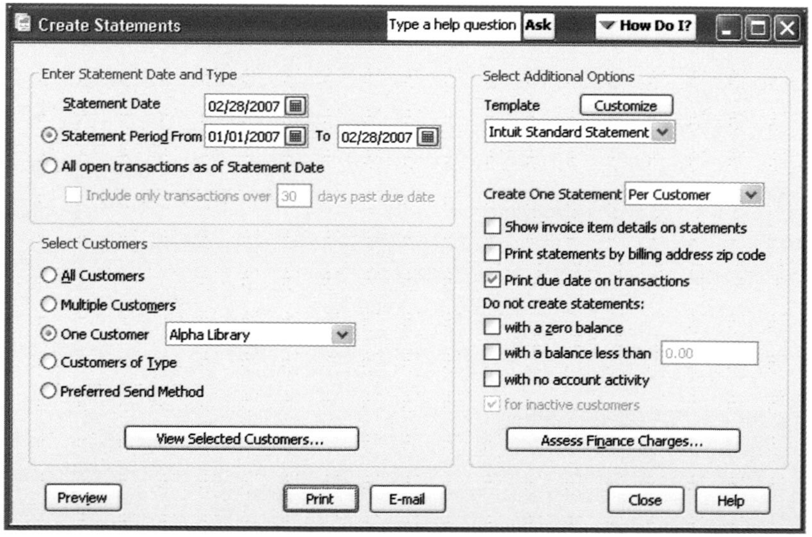

Figure 6-13: ***You can e-mail, mail, or fax statements, as you can all forms in QuickBooks.***

NOTE

QuickBooks sorts invoices according to date, not according to invoice number.

4. In the Select Customers section, you have the choice of all, multiple, type, or preferred send method. Click the **One Customer** option, and a drop-down menu will appear to the right. Click the down arrow and click your customer, for example, **Alpha Library**.
5. Click the **Preview** button. A preview window opens, as shown in Figure 6-14.
6. Click **Print**. A dialog box will appear, asking if your statements printed correctly. Click **Yes** or **No** as appropriate. A dialog box may appear, informing you of the option to e-mail your statements. Click **OK** if this happens.

Enter Sales Receipts

Sales receipts are used for any sale paid in full at the time of the transaction, whether paid by cash, check, or credit card. To process sales, you can use a cash register or have a computer set up at your checkout stand. While entering all sales receipts directly into QuickBooks results in more accurate reporting, it may not be practical in terms of employee training and customer volume. Determine if it will work for your business.

To enter sales receipts:

1. Click the **Customers** menu and click **Enter Sales Receipts**. A Merchant Account Service dialog box may appear, asking if you use credit cards. Click the relevant answer for your business, and the Enter Sales Receipts window opens (see Figure 6-15).
2. Type your customer's name, for example, Alpha Library. Since it is a previous customer, the company name should appear automatically as soon as you type A. If there are multiple names starting with the same letter, continue typing until the name you are seeking appears. If you can't find it by typing, you can click the down arrow to select it from the list.
3. Click in the **Date** field to enter the correct date, if necessary.
4. Press the **TAB** key to move to the Sale No. field. If this is the first time you've used QuickBooks, your sales receipt number will be 1. This field will automatically increase by one each time you enter a sales receipt.

Figure 6-14: ***Zoom in or out by clicking in the statement. Click Close to return to the Create Statements window, where you can edit parameters or e-mail the statement.***

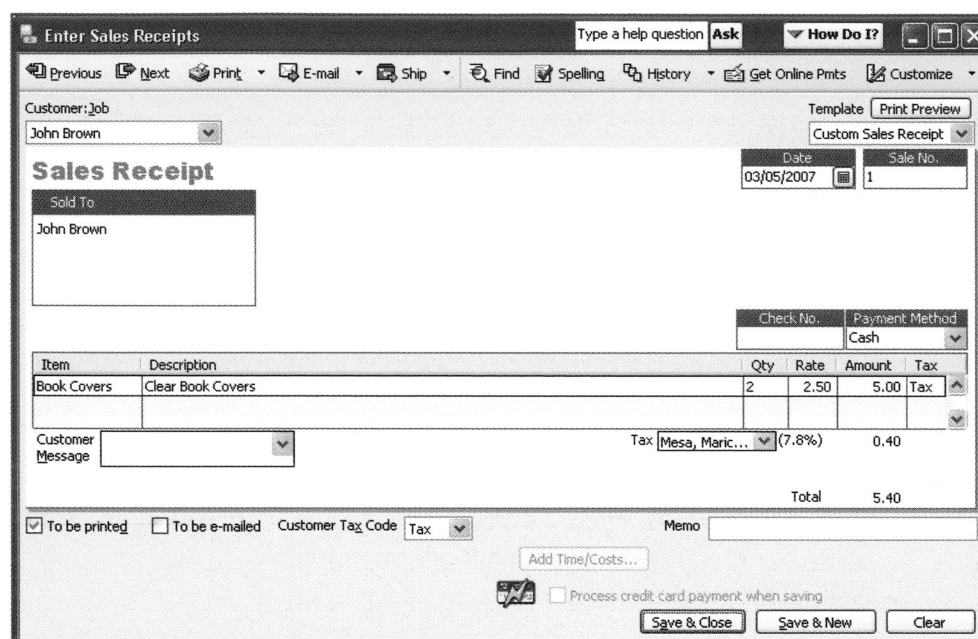

Figure 6-15: ***You can choose to leave the Enter Sales Receipts window open if you are using a computer as a cash register.***

5. Press **TAB** to move to the Sold To field, which will be automatically filled from the Customer information if present. Confirm that the information is accurate.
6. Click in the **Item** field. Begin typing the item name, such as B, for Book Covers. If already created, the item name should appear automatically in the drop-down list.
7. Press **TAB** to move to the Description field. QuickBooks automatically enters the price and calculates the total for you.
8. Press **TAB** to move to the Qty (Quantity) field, and type the quantity of items sold, for example, 2.
9. Confirm the **Tax** at the bottom of the form. If it is not correct, click the Tax down arrow and click the correct tax. The tax owed appears just above the total amount due.
10. Upon taking the payment from the customer, click the **Payment Method** down arrow, and click the correct payment method, such as **Cash**.
11. Click the **Print** button near the top of the sales receipt to immediately print a copy for the customer.

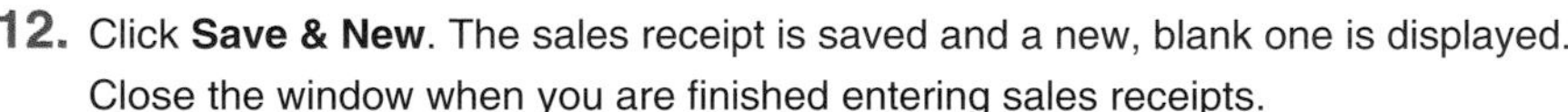

12. Click **Save & New**. The sales receipt is saved and a new, blank one is displayed. Close the window when you are finished entering sales receipts.

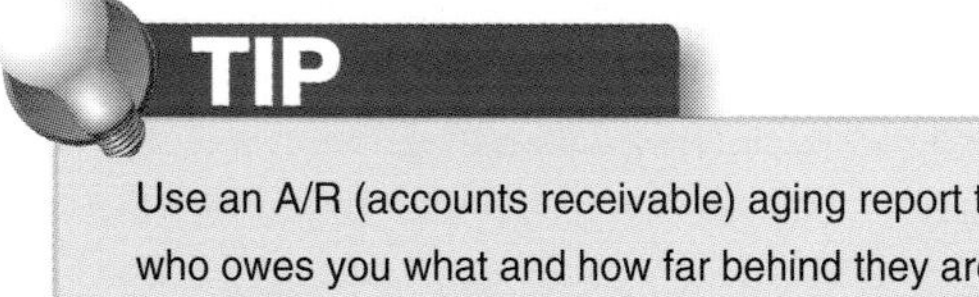

Use an A/R (accounts receivable) aging report to see who owes you what and how far behind they are. Send regular statements and have a policy in place to escalate the collection attempts and receive your money as soon as possible.

Create Estimates

If you create estimates for your business or do project work that has phases over time, use QuickBooks to generate an estimate, and then create invoices based on the estimate as work is completed.

ACTIVATE ESTIMATES

If you don't have an option for creating estimates, check your Preferences settings in QuickBooks.

TIP

If your sales flow is too great to use QuickBooks for each sales receipt, you can use a cash register or other method. Then, at the end of the day, one large sales receipt can be prepared. Make sure you use the correct items and amounts at the end of the day in order to have accurate tracking of items sold and inventory counts. If you use this method, enter your taxes on separate lines as well.

TIP

Regardless if you use a computer or cash register, if you have a cash drawer, count it out at the end of every shift, and make sure your actual cash matches your cash sales. Errors are easier to find on the day they occur as opposed to the end of the week or month.

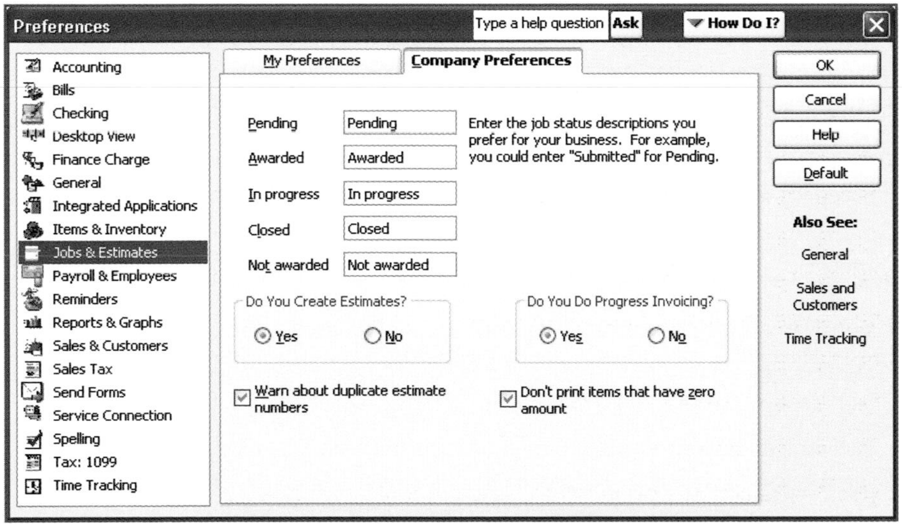

Figure 6-16: ***Customize the names for your estimate procedure to match your business.***

To activate the Estimates feature:

1. Click the **Edit** menu and click **Preferences**. The Preferences window opens.
2. Click **Jobs & Estimates** on the left, and click the **Company Preferences** tab, as shown in Figure 6-16.
3. Click **Yes** in the Do You Create Estimates? area.
4. Click **Yes** in the Do You Do Progress Invoicing? area if desired.
5. Make any other changes for your company, and click **OK** to save and close the Preferences window. If QuickBooks notifies you that it must close all open windows, click **OK**.

CREATE ESTIMATES

To create an estimate:

1. Click the **Customers** menu and click **Create Estimates**. If QuickBooks notifies you about tracking Change Orders, templates, and forms, read the information and click **OK**. The Create Estimates window opens (see Figure 6-17).
2. Click in the **Customer:Job** drop-down list, and type your customer name. For example, since Jeanne Bishop is a previous customer, typing B should cause "Bishop, Jeanne" to automatically appear. You can also Quick Add customers here as in any form in QuickBooks.
3. Click in the **Date** field. Confirm the date.
4. Press **TAB** to move to the Estimate # field. You can leave it as 1 if you will use it only for internal use, or you can change it to a larger number if you want. The number will automatically increase by one each time you create a new estimate.
5. Press the **TAB** key to move to the Name/Address field. Type the customer's address if it's not already filled in. This information is optional, but it will be carried over to the invoice and all other customer-related areas.
6. Press **TAB** to move to the Item field. Enter an existing item, such as Research, or a new item. See the "Set Up Service Items" or "Set Up Non-Inventory Items" section of this chapter for further clarification.

1 2 3 4 5 6 7 8 9 10

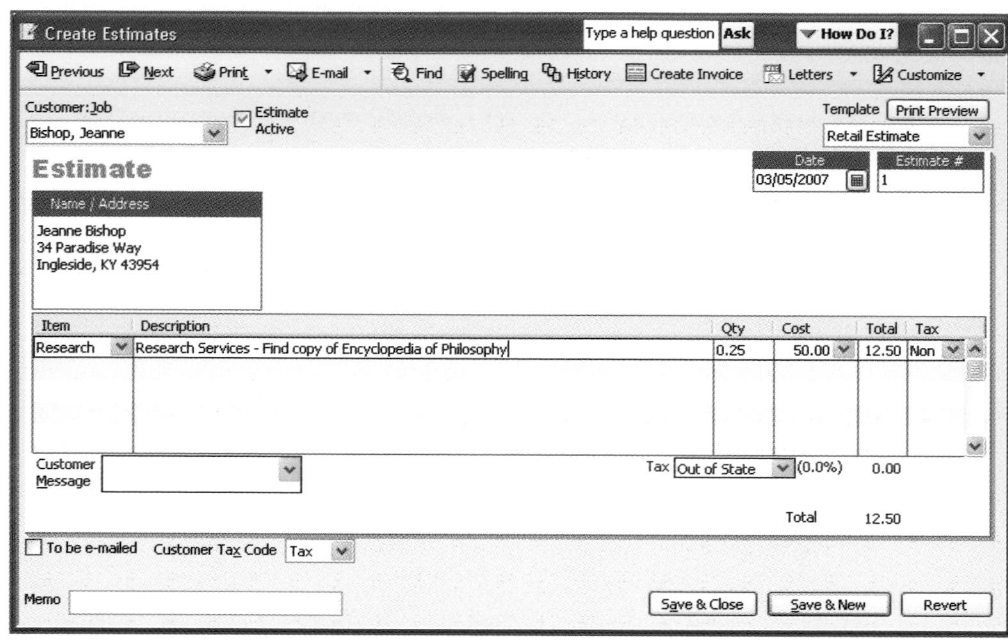

Figure 6-17: ***The Amount and Markup columns will not be printed or transferred to any invoice created unless you change the template.***

7. Press **TAB** to move to the Description field, and all information pertaining to the Research item will populate the other fields automatically based on what you entered when this item was created. Click at the end of the words "Research Services," and type - Find copy of Encyclopedia of Philosophy.
8. Press **TAB** to move to the Quantity column, and type the quantity (which is time in this case), for example, .25.
9. Press **TAB** to move to the Cost field. You can change the cost manually, create price levels for this cost, or accept the item's default cost. QuickBooks automatically calculates the total for you.
10. Click the **Print** button if you want to print this estimate.
11. Click the **Save & Close** button. If you changed the address and want to save the changes, click **Yes** when prompted.

This estimate is now active for this customer. You can create an invoice directly from this estimate by clicking the **Create Invoice** button at the top of the estimate form. In the next section, you will create an invoice based on this estimate from the Invoice window.

TIP

An estimate can be marked as inactive if it is not accepted and you don't want to delete it.

CREATE INVOICES FROM ESTIMATES

QuickBooks has three options by which you can create an invoice from an estimate:

- **Full Amount** directly copies all of the estimate information to the current invoice.
- **Percentage of Full Amount** gives you the option of entering a flat percentage, which will then be entered along with the item names for all of the items on the estimate.
- **Selected Items and Specific Amounts** opens an additional window in which you will enter specific amounts and/or percentages for each item on the estimate.

To create an invoice from an estimate:

1. Click the **Customers** menu and click **Create Invoices**. The Create Invoices window opens.
2. Click in the **Customer:Job** drop-down list, and type your customer name, or click the down arrow to select from the list.
3. Press the **TAB** key. The Available Estimates window opens, displaying a list of existing estimates for this customer.
4. Click the estimate you want to use for your invoice. Click **OK**. The Create Progress Invoice Based On Estimate window opens, displaying the three options referred to previously.
5. Click **Create invoice for the entire estimate (100%)**, and click **OK**. The Create Invoice window now contains the estimate information in a Progress Invoice layout, so you may see additional fields. Click the **Template** down arrow to choose a different invoice layout for your customer.
6. Click **Save & Close**.

You can choose from multiple estimates for the same customer, so you can create estimates as needed and then convert them to invoices after they have been accepted by the customer.

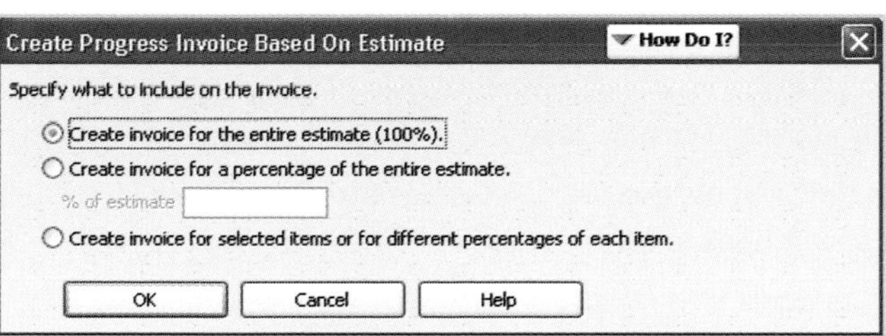

TIP

If you don't want to base an invoice on an existing estimate, click **Cancel** in the Available Estimates window and continue creating an invoice as usual.

TIP

Regardless of which method you use to sell services or products, you will still need to ultimately deposit the funds into a bank account.

Receive Payments

Sales receipts should only be used when payment is received in full at the time of the service being performed or the purchase being made. Invoices are used when some or all of the payment is delayed. When you receive payments against these invoices, you will use the Receive Payments window to enter the payment information and apply them to the correct invoices.

Process Cash Payments and Checks

Cash and checks are handled in a similar fashion. The only difference is you need to enter a check number when receiving a payment by check. QuickBooks provides you with an option to enter a reference number (such as a cash receipt number) when entering cash payments, but this is not required.

1 2 3 4 5 6 7 8 9 10

CAUTION

Always use the Receive Payments window to enter payments into QuickBooks before depositing the money to ensure accurate sales reports.

Underpayment $20.00. When you finish, do you want to:

- ◉ Leave this as an underpayment
- ○ Write off the extra amount

[View Customer Contact Information]

To receive payments by check:

1. Click the **Customers** menu and click **Receive Payments**. The Receive Payments window opens (see Figure 6-18).
2. Click in the **Received From** field. Type your customer name, such as Alpha Library. They have one outstanding invoice appearing in the bottom.
3. Press the **TAB** key to move to the Amount field, and type the amount of the payment you have received, for example, 143.79.

Overpayment $20.00. When you finish, do you want to:

- ◉ Leave the credit to be used later
- ○ Refund the amount to the customer

[View Customer Contact Information]

4. Press **TAB** to move to the Date field. QuickBooks automatically marks the outstanding invoices (located in the middle of the window) as paid. Always confirm that the payments are correctly applied. Type the date you received the payment.
5. Press **TAB** to move to the Payment Method field. Type the payment method; for example, typing Ch will cause **Check** to be selected.
6. Press **TAB** to move to the Check # field. Type the check number, for example, 3847. Verify that all other information is correct.
7. Click **Save & Close**, and the window closes. If you have received several checks, click the **Save & Next** button to continue entering customer payments.

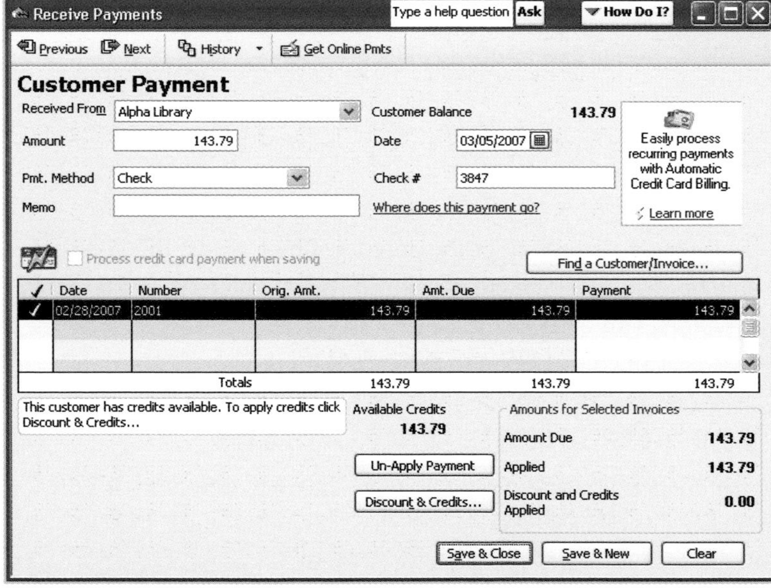

Figure 6-18: ***Use the Receive Payments window to apply credits and discounts to customers.***

Process Credit Card Payments

Credit card payments must be processed in a separate deposit, since they are not funds you physically have in your hands as you do with cash and checks.

To receive payments by credit card:

1. Click the **Customers** menu and click **Receive Payments**. The Receive Payments window opens.
2. Click in the **Received From** field, and type your customer's name. For example, since Jeanne Bishop is a previous customer, typing B should cause "Bishop, Jeanne" to automatically appear (she has one outstanding invoice).

ACCEPTING CREDIT CARDS FROM CUSTOMERS

Credit cards are convenient for clientele and may help boost sales if consumers are your primary market. Unfortunately, accepting credit cards can be inconvenient and expensive and can impede cash flow for you as the merchant.

Accepting credit cards requires that you:

- Have a merchant account set up (you can use PayPal, QuickBooks, or traditional merchant services)
- Have a credit card machine and perform a manual authorization every time (or use QuickBooks' built-in authorization)
- Perform a nightly batch-transfer of all transactions if you use a credit card machine (no money will be disbursed until you do this)
- Receive payments separately from cash and checks
- Track payments separately from cash and checks

When you accept credit card payments, merchant authorization usually involves setting up a deposit directly into your bank account. This "deposit" usually takes place three to five days after the actual transaction. In some cases, this is automatic, but in others (such as through PayPal), you will need to initiate the transfer. This "deposit" made by the credit card company will have the transaction fees already removed, so that the amount shown on your bank statement will not match the invoice or sales receipt amount unless you have accounted for this charge. If your primary customers are businesses, you may not have enough volume in credit card transactions to justify the numerous fees, including application fees, monthly fees, and per-transaction fees.

3. Press the **TAB** key to move to the Amount field, and type the amount of the payment you received, for example, 12.50.
4. Press **TAB** to move to the Date field. QuickBooks automatically marks the outstanding invoice (located in the middle of the window) as paid.
5. Click in the **Date** field, and type the date on which you received the payment.
6. Press the **TAB** key to move to the Payment Method field. Type the payment method; for example, typing V will cause **Visa** to be selected.

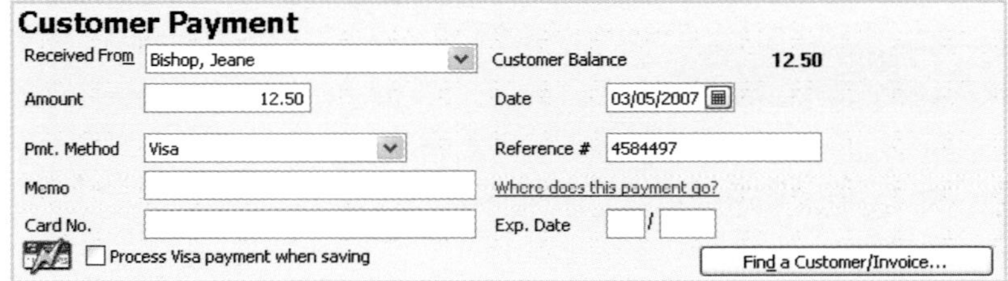

7. Press **TAB** to move to the Reference # field. If you have run the credit card manually, you can type the approval number, for example, 4584497. Otherwise, if you have a merchant account set up with QuickBooks, you need to enter the card number and the expiration date and click the **Process Visa Payment When Saving** check box.
8. Click **Save & Close**. The window closes, and the transaction is saved.

Make Deposits

Making a deposit was covered in Chapter 4. The difference this time is that you now have outstanding payments that have been received against invoices but that have not yet been deposited in your bank account.

1. Click the **Banking** menu and click **Make Deposits**. The Payments to Deposit window opens, as shown in Figure 6-19.
2. Click in the column indicated by a check mark next to all check and cash payments (the payments from John Brown and Alpha Library in this example). These can be combined into one deposit, but credit card payments must be entered in a separate deposit.
3. Click **OK**. The Make Deposits window opens (see Figure 6-20) with the selected payments displayed.

1 2 3 4 5 6 7 8 9 10

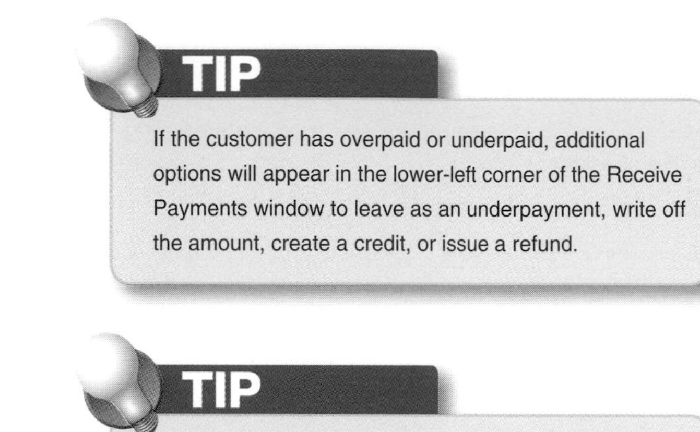

TIP
If the customer has overpaid or underpaid, additional options will appear in the lower-left corner of the Receive Payments window to leave as an underpayment, write off the amount, create a credit, or issue a refund.
TIP
You can double-click any invoice to open it for review.

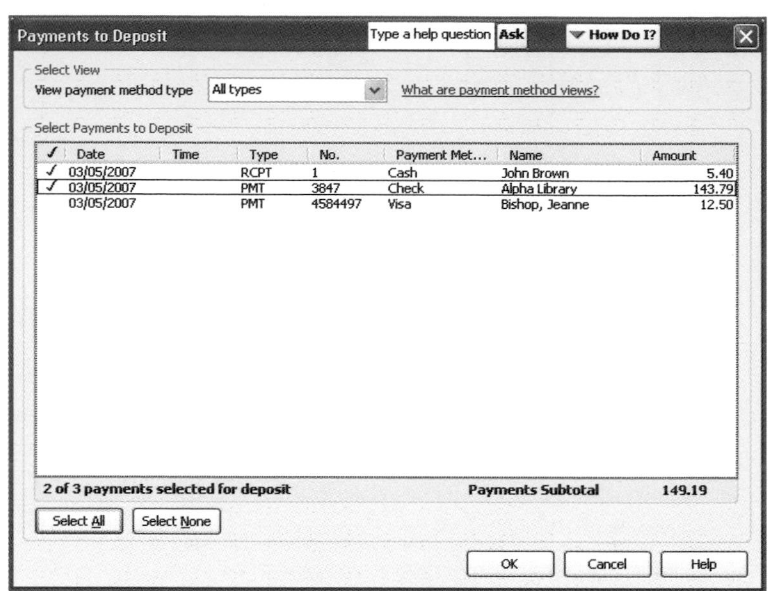

Figure 6-19: ***Use the View Payment Method Type drop-down list to see only certain types of payments.***

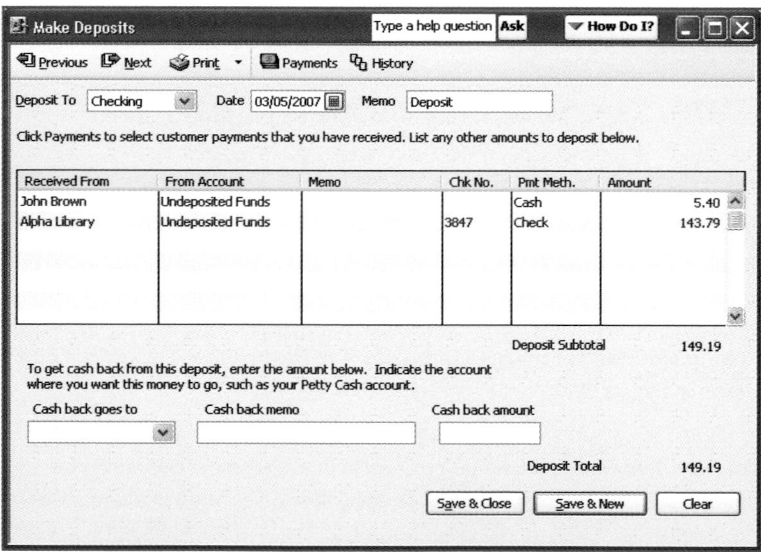

Figure 6-20: ***Confirm that the deposit total matches your actual cash and checks in hand.***

4. Click the **Print** button to print a deposit slip. The Print Deposit dialog box appears. Click one of the following options:
   - **Deposit Slip And Deposit Summary** to use a preprinted deposit slip
   - **Deposit Summary Only** to use as a reference when handwriting your deposit slip

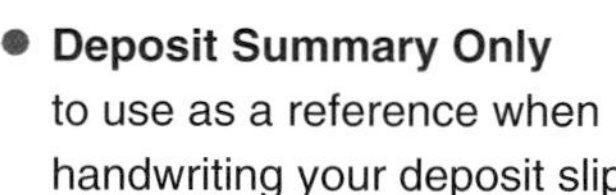

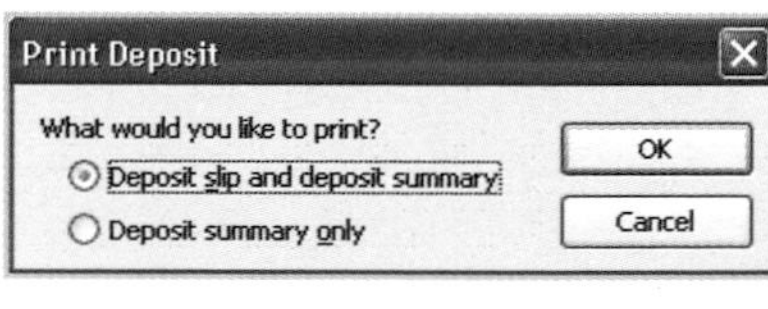

5. Click **OK**. Place a deposit slip in your printer if you are using preprinted deposit slips. The Print Deposit Slips window opens. Review the printer information and click the relevant options for your deposit slip.
6. Click **Print**. Your deposit information is printed, and you are returned to the Make Deposits window.
7. Click the **Save & New** button. The current deposit is saved, and you are returned to the Payments To Deposit window. Notice that the outstanding credit card payment is the only deposit remaining in the window.

8. Click the **Select All** button, or click the single payment. Click **OK**. The Make Deposits window opens with the credit card deposit displayed. Depending on how your merchant account is set up, you may have to wait to deposit this amount until you receive a statement or post it a few days in the future so that you don't show money in your bank account that is not there. Change the date, if desired, and print the deposit, if desired.
9. Click **Save & Close**.

Issue Credit Memos

Occasionally, you will have to issue a refund to a customer. QuickBooks accomplishes this using credit memos so that refunds are credited to the correct items and accounts. Credit memos can then be used to create a refund check or to apply a credit toward future purchases.

To issue a credit memo:

1. Click the **Customers** menu and click **Create Credit Memos/Refunds**. The Create Credit Memos/Refunds window opens, as shown in Figure 6-21.

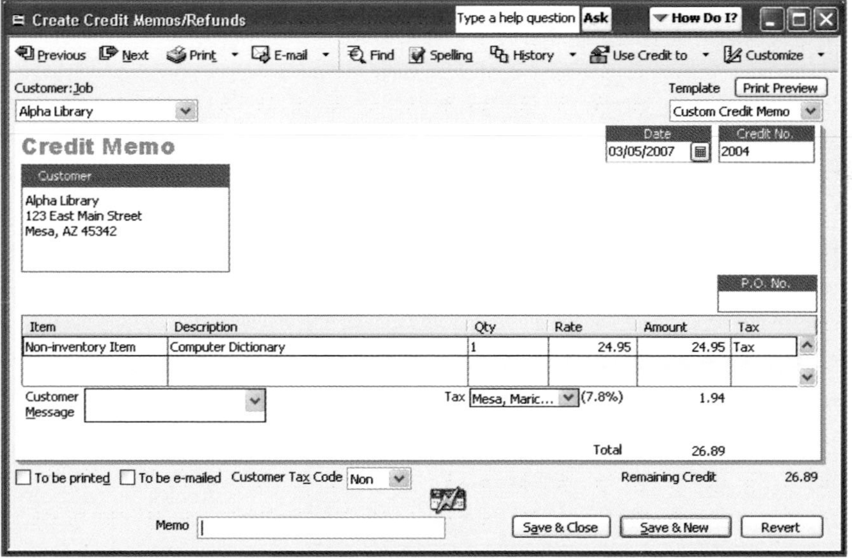

Figure 6-21: ***Refer to the original invoice or sales receipt to ensure an accurate entry when issuing a credit memo.***

TIP

If you accept checks, be sure you have a policy in place for bad checks. Review the customer's status in the event that you need to halt a shipment, place him or her on COD status, or take other action. Contact the customer immediately to arrange for him or her to pay the amount due, as well as any processing fees stated in your policies.

TIP

If you're not processing payments through QuickBooks, don't save your customers' credit card numbers, since there is no need and you may put yourself at greater liability.

TIP

If you don't have a merchant account and click the **Process Visa payment when saving** check box, a window will open, displaying more information on how you can apply and set up a merchant account.

TIP

Deposit all monies received in a timely matter. Some businesses do this on a daily basis. Make it no longer than one week to ensure good cash flow, reduce the risk of theft or loss, and prevent customers from wondering about their checks.

1 2 3 4 5 6 7 8 9 10

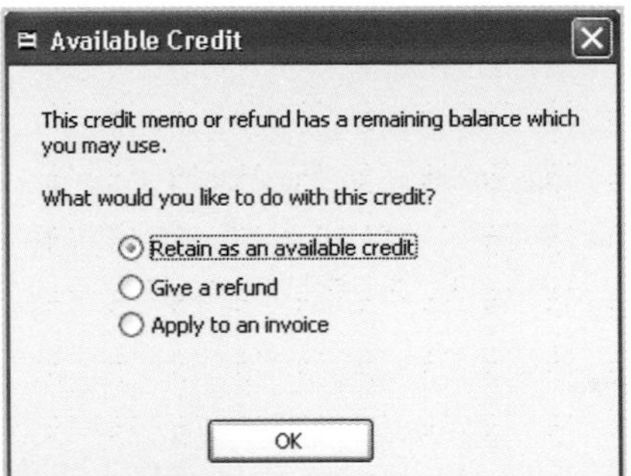

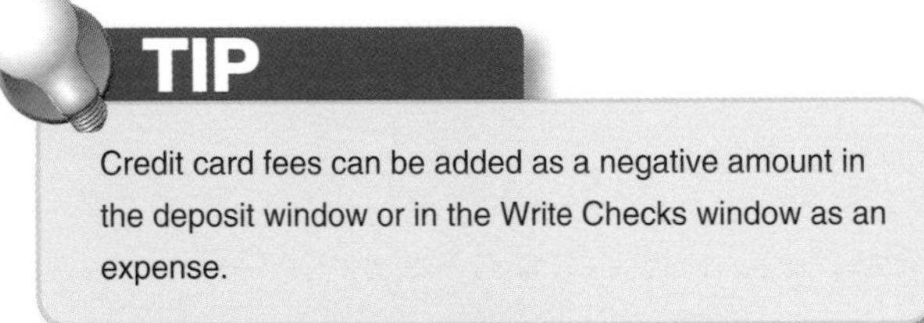

TIP

Credit card fees can be added as a negative amount in the deposit window or in the Write Checks window as an expense.

TIP

Even though QuickBooks provides a place for cash back on your deposit, a more accurate business practice is to deposit all items received and take cash out separately.

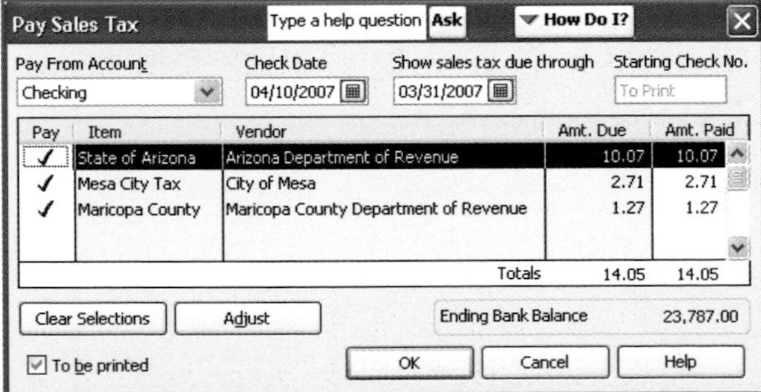

Figure 6-22: ***Returns and credits against your liabilities will be listed in the Pay Sales Tax window as well as liabilities.***

2. Referring to the invoice or sales receipt you are generating the credit memo against, enter the corresponding information for your customer and the item(s) being returned. Be sure to confirm the tax settings and quantities, as well as price.
3. Click the **Print** button if you want to print a copy of the credit memo for the customer.
4. Click **Save & Close**. If the spell check appears, click **Close**. The Available Credit dialog box appears with **Retain as an available credit** selected by default.
5. Click **OK**, and the credit memo process will be complete.

To apply this credit memo to future purchases, in the Receive Payments window, click the **Discounts & Credits** button after you have entered the customer name.

Review and Pay Sales Taxes

If you charge sales tax, you need to pay the related tax agencies on a regular basis. A monthly basis is the most common time frame, but check your local requirements.

To pay sales tax:

1. Click the **Vendors** menu, click **Sales Tax**, and click **Pay Sales Tax**. The Pay Sales Tax window opens, as shown in Figure 6-22.
2. Click the **Pay From Account** down arrow, and click the relevant bank account.
3. Press the **TAB** key to move to the Check Date field. Type the date to be printed on the check.
4. Press the **TAB** key to move to the Show Sales Tax Due Through field. Type the closing date of the sales tax for which you are paying.
5. Click the sales tax items you want to pay to place a check mark in the leftmost column.
6. Click the **To Be Printed** check box, or type a check number in the Starting Check No. field if you are printing them.
7. Click **OK**. The window closes, and checks have now been generated for the relevant vendors.

To print the checks later, click the **File** menu, click **Print Forms**, and click **Checks**. Send them online using the Online Banking Center.

Be sure to keep on top of your tax payments. QuickBooks makes it easy to create checks for the correct amounts, as long as all of your entries are being made correctly.

How to...

- *Activate Inventory in Preferences*
- *Create Inventory Items*
- *Create and Build Inventory Assembly Items*
- *Create Groups*
- *Understanding Item Types*
- *Use Purchase Orders*
- *Receive Items*
- *Ship Items*
- *Use the QuickBooks Shipping Manager*
- *Take Inventory*
- *Manually Adjust Inventory*

Chapter 7 Managing Inventory Items

Inventory can include raw materials, works in progress, and finished goods. Some companies may just buy and sell specific items, while others combine or assemble items. Smaller service companies may not need to track inventory if they purchase items specifically for customers and do not keep any items on hand. This chapter will review the inventory-tracking feature QuickBooks provides that allows you to order, receive, build, and sell inventory items while tracking all information along the way. The chapter will also examine purchase orders and shipping.

Create and Purchase Inventory Items

The buying and selling of non-inventory items is best carried out by accurately entering them as expenses and charging them back to customers (see Chapters 5 and 6). However, if you handle a number of items on a regular basis and keep them in stock, inventory items can be tracked as well. Inventory Part and Inventory Assembly are items available on the Item Type List when the Inventory feature is activated in the Preferences settings.

An *inventory assembly* (available only in Premier or Enterprise editions) is a compilation of inventory items. If you don't want to use inventory assemblies (or don't have the correct edition), groups can serve the same function.

Activate Inventory in Preferences

Before you can use the Inventory feature in QuickBooks, you must first activate it from within the Preferences settings.

1. Click the **Edit** menu and click **Preferences**. The Preferences window opens (see Figure 7-1).
2. Click **Items & Inventory** on the left side, and click the **Company Preferences** tab.
3. Click the **Inventory and purchase orders are active** check box.
4. Review the following choices and select according to your business needs:
   - **Warn about duplicate purchase order numbers** helps prevent errors, but will take more time for each purchase order to save while QuickBooks checks for duplicates.
   - **Quantity reserved for pending builds** for calculating quantity available will warn you if you have enough items on hand, but those items are already earmarked for use in building assemblies.
   - **Quantity on Sales Orders** (only available in Premier and Enterprise) will warn you if you have enough items on hand, but those items are already earmarked for sale to a customer.
   - **When the quantity I want to sell exceeds the Quantity On Hand** will warn you only if you are physically out of the items you wish to sell.
   - **When the quantity I want to sell exceeds the Quantity Available** will warn you if you have committed more than you want to sell. Selecting this option would make it possible for QuickBooks to say you are out of items, but still have some on the shelf.

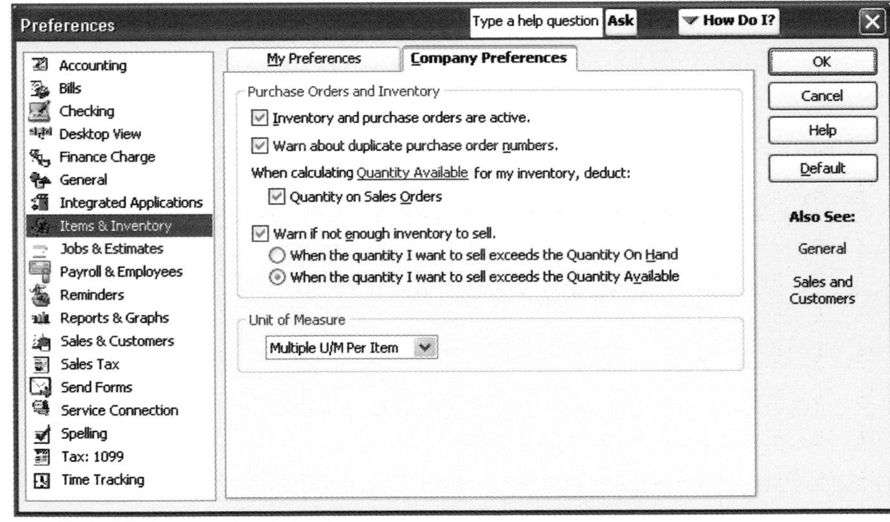

Figure 7-1: ***Inventory warnings can be turned off, but this is not recommended.***

5. Click the **Enable** button. The Unit of Measure window will appear. With unit of measure turned on, you can show what quantities, prices, rates, and costs are based on. For example, if you enter a quantity of 25 on an invoice for a Book Cover item, the unit of measure can show whether that quantity means 25 individual book covers, 25 dozen book covers, or 25 cases of 144 book covers.

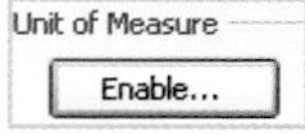

TIP

If you have *even one* item that you buy, stock, or sell in more than one unit of measure, you must select Multiple U/M Per Item.

6. Select one of the following:
   - **Single U/M Per Item** *only* if you buy, stock, and sell *all* items using the same unit of measure, such as buying and selling items by the case.
   - **Multiple U/M Per Item** if you buy, stock, and sell *any* item in more than one unit of measure, such as buying by the case and selling items individually.
7. Click **Finish**. The Unit of Measure window will close.
8. Click **OK** to save your preferences and close the window. Click **OK** if you receive a warning message that QuickBooks needs to close all open windows. You now have the ability to use inventory items and purchase orders in QuickBooks.

NOTE

See Chapter 6 for information on creating non-inventory items, service items, tax items, and tax groups.

Create Inventory Items

The Inventory Part item is used for inventory you buy, track, and sell.

1. Click the **Lists** menu and click **Item List**. The Item List is displayed. Alternatively, you can click **Items & Services** on the Home page.
2. Click the **Item** menu button, and click **New**. The New Item window opens (see Figure 7-2).
3. Click **Inventory Part** in the Type field.
4. Press the **TAB** key to move to the Item Name/Number field. Type the item name, for example, Coffee Mugs.
5. Click in the **Unit of Measure, U/M Set** field. Click **Add New**. The Unit of Measure window will open. Choose the appropriate measurement, such as Count, and click **Next**.
6. Click the appropriate base unit of measure, such as **Each**, and click **Next**.

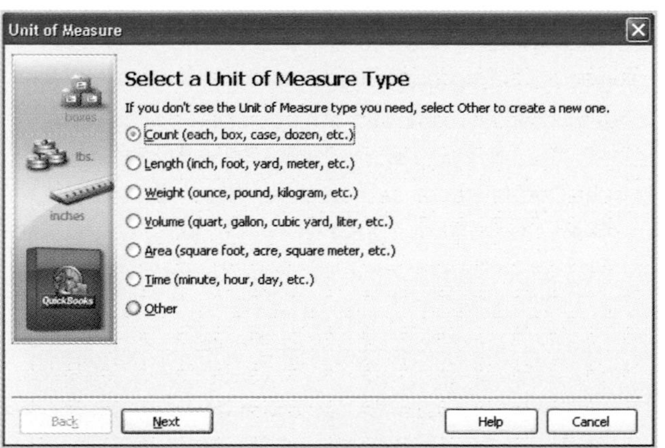

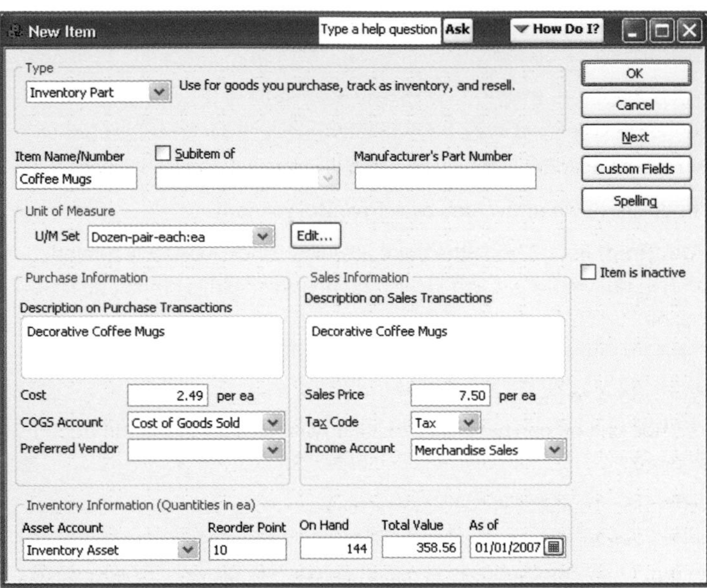

Figure 7-2: ***You can enter multiple items by clicking the Next button instead of the OK button.***

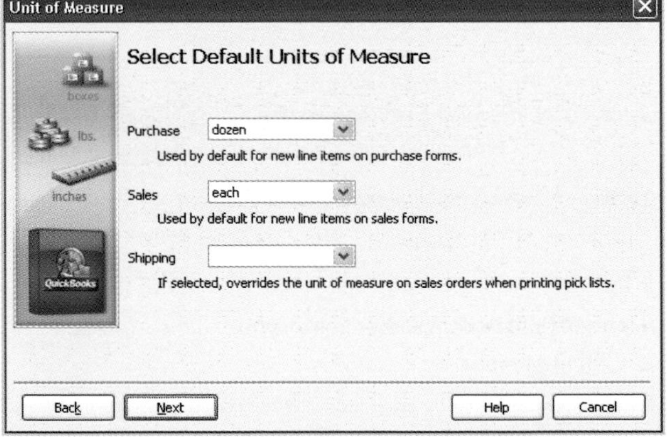

7. Click the appropriate Related Units, such as **pair** and **dozen**. If you prefer, you can choose additional related units and enter the related number of base units, then click **Next**.

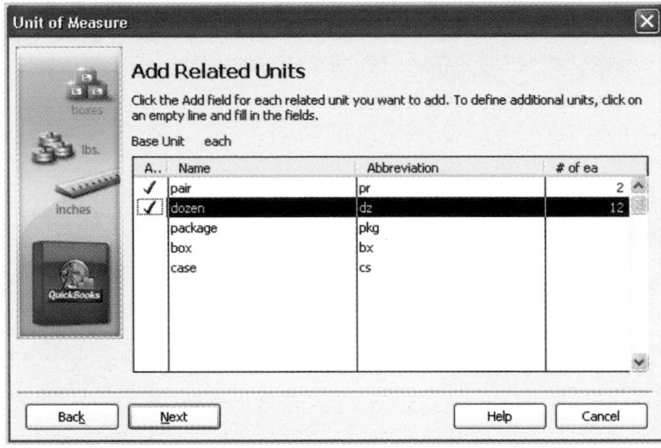

8. Select default units of measure for purchase and sales transactions and click **Next**. You can override these defaults; for example, you can sell a dozen to someone instead of a single item.
9. Type a name for this unit description, such as <u>Dozen-pair-each</u> so that you can reuse this unit description if you need to, and click **Finish**.
10. Click in the **Description on Purchase Transactions** field. Type a description, for example, <u>Decorative Coffee Mugs</u>.
11. Press **TAB** to move to the Cost field. The text in the Description on Purchase Transactions field is copied to the Description on Sales Transaction field. Type the cost of the item (that is, the price the item cost you), for example, <u>2.49</u>.
12. Press **TAB** to move to the COGS Account field. Click the down arrow and click **Cost Of Goods Sold**. This is the Cost of Goods account to which purchases using this item will be recorded.
13. Click the **Preferred Vendor** down arrow, and click the vendor you normally purchase from (this field is optional).
14. Click in the **Sales Price** field. Type the price of the item (that is, what the customer must pay), for example, <u>7.50</u>.

Since you can run reports by either item or account, there is no reason to have a large number of separate income accounts when you can easily view sales information by items sold.

15. Press **TAB** to move to the Tax Code field. Click the down arrow and click **Tax** (provided the item is a taxable item).
16. Press **TAB** to move to the Income Account field. Click the down arrow and click the income account to which you assign your inventory items, such as **Merchandise Sales**. This is the income account to which all sales using this item will be recorded.
17. Click the **Asset Account** down arrow, and click **Inventory Asset**.
18. Click in the **Reorder Point** field. This is the point at which QuickBooks will remind you to reorder when your inventory reaches this amount (this field is optional). Type an amount that will be sufficient to fulfill orders while waiting for a new shipment, for example, 10.
19. Press the **TAB** key to move to the On Hand field. If you had inventory already when you started your business, you can enter it here. Otherwise, inventory will be added when you receive items.
20. Press **TAB** to move to the Total Value field. QuickBooks automatically computes this amount for you based on the amount in the Cost field. Adjust it if it is not accurate because of a discount or some other reason. Confirm the date on which the inventory was obtained in the **As Of** field. Type your start date in this field if the inventory was purchased before then.
21. Click **OK** to save your selections and close the window, or click **Next** to continue entering items. The inventory item is created and will appear in the Item List, along with the inventory balance.

Once you have created an inventory item, you will be able to use it on purchase orders, invoices, estimates, sales orders, credit memos, and sales receipts.

A second inventory item, Gift Baskets, has been entered in the sample file with no Unit of Measure, as they are bought and sold singly. They cost $1.49, the sale price is $7.95, the reorder point is 10, and the on-hand quantity is 50. You can add this item to QuickBooks for practice purposes if you want.

Create and Build Inventory Assembly Items

To package items together, you can use an inventory assembly or an item group. There are two parts to creating an assembly: creating the item and then building it.

> **NOTE**
>
> See Table 7-1 later in this chapter for a comparison between inventory assembly items and item groups.

> **NOTE**
>
> The build point will cause QuickBooks to notify you when you need to "build" more items, just as the reorder point tells you when to order more items. For example, you might have all the supplies in your store but only have four Coffee Gift Packs left for sale, so QuickBooks will warn you that you need to "build" more of these assembly items.

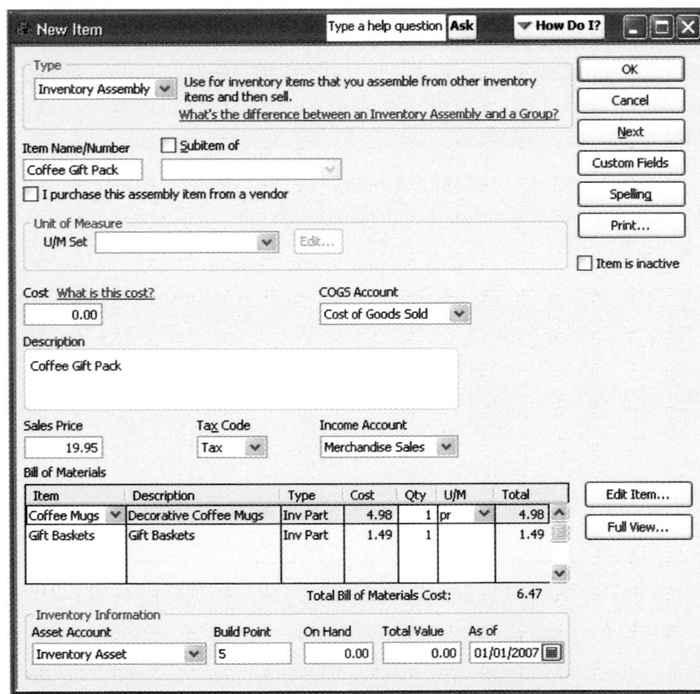

Figure 7-3: ***The New Item window changes, depending on the item type selected.***

CREATE AN INVENTORY ASSEMBLY ITEM

An inventory assembly item (only available in QuickBooks Premier or Enterprise Edition) can only include items that have been created. Once incorporated into the assembly, inventory items used in the component will be decreased accordingly. You can set any price you like for the assembly, regardless of the costs of the components used for the assembly, whereas groups will automatically sum the cost of the components.

To create an inventory assembly item:

1. Click the **Lists** menu and click **Item List**. The Item List is displayed.
2. Click the **Item** menu button, and click **New**. The New Item window opens (see Figure 7-3).
3. Click the **Type** down arrow, and click **Inventory Assembly**. This assembly will contain two coffee mugs with certificates for one free order of coffee, placed in a basket, covered with cellophane, and tied with a ribbon. The coffee mugs and baskets are inventory items; the gift certificates, cellophane, and ribbon are supply items.
4. Press the **TAB** key to move to the Item Name/Number field. Type the item name, for example, Coffee Gift Pack.
5. Click in the **Description** field. What you type in this field will be displayed on your invoices. Type a description, for example, Coffee Gift Pack.
6. Press **TAB** to move to the Sales Price field. Type the price for the customer, for example, 19.95.
7. Click the **Income Account** down arrow, and click **Merchandise** (a subaccount of Sales).
8. Verify that the COGS Account field lists **Cost Of Goods Sold**, the Tax Code field lists **Tax** (provided the item is a taxable item), and the Asset Account field lists **Inventory Asset**.
9. Click in the **Item** field in the Components Needed area. Type C and "Coffee Mugs" will appear automatically, since this is a previously created item.
10. Press the **TAB** key to move to the Qty (Quantity) field. QuickBooks fills in the Description, Type, Cost, and Total fields for the item (you cannot edit this information in this field). Type a quantity for this assembly, for example, 2.

CAUTION

If you enter a quantity on hand for inventory assembly items in the New Item window, QuickBooks will assume those assemblies have already been created from other items and will not use existing inventory items, but will add those as an inventory adjustment. Therefore, make sure you don't enter your items twice.

NOTE

If you need to track a detailed history of assemblies, labor, or other items involved in manufacturing items, you should track the process in some other manner, as QuickBooks will only track the combined costs of the inventory assembly items.

11. Press the **TAB** key to move to the U/M (Unit of Measure) field. Click the down arrow to choose a Unit of Measure for this assembly, for example, **pr** (pair). Notice that this might change your quantity to .5, so confirm that your quantity is 1 if your U/M is a pair.
12. Press **TAB** to move to a new line in the Item field. Type Gift Baskets (if you entered this item as previously suggested).
13. Press **TAB** to move to the Qty (Quantity) field. Type a quantity for this assembly, for example, 1. Notice there is no choice for U/M if you didn't enter one when you created this item.
14. Click in the **Build Point** field. This is the point at which QuickBooks will remind you to reorder when your inventory reaches this amount (this field is optional). Type a number, for example, 5. This example leaves the On Hand empty, as none have yet been assembled (built).
15. Click **OK** to save the inventory assembly item and close the window.

You will now see the Item List with your two new inventory items and the new inventory assembly item displayed, as shown in Figure 7-4.

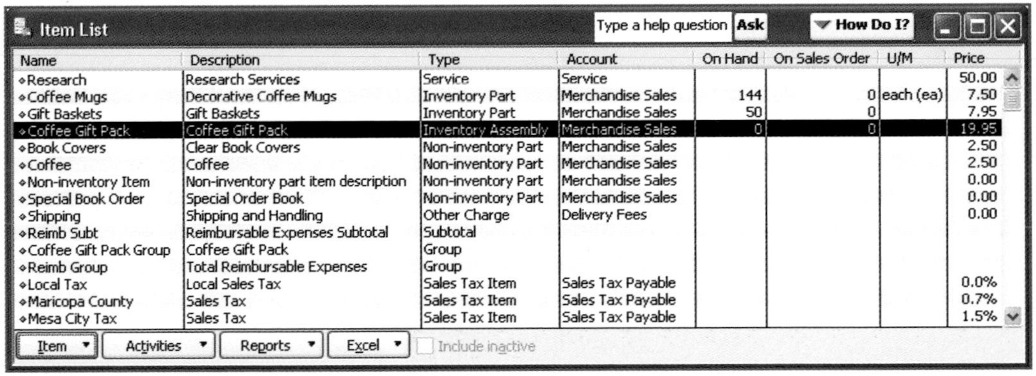

Item List — Type a help question | Ask | How Do I?

Name	Description	Type	Account	On Hand	On Sales Order	U/M	Price
◆Research	Research Services	Service	Service				50.00
◆Coffee Mugs	Decorative Coffee Mugs	Inventory Part	Merchandise Sales	144	0	each (ea)	7.50
◆Gift Baskets	Gift Baskets	Inventory Part	Merchandise Sales	50	0		7.95
◆Coffee Gift Pack	Coffee Gift Pack	Inventory Assembly	Merchandise Sales	0	0		19.95
◆Book Covers	Clear Book Covers	Non-inventory Part	Merchandise Sales				2.50
◆Coffee	Coffee	Non-inventory Part	Merchandise Sales				2.50
◆Non-inventory Item	Non-inventory part item description	Non-inventory Part	Merchandise Sales				0.00
◆Special Book Order	Special Order Book	Non-inventory Part	Merchandise Sales				0.00
◆Shipping	Shipping and Handling	Other Charge	Delivery Fees				0.00
◆Reimb Subt	Reimbursable Expenses Subtotal	Subtotal					
◆Coffee Gift Pack Group	Coffee Gift Pack	Group					
◆Reimb Group	Total Reimbursable Expenses	Group					
◆Local Tax	Local Sales Tax	Sales Tax Item	Sales Tax Payable				0.0%
◆Maricopa County	Sales Tax	Sales Tax Item	Sales Tax Payable				0.7%
◆Mesa City Tax	Sales Tax	Sales Tax Item	Sales Tax Payable				1.5%

Item ▾ | Activities ▾ | Reports ▾ | Excel ▾ | Include inactive

Figure 7-4: ***Inventory items and inventory assemblies show you the current on-hand and on-order (if Premier Edition) amounts; while non-inventory items, service, tax, and other items used throughout QuickBooks are listed more simply.***

1 2 3 4 5 6 7 8 9 10

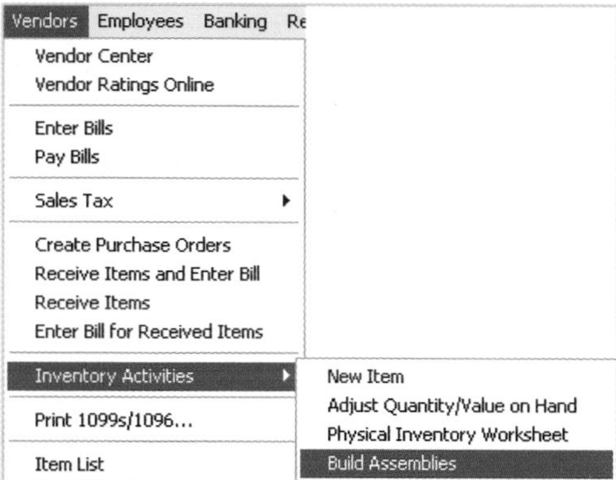

TIP

You can disassemble these inventory assemblies by reopening this window and reducing the quantity, or deleting the transaction altogether, if the gift packs are not selling.

BUILD AN INVENTORY ASSEMBLY ITEM

Now that you have created an inventory assembly item, you need to use the Build Assemblies window to create it. This "adds" assembly item units and "deducts" inventory items. You will see this change in the Quantity column of the Item List, as well as on inventory reports.

1. Click the **Vendors** menu, click **Inventory Activities**, and click **Build Assemblies**. The Build Assemblies window opens (see Figure 7-5).
2. Click the **Assembly Item** down arrow, and click the item you want to build, such as **Coffee Gift Pack**, if it is not already selected.
3. Press the **TAB** key to move to the Quantity to Build field, and type the number of items you have actually created, for example, 10.
4. Press the **TAB** key to move to the Date field, and type the date on which the items were created.
5. Press **TAB** to move to the Build Ref. field, and enter any number you may use internally to track build orders for your employees.
6. Press **TAB** to move to the Memo field, and type any pertinent information.
7. Click the **Build & Close** button.

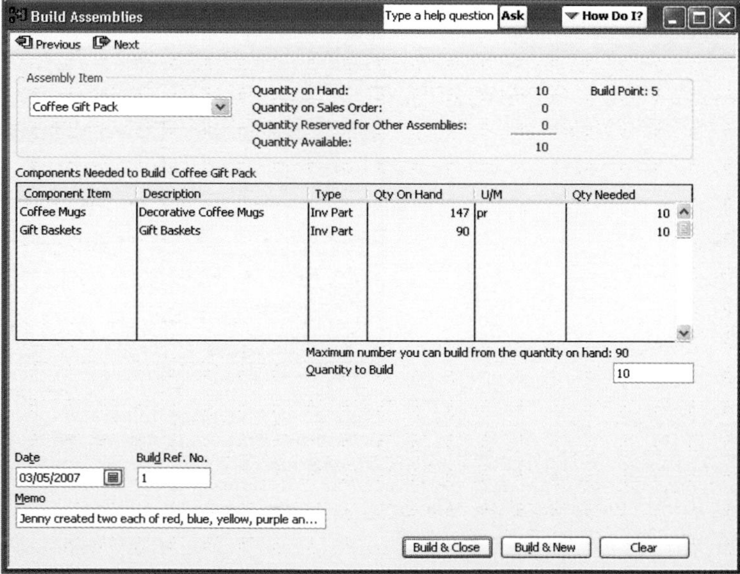

Figure 7-5: ***Use the Memo field (located at the bottom) for notes regarding the assembly.***

Your Item List will now show an increase in the assembly items on hand (10) and a decrease in the baskets (40) and coffee mugs (124), since those inventory items are no longer available for individual sale. Cellophane, coffee coupons, and ribbons are not accounted for in this procedure, although you could set up inventory items for each. Labor is also not accounted for in this procedure. Determine if this will work for your company.

Create Groups

Another method whereby you can create a product that consists of multiple items, especially if those items are not all inventory items, is to create a group. This section will show you how to create the same gift basket that was created as an inventory assembly item in the preceding section as an inventory group. (Assembly items and groups work interchangeably.)

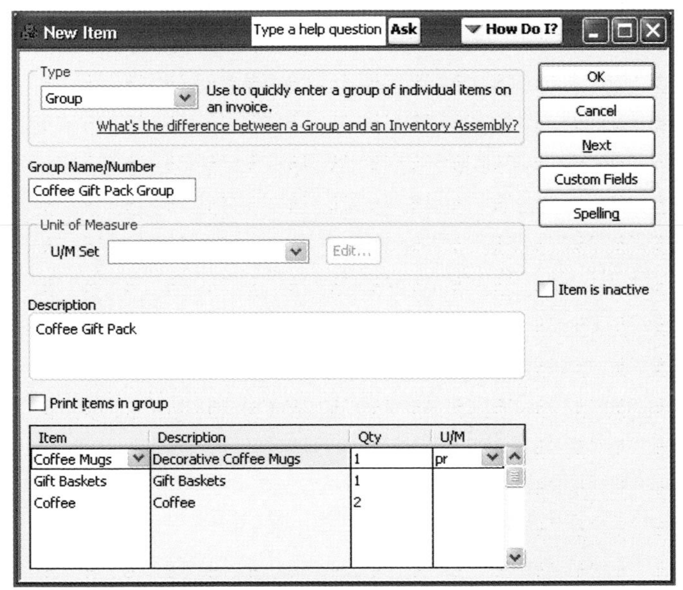

Figure 7-6: ***You don't see sales price, income account, cost of goods sold account, tax code, and asset account information, as you do on other items, because each of these fields will be pulled from the items used in the group.***

1. Click the **Lists** menu and click **Item List**. The Item List is displayed.
2. Click the **Item** menu button, and click **New**. The New Item window opens (see Figure 7-6).
3. Click **Group** in the Type field.
4. Press the **TAB** key to move to the Group Name/Number field. Type a group name, for example, Coffee Gift Pack Group (note that you can't use the same name as an existing item, although you can use the same description).
5. Press the **TAB** key to move to the Description field. What you type in this field will be displayed on your invoices. Type a description, for example, Coffee Gift Pack.
6. Click in the **Item** field (located at the bottom of the window). Type C and "Coffee Mugs" will appear automatically, since this is a previously created item.
7. Press the **TAB** key to move to the Qty (Quantity) field. Type a quantity for this group, for example, 2 if you use U/M each or 1 if you use U/M pair.
8. Press the **TAB** key to move to the U/M (Unit of Measurement) field. Click the down arrow to select a unit of measurement for this group, for example, each if your quantity is 2 or pair, if your quantity is 1. Confirm your quantity if you change your U/M.
9. Press **TAB** to move to a new line in the Item field. Type Gift Baskets (if you entered this item previously as suggested).
10. Press **TAB** to move to the Qty (Quantity) field. Type a quantity for this group, for example, 1.

1 2 3 4 5 6 7 8 9 10

UNDERSTANDING ITEM TYPES

QuickBooks contains many types of items used to ensure consistency, ease of entry, and accurate account credit:

- **Service** Non-tangible services you provide, such as labor, consulting, and professional fees.
- **Inventory Part** Any items you purchase, track as inventory, and then resell.
- **Inventory Assembly** Assembled items built or purchased, which you track as inventory and resell (available in Premier and Enterprise editions only).
- **Non-Inventory Part** Supplies or specific purchases that may be charged back to your customer.
- **Other Charge** Any item not covered elsewhere, such as delivery, setup, or service fee.
- **Subtotal** An automatic item; the subtotal is automatically calculated based on the items above it on a form, up to the last subtotal, which can then be used for project sections or to apply a percentage discount or surcharge to the subtotaled items.
- **Group** Associates and totals individual items to be listed as a group or individually on any form.
- **Discount** A negative amount used on invoices or cash receipts to subtract either a percentage or a fixed amount from the item on the line directly above it, which can be a single item or a Subtotal item.
- **Payment** Used on invoices when partial payment is made at the time of sale.
- **Sales Tax Item** Calculates and tracks a single sales tax.
- **Sales Tax Group** Calculates and tracks two or more sales tax items as a single group item on a sales form and individually in the Tax Liabilities section.

11. Press **TAB** to move to a new line in the Item field. Type Coffee (if you previously entered this item). When creating Groups, you can mix inventory with non-inventory items, as well as service items, which cannot be done with inventory assembly items.
12. Press **TAB** to move to the Qty (Quantity) field. Type a quantity for this group, for example, 2.
13. Click **Print Items In Group** if you want to show the items individually. In some cases, you may want to show the group list; while other times, such as with this gift basket, you may prefer that the group appear as a single line item on an invoice or sales receipt.
14. Click **OK** to save the group and close the window.

You will now see the Item List with your new group item displayed. The biggest difficulty with this method is that the total price comes completely from the total cost of the items as entered in an invoice; however, you could add an additional item to increase or decrease the price.

You can return to a group and add more items as needed, and if the item has not yet been entered into QuickBooks, you can add it on the fly. Consider adding employee labor time (as a Service item) and a Discount item or Other Charge item to bring the total customer price of the group to your desired price level. Table 7-1 provides a comparison of assembly items to groups to help you determine when one would work better for you than the other.

Use Purchase Orders

Purchase orders are a written request by your business for goods or services, containing product description, quantities, terms, shipping instructions, prices, and approvals. Even if you don't specifically track inventory, using purchase orders helps ensure that the supplies you order are received and paid for without paying for items you didn't order. The larger your company, the more important it is to have purchase-order procedures in place. If you're the only employee in your business, you will likely remember what you ordered and when, but when one person is responsible for ordering items, another receives them, and a third pays for them, purchase orders will help make sure everyone is on the same page.

GROUP ITEM	INVENTORY ASSEMBLY ITEM
Can include any combination of item types, except other groups.	Can include only service, inventory part items, non-inventory items, other charges, and other inventory assembly items.
Option to list individual items or just the group item.	Lists only the assembly item name, not the individual items.
No preset reports, but more detailed custom reports can be created.	Included in standard preset inventory reports, including build status reports.
Quantity on hand is adjusted for each item at the time of sale.	Quantity on hand is adjusted for each item at the time of inventory assembly item being built.
Sales tax is calculated individually for each item in the group item.	Sales tax is calculated for single assembly item, even if each item's tax code differs.
Group items cannot be included in other group items or in inventory assembly items.	Assembly items can be used within other assembly items and group items.
Inventory is tracked individually, so items may show as available to sell individually even if they have been combined in a group.	Inventory is tracked separately, so items in an assembly item do not show as available to sell individually.
Group item price is calculated as the total sum of items in the group (which can include discounts or additional-charge items).	Assembly item price is set to anything you specify.
Group item can include any combination of taxable and non-taxable items.	Single assembly item must be designated as a single tax type.
Easy to keep detailed records of your inventory; and customers receive clear, easy-to-read invoices.	Gives you information such as the date that items were assembled, quantity, cost, and component lists; customers receive a single-line-item invoice.
If you show each item in your group, you can quickly enter a lot of line-item detail. Just type the group name, and all the details will appear for the customer, such as a complete list of all parts in a computer.	Shows assembled items as separate from individual inventory items. If you have things packaged together, you won't mistake a part (as in a group) as individually available, since the component parts will have already been deducted from the quantity on hand.
You can sell items as part of a group or on an individual basis. Best for package deals.	You can set reminders to create new assembly items as you sell them.

Table 7-1: ***Comparison of Assembly Items to Groups***

To create a purchase order:

1. Click the **Vendors** menu and click **Create Purchase Orders**. The Create Purchase Orders window opens, as shown in Figure 7-7.
2. Click the **Vendor** down arrow, and click the name of the vendor from whom you want to purchase an item or add a new vendor, for example, <u>Mug-O-Rama</u>. QuickBooks will automatically fill in any existing information for this vendor or ask if you would like to QuickAdd. Confirm the name and address, or type it in the fields if it is not complete. Confirm the address in the **Ship To** field as well, which should be your company's address.

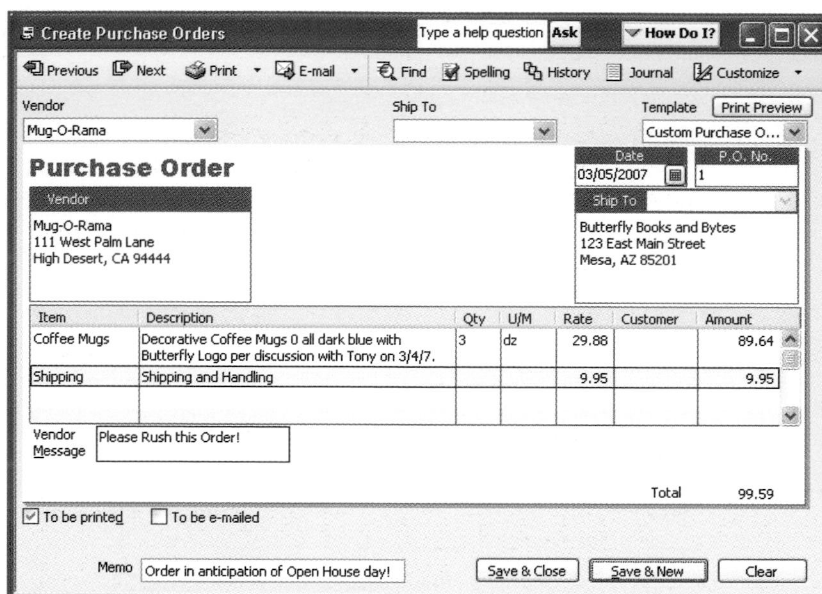

Figure 7-7: ***Forms look similar throughout QuickBooks. The same items are used on purchase orders as are used on all other forms.***

3. Click in the **Item** field. Type Coffee Mugs. The preset information is filled in.
4. Press the **TAB** key to move to the Description field. Edit if necessary, such as adding color, description, or part number—anything that will ensure an accurate delivery from your vendor.
5. Press **TAB** to move to the Qty (Quantity) field. Type the quantity you are ordering, for example, 3, and select the appropriate Quantity if applicable, such as dz (dozen).
6. Press **TAB** to move to the U/M (Unit of Measurement) field. Click the down arrow to convert your unit of measurement if desired.
7. Press **TAB** to move to the Rate field. Confirm or edit your price from the vendor.
8. Press **TAB** to move to the Customer field. If you are ordering these items for a specific customer, type his or her name here, for future chargeback. If this is just a standard inventory order, this field can be left blank.
9. Press **TAB** to move to the Amount field. QuickBooks automatically calculates the figure in the Amount field. If you change the amount, QuickBooks will divide the amount by the quantity and will change the rate accordingly.
10. Press **TAB** to move to a new line in the Item field, and type Shipping to add the shipping costs to send this product to your customer.
11. Press **TAB** to move to the Description field. The Item Not Found dialog box appears, since an item called "Shipping" is not in the Item List. Click **Yes** to add this item to your Item List. The New Item window opens (see Figure 7-8).
12. In the New Item window, click the **Type** down arrow, and click **Other Charge**.
13. Press **TAB** to move to the Item Name/Number field. QuickBooks automatically inserts the Shipping item here.
14. Click the **This Item Is Used In Assemblies Or Is A Reimbursable Charge** check box. This will allow you to use this item on purchase orders and invoices. The Purchase Information area will appear in the New Item window, as seen in Figure 7-8.

TIP

Check to see if your vendor supports drop shipping, which allows you to send a product directly to your customer from your supplier using the Ship To drop-down box. This is especially useful for Internet-based companies.

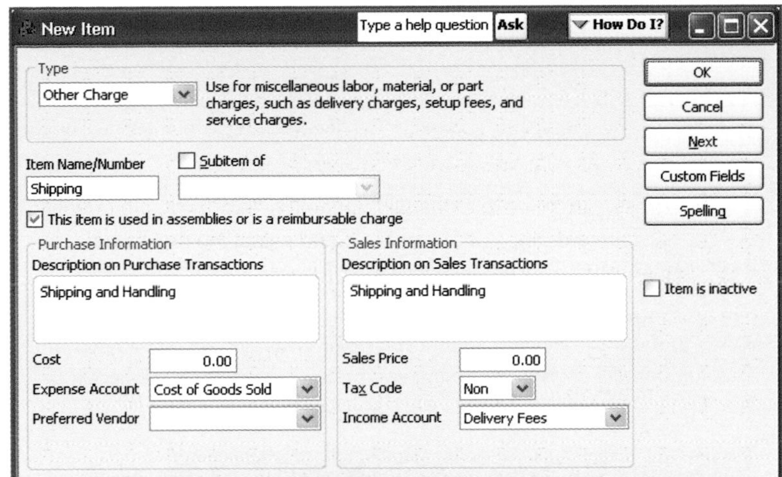

Figure 7-8: ***When you use the Quick Add feature to add an item that you suddenly realize you need, such as shipping, you can always edit it later.***

15. Click in the **Description On Purchase Transactions** field. Type the item name as you want it to appear on your purchase order, for example, <u>Shipping and Handling</u>.
16. Press **TAB** to move to the Cost field. If you have a standard cost, type it here or simply leave blank. You can always edit the Description and Amount fields each time you use this item. Confirm that **Cost Of Goods Sold** is displayed in the Expense Account field, or you can create a new shipping account.
17. Click the **Tax Code** down arrow, and click **Non-Taxable Sales**.
18. Click the **Income Account** down arrow, and click **Delivery Fees**. All other fields in this window are optional.
19. Click **OK** to save this item and return to the Create Purchase Orders window.
20. Press the **TAB** key twice to move to the Rate field. Type the cost of shipping, for example, <u>9.95</u>.
21. Press **TAB** to move to the Customer field. Type the customer name only if this will be charged back to the customer. Click **No** if prompted to update the shipping cost.
22. Click in the **Vendor Message** field. Type a relevant message for the vendor, if desired.
23. Press **TAB** to move to the Memo field. Type a relevant note for internal use regarding this purchase order, if desired.
24. Click the **Save & Close** button. If the spell check appears, use it to check your spelling, or click **Close**. If the Name Information Change dialog box appears, click **Yes** to accept the address change.

Receive Items

When deliveries arrive from vendors, you need to receive the items in QuickBooks, either as inventory items or as regular items. The purchase orders will then be marked as received, inventory will be added (if applicable), and a bill will be generated for payment. The receipt of special orders is handled just as the receipt of inventory is; however, the items are not marked as inventory, so consider creating the invoice to send to your customer at the time you place the order (use the Sales Order feature in the Premium edition) or upon receiving the special-order item.

Vendors | Employees | Banking | Re
Vendor Center
Vendor Ratings Online
Enter Bills
Pay Bills
Sales Tax
Create Purchase Orders
Receive Items and Enter Bill
Receive Items
Enter Bill for Received Items
Inventory Activities
Print 1099s/1096...
Item List

RECEIVE ITEMS AND ENTER BILLS

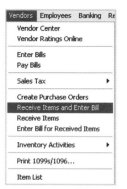

If you've received items along with an invoice from your vendor, use the Receive Items and Enter Bill feature. If you've only received a packing slip and not a bill, use the Receive Items feature.

1. Click the **Vendors** menu and click **Receive Items and Enter Bill**. The Enter Bills window opens (see Figure 7-9).
2. Click the **Vendor** down arrow, and click the vendor name from whom you have received a shipment, for example, **Mug-O-Rama**.
3. Press the **TAB** key to move to the Date field. If you have an open purchase order for this vendor, a dialog box will appear, informing you that you have open, or pending, purchase orders and asking you if you want to receive against them.

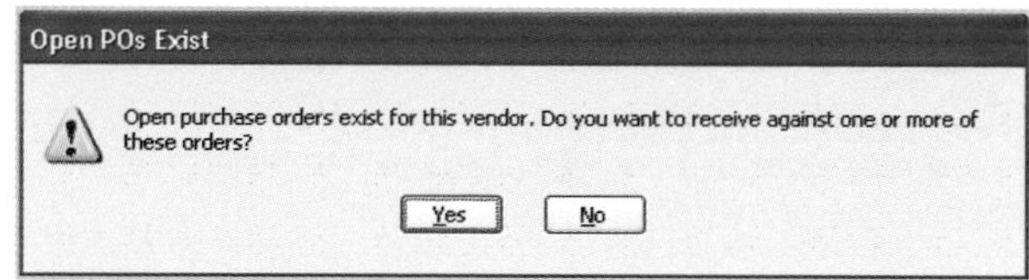

4. Click **Yes**. The Open Purchase Order window opens, listing all outstanding purchase orders for this vendor. Click the purchase order that matches the items received.

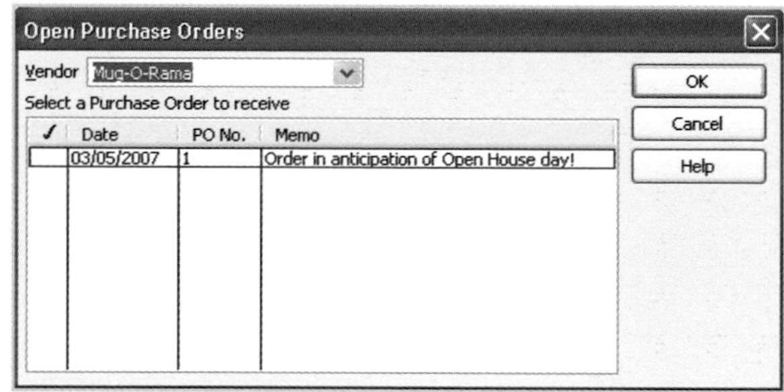

5. Click **OK**. You are returned to the Enter Bills window. The items from the purchase order are entered into the Item List at the bottom of the window. If this was a partial shipment, you could adjust the quantity received.
6. Click the **Save & Close** button.

If this order includes inventory items, they are added to inventory, and a bill has been entered for payment.

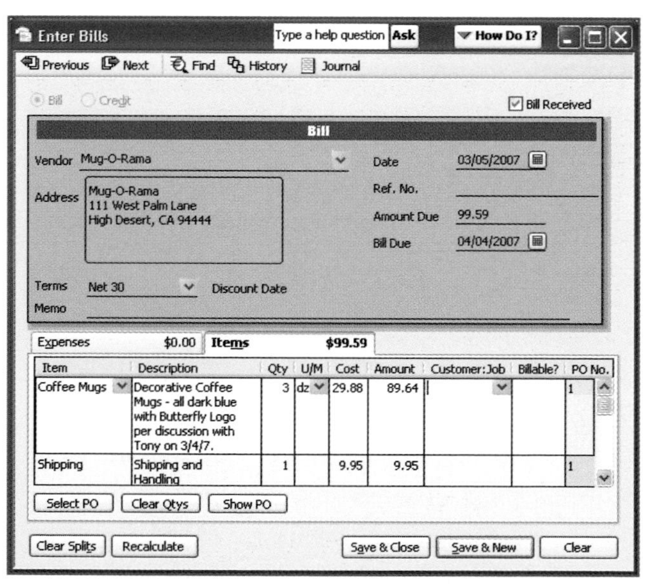

Figure 7-9: ***From the Enter Bills window, you can use the Select PO button (located near the bottom) to review pending purchase orders.***

Ship Items

Some businesses may offer shipping. With QuickBooks you can create packing slips and also connect directly to UPS and FedEx for estimates and to create shipping labels with those companies.

> **NOTE**
>
> Printing a packing slip from a sales receipt requires customizing a form and printing the sales receipt twice—once with the prices, once without.

SET SHIPPING PREFERENCES

1. Click the **Edit** menu. Click **Preferences**. The Preferences window opens, as shown in Figure 7-10.
2. Scroll down the left side, and click **Sales & Customers**. Click the **Company Preferences** tab.
3. Click the **Usual Shipping Method** down arrow and select your default shipping method. DHL, Federal Express, UPS, and US Mail are included, or you can create your own, like Speedy Delivery, by clicking **Add New**.
4. Enter your FOB (Freight Origin) if used by your shipper.
5. Click the **Choose Template for Packing Slips** down arrow, and click **Intuit Packing Slip**. You can choose any invoice template, including those you customize.
6. Click **OK**.

> **TIP**
>
> If you marked all your invoices to be printed, they will be listed in your Reminders List. From here, you can review and choose the invoices for which you need to print packing slips. These packing slips can also be used as pick slips in a warehouse.

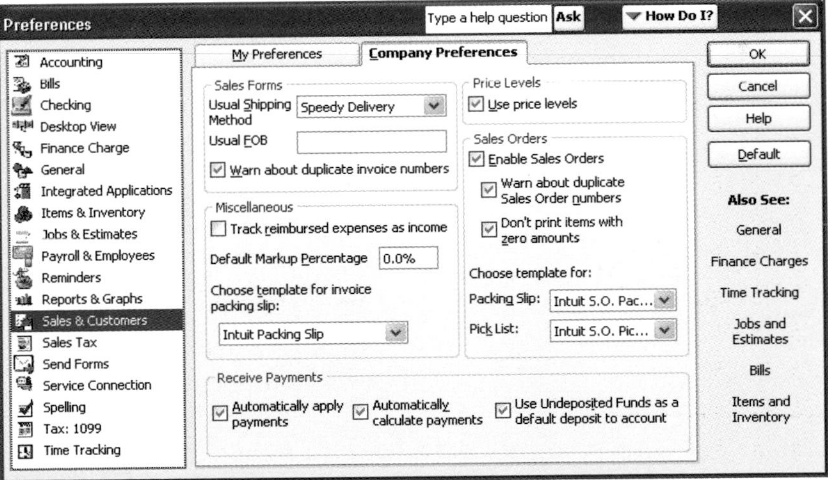

Figure 7-10: ***You can change these preferences at any time and also change individual invoices as needed.***

1 2 3 4 5 6 7 8 9 10

1 2 3 4 5 6 7 8 9 10

> **TIP**
>
> You can e-mail invoices by clicking the **E-Mail** button, and you can tie in with UPS and FedEx by clicking the **Ship** button in the Invoice window. Click the drop-down menus for more information.

> **CAUTION**
>
> If you printed the invoice, the To Be Printed check box has now been cleared on the invoice. Be sure to select it if you still need to print the invoice for the customer, or you can print that invoice now by clicking the **Print** button.

CREATE PACKING SLIPS

Packing slips typically include all the product information and quantities but not the price information. Thus, it is simply a modified invoice or sales receipt form. QuickBooks includes a default packing slip, or you can create your own by customizing your forms (see Chapter 8).

To print a shipping label from the Create Invoices window:

1. Open an invoice for which you want to print a packing slip.
2. Click the **Print** down arrow, and click **Print Packing Slip**. A dialog box may appear regarding shipping labels, which are also available on the Print menu.
3. Click **OK**. The Print Packing Slip dialog box appears, as shown in Figure 7-11.
4. Click the **Print** button.

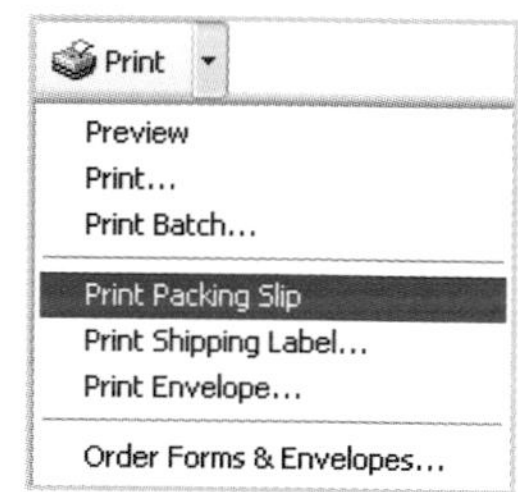

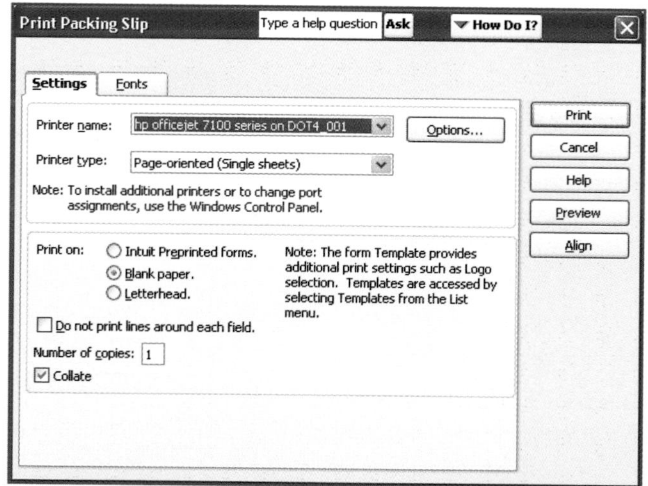

Figure 7-11: ***Click the Preview button (on the right) if you want to see the layout of your packing slip and check it for accuracy before printing.***

Figure 7-12: ***Click the Green buttons to expand sections for more options. Click the Red buttons to minimize sections.***

Use the QuickBooks Shipping Manager

QuickBooks can be integrated with FedEx and UPS so that you can create relevant shipping labels directly from your QuickBooks invoice.

SEND A PACKAGE VIA UPS

1. Open the **Invoice** requiring shipment.
2. Click the **Ship** down arrow, and click **Ship UPS Package**. The first time you use the QuickBooks Shipping Manager for UPS, you will need to set up your account. After that, a window will open, displaying a shipping form (see Figure 7-12).

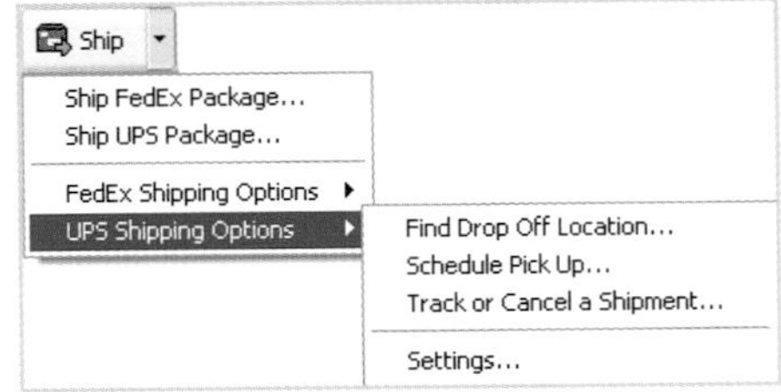

3. In the To area, enter your customer's name and address.
4. Click the **Service** down arrow, and click your shipping method (for example, **UPS Ground**).

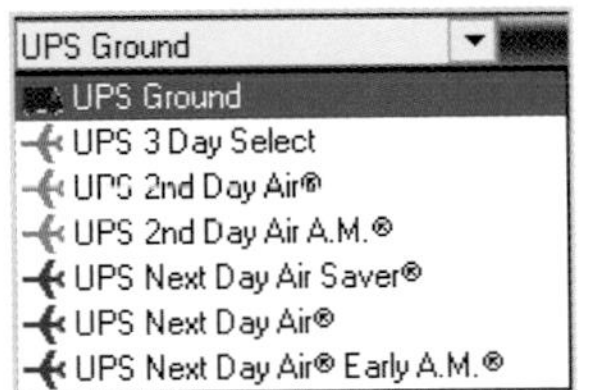

5. In the Package area, click in the **Weight** field. Type the package weight in pounds, for example, 2.
6. In the Package area, click in the **Declared Value** field. Type the package value in your currency, for example, 30.

TIP

Create a reference chart of standard items you ship with sizes and weights.

CAUTION

If this is your first time using the QuickBooks Shipping Manager, you'll need to fill in a form with your UPS and/or FedEx account number and choose your printer. UPS requires that you have an account before using this process. Fed Ex allows you to sign up online.

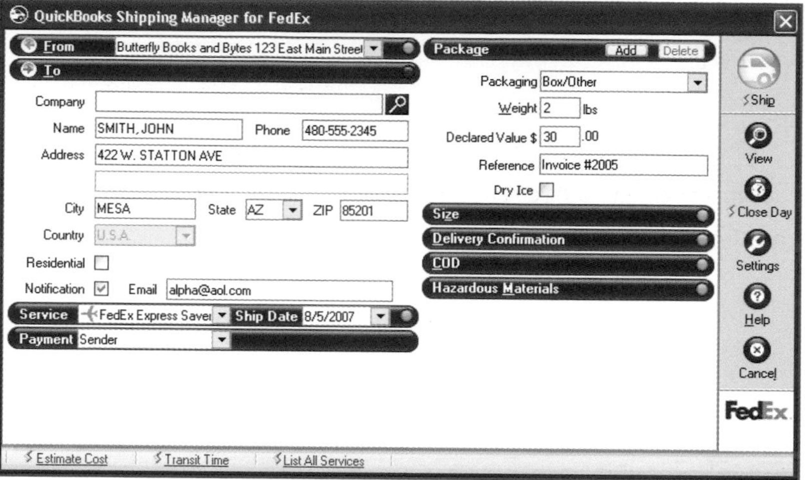

Figure 7-13: ***Enter your information, as it is not copied over from the invoice.***

7. Click the **Estimate Cost** (located near the lower-left area of the window). An estimate replaces the Estimate Cost section. If the estimate is more than you're willing to pay, you can click **Cancel** to stop the shipping process at this point.

UPS Ground : $ 4.02

8. If you are satisfied with the rate quote, click **Ship**. A label is sent to your printer. The QuickBooks Shipping Manager closes, and you are returned to the Create Invoices window.

9. Click **Save & Close**.

SEND A PACKAGE VIA FEDEX

1. Open the **Invoice** requiring shipment.

2. Click the **Ship** down arrow, and click **Ship FedEx Package**. The first time you use the QuickBooks Shipping Manager for FedEx, you will need to set up your account. After that, a window will open, displaying a FedEx shipping form (see Figure 7-13).

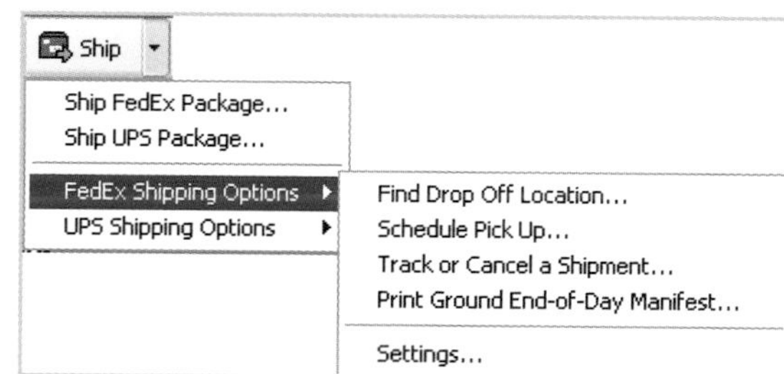

3. In the To area, enter your customer's name and address.

4. Click the **Service** down arrow, and click your shipping method (for example, **FedEx Express Saver**). The screen will change accordingly.

5. Confirm the date on which you want your package shipped and who will pay for it.

6. On the right side of the screen, choose the type of service and packaging, type the package weight in pounds (if applicable), type the package value in U.S. dollars (if applicable), and type any other special handling or shipping options you require.

FedEx Express Saver® : $ 9.59

7. Click the **Estimate Cost** (located near the lower-left area of the window). An estimate replaces the Estimate Cost section. If the estimate is more than you're willing to pay, you can click **Cancel** to stop the shipping process at this point.
8. If you are satisfied with the rate quote, click **Ship**. A label is sent to your printer. The Shipping Manager closes, and you are returned to the Create Invoices window.
9. Click **Save & Close**.

TIP

You can click use other options on the right to track your packages in transit, request pickups, change your settings, or get help on this feature.

Monitor and Maintain Inventory Items

QuickBooks provides options for you to take physical inventory and adjust for errors, theft, breakages, or other inaccuracies in your inventory. If you have slow-moving or large items, you can take inventory on an infrequent basis. If you have small, expensive items, you may want to closely monitor storage and do random or frequent inventories.

Take Inventory

To take inventory, you need a list of your inventory items. You should do a monthly inventory, if possible—at the very least, take your inventory at least once a year.

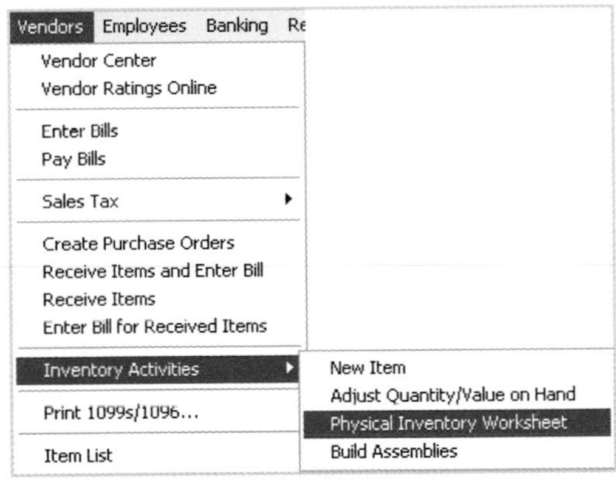

1. Click the **Vendors** menu, click **Inventory Activities**, and click **Physical Inventory Worksheet**. A Physical Inventory Worksheet report appears, as shown in Figure 7-14.
2. Click **Print**. The Print dialog box appears. Click **Print** again.
3. Click the **Close** button (the X in the upper-right corner) to close the report window. If QuickBooks prompts you to memorize this report, click **No**.

You can now use this inventory worksheet to physically check your inventory against what you have listed in QuickBooks.

TIP

You can group your items using subitems. Consider grouping them by location to facilitate inventory checks.

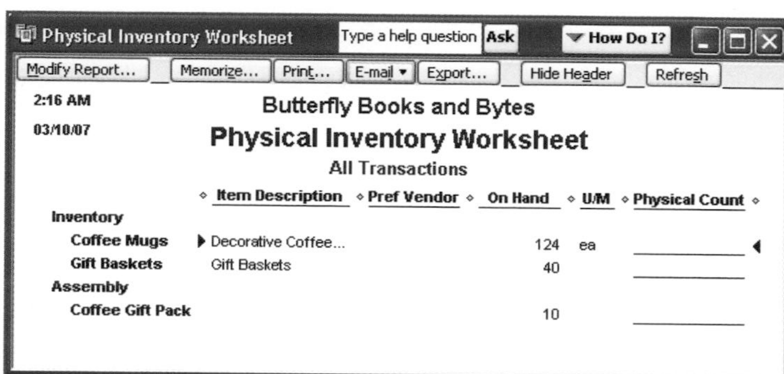

Figure 7-14: ***In the Physical Inventory Worksheet report, inventory items and inventory assemblies are grouped separately.***

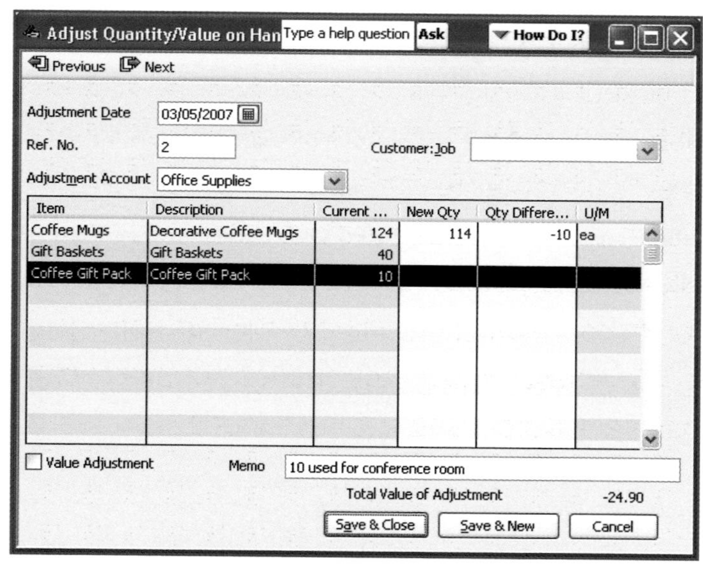

Figure 7-15: ***Use the Customer:Job field to correct errors involving any incorrect entries of items so that they can be charged correctly for job-costing reports.***

Manually Adjust Inventory

When you have completed your physical inventory, you can adjust it in QuickBooks if necessary.

1. Click the **Vendors** menu, click **Inventory Activities**, and click **Adjust Quantity/Value On Hand**. The Adjust Quantity/Value On Hand window opens, as shown in Figure 7-15.
2. Click in the **New Quantity** field in the Coffee Mug row. Type the actual count of mugs, for example, 114.
3. Click the **Adjustment Account** down arrow, and click **Office Supplies**. In this case, these mugs were taken for office use. If they had been broken or lost, however, you could create an expense account to reflect that.
4. Click **Save & Close**.

Your inventory has now been updated and the appropriate expense account charged. If you need to use multiple expense accounts, click the **Save & New** button, and add multiple inventory adjustments, each with its own account.

How to...

- *Automate Your Backups*
- *Restore Your Data*
- *Verify Your Data*
- *Work with an Accountant's Copy*
- *Storing Your Backups*
- *Close Your Books*
- *Network Your QuickBooks File*
- *Customize Company Preferences*
- *Customize My Preferences*
- *View Reminders*
- *Use the Find Feature*
- *Write Collection Letters to Customers*
- *Create Mailing Labels*
- *Customize Forms*

Chapter 8
Customizing and Maintaining QuickBooks

QuickBooks can be customized to meet your specific needs and adjusted to fit your interaction with it. Commonly used preferences will be covered in this chapter, as well as other features, such as customizing forms, networking your files, maintaining your data, and communicating with your customers. Each QuickBooks company file can be customized to meet your needs and preferences. Experiment with the various settings to determine what works best for you. Any change you make can be easily changed back if it doesn't suit your needs.

Maintain and Access Your Data

The most important thing in accounting is to maintain your data. All of your QuickBooks data is stored in a single file with a .qbw file extension. When you back it up, it is compressed into another single file with a .qbb file extension. Backing up your data is covered in Chapter 1. If you need to restore your data, you need to uncompress your .qbb file back into a .qbw file.

TIP

It's a good idea to make sure that everyone using QuickBooks closes the company file at the end of every day to avoid power outages causing data corruption, and everyone *must* be out of the file for automatic backups to occur.

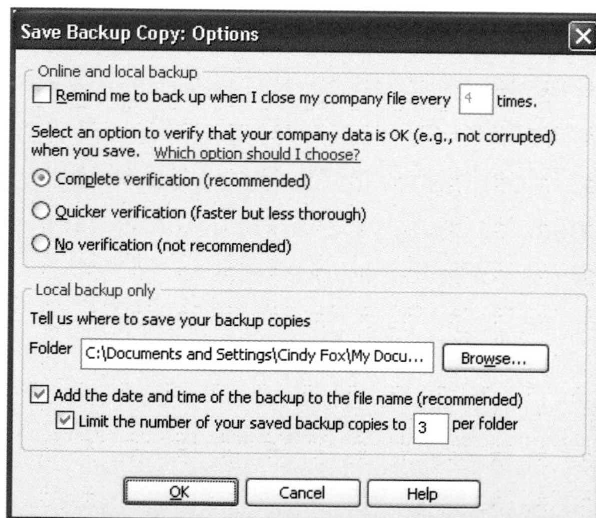

Figure 8-1: ***Be sure you are fully aware of where your backup is being stored in case you ever need to restore it.***

Automate Your Backups

Chapter 1 covered manual backups. If you want QuickBooks to back up your data every day or every time you use your file, you can schedule automatic backups. QuickBooks provides you with two options:

- **Set automatic backups** that take place when you close the company file (every time or at set intervals).
- **Schedule regular backups** at specific times. Make sure these are times that the computer will be on and the file will be closed on all computers. QuickBooks can be open or closed, but make sure the file to be backed up is closed.

SET REMINDERS, AUTOMATIC AND REGULAR BACKUPS

1. Click the **File** menu and click **Save Copy or Backup**. The Save Copy: Type window opens.
2. Click **Backup Copy** and click **Next**. You have the option here to save files online or locally. You should also be backing up all of your data online or onto a removable medium, such as a CD, an external USB hard drive, or a tape, and storing some copies offsite. You may receive a warning to switch to single-user mode. If so, make sure everyone is out of your file and click the **File** menu and click **Switch to Single-user Mode**.
3. Click **Options**. The Save Backup Copy: Options window opens as in Figure 8-1.
4. Confirm the following items:
   - Click the **Remind me to back up when I close my company file every _ times** check box to clear the selection box. If you will be saving the file automatically, you don't need to be reminded.
   - Select a verification level to ensure accuracy in your data file. This will apply to all your backups.
   - Type your file storage location or click **Browse** to open a Browse for folder window that will allow you to select a location to store your backups on a regular basis. Select your folder, and then click **OK** to save this location and return to the Save Backup Copy: Options window.
   - Confirm that **Add the date and time of the backup to the file name** is selected.
   - Confirm that **Limit the number of your saved backup copies to _ per folder** is selected and choose a number in order to save space. If this choice is not selected, QuickBooks will continue to back up new copies without removing the old copies.
5. Review your choices and click **OK** when you are satisfied to return to the Save Backup: Method window.

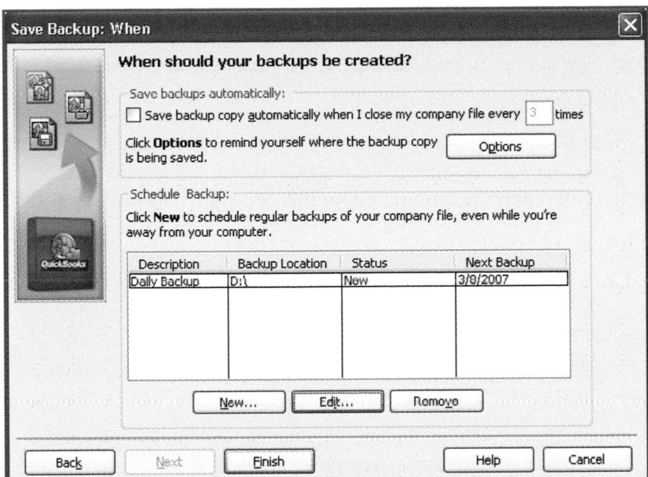

Figure 8-2: ***Back up your company file to a thumb drive or other removable drive for the most security, but make sure it is in the computer each night.***

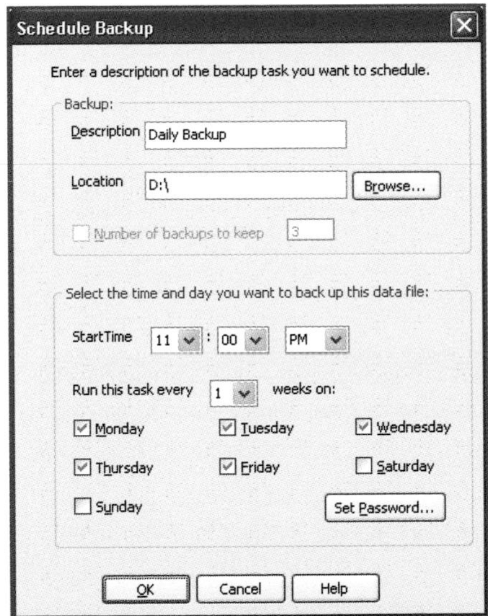

Figure 8-3: ***Back up your company file to a thumb drive or other removable drive for the most security, but make sure it is in the computer each night.***

6. Click **Next** to move to the Save Backups: When window.
7. You can choose to save right now if you wish to; otherwise, click **Only schedule future backups** and click **Next** to move to the scheduling area as seen in Figure 8-2.
8. Click the **Save backup copy automatically when I close my company file every _ times**. Click in the **Times** field, and type how often you want the backup to occur, for example, 1 (every time you close the file). If you type 2, QuickBooks will back up the file every other time it is closed.
9. Click the **New** button, located near the bottom of the window. The Schedule Backup window opens (see Figure 8-3).
10. Confirm the following items:
    - In the **Description** field, type a description for your backup, for example, Daily Backup.
    - In the **Location** field, enter a name or click the **Browse** button. A Folder List dialog box appears. Select a destination for your backup. Click **OK** to close the Folder List and return to the Schedule Backup window.
    - The **Number of Backups to Keep** is the maximum number of old backups that will be stored. After this number is reached, such as 3, whenever a new backup is created, the oldest backup will be deleted. This helps prevent filling up a disk with too many backups.
    - In the **Start Time** area, click the **hour** down arrow, and click the hour you want the backup to occur, for example, **11**. Repeat for the **minute** down arrow, and the **AM/PM** down arrow, and click the desired time of day, such as **PM**.
    - Click the **Run this task every** down arrow, and select how often you want to run backups, for example, once a week.
    - Click the days on which you want your backup to run; for example, click **Monday**, **Tuesday**, **Wednesday**, **Thursday**, and **Friday** to back up each weekday. If you're backing up to your hard disk, make sure you have a system-wide backup running on a regular basis to copy all your data to another location in case of corruption.
    - Click the **Set Password** button. The Enter Windows Password dialog box appears. If you are required to enter a password when Windows starts up (this is different from your QuickBooks password), type it here. Unattended backups cannot take place unless you provide your Windows user name and password.

Enter Windows Password

Enter the login information for a user. The scheduled backup will run based on the Windows privileges of that user.

Username: Cindy Fox

Password: ••••••

Confirm Password: ••••••

OK Cancel

11. Click **OK** to close the Enter Windows Password window.
12. Click **OK** to close the Schedule Backup window. You'll see your scheduled backup listed in the Schedule Backup window as in Figure 8-2.
13. Click **Finish** to close the QuickBooks Backup window. A small window may inform you that Backups have been scheduled as specified. Click **OK**.

CAUTION

Don't overwrite a newer copy of your data with an older backup. Always rename your current working file before restoring another file in case of any problems.

Restore Your Data

You will need to restore your data if, for example, you have a hard disk crash, a stolen computer, or a possible corrupt company file. After remedying whatever situation caused you to lose your data, you may need to reinstall QuickBooks and then restore your data.

1. Click the **File** menu and click **Open or Restore Company**. The Open Company:Type window opens (see Figure 8-4).
2. Click **Restore a backup copy** and click **Next**. The Restore Backup: Method screen opens.
3. Click **Local Backup** (or online as appropriate) and click **Next**. The Open window opens.
4. Select your location and file, and click **Open**. You will return to the Restore Backup: To Location window.
5. Click **Next**. The Restore To window will appear.
6. Select your location and file, and click **Save**. The default file will already be selected. If you are choosing to overwrite an existing file, a warning will display, prompting you to confirm this action. (If you are unsure, click **No** to return to the Restore To window, and choose another name for your restore file.)

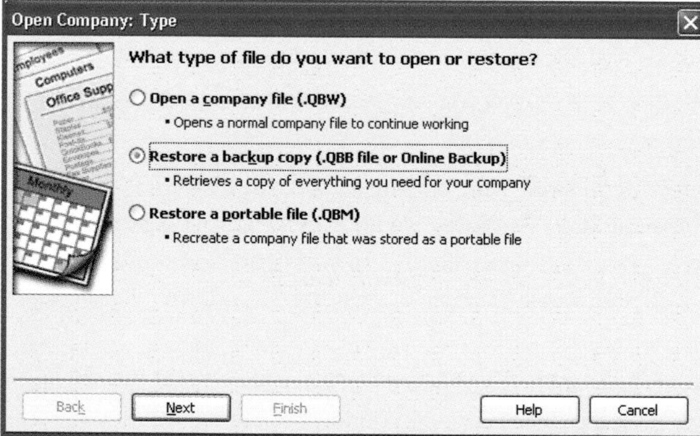
Open Company: Type
What type of file do you want to open or restore?
Open a company file (.QBW)
• Opens a normal company file to continue working
Restore a backup copy (.QBB file or Online Backup)
• Retrieves a copy of everything you need for your company
Restore a portable file (.QBM)
• Recreate a company file that was stored as a portable file
Back
Next
Finish
Help
Cancel

Figure 8-4: ***Choose Restore a backup copy or Restore a portable file, depending which type of file you want to restore.***

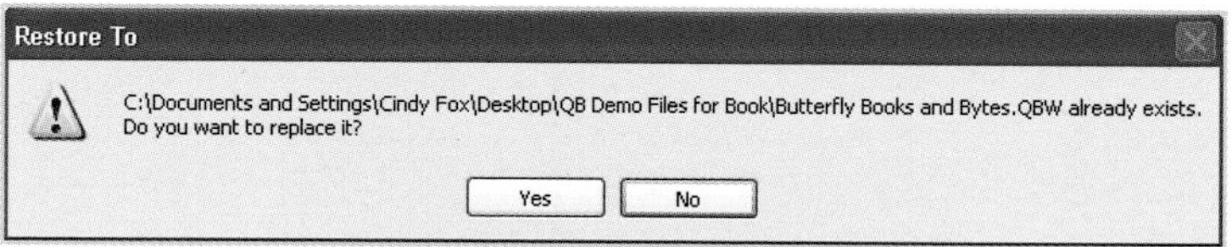
Restore To
C:\Documents and Settings\Cindy Fox\Desktop\QB Demo Files for Book\Butterfly Books and Bytes.QBW already exists.
Do you want to replace it?
Yes
No

7. Click **Yes**. A Delete Entire File dialog box appears, asking you again to confirm this action.

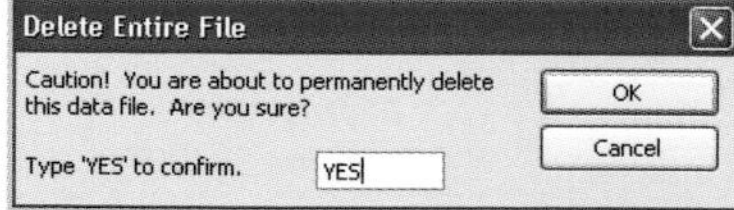
Delete Entire File
Caution! You are about to permanently delete this data file. Are you sure?
Type 'YES' to confirm.
YES
OK
Cancel

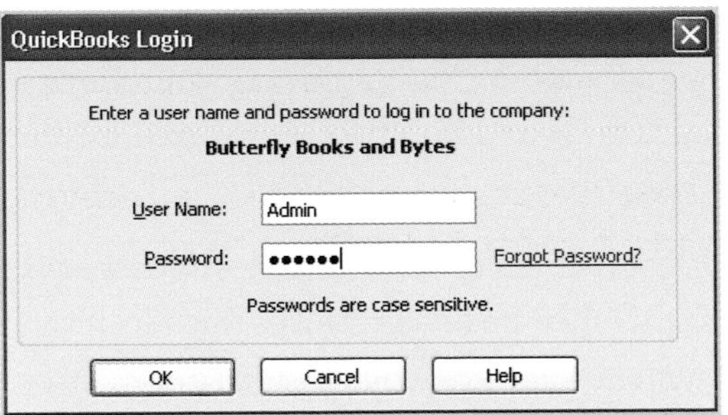

8. If you are sure you want to proceed with the deletion, type YES in the confirmation box. Click **OK**. The restore operation begins, and the QuickBooks Login dialog box appears.
9. Type your password, if required, and click **OK**. The restore operation continues, and a final dialog box appears when the restoration is complete, informing you of a successful restore.
10. Click **OK**.

Verify Your Data

If you have any concerns that your data might be corrupt, such as strange entries or links not working correctly, you can check it by verifying your data at any time.

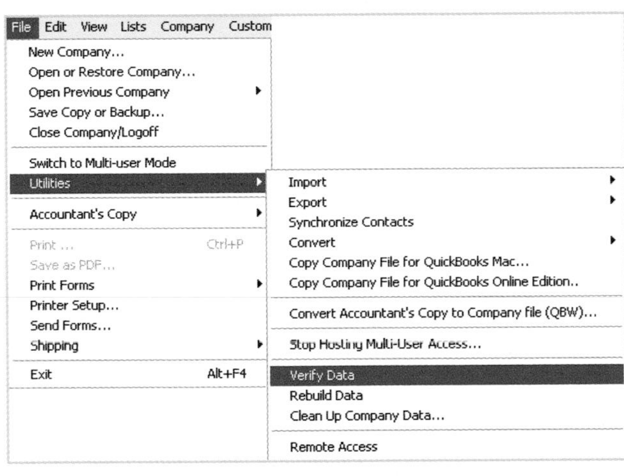

1. Click the **File** menu, click **Utilities**, and click **Verify Data**. A Verify Data dialog box may appear, notifying you that QuickBooks needs to close all open windows before proceeding.
2. Click **OK**. If all is well, a dialog box will appear, informing you that QuickBooks found no problem with your data.

If you see a dialog box stating that your data is corrupt, you will be directed to use the Rebuild Data feature (you can also access this feature by clicking the **File** menu and clicking **Utilities**). If the Rebuild Data feature fails, you should contact Intuit for support.

Work with an Accountant's Copy

In addition to creating a backup for emergencies, you may need to give a copy of your data to your accountant. You can accomplish this in one of three ways:

- **Create a normal backup** to give to your accountant for review.

  –Or–

- **Create a portable company file** of your data to give to your accountant for review.

  –Or–

- **Create an accountant's copy** of your data to give your accountant, which can then be returned and reintegrated into your QuickBooks company file.

STORING YOUR BACKUPS

It's convenient and easy to store all your financial data in one file, but when (not if) a computer crashes, computer programs can be restored, but data cannot unless you have a backup.

A *backup* is a compressed copy of your data. You can store your data on a CD-ROM, DVD, a flash drive, or online. Keep this backup file offsite in case of flood, fire, or theft.

STORE YOUR BACKUP ONLINE

Online storage of your backup is easy when you have a high-speed connection and can automatically store the backup offsite. Intuit offers its own service, but a popular option is www.ironmountain.com for automated backup of all of your data.

STORE YOUR BACKUP ON TAPE

If you have a tape drive that backs up your entire computer system, make sure your QuickBooks file is included. If you ever need to retrieve that data, you will need to have the same type of tape drive and software to access that drive.

STORE YOUR BACKUP ON CD-ROM OR DVD

CD-ROM and DVD media are convenient and supported by most computers. For example, Windows XP can automatically write to CDs, which can then be easily read on any other computer, but always test your backups by placing them in another computer and making sure you can open that file.

STORE YOUR BACKUP ON FLASH DRIVES

Flash drives (also known as thumb drives or memory sticks) are small devices (less than 1 × 3 inches) that plug directly into your USB connection and that are recognized by Windows XP as an additional hard drive, similar to camera memory cards. They can be reused indefinitely and are available in a variety of sizes, from 16MB and up.

Whichever method you choose, make a note as to where you save the file so you can easily transfer it to your accountant. You can e-mail your file to your accountant or physically deliver it on your accountant's preferred medium, such as a floppy disk, CD, or flash drive.

If you use a backup or portable company file, this will give your accountant the greatest amount of control, but when he or she returns this file, it cannot be merged back into your company file, so you will have to stop work on your company file while your accountant has his or her copy.

To create a portable company file:

Click the **File** menu, click **Save Copy or Backup**, select **Portable Company File**, and click **Finish**.

To create an accountant's copy:

Click the **File** menu, click **Accountant's Review**, and click **Create Accountant's Copy**.

While you have an accountant's copy in existence, you *can* use your QuickBooks file to:

- Create, edit, and delete transactions
- Add and edit list items

While you have an accountant's copy in existence, you *cannot* use your QuickBooks file to:

- Delete, move, or rename a list entry

Table 8-1 lists the actions that your accountant can and cannot perform on an accountant's copy of your QuickBooks file. Table 8-2 provides an explanation of the most common file extensions used in QuickBooks and their meanings.

When your accountant returns your file, you need to reintegrate it into your company file.

To import your accountant's changes:

Click the **File** menu, click **Accountant's Review**, and click **Import Accountant's Changes**; or, alternatively, click **Cancel Accountant's Changes** if no file is returned.

TIP

To transfer QuickBooks data from one system to another, you can use either the portable company file or backup copy. All information will be preserved in either file, but portable company files remove indexes and other technical information and then rebuild some of them upon restore, which causes this type of file to take longer to create and restore but results in a smaller file for ease of e-mailing or other transfer. Some information is not restored, such as checkpoints within the file, which are used for recovering your information in the event of a corrupted database. However, if you are very good about making backups, then the checkpoint information you lose in a portable data company is not that important.

TIP

You may use the portable company file for transfers of information, but be sure to use the backup feature on a regular basis in the event of any emergency.

ACCOUNTANT CAN	ACCOUNTANT CANNOT
View lists, transactions, and reports; add new items to the Chart of Accounts, Item list, and To Do Notes list; edit account and tax information for existing items	Delete, reorganize, or make list entries inactive, including memorized reports
Enter and memorize general journal transactions, adjust inventory value and quantities	Enter, edit, delete, or memorize any transaction other than general journal and inventory adjustment entries
Create and print new reports, including 1099, 941, 940, and W-2 forms	Export any changes made to 1099, 941, 940, or W-2 forms or employee YTD payroll setup transactions back to your copy

Table 8-1: ***What Accountant Can and Cannot Do with the Accountant's Copy of Your File***

Close Your Books

Unlike many accounting programs, QuickBooks allows you to make changes to your accounting files at any time. Although this is convenient, it can be a problem if information is changed after it has already been filed with the IRS or other agencies.

EXTENSION	FILE TYPE AND DESCRIPTION
.qbw	**QuickBooks company file** is your daily company file.
.qbb	**QuickBooks backup file** can be used at other locations and then restored over current QBW file if no changes were made in it.
.qbm	**QuickBooks portable company file** can be used at other locations and then returned to be used if no changes were made in the company QBW file.
.qbx	**Accountant export file** is the file you give your accountant to review while you continue to use QuickBooks.
.qba	**Accountant review copy** is used by your accountant when he or she restores your .qbx file.
.aif	**Accountant import file** is the file your accountant will return to you to import his or her changes.
.iif	**Intuit interchange format file** is for importing or exporting data, such as lists and transactions, between QuickBooks and other programs.
.nd	**Network data file** tracks network configuration information (do not delete).
.tlg	**Transaction log file** aids in recovery by technical support personnel if needed.

Table 8-2: ***Common QuickBooks File Extensions and Their Meanings***

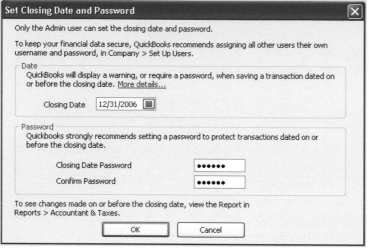

Set Closing Date and Password

Only the Admin user can set the closing date and password.

To keep your financial data secure, QuickBooks recommends assigning all other users their own username and password, in Company > Set Up Users.

Date

QuickBooks will display a warning, or require a password, when saving a transaction dated on or before the closing date. More details...

Closing Date 12/31/2006

Password

Quickbooks strongly recommends setting a password to protect transactions dated on or before the closing date.

Closing Date Password ••••••

Confirm Password ••••••

To see changes made on or before the closing date, view the Report in Reports > Accountant & Taxes.

OK Cancel

To prevent changes before a certain date:

1. Click the **Company** menu and click **Set Closing Date**. The Preferences window opens (see Figure 8-5) in the Accounting Company Preferences.
2. In the Closing Date area, click the **Set Date/Password** button and the Set Closing Date and Password window opens.
3. Click in the **Closing Date** field, and type the end date of your prior fiscal year.
4. Click in the **Closing Date Password** field and type a password you will remember.
5. Click in the **Confirm Password** field and retype your password.
6. Click **OK** to close the Set Closing Date and Password window.
7. Click **OK** to close and save your preferences.

Changes made before this closing date will require the use of the password, which will help ensure that no accidental changes are made.

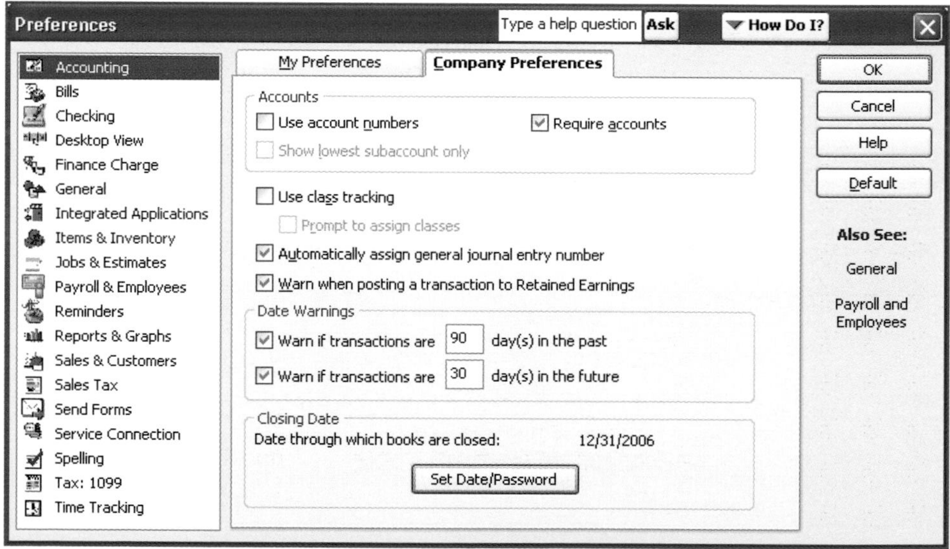

Figure 8-5: ***Only the Administrator user of QuickBooks can change or modify company preferences, and this person must be in single-user mode.***

Network Your QuickBooks File

If you have purchased a multiuser pack, more than one person can use QuickBooks at one time (the Basic edition does not support this feature). This is useful, as it would, for example, allow the owner, a bookkeeper, and a person at the checkout counter to all enter transactions at the same time.

SET UP MULTI-USER ACCESS

1. Connect your computers together using a network (use a contractor if you are not comfortable with this).
2. Determine on which computer the data file will reside. This computer must have a copy of QuickBooks installed on it and be on at all times when others need to access the file. It should be the most stable computer and not need to be rebooted. Preferably, no one uses this computer for daily work.
3. Install the QuickBooks program (the same version) on all of the computers that need access. Update the file (click **Help** and click **Update QuickBooks**) on each computer to make sure they are the same version.
4. Open QuickBooks on the computer on which the company file (.qbw) is installed. Be sure you are on the *host* computer.
5. Click **File**, then click **Utilities**, and click **Host Multi-User Access** (see Figure 8-6). A warning will appear that you will be allowing others to access your company file and asking if you wish to continue.
6. Click **Yes**. A warning will appear that QuickBooks needs to change to single-user mode to make changes.
7. Click **Yes**. A notice will appear that the setup is complete. This includes a warning to remind you that you must leave this computer on and active (not in standby or hibernate mode) but that QuickBooks does not need to be running.
8. Click **OK**.

Now that your system is set up for hosting your Company File, be sure to set up multiple users (see Chapter 2) and switch to multi-user mode. Others can now access the file as well.

TIP

If you have more than one Company file, be sure to store them all on the same computer and open each file on the host computer before opening on other systems.

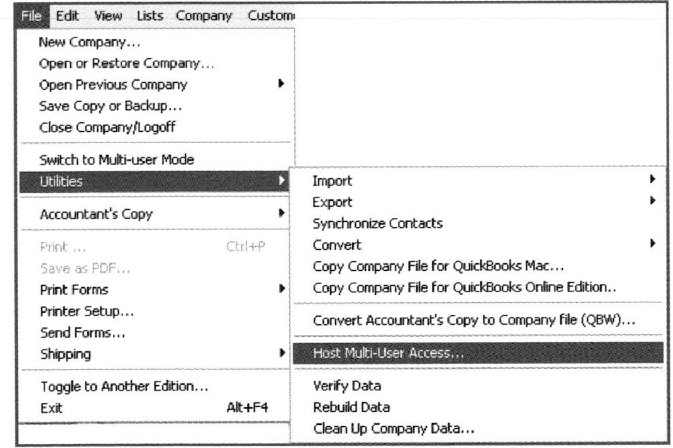

Figure 8-6: ***Be sure to select Host Multi-User Access only on the computer you wish to host the file. This should not be activated on any other system.***

1 2 3 4 5 6 7 8 9 10

1 2 3 4 5 6 7 8 9 10

CAUTION

Shut down QuickBooks at the end of each day to avoid data corruption that can be caused by losing power overnight.

SHARING FILES

When sharing a file with others, there are two modes for access:

- Multi-user mode allows everyone to access the file and is the default way to open and use a shared file. Make sure you are in multi-user mode for daily work.
- Single-user mode limits access and changes to one person, but switching to single-user mode can speed some tasks, such as running big reports.

Single-user mode must be used for the following tasks:

- File operations, including backups and exporting data
- Certain list changes, such as deleting a list item
- Setting up new features and setting company preferences
- Online banking

If you are working in multi-user mode and try to do something that can only be done in single-user mode, a dialog box will notify you when this is necessary. You can then easily switch to single-user mode, complete your task, and switch back to multi-user mode, but others will need to exit the file before you do this.

To switch from single-user to multi-user mode:

Click **File** and click **Switch to Multi-User mode** (as seen in Figure 8-6).

To switch from multi-user to single-user mode:

Click **File** and click **Switch to Single-User Mode**. This is a toggle.

Edit Your QuickBooks Preferences

Preference settings are available in QuickBooks for the entire company file (Company Preferences tab) or for the current user (My Preferences tab). Some preferences require that you close all open windows before making changes, so finish any transactions in progress before changing your preferences.

Customize Company Preferences

Company preferences affect the entire company file and should only be changed by the business owner or accountant after careful consideration.

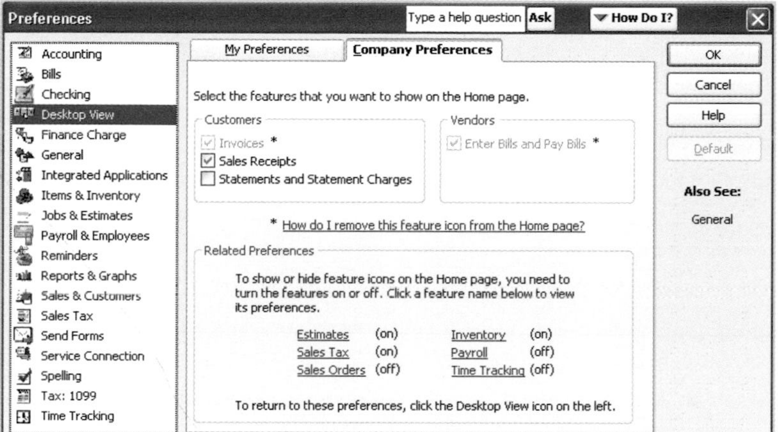

1. Click the **Edit** menu and click **Preferences**.
2. Click the icon on the left side for the section you want to change, and click the **Company Preferences** tab.
3. Make your selections. When finished, either:
   - Click **OK** to save and close.

     –Or–
   - Click **Cancel** if you have made an error.

Table 8-3 lists the specific company preferences in QuickBooks that you can change. Keep in mind that a change to your company preferences affects all QuickBooks users.

Customize My Preferences

Personal preferences are unique to each user in QuickBooks.

1. Click the **Edit** menu and click **Preferences**.
2. Click the icon on the left side for the section you want to change, and click the **My Preferences** tab.
3. Make your selections. When finished, either:
   - Click **OK** to save and close.

     –Or–
   - Click **Cancel** if you have made an error.

Table 8-4 lists the specific user preferences in QuickBooks that you can change. Changes made here only affect the currently logged-in user.

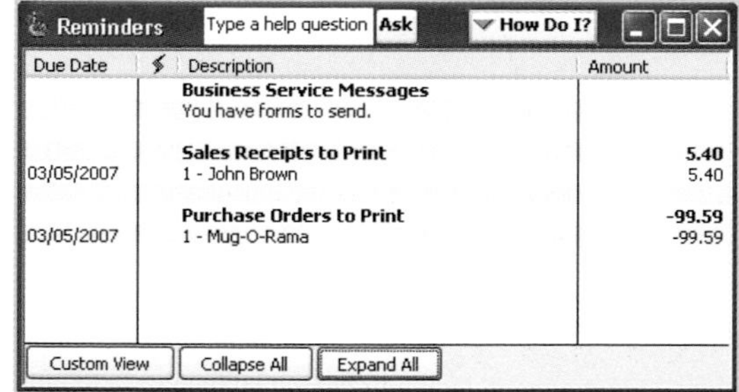

View Reminders

You can view the Reminders List at any time, but it's convenient when reminders appear each time you open QuickBooks, especially if you do not use QuickBooks every day.

PREFERENCE	COMPANY PREFERENCES
Accounting	Account numbers, classes, general journal entries, retained earnings, date warnings, and closing date (with password).
Bills	Bill due dates, duplicate warning, and using discounts and credits.
Checking	Voucher account names, check updating when printed, field start order, duplicate check number warning, autofill payee information, default accounts for paychecks and payroll liabilities, and creating payee aliases for online banking.
Desktop View	Customize home page features and turn related preferences on or off.
Finance Charge	Annual interest rate, minimum finance charge, grace period, finance charge account, finance charge calculations on finance charges, date calculation, and printing.
General	Time and year format; turn off name update (not recommended).
Integrated Applications	Control access to your QuickBooks file from other programs (such as the Intuit Customer Manager).
Items and Inventory	Activate inventory and purchase orders, warn about quantity on hand, and set Unit of Measure (see Chapter 7 for information on inventory).
Jobs and Estimates	Edit estimate titles, warn about duplicate numbers, hide zero amounts, and activate estimates and progress invoicing.
Payroll and Employee	Activate payroll and set preferences for printing pay stubs and vouchers, workers' compensation information, and Employee List (see Chapter 9).
Reminders	Set lists or summaries for each section and reminder dates (see the section "View Reminders" in this chapter for more information).
Reports and Graphs	Set accrual or cash basis for reports and set account names, aging report options, format, and cash flow accounts (see Chapter 10).
Sales & Customers	Set sales forms, shipping options, price levels, sales orders, reimbursed expenses, default markup, and receive payment settings (see Chapter 6).
Sales Tax	Set sales tax, codes, and payments (see Chapter 6 for information on charging sales tax and Chapter 9 for information on paying sales tax).
Send Forms	Customize default text for e-mailing forms.
Service Connection	Set automatic login to business services and downloading of messages.
Tax:1099	Set thresholds for 1099 creation and relate to accounts (see Chapter 5).
Time Tracking	Turn on time tracking and set day of week (see Chapter 9).

Table 8-3: ***Company Preferences***

PREFERENCE	MY PREFERENCES
Accounting	Autofill memos for general journal entry.
Checking	Account associations for writing checks, paying bills, paying sales tax, making deposits, and online banking Add To Register option.
Desktop View	View single or multiple windows; change desktop settings, color scheme, and links to operating system monitor and sound settings.
General	Field movement, drop-down lists, sounds, decimal point placement, warnings for editing or deleting a transaction, one-time messages, turn off pop-up messages, show ToolTips, recall transactions, set default date, set custom item information.
Reminders	Show Reminders List when opening a company file.
Reports and Graphs	Refresh report settings, prompt for report option modification each time you run a report, graph options for slower computers.
Sales & Customers	Set Time/Costs options for jobs.
Send Forms	Set E-Mail autocheck.
Service Connection	Option to save files and whether to close your browser when using Web Connect.
Spelling	Turn spell check on or off and control what it does or does not check.

Table 8-4: ***My Preferences***

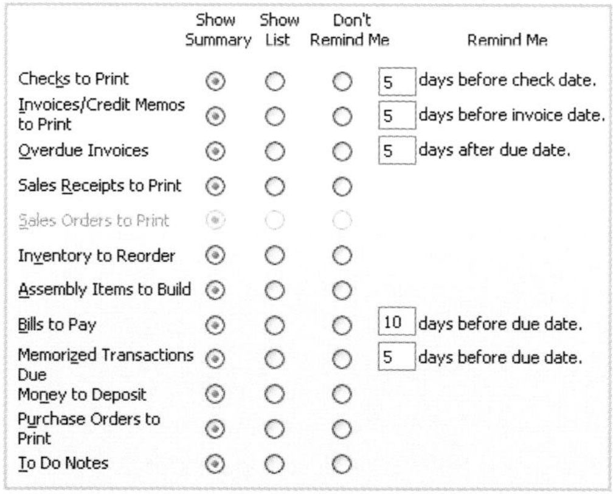

VIEW REMINDERS AT ANY TIME

To view your Reminders List:

Click the **Company** menu and click **Reminders**.

	Show Summary	Show List	Don't Remind Me	Remind Me
Checks to Print	⦿	○	○	5 days before check date.
Invoices/Credit Memos to Print	⦿	○	○	5 days before invoice date.
Overdue Invoices	⦿	○	○	5 days after due date.
Sales Receipts to Print	⦿	○	○	
Sales Orders to Print	⦿	○	○	
Inventory to Reorder	⦿	○	○	
Assembly Items to Build	⦿	○	○	
Bills to Pay	⦿	○	○	10 days before due date.
Memorized Transactions Due	⦿	○	○	5 days before due date.
Money to Deposit	⦿	○	○	
Purchase Orders to Print	⦿	○	○	
To Do Notes	⦿	○	○	

Double-click any bold section header to expand the section and see section items. Double-click any section item to open that item to review, print, or update it.

CUSTOMIZE REMINDERS

To customize the Reminders List:

1. Click the **Edit** menu and click **Preferences**.
2. Click the **Reminders** icon on the left.
3. Click the **My Preferences** tab, and click **Show Reminders List when opening a Company file**.
4. Click the **Company Preferences** tab. For each item on the list, choose one of the following:
   - **Show Summary** lists the section header with items hidden.
   - **Show List** lists each item in the section.
   - **Don't Remind Me** does not show any item or header in the section.

1 2 3 4 5 6 7 8 9 10

5. For items with dates, type the number of days for each reminder in the relevant field.
6. Click **OK** to save your change and close the Preferences window.

VIEW TO DO LIST

To Do items are listed as a section of the Reminders List, or you can view them individually.

Click the **Company** menu and click **To Do List**.

TIP

You can use keyboard shortcuts to quickly open windows you use often; for example, press **CTRL+F** to open the Find window.

Use the Find Feature

The Find feature in QuickBooks can be used to quickly find a transaction. It has a Simple tab and an Advanced tab. Try both methods of searching and use whichever one you find works better for you. There is also a Search feature included if you chose to install Google Search during your QuickBooks installation.

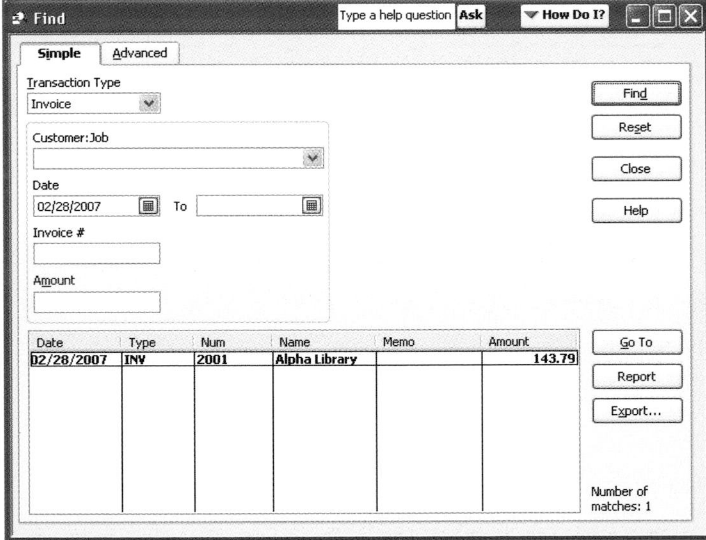

Figure 8-7: ***When conducting a search from the Find window, click the Reset button to clear all entries and start a new search.***

THE SIMPLE TAB

1. Click the **Edit** menu and click **Find**. The Find window opens (see Figure 8-7).
2. Click the **Simple** tab (if it is not already active).
3. Enter any combination of the options, including Transaction Type, Customer: Job, Date, Invoice Number, and Amount. Note that *all* criteria you select must be met for a transaction to appear in the list below.
4. Click **Find**.
5. The Find window will display a list of all transactions for the criteria you selected. Double-click any item to open the transaction. If you get a large list, you can add more restrictions, such as date range, invoice number, or amount. If you want to see all transaction types at the same time, you'll need to use the Advanced tab. The Simple tab can only search for one type of transaction at a time.

THE ADVANCED TAB

1. Click the **Edit** menu and click **Find**. The Find window opens.
2. Click the **Advanced** tab (see Figure 8-8). For each filter you click in the list, the options to the right of the Filter List will change accordingly. If you find too many transactions, add more filters; if you find too few, remove some of your filters.

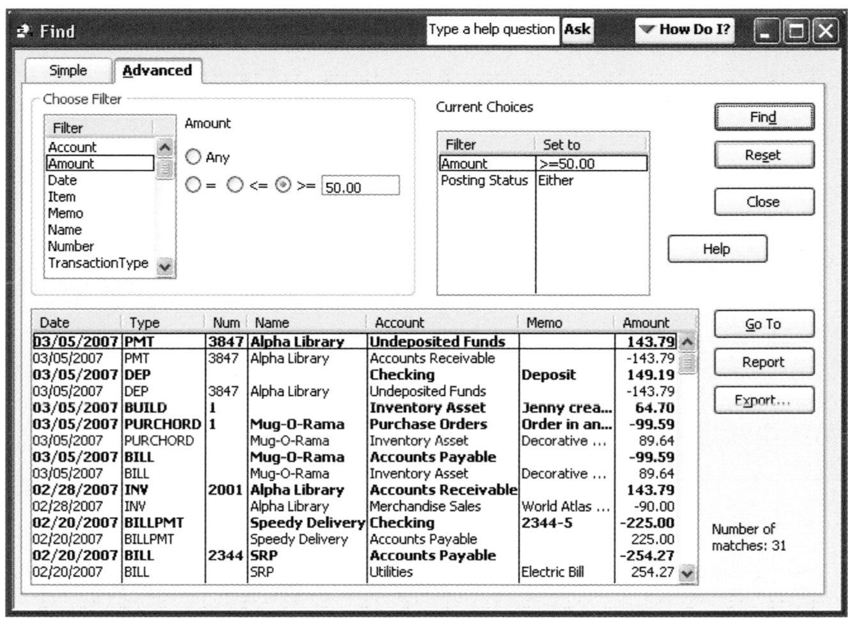

Figure 8-8: ***The Advanced tab has a list of filters showing all the searchable fields in QuickBooks.***

3. Click a filter, such as **Amount**, in the Filter List.
4. Click an option, such as **>=**, and enter any additional criteria, such as typing 50 in the Amount box.
5. Click **Find**.

The Find window displays all transactions in bold, as well as all line items associated with the customer you selected. Double-click any transaction in the Find window to open that transaction for reviewing, editing, or printing. Close the Find window when finished.

TIP

Click the **Report** button to generate a report based on the items retrieved using the Find feature.

Communicate with Customers

When communicating with your customers in writing, you can print (and send by regular mail), e-mail, or fax forms and letters. When sending forms (such as invoices) by e-mail, you can customize the default e-mail text aimed at customers in the Preferences section. Click the **Edit** menu, click **Preferences**, click **Send Forms**, and click **Company Preferences**.

TIP

You can write letters to vendors, employees, people on the Other Names List, and customers, using existing QuickBooks templates, or create your own customer letter.

1 2 3 4 5 6 7 8 9 10

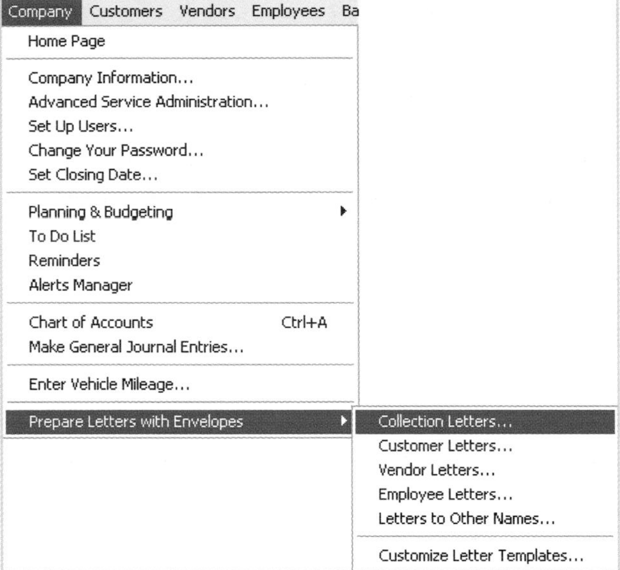

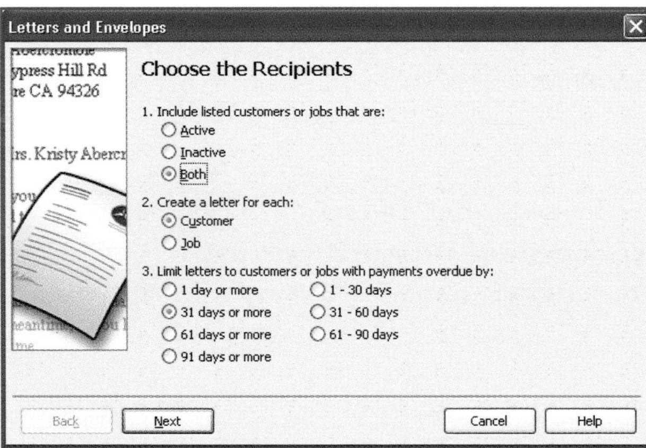

Figure 8-9: ***The Letters and Envelopes Wizard can help make your collection efforts easier by providing form letters that you customize.***

Write Collection Letters to Customers

Collection efforts can be unpleasant, but they need to be done. To make it easier, QuickBooks provides you with collection reports (see Chapter 10), statements (see Chapter 6), and form letters you can use when writing collection letters to your customers. You can customize these form letters to meet your company's specific needs.

To write a collection letter:

1. Click the **Company** menu, click **Prepare Letters With Envelopes**, and click **Collection Letters**. If you did a nonstandard QuickBooks installation, you may see a message prompting you to copy the letter templates or to browse to them.
2. The Letters and Envelopes Wizard starts, as shown in Figure 8-9.
3. Select your desired options.
4. Click **Next**. A list of customers that met your criteria is displayed along with their amounts due, as shown in Figure 8-10. They are all selected by default. Click the check mark in the left column to select or deselect a customer.
5. Click **Next**. Click the type of letter you want to send (**Formal**, **Friendly**, **Harsh**, or a custom letter you've created).

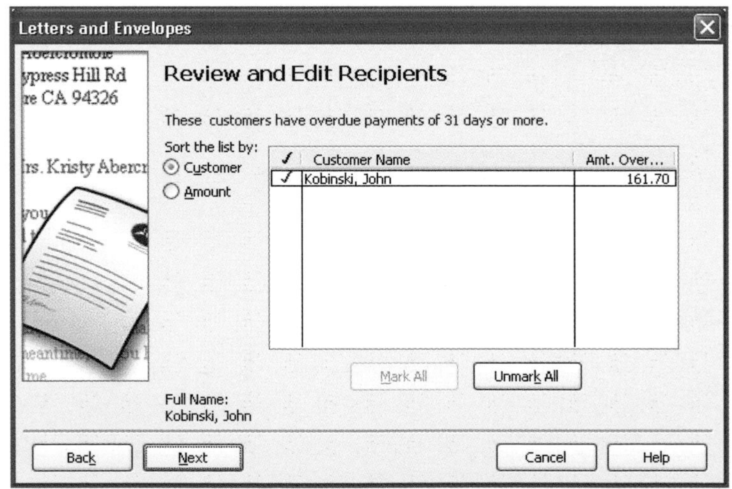

Figure 8-10: ***You can click the Back button if the list of customers is not what you expected.***

Butterfly Books and Bytes
123 East Main Street
Mesa, AZ 85201

March 8, 2007

Kobinski, John

Dear **MISSING*INFORMATION** **MISSING*INFORMATION**,

Although we have contacted you about the outstanding balance on your account, we still have not heard from you. You have an outstanding balance of $161.70. The following invoices are overdue:

Inv. No.	Inv. Date	Due Date	Inv. Amount	Balance
2006	01/07/2007	01/07/2007	$161.70	$161.70

If you have already sent payment in full, we ask that you call and let us know. Otherwise, please call me to discuss what you plan to do to settle your account.

Thank you for your prompt attention to this matter.

Sincerely,

Cindy Fox
Owner
Butterfly Books and Bytes

Figure 8-11: ***Edit the missing information (in this case, first name and last name) in the customer information area if it exists.***

CAUTION

The letter-writing feature in QuickBooks requires you to have Microsoft Word 2000 or later.

TIP

In the Customer Center, click the **Word** down arrow and click **Prepare Customer Letters** to send out your custom templates, or the included templates, such as Accept/Deny Credit App, Bounced Check, Contract Transmittal, Customer Apology, Birthday, Fax, Inactive Customer, or Thanks For Business.

6. Click **Next**. Type your name and title in the fields provided, or leave these blank if you don't have a title or don't want your name on the letter.
7. Click **Next**. QuickBooks creates the letters and opens Microsoft Word. If any information is missing, QuickBooks will notify you. Click **OK** if this occurs.
8. Your letter is displayed with any missing information indicated, as shown in Figure 8-11. You can now edit the letter directly in Word and print, save, or otherwise manipulate the letter.
9. In Word, click the **File** menu and click **Print**.
10. In Word, click the **Close** button (the X in the upper-right corner). Save the document when Word prompts you, if desired. The letter will be saved in a Company Letters Folder in the same directory as your Company File.
11. Return to the QuickBooks window and to the Letters and Envelopes Wizard. If you use window envelopes, you can click the **Cancel** button at this point to skip printing envelopes.
12. Click **Next**. The Envelope Confirmation window opens. Review the information shown and click the **Delivery Point Barcode** check box if you so desire.

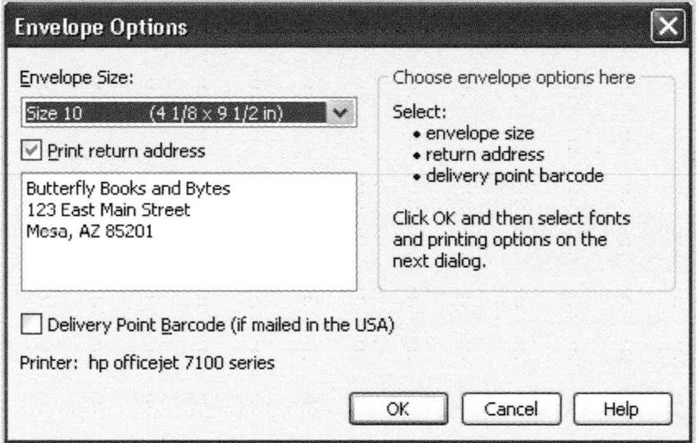

13. Click **OK**. Word opens again so that you can print your envelopes. Load your envelopes into your printer.
14. Click **OK**. Your envelopes are printed and you are returned to QuickBooks. If your envelope did not print correctly, click the **Previous** button on the wizard to try again.
15. Click **Finish**.

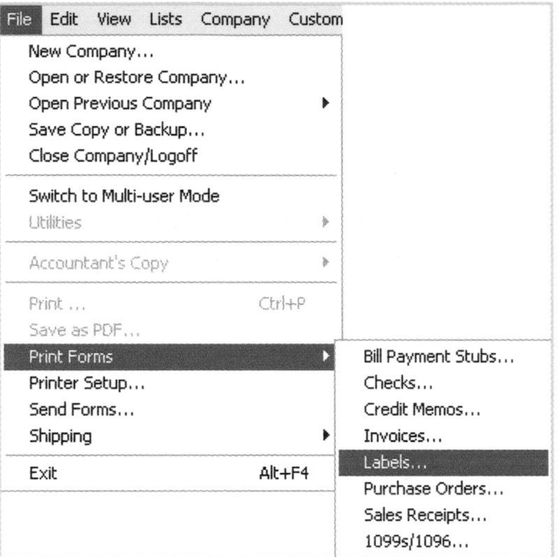

Create Mailing Labels

If you don't have Word or want to send a flyer or other item requiring a label instead of writing a letter, you can easily create mailing labels in QuickBooks.

1. Click the **File** menu, click **Print Forms**, and click **Labels**. The Select Labels to Print window opens, as shown in Figure 8-12. Select the relevant options for printing and/or sorting your labels.
2. Click **OK**. The Print Labels dialog box appears.
3. Click the **Label Format** down arrow, and click your label type, for example, **Avery #5261 Intuit Std. Mailing Label**. Make sure your labels are loaded correctly in the printer.
4. Click **Print**. Your mailing labels are printed.

Avery #5261 Intuit Std Mailing label
✓ Avery #5261 Intuit Std Mailing label
Avery #5163 Mailing label
Avery #5260 Mailing label
Avery #5262 Mailing label
Avery #5261 Intuit Std Name & Phone
Avery #5163 Name and Phone
Avery #5260 Name and Phone
Avery #5262 Name and Phone
2 1/4" x 4" Rolodex cards
3" x 5" Rolodex cards
Intuit Pre-printed Shipping label
File folder label (2/3" x 3 7/16")

> **TIP**
>
> Print your labels on plain paper first to make sure they will correctly line up.

> **TIP**
>
> You can click Preview to review labels for complete addresses before printing.

> **TIP**
>
> QuickBooks provides standard templates with the most commonly used options. You can edit this template to have all (or alternative) options available.

Customize Forms

All of the sales forms in QuickBooks can be customized to meet your needs. This section will demonstrate how to create a new custom invoice, but the procedure is the same for Estimates, Sales Receipts, Statements, Credit Memos, Sales Orders, and Purchase Orders.

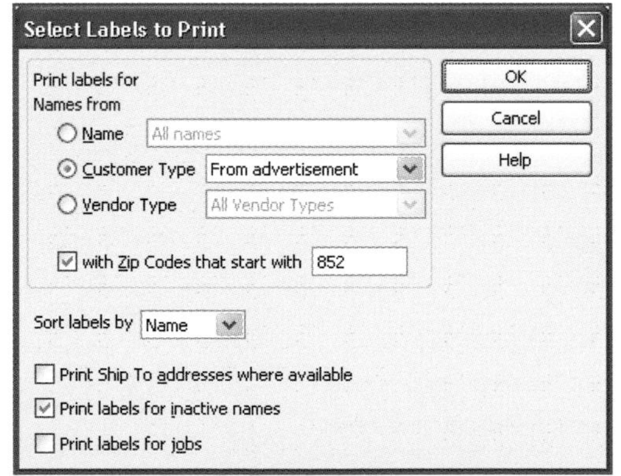

Figure 8-12: ***You can print and sort labels according to type or ZIP code.***

CREATE A NEW INVOICE TEMPLATE

1. Click the **Lists** menu and click **Templates**. The Templates List is displayed.
2. Click the **Templates** menu button (located near the bottom), and click **New**. The Select Template Type dialog box appears, asking you to choose the type of template you are creating.
3. Click **Invoice** and click **OK**. The Basic Customization window opens, displaying basic choices on the left and a layout example on the right as seen in Figure 8-13. Change any option on the left to see your changes on the right.

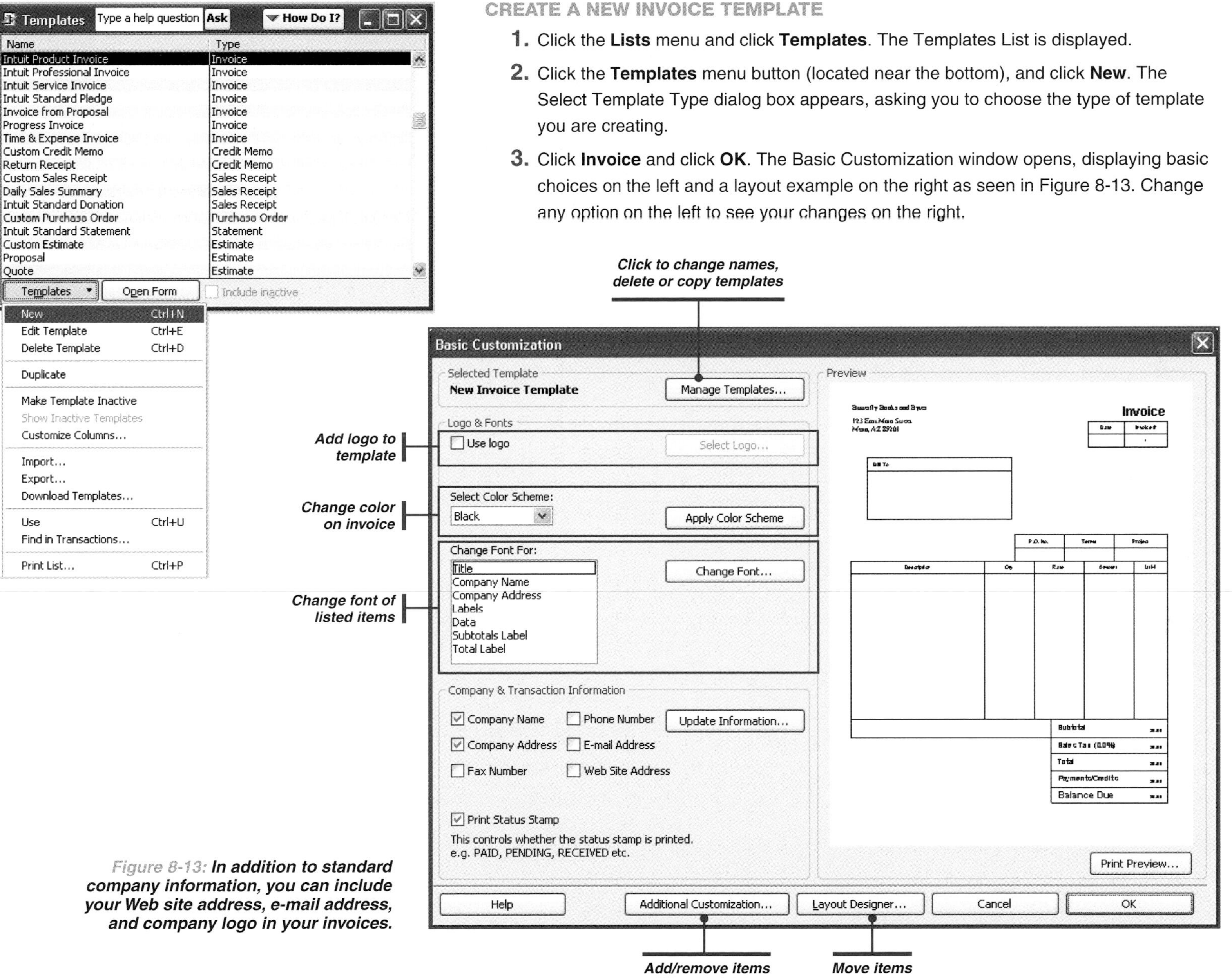

Figure 8-13: ***In addition to standard company information, you can include your Web site address, e-mail address, and company logo in your invoices.***

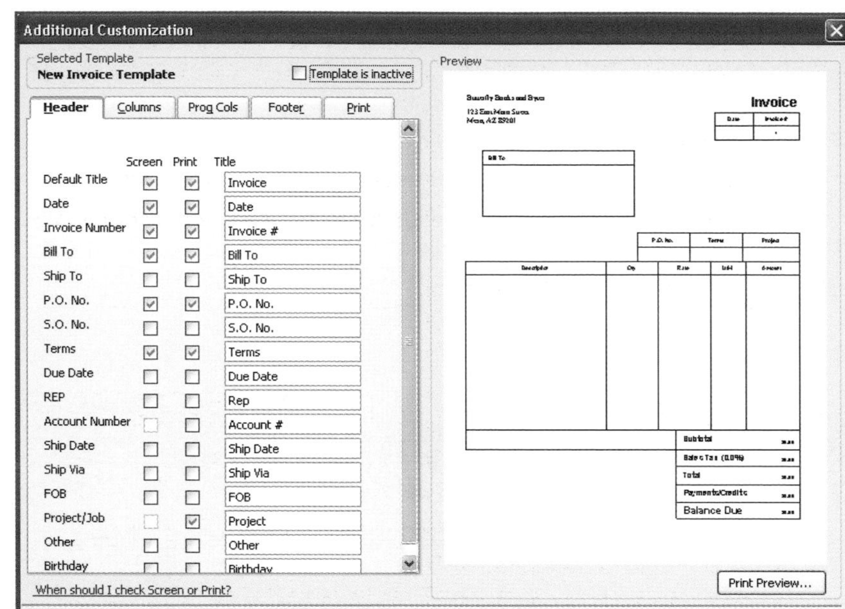

Figure 8-14: ***Click Screen check boxes to track information on screen and click Print check boxes for only those items you wish to appear on your template.***

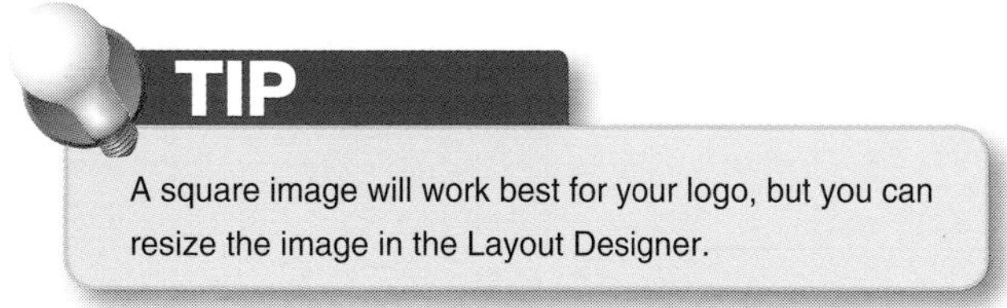

TIP

A square image will work best for your logo, but you can resize the image in the Layout Designer.

4. Click the **Manage Templates** button near the top and click in the **Template Name** field on the right. Highlight the current name (such as Copy of: New Invoice Template), and type the name of your new invoice, for example, Online Invoice.
5. Click **OK** to return to the Basic Customization window.
6. Click the **Additional Customization** button to open the Additional Customization window as seen in Figure 8-14.
7. Click each of the five tabs to review your customizing options, and makes any changes you desire. See Table 8-5 for a description of each tab's contents.
8. Click **OK** to return to the Basic Customization window.
9. Click **OK** to close and save your changes. The new Online Invoice form is now in the Templates List.

USE THE LAYOUT DESIGNER

To move or resize objects on your form, use the Layout Designer. This feature is especially useful when using window envelopes for invoices. You can arrange the layout, print the document, and fold and stuff it into a test envelope, thus saving yourself time addressing envelopes.

To use the Layout Designer:

1. Click the **Lists** menu and click **Templates**. The Templates List is displayed.
2. Double-click the form you want to customize using the Layout Designer, for example, **Online Invoice**. The Customize Invoice window opens.
3. Click the **Layout Designer** button. The Layout Designer opens, as shown in Figure 8-15.
4. You now have the following options:
   - Drag any item to a new location.
   - Click any item and press the **DEL** key to remove it from the layout view (some items cannot be removed).
   - Right-click anywhere in the layout view to see a menu of commands, for example, Undo. You can also add fields, images, or text boxes anywhere you like.

TAB	DESCRIPTION
Header	Fields that will print on the top of every page of the form (Default Title, Date, Invoice Number, Bill To, Ship To) and can include custom fields.
Columns	The main part of the invoice where items, a description, and amount are listed.
Prog Cols	Progressive columns can be included to give more information on related estimates when creating a progressive invoice.
Footer	Fields that will print on the bottom of each page of the form; includes a text box that you can use to include warranty or return information on every invoice.
Print	Option to use the default printer settings or to specify specific printer settings for this form.

Table 8-5: **Options for Additional Customization of a Form**

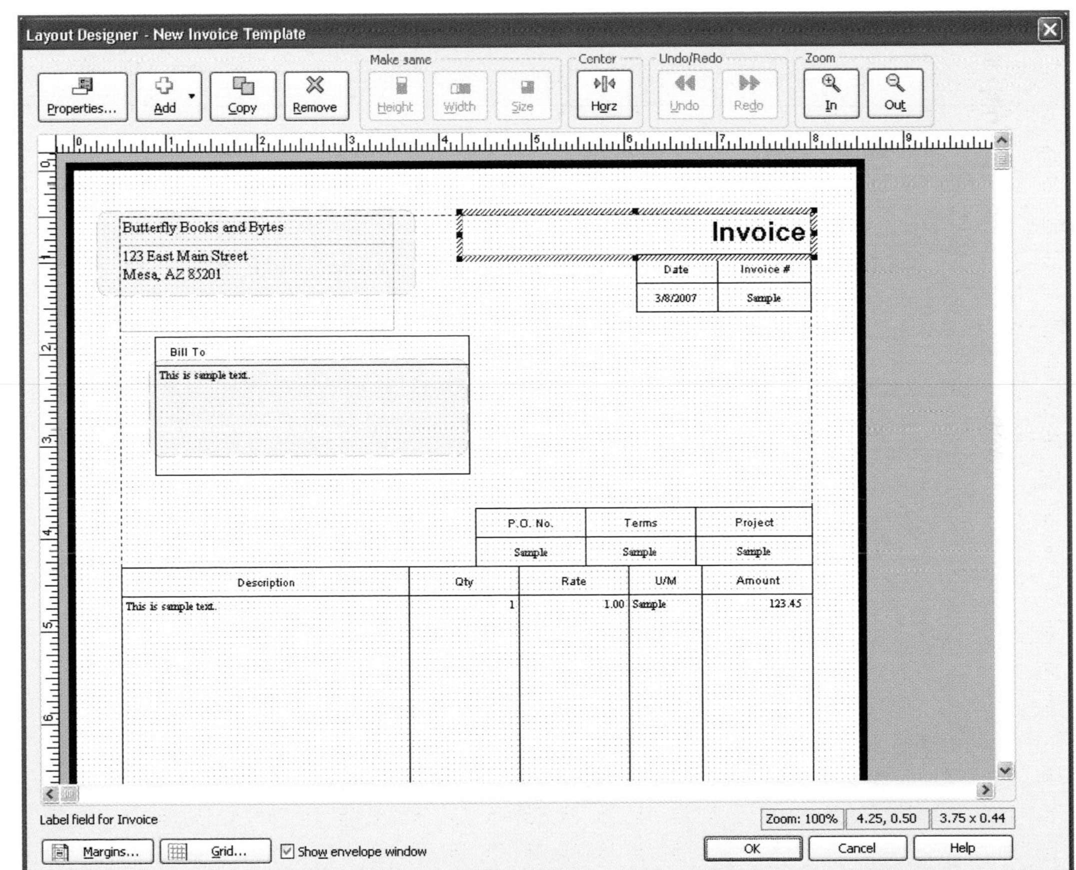

Figure 8-15: ***The green shaded areas represent standard window envelope placement. The form title, "Invoice," is currently selected and can be easily moved or deleted.***

5. When you are finished editing, click **OK** to save your changes (or click **Cancel** if you want to discard your changes). Your changes are saved, and you will exit the Layout Designer. (If you click Cancel, a dialog box appears, prompting you to confirm that you want to discard your changes, and you will then exit the Layout Designer.)
6. Click **OK** to save your changes and exit the Basic Customization window.

You can create as many customized forms as you like, but it is best to have one form of each type for ease of readability, and only create extra forms if needed for specific customers or purposes.

How to...

- *Activate Payroll in Preferences*
- *Select a Payroll Service*
- *Comparing Payroll Options*
- *Set Up Company Information*
- *Enter and Review Employee Information*
- *Set Up Payroll Taxes*
- *Setting Year-to-Date Amounts*
- *Create and Print Paychecks*
- *Edit or Void Paychecks*
- *Entering a Single Activity*
- *Turn On Time Tracking*
- *Enter Weekly Timesheets*
- *Review and Pay Payroll Taxes*

Chapter 9 Paying Employees and Taxes and Tracking Time

Employees help a business grow, but having employees requires a whole new area of tracking. Companies need to track employee information, hours, and payroll items. In addition to tracking your employee hours for payroll purposes, you can use time tracking to track billable hours to charge back to customers. This chapter will cover both uses of time tracking. Payroll can be set up manually or automated through any of Intuit's payroll services. Both methods will be addressed in this chapter. You also need to pay payroll taxes and sales taxes, which this chapter will also discuss.

Set Up Payroll Options

Before you can use any payroll feature, you need to make sure payroll is enabled in your QuickBooks company file, choose which payroll method you will use (see the "Comparing Payroll Options" QuickFacts), and then set up employees in QuickBooks.

1
2
3
4
5
6
7
8
9
10

NOTE

An Employer Identification Number (EIN) is required to run payroll. This number is assigned by the IRS upon request. Visit www.irs.gov to obtain the necessary paperwork.

CAUTION

The QuickBooks payroll feature is not compatible with QuickBooks Online Edition, QuickBooks Simple Start Edition, or QuickBooks Pro for Mac.

Activate Payroll in Preferences

The first step in setting up payroll is to make sure it is enabled in the Preferences window. Once you've done this, you'll need to choose a payroll service, set up your company and employees, enter any year-to-date (YTD) information (if you have been running payroll another way), and then check your payroll data.

To activate payroll:

1. Click the **Edit** menu and click **Preferences**. The Preferences window opens.
2. Click the **Payroll & Employees** icon on the left, and click the **Company Preferences** tab. The Payroll & Employees Company Preferences are displayed (see Figure 9-1). QuickBooks will display a message stating if you need to switch to single-user mode or log in as the Administrator user for this task.
3. Click the **Full Payroll** option in the QuickBooks Payroll Features area to activate payroll and have additional options made available on this tab.
4. Click **OK** to close the Preferences window. If a message appears, stating that QuickBooks must close all windows to make this change, click **OK**.

You can come back to this window at any time if you need to change your preferences, including printing, workers' compensation, or employee defaults.

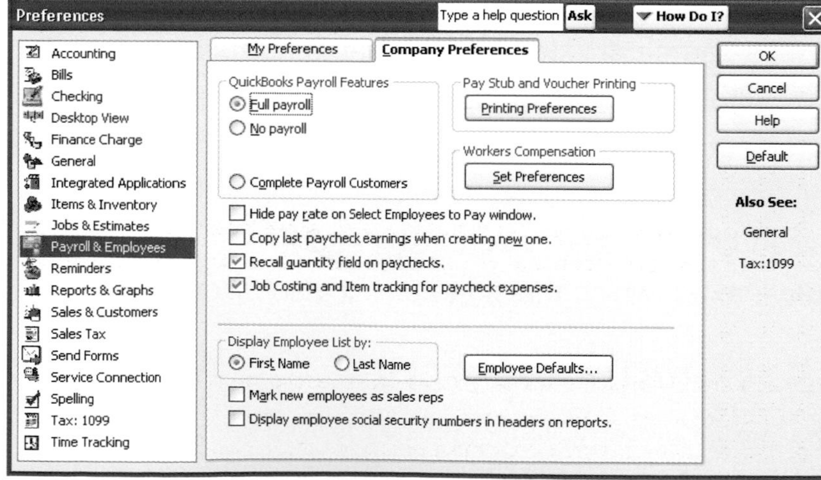

Figure 9-1: ***The default preference settings (shown here) are correct for most companies.***

Select a Payroll Service

QuickBooks provides a Payroll Setup Interview that walks you through your initial setup. You can exit the Payroll Setup Interview at any time and return later to complete the setup if needed.

To set up your payroll:

1. Click the **Employees** menu, click **Payroll**, and click **Order Payroll Service**. The Payroll Setup window opens, as shown in Figure 9-2.
2. Click **Buy Now** under the payroll service you want. If you want to use manual calculations, click the **Learn More** link *under* the Help Me Choose section, and click **Set QuickBooks To Enable Manual Paycheck Entry**. See the "Comparing Payroll Options" QuickFacts for more information on what you should choose.

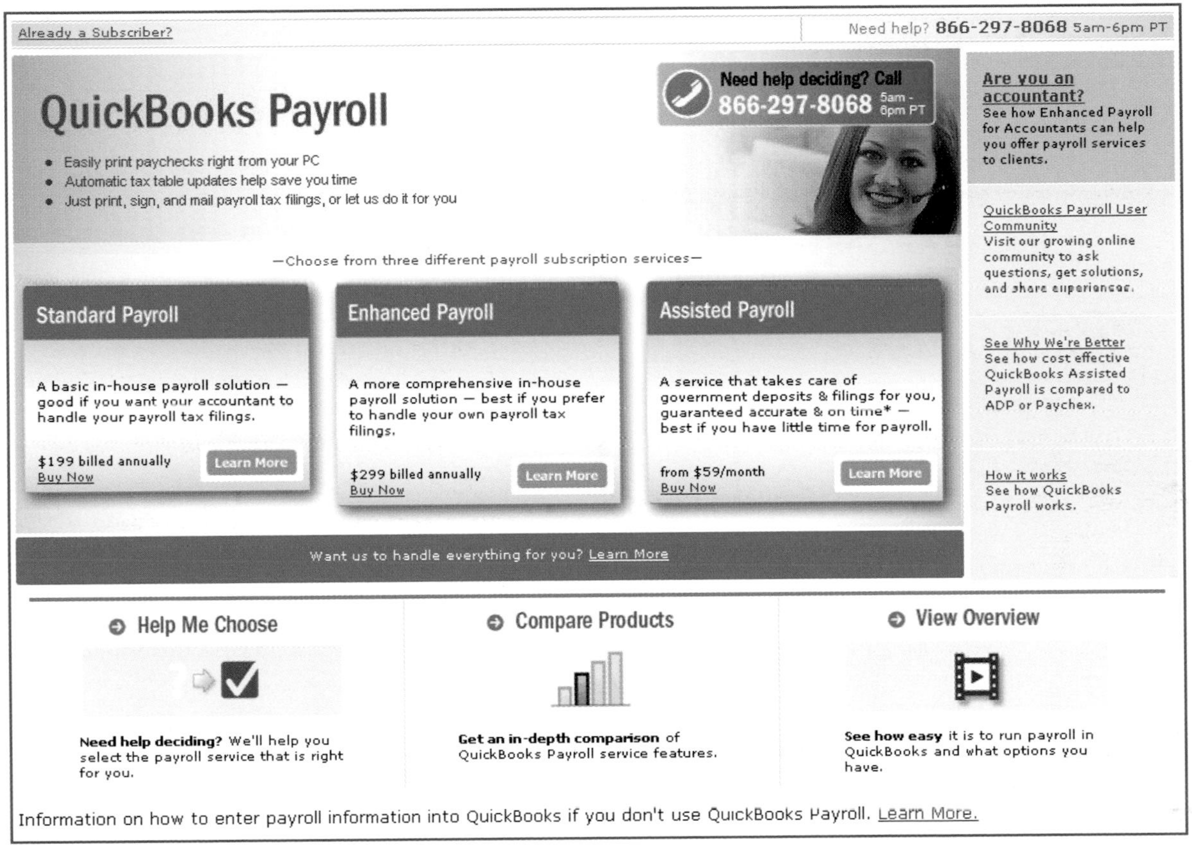

Already a Subscriber?

Need help? 866-297-8068 5am-6pm PT

QuickBooks Payroll

- Easily print paychecks right from your PC
- Automatic tax table updates help save you time
- Just print, sign, and mail payroll tax filings, or let us do it for you

Need help deciding? Call 866-297-8068 5am - 6pm PT

Are you an accountant? See how Enhanced Payroll for Accountants can help you offer payroll services to clients.

QuickBooks Payroll User Community Visit our growing online community to ask questions, get solutions, and share experiences.

See Why We're Better See how cost effective QuickBooks Assisted Payroll is compared to ADP or Paychex.

How it works See how QuickBooks Payroll works.

—Choose from three different payroll subscription services—

Standard Payroll

A basic in-house payroll solution — good if you want your accountant to handle your payroll tax filings.

$199 billed annually Buy Now Learn More

Enhanced Payroll

A more comprehensive in-house payroll solution — best if you prefer to handle your own payroll tax filings.

$299 billed annually Buy Now Learn More

Assisted Payroll

A service that takes care of government deposits & filings for you, guaranteed accurate & on time* — best if you have little time for payroll.

from $59/month Buy Now Learn More

Want us to handle everything for you? Learn More

Help Me Choose

Need help deciding? We'll help you select the payroll service that is right for you.

Compare Products

Get an in-depth comparison of QuickBooks Payroll service features.

View Overview

See how easy it is to run payroll in QuickBooks and what options you have.

Information on how to enter payroll information into QuickBooks if you don't use QuickBooks Payroll. Learn More.

Figure 9-2: ***To learn more before choosing a payroll service, click Help Me Choose, Compare Products, or View Overview.***

TIP

One payroll subscription can be used for up to three company EINs. To set up additional companies after you set up the first one, open the relevant company file, click the **Employees** menu, click **Add Payroll Service**, and click **Use My Existing Payroll Service**.

3. If you chose to calculate your payroll manually, you will see a message that your company file is now set up for this as in Figure 9-3. Click OK to exit the Payroll Setup Interview.

   –Or–

   If you choose any of the paid services, you will see a description of the service. Click the **Continue** button and follow the steps. The following steps use the QuickBooks Enhanced payroll service, which is the most commonly chosen type.

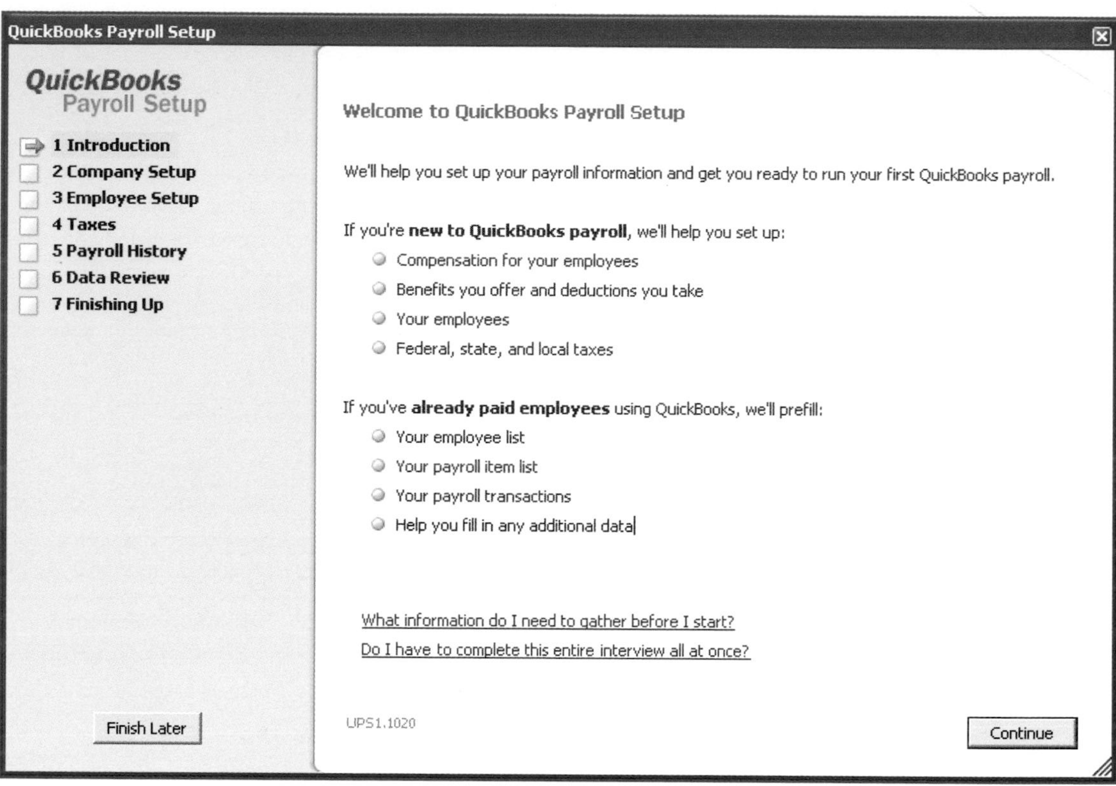
QuickBooks Payroll Setup
QuickBooks
Payroll Setup
1 Introduction
2 Company Setup
3 Employee Setup
4 Taxes
5 Payroll History
6 Data Review
7 Finishing Up
Finish Later
Welcome to QuickBooks Payroll Setup
We'll help you set up your payroll information and get you ready to run your first QuickBooks payroll.
If you're new to QuickBooks payroll, we'll help you set up:
Compensation for your employees
Benefits you offer and deductions you take
Your employees
Federal, state, and local taxes
If you've already paid employees using QuickBooks, we'll prefill:
Your employee list
Your payroll item list
Your payroll transactions
Help you fill in any additional data
What information do I need to gather before I start?
Do I have to complete this entire interview all at once?
UPS1.1020
Continue

Figure 9-3: ***This screen displays the steps to set up your company's payroll. You will see fewer steps if you have not purchased a payroll subscription.***

TIP

You can switch from manual payroll to using a service or vice versa at any time.

CAUTION

If you choose a QuickBooks payroll service, you will need to go online to activate your payroll, which will require a credit card payment and your federal EIN. You can choose to calculate your payroll manually, set up payroll now, and then choose a QuickBooks payroll service later.

4. Read the required items for your selected payroll service, and click **Continue**. If you don't have your EIN or credit card information, you can cancel at this point and return to the process later. If you don't have your bank account information for direct deposit, you can set it up later as well.
5. Confirm your company information (if you previously entered it in QuickBooks), or enter your correct company information, and click **Continue**. It will be updated in your company file.
6. Enter the contact information of the owner (or officer) and payroll administrator, and click **Continue**.
7. Enter your banking information to activate direct deposit, if desired, or leave this information out, and click **Continue**.
8. Enter your credit card information to pay for your subscription, and click **Continue**.

QUICKFACTS

COMPARING PAYROLL OPTIONS

QuickBooks offers five payroll options. Table 9-1 compares the features of the Payroll Services, while Table 9-2 shows the estimated costs for comparison.

- **Manual Payroll** requires that you manually calculate and enter the tax rates for your employees. Your accountant can give you the correct amounts to enter for withholding. There is no charge for this and no guarantees of accuracy.
- **Standard Payroll** allows you to fully control the payroll process and includes tax tables that are updated on a regular basis to automatically calculate withdrawal amounts.
- **Enhanced Payroll** includes all the Standard Payroll features, as well as information for state tax forms. This level is recommended for companies with 1 to 250 employees.
- **Assisted Payroll** includes more features than Enhanced Payroll, such as making federal and state payroll tax payments from your payroll bank account; filing all required federal and state payroll tax forms; preparing, printing, and mailing employee W-2 forms; and filing your company's W-3 forms with the IRS.

Continued . . .

9. Review your order and click **Place My Order** to activate your subscription. QuickBooks will automatically activate your subscription online in a minute or so.
10. Click **Return To QuickBooks** after your order is completed, and QuickBooks will download the updated tax tables and associated state forms.
11. Click **OK** to read about new tax table updates when the download is complete. The Payroll Update window will now open, but the Payroll Setup window may open on top of it. Read the information provided and close the Payroll Update window if this happens. You can read the Getting Started Guide by clicking the link. Then click Continue To Setup when you are ready and continue on to the next section to complete the Payroll Setup Interview.

Set Up Company Information

Payroll setup includes payroll items, such as salary, hourly wage, benefits, and garnishes; federal and state agency identification numbers, withholding percentages, and agency payment vendors; and default settings for new employees. Once you've activated the payroll feature in QuickBooks, whether you're doing it manually or using a paid subscription, your Employees menu, Employee Center, and home page will have additional options available. If you ordered a payroll subscription, you will also have an additional feature called Payroll Center.

SET UP PAYROLL ITEMS

Payroll items include compensation, benefits and other payments, and deductions—basically, anything you find on a paycheck. Typical items include salary, hourly wages, commission, taxable fringe benefits (such as use of a company car), insurance, retirement, union dues, wage garnishments, cash advances, and mileage reimbursement.

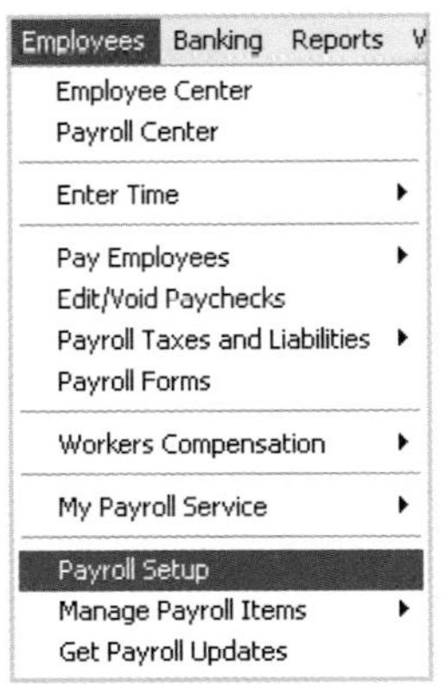

1. After subscribing to a QuickBooks payroll service, the QuickBooks Payroll Setup window opens, as seen in Figure 9-3. Alternately, you can click the **Employees** menu and click **Payroll Setup**. If you don't see Payroll Setup, return to the section "Select a Payroll Service" in this chapter and follow the steps.

QUICKFACTS

COMPARING PAYROLL OPTIONS

(Continued)

- **Complete Payroll** is an Intuit service that is fully outsourced; you do not need to enter your payroll information into QuickBooks. You can call in your information, and the service processes, prints, and delivers your paychecks to you. They will also prepare and file payroll tax forms, make payroll tax deposits on your behalf, and provide reports. This service does *not* directly integrate with QuickBooks, but you can import information into your company file from the Internet for QuickBooks reporting.

To learn more about any service or to find pricing information:

Click the Employees menu, click Payroll Services, and click Learn About Payroll Options.

Although you can choose to receive updates on a CD-ROM and subscribe to a payroll service over the phone, Internet access is required to use direct deposit, to download payroll updates, or to use Assisted Payroll.

Set up insurance benefits

What kinds of **insurance benefits** do you provide for your employees? Choose all that apply:

- [ ] Health insurance
- [x] Dental Insurance
- [x] Vision insurance

Other Insurance

- [ ] Group Term Life — Explain
- [ ] Health Savings Account — Explain
- [ ] S Corp Medical — Explain
- [ ] Other Insurance
- [ ] Medical Care FSA — Explain
- [ ] Dependent Care FSA

2. Click **Continue** to move to Compensation and Benefits.
3. Click **Continue** to enter compensation items. A window opens, displaying typical compensation items. Click the check box next to each item you want to add.

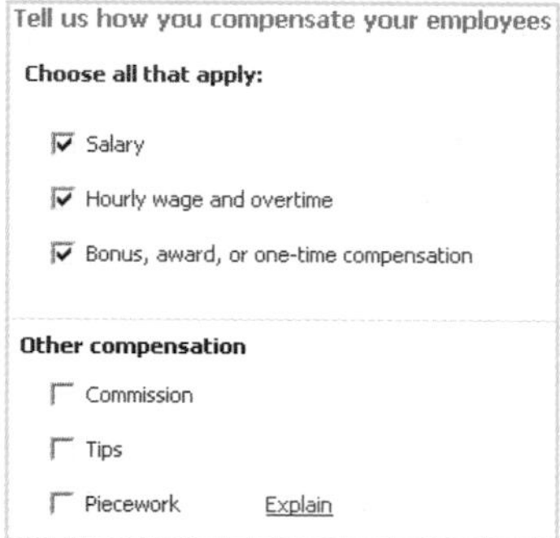

4. Click **Next**, if it appears, to review other compensation options; otherwise, click the **Finish** button to save and review your choices. You can click any of your items and then click the **Delete** or **Edit** button below the list to remove or edit the item. Click the **Add New** button to add additional items.

Compensation	Description
Hourly wage	Hourly
Hourly wage overtime (x1.5)	Overtime Hourly
Hourly wage overtime (x2)	Overtime Hourly
Salary	Salary
Bonus	Bonus

5. Once you are satisfied, click **Continue** to enter employee benefit items.
6. Click **Continue**. A window opens, displaying typical insurance benefit items.
7. Click the check box next to each item you want to add. Click **Next**, if it appears, to enter additional information, such as percentage paid by employer and employee, company to whom benefit is paid, and account number. Then click the Finish button to save your choices.

PAYROLL FEATURES	STANDARD	ENHANCED	ASSISTED	COMPLETE
QuickBooks payroll reports (Complete Payroll provides data-import option with 40 additional reports online)	√	√	√	√
Print paychecks and pay stubs from QuickBooks (Complete Payroll can also print for you for an additional fee)	√	√	√	√
Integrated direct deposit ability (for an additional fee)	√	√	√	√
QuickBooks Employee Organizer (or "HR Assistant") provides employee management tools (for an additional fee)	√	√	√	√
QuickBooks payroll calculations, with automatic update of federal and state payroll tax table and withholding limits	√	√	√	
Full QuickBooks integration	√	√	√	
Generate and print latest federal forms, such as 940, 940EZ, 941, W-2, W-3, 1099-MISC, and 1096	√ Completed by Company	√ Completed by Company	√ Completed by Service	√ Completed by Service
Generate and print latest state forms		√ Completed by Company	√ Completed by Service	√ Completed by Service
Track workers' compensation		√	√	√
Enter all employee hours on one screen		√	√	√
Calculate net-to-gross paycheck amounts		√	√	√
Phone support included			√	√
Federal and state electronic payroll tax deposit and filing completed for you with "No Penalties" guarantee			√	√
Local payroll tax deposit and filing completed for you				√
Enter payroll information online or by phone (additional fee for phone use)				√
Preparation and filing of state new-hire reports and calculation and preparation of third-party checks (such as garnishments)				√

Table 9-1: ***Comparison of Payroll Services Features***

STANDARD PAYROLL	ENHANCED PAYROLL	ASSISTED PAYROLL	COMPLETE PAYROLL
$17/month ($199 annual fee); unlimited employees	$25/month ($299 annual fee); unlimited employees	$59/month for up to 15 employees plus $2 per employee per pay period for additional employees over 15.	$100/month for up to 5 employees. Call for pricing on additional employees.

Table 9-2: ***Comparison of Average Costs of Payroll Services for Biweekly Payroll Services***

1 2 3 4 5 6 7 8 9 10

NOTE

Each paycheck tracks both the employer and employee contributions for taxes, benefits, and withholdings, so enter both the employer and employee shares of each payroll item.

TIP

Click the **Employee List** button in the Employee Setup window to display the Employee List. You can also click the **Employees** menu and then click **Employee Center** to access the Employee Center at any time, but it is easier to return to the Payroll Setup window to set up new employees and ensure that all payroll information is entered.

CAUTION

If you have used an alternative payroll system during your current calendar year, you will need to either enter all paychecks into QuickBooks or enter current-year balances for all payroll items in order for your end-of-year reports and forms to have the correct amounts.

8. Review your choices. You can click any of your items, and click the **Delete** or **Edit** button below the list to remove or edit the item. You can click the **Add New** button to add additional items. Once you are satisfied, click **Continue**.
9. Repeat Steps 7–8 for retirement benefit, paid time off, and miscellaneous items. At this point, you are simply entering the available options. You will be able to use these options individually for each employee.

You've now completed the Compensation and Benefits setup. To add items in the future, you can repeat this process or click the **Lists** menu and click **Payroll Item List**.

Enter and Review Employee Information

In order to pay employees, you must first set them up in QuickBooks. Use the Payroll Setup window to initially set up employees, and then use the Employee Center to manage or add new employees. The Employee Center gives you an overview and links to employee tasks and information, while the Payroll Center lets you easily process payroll.

SET UP EMPLOYEES

To set up employees from the Payroll Setup window:

1. Click **Continue** on the Payroll Setup window. The Employee List window opens if you already have employees entered; the Employee <Name> window (see Figure 9-4) will open if you have not yet added employees.
2. If the Employee List window opens, click the **Add New** button. The Employee <Name> window opens.
3. Click in the **First Name** field, and type the employee's first name.
4. Press the **TAB** key to move through the fields, entering information in the required fields and any other fields you want to use. If you skip a required field, QuickBooks will highlight it in yellow, with a note of what you need to enter. If you don't know it, you can leave it blank at this point and fill it in later. You won't be able to run payroll until you enter this information, but you can complete the setup with the information you know now.
5. Click **Next** to continue entering information.

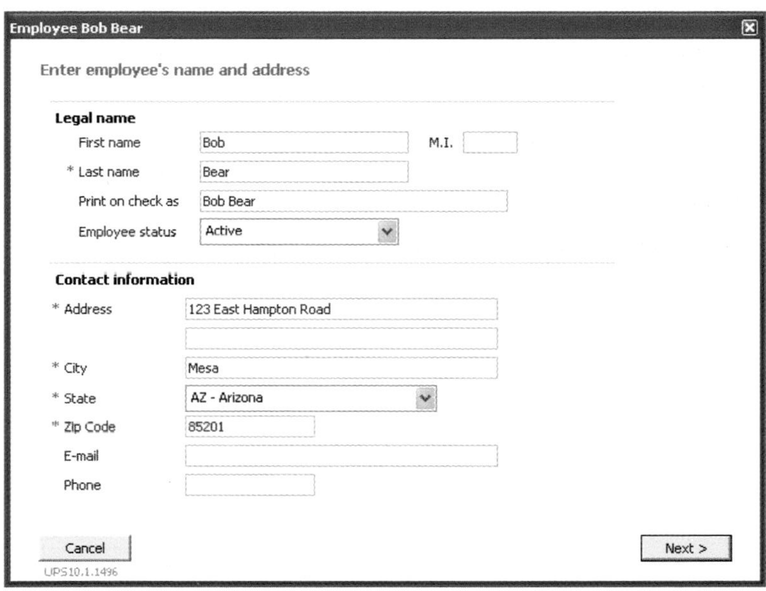

Figure 9-4: ***Fields with an asterisk (*) are required. The other fields are optional.***

6. Select the employee's tax type and enter his or her Social Security number and hire date. The release date will be provided when the employee leaves the company. Fill in the birth date and gender fields, if desired.
7. Click **Next** and enter the employee's pay frequency, wage or salary, and other items, as shown in Figure 9-5. You can change this information on each paycheck and do not have to use all the items you choose, so just use what is most frequently the case for this employee.
8. Click **Next** and enter the employee's benefit items, if applicable. Repeat this step for additional benefits, including sick and vacation time. Be sure to enter the correct amount for both the company and employee portions if costs are shared.
9. Click **Next** and enter information for direct deposit, if desired. Direct Deposit requires an additional fee.
10. Click **Next** and enter the employee's withholding and unemployment state information, where he or she lives and works.

TIP

Be sure to confirm your new employee's information. Referring directly to a copy of the employee's Social Security card and driver's license is a good assurance of accuracy.

Employee Bob Bear

Tell us about wages and compensation for Bob Bear

Pay frequency: Every other week (Biweekly)

What regular compensation does Bob Bear receive?

- (•) **Employee is paid hourly**
- ( ) Employee is paid on salary
- ( ) Employee does not have any base compensation

Hourly wage: 9.50

	Regular wages	Amount	Description
☑	Hourly wage overtime (x1.5)	14.25	
☐	Hourly wage overtime (x2)		
☐	Bonus		

One of the ways I pay this employee isn't on this list. What should I do?

Cancel | < Previous | Next >

UPS10.3.1174

Figure 9-5: ***All employee information can be edited later.***

Be sure to confirm your state tax obligations.

TIP

Highlight any employee in your list, and click the **Summary** button to view a printable summary of your employee. Consider printing and filing employee summaries, along with the papers your employee filled out, for future reference.

QuickBooks will automatically add the agency names for your state to your Vendor List if they are available in Intuit's database.

11. Click **Next** and enter the employee's federal tax information from the W-4 form (and W-5 form, if applicable) filled out by the employee.
12. Click **Next** and enter employee's state tax information from the relevant state withholding forms filled out by the employee.
13. Click **Finish** to return to the Payroll Setup window.
14. Repeat Steps 2–12 to add additional employees.
15. The Employee Setup section is finished. Click the **Continue** button to move to the Taxes section of the Payroll Setup Interview.

Set Up Payroll Taxes

The next section in the Payroll Setup Interview has to do with federal, state, and local taxes. Be sure you have your federal Employer Identification Number (EIN) and any state identification numbers for this section, as well as information on local taxes you might need to pay.

SET UP FEDERAL PAYROLL ITEMS

1. Click **Continue** to move to the federal income tax section of the Payroll Setup Interview.
2. Review the list of taxes that appears. You can select any tax and click **Edit** to review or change details.

Federal Tax	Description
Federal Withholding	Also known as Federal Withholding Tax
Advance Earned Income Credit	Also known as AEIC
Federal Unemployment	Also known as FUTA.
Medicare Company	Medicare Tax
Medicare Employee	Medicare Tax
Social Security Company	Also known as FICA.
Social Security Employee	Also known as FICA.

3. Click **Continue** to move to the state tax area, if applicable.

SET UP STATE PAYROLL ITEMS

1. Enter your state income tax, unemployment tax, and any other items required by your state.
2. Click the **Continue** button. If you chose multiple states, you will be prompted to enter the pertinent information for each one. Enter the information and click the **Continue** button.

NOTE

Providing year-to-date (YTD) information is a one-time process that only needs to be completed *if* your company was in operation and paying employees *and if* you are starting to use QuickBooks mid-year. If you have not yet paid any employees since the beginning of your fiscal year, you can skip this section.

QUICKSTEPS

SETTING YEAR-TO-DATE AMOUNTS

If your company has employees who have been paid through some prior payroll method, you will need to adjust the current balance of liabilities to ensure correct year-to-date totals on the paychecks.

1. Click **Continue** to move to the payroll history section of the Payroll Setup Interview.
2. Click **Yes** or **No** to indicate whether you have already paid payroll in this year and click **Continue**. If you choose No, skip to the next section.
3. Click **Yes** or **No** for each of the following items:
   - Created paychecks
   - Paid payroll liabilities
   - Paid non-tax liabilities
4. Click **Continue** to enter the first quarter's information.
5. If you selected paychecks, you will see a list of your employees. Select each employee and click Edit to enter amounts and dates paid for this quarter and click **Continue**.

Continued . . .

SET PAYMENT FREQUENCY

1. Click **Continue** to open the Schedule Tax Payment window and click **Next** to open the **Schedule Payment** window for the Federal 940.

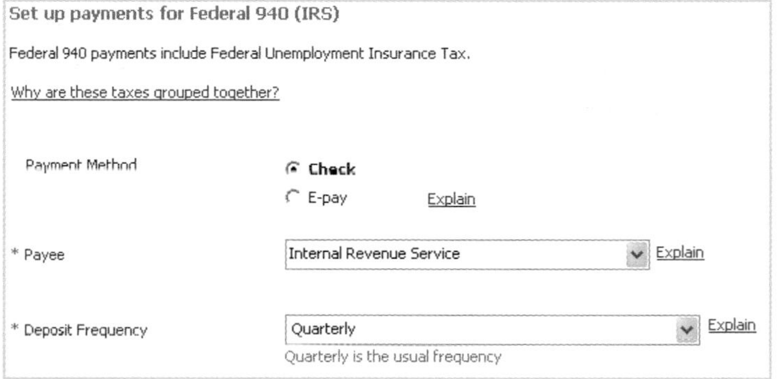

2. Select whether you wish to use E-Pay or Check to pay your liability, and then confirm the Payee and Deposit Frequency.
3. Click **Next** and repeat for each tax item.
4. Click Finish to move to E-Pay accounts. If you chose to use E-Pay in the earlier section, click the account and click **Edit** to enter your bank account and routing number before clicking **Finish**.
5. If you activated accounts for E-Pay, a View Enrollments screen will appear for review of information for the agencies you will be using E-Pay with. Read the information and close the window. You will see a summary of your agency enrollments, along with a note for any that need further action.

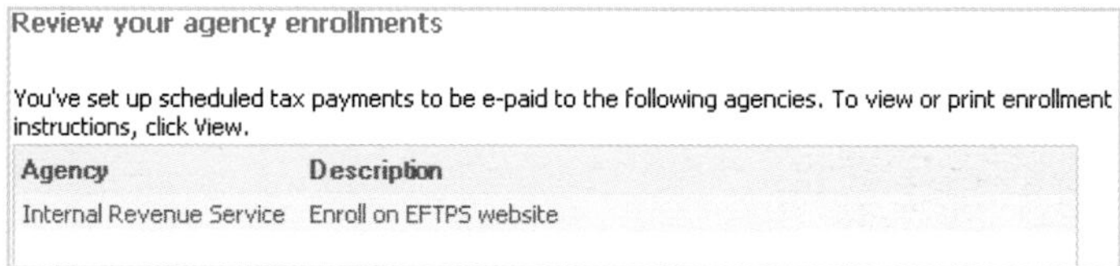

6. Click **Continue** to move to the Payroll History section.

   If you've set up manual payroll, you will now see a Congratulations page with information about where to edit your payroll information in the future. In this case, click **Continue** twice more and then click **Go To The Employee Center**. The Employee Center is displayed.

1 2 3 4 5 6 7 8 9 10

QUICKSTEPS

SETTING YEAR-TO-DATE AMOUNTS

(Continued)

6. If you selected payroll liabilities, QuickBooks will now display each of your tax vendors for you to enter tax payments to date. Enter any amounts you have paid for the fiscal quarter displayed, and click **Continue**.
7. If you selected non-tax liabilities, enter any non-tax payments made for this quarter and click **Continue**.
8. Repeat Steps 5–7 for each quarter that you paid taxes for this year.

You've now completed the payroll history portion of the Payroll Setup Interview. Be sure to review and check your data when you run payroll for the first time. After a few payroll periods, you will be more comfortable with the mechanism of running payroll and more confident of your payroll settings.

TIP

If you are upgrading, you may have data already entered. This cannot be edited in the Payroll Setup Interview.

DATA REVIEW

Now that you have entered all of your payroll data, Quickbooks can review your entries for accuracy.

1. Click **No** to skip this section; or click **Yes** to have QuickBooks review your payroll entries, and click **Continue**.
2. Click **Continue** and your prior quarter wages will be examined for errors. You'll receive a congratulations or information if there is any problem.
3. Click **Continue** and your current quarter wages will be examined for errors. You'll receive a congratulations or information if there is any problem.
4. Click **Continue** and you'll be given the opportunity to reconcile your 941 to current information.
5. Click **Continue** and click **Yes** or **No** as to whether you have filed a 941.
6. Click **Next**, enter all relevant information, click **Next**, enter the rest of the requested data, and click **Finish**. You'll receive a congratulations or information if there is any problem.
7. Click **Continue** and the Payroll Center example will appear.
8. Click **Continue** and then click **Go to the Payroll Center**.

USE THE PAYROLL CENTER

The Payroll Center is available for customers who have a subscription to one of the QuickBooks payroll solutions (Standard, Enhanced, or Assisted). The options available vary based on your payroll solution level.

To view the Payroll Center:

Click the **Employees** menu and click **Payroll Center**. The Payroll Center opens, as shown in Figure 9-6.

From here, you can run payroll, pay liabilities, or process payroll forms. Click the **Close** button (the X in the upper-right corner) when finished.

SET UP PAYROLL SCHEDULE

Before you can run payroll the first time, you need to set up at least one payroll schedule. Some companies will use multiple payroll frequencies to handle biweekly, weekly, monthly, or quarterly payments for employees.

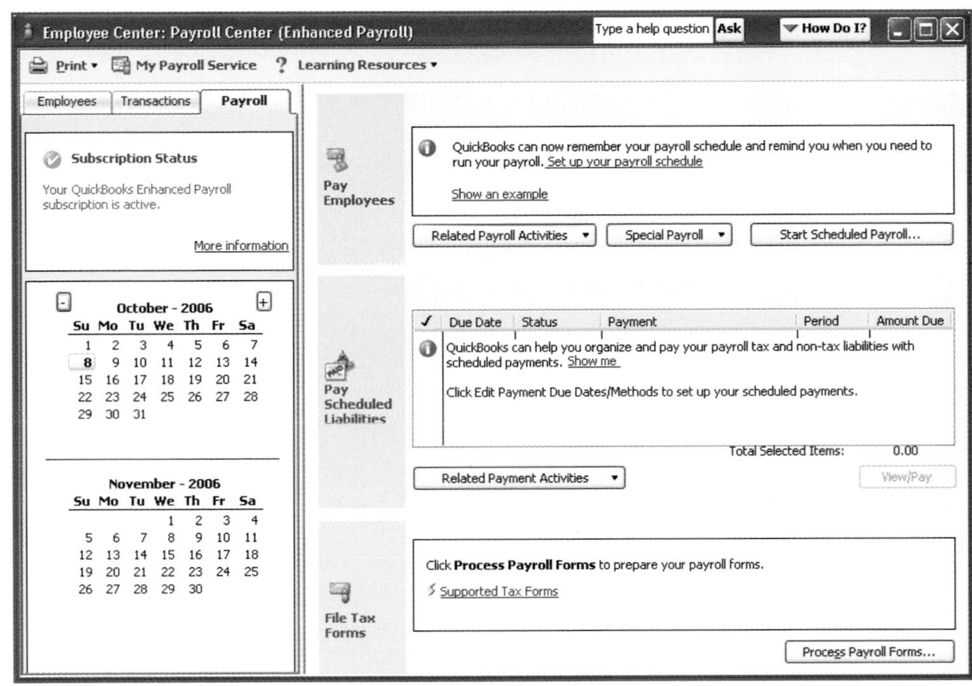

Figure 9-6: ***Access time, employee, and payroll functions from the Payroll Center as well as the Employees menu.***

1. Click **Set up your payroll schedule** in the Pay Employees section on your employee center (see Figure 9-7) and the Edit Pay Schedule window will open.
2. Type your Payroll Schedule name, such as Bi-Weekly, in the name field.
3. Click the Frequency down arrow and click the appropriate frequency, such as **Biweekly**.
4. Press **Tab** to move to the Pay Period End Date field and enter the appropriate date.
5. Press **Tab** to move to the Next Paycheck Date field and enter the appropriate date.
6. Press **Tab** to move to the Day of the week field and QuickBooks will update the day to match your paycheck date.

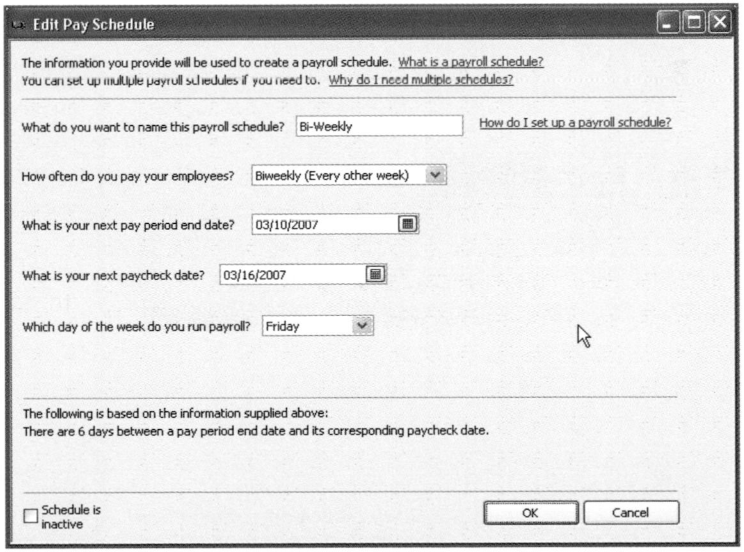

Figure 9-7: ***Create Payroll schedules as needed to match your company's practices.***

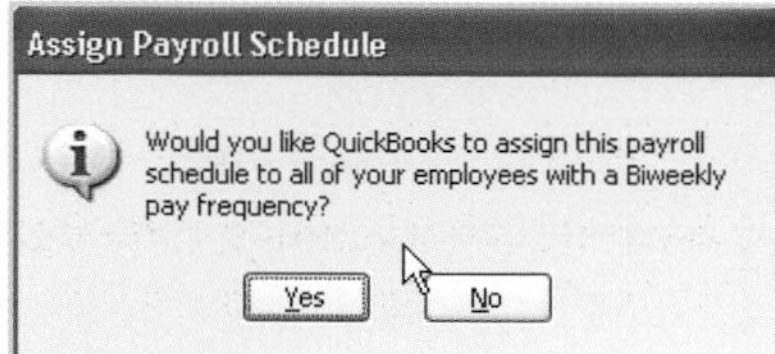

TIP

QuickBooks offers an Employee Organizer, which is integrated with QuickBooks to provide you access to up-to-date state and federal employment laws; additional reports; and selected forms, letters, and templates; as well as an e-mail-based help line for all employee-related questions. Visit www.payroll.com/services/employeeorganizer for more information.

TIP

If you see the Payroll Center when you click Employee Center, click the **Employees** tab in the upper-left area. They are just different tabs in the same window.

NOTE

Once you've activated employees and payroll, you'll have an additional employee section on your home page.

7. Review your information and click **OK**. A message may appear asking if you wish to apply this schedule to all of your employees that appear to match your choices. Click **Yes** and a message will appear informing you of how many employees were affected. Click **OK**.

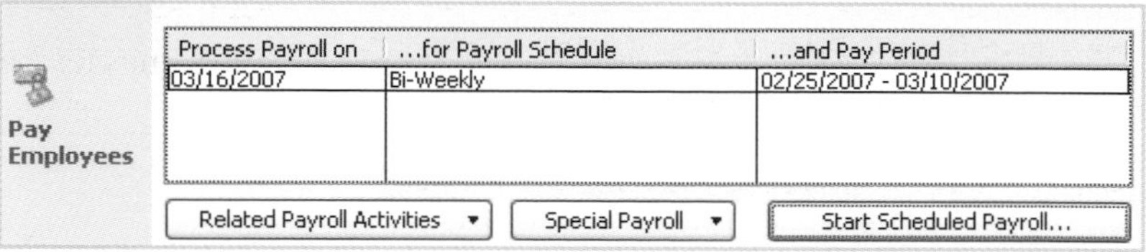

Your Pay Employees section will now have a Payroll schedule listed with the effective dates.

ACCESS THE EMPLOYEE CENTER

The new Employee Center is similar in look and function to the Customer and Vendor Centers. To access the Employee Center:

Click the **Employees** icon on the home page (or click the Employees menu and select **Employee Center**). The Employee Center is displayed (see Figure 9-8).

From here, you can work with all employee-related reports, activities, forms, and timesheets. Click the **Close** button (the X in the upper-right corner) when finished.

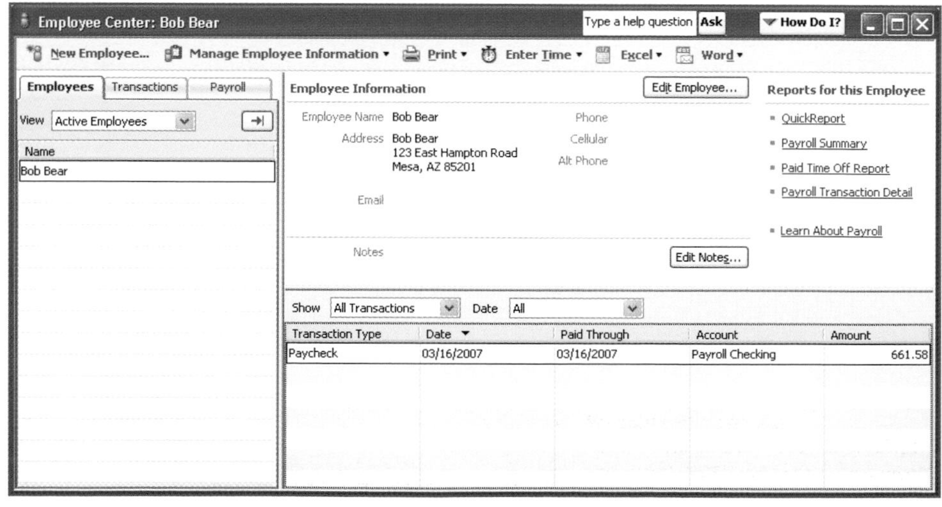

Figure 9-8: ***Double-click any transaction to open it for review or editing.***

Run and Maintain Payroll

To run payroll, you must use the Create Paycheck feature and *not* the Write Checks feature in order to have accurate withholdings, although you can use the same checking account.

Create and Print Paychecks

To create paychecks:

1. On the Payroll Center, click the Payroll Schedule you wish to run in the Pay Employees section and click the **Start Scheduled Payroll** button. The Enter Hours window opens, as shown in Figure 9-9. If you get an error message, you have the option to click **Go to Payroll Setup**, as described earlier in the chapter. QuickBooks will remind you to update your payroll tax tables on a regular basis and may update automatically before allowing you to create paychecks. You can also do a manual update (click the **Employees** menu and click **Get Payroll Updates**).

CAUTION

You may see a dialog box regarding year-to-date amounts. Confirm that you do not need to enter them, or return to the Setup YTD Amounts window before creating paychecks. Do *not* create paychecks before entering YTD amounts if they need to be entered.

NOTE

In the Enter Hours window, you will *not* see vendors (subcontractors), employees identified as owners, inactive employees, or employees with a release date earlier than the current pay date.

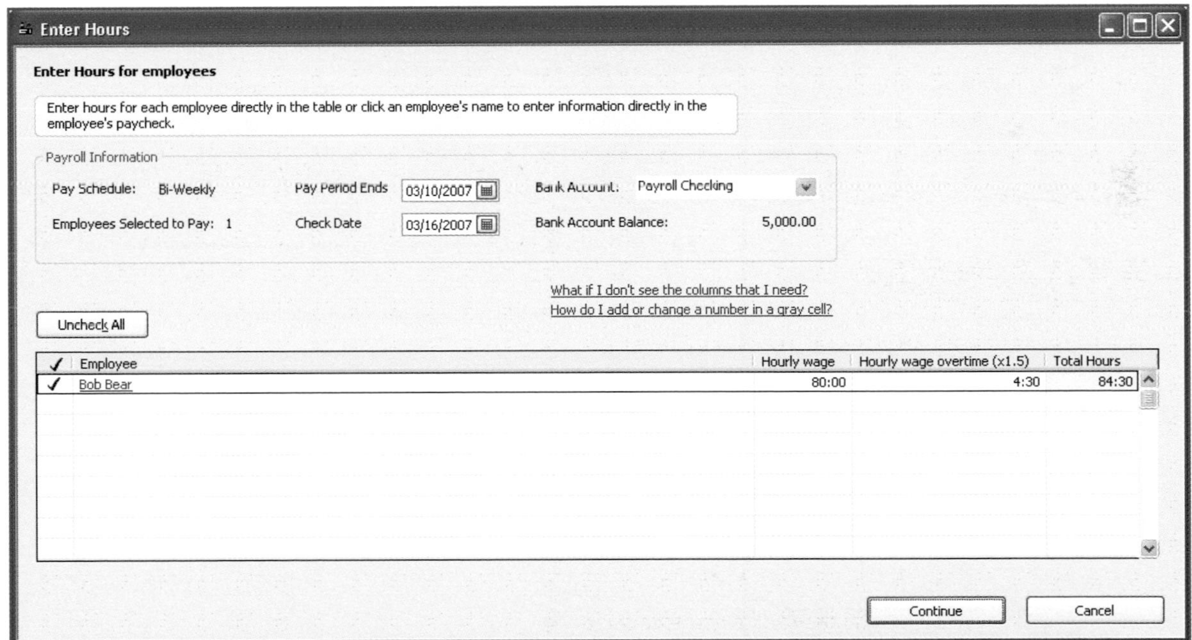

Figure 9-9: ***It's easy to enter all employee hours here in the hourly wage and overtime wage columns.***

TIP

Each time you create a paycheck, you are incurring a liability against your company to be paid later. This liability includes state and federal taxes and any shared expenses, like medical benefits. Be sure to allow for this expense.

2. Click the **Bank Account** down arrow, and click the bank account against which you are writing payroll checks. If you only have one bank account, you can use it for regular checks and payroll checks, but just make sure to always create paychecks using this window.
3. Confirm the dates in the **Check Date** field and **Pay Period Ends** field.
4. Ensure the employee names you will be entering paychecks for are selected. If the employee is a salaried employee, the salary amount will be entered. If he is an hourly employee, you will need to enter the amount of hours (and overtime hours).
5. Enter hours worked in the appropriate columns for regular wages and overtime wages.
6. Click the **Continue** button. The Review and Create Paychecks window opens as shown in Figure 9-10.
7. Click on each employee name to open the Review or Change paycheck window as seen in Figure 9-11 and click **Close** when finished reviewing or editing. Payroll deductions will be automatically entered for you if a payroll service has been activated. Otherwise, you will need to manually enter the amounts.

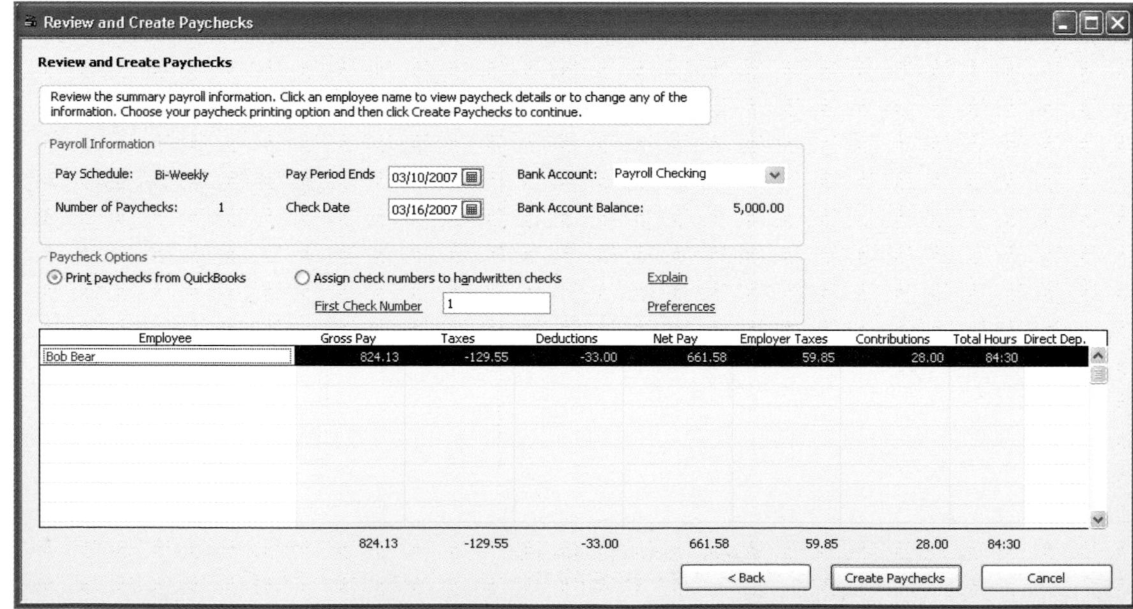

Figure 9-10: ***Click any employee name to review the detailed paycheck.***

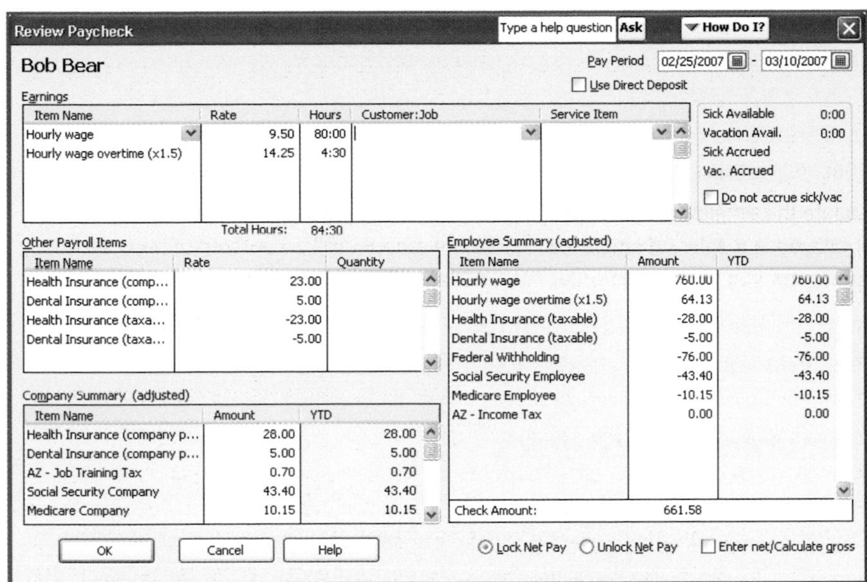

Figure 9-11: ***Review and edit any amounts needed, with the exception of YTD amounts.***

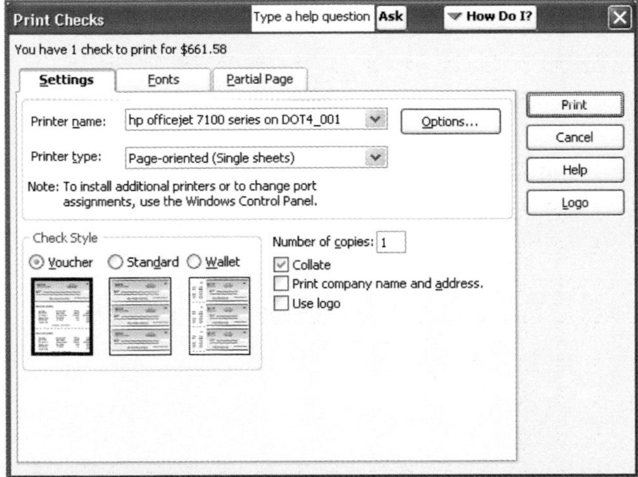

Figure 9-12: ***If your company name, address, and logo are not already printed on the check, click the Print Company Name and Address and Use Logo check boxes.***

8. Click **Print Paychecks from QuickBooks** unless you are using handwritten checks.
9. Click **Continue** and a Confirmation and Next Steps window will open. The paychecks have been created and are ready for printing. The process of creating them calculates taxes, tracking both the employee balances and what you owe the tax agencies. You can now print paychecks or close this window.
10. Click **Print Paychecks** to open the Select Paychecks to print window. Confirm that the check number is correct and the employee checks are all selected.
11. Click **OK** and the Print Checks window will open as seen in Figure 9-12. Load your checks correctly in the printer, and verify that the correct printer is selected in the Printer Name field.

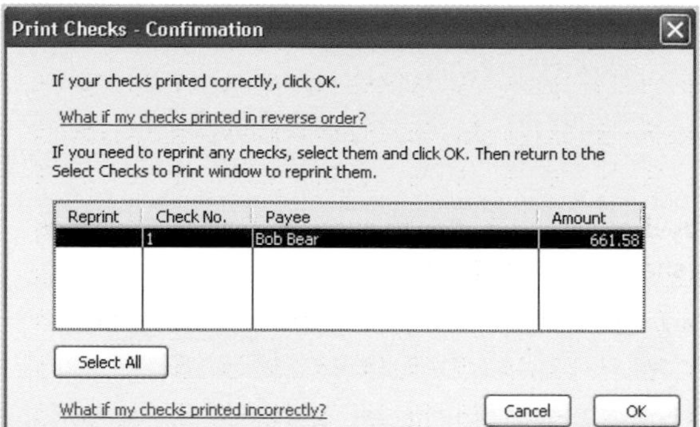

CAUTION

Make sure your year-end closing date is set so that you do not accidentally edit payroll checks on which you have already paid company taxes. See Chapter 8 for more information on closing dates.

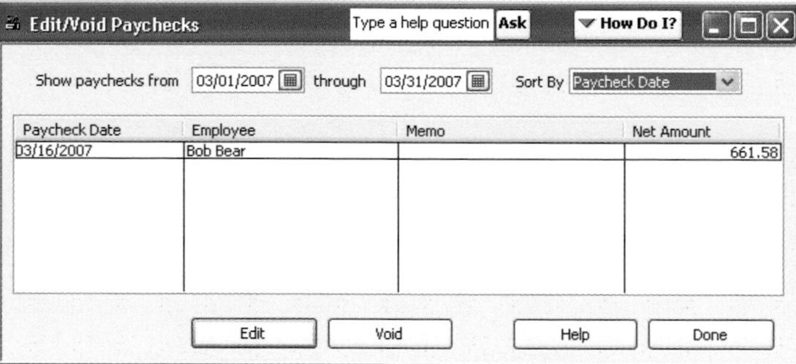

12. In the Check Style area, click the option that corresponds to the type of check you have. Most paychecks are printed on voucher-style checks, which have a check on the top and the deduction information on the bottom of an 8.5" × 11" sheet.
13. Click **Print**. The check is sent to your printer, and the Print Checks – Confirmation window will open. If any check did not print correctly, click that check to mark it.
14. Click **OK**. The dialog box closes and the paycheck is updated with the check number, or continues to be marked To Be Printed if selected. Close the Confirmation window if it still open.

Once paychecks are created, you can also print them by clicking the **File** menu, clicking **Print Forms**, and clicking **Paychecks**.

Edit or Void Paychecks

With QuickBooks, you can edit, void, review, or reprint a paycheck. If an employee has lost a paycheck, or if you need to make changes after creating it but before printing, you can make those changes, but don't change a check that is unaccounted for.

To edit or void a paycheck:

1. Click the **Employees** menu and click **Edit/Void Paychecks**. The Edit/Void Paychecks window opens.
2. Click in the beginning and ending date fields, and choose the date range during which the paycheck you are looking for was written.
3. Click the check you want to void or edit. Then, either:
   - Click the **Void** button and then confirm your choice by typing YES in the next screen.

     –Or–
   - Click the **Edit** button to view the check for reviewing, editing, or printing, as shown in Figure 9-13.

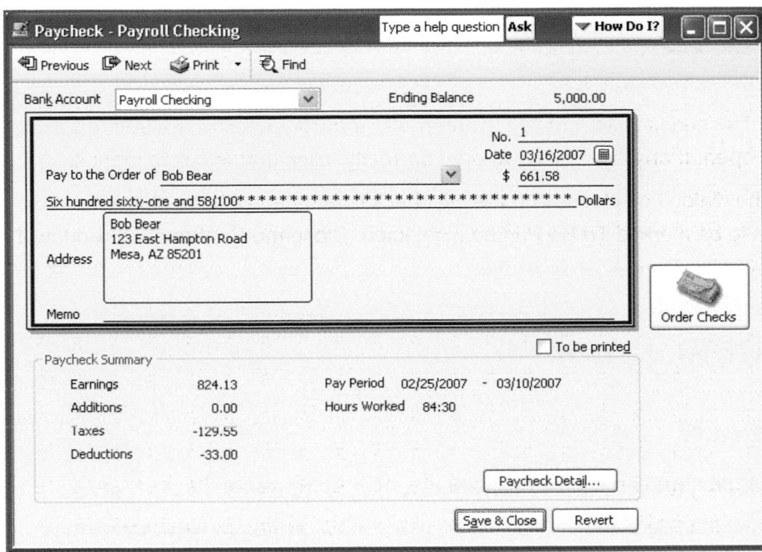

Figure 9-13: ***A paycheck looks different from an average check and has additional details available.***

4. After editing your check, you can:
   - Click the **Print** button to print the check now.
   - Click the **To Be Printed** check box if you want to print the check later.
   - Click the **Paycheck Detail** button to open the Review Paycheck window, as shown in Figure 9-14.
5. After making any changes necessary, click **OK** to return to the Paycheck window.
6. Click **Save & Close** to save your changes and close the window. Confirm that you want to save your changes if asked.
7. Click the **Done** button to close the Edit/Void Paychecks window.

You can discard changes by clicking the **Revert** button or by clicking **No** when QuickBooks asks if you want to save your changes.

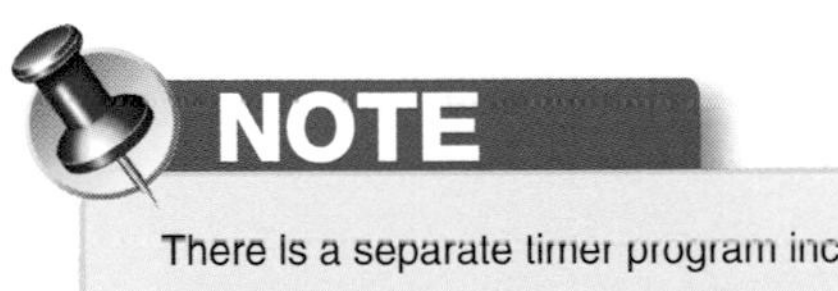

There is a separate timer program included with QuickBooks (all editions but Simple Start). Use this program if you need to specifically track a lot of small periods of time for many people.

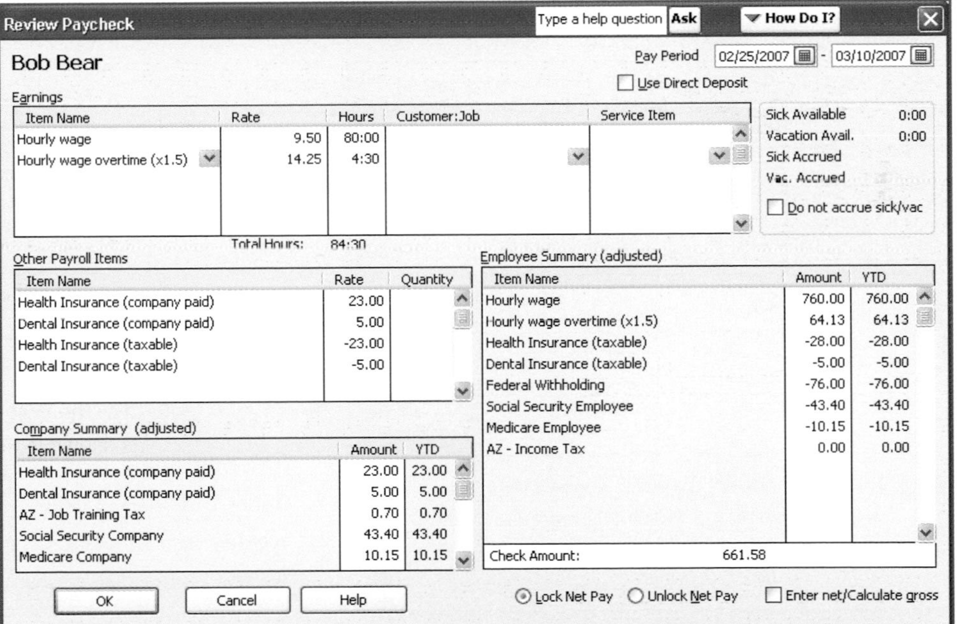

Figure 9-14: ***From the Review Paycheck window, you can edit any item entered incorrectly and then reprint the check.***

> **NOTE**
>
> Activities will appear on both single-activity and weekly timesheets, so it doesn't really matter which way you enter them; use whichever method is more convenient for you.

> **QUICKSTEPS**
>
> **ENTERING A SINGLE ACTIVITY**
>
> Enter a single activity for individual entries or to time an event. Use the weekly timesheets (see "Enter Weekly Timesheets") to enter hours for the week.
>
> 1. Click the **Employees** (or **Customers**) menu, click **Enter Time**, and click **Timer / Single Activity**. The Time/Enter Single Activity window opens.
>
> 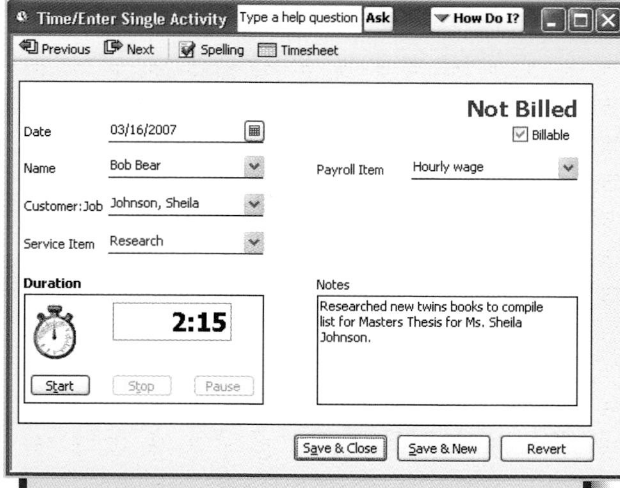
>
>
> 2. Confirm or correct the date. Today's date is displayed by default, which you *must* use to use the timer.
>
> *Continued . . .*

Track Time

The ability to track time is not available in QuickBooks Simple Start edition, but it is available in all other editions.

It is used to enter employee hours for payroll, billable hours for customer billing, or both. Time can be tracked within QuickBooks as a single entry for each activity or as a weekly timesheet.

Turn On Time Tracking

Before you can use the time-tracking feature, you need to activate it in the Preferences window.

1. Click the **Edit** menu and click **Preferences**.
2. Click the **Time Tracking** icon on the left, and click the **Company Preferences** tab.
3. In the Do You Track Time? area, click **Yes**.

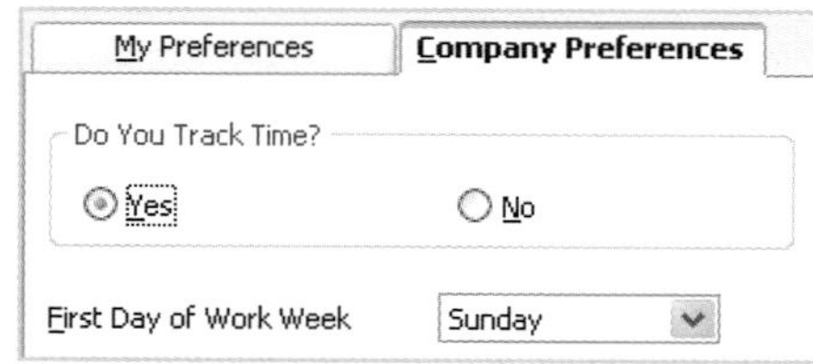

4. Click the **First Day Of Work Week** down arrow, and choose the day you will use as your first day of the week for payroll. This will be used for entering time on a weekly basis.
5. Click **OK**. Your preferences are saved and the window closes.

Enter Weekly Timesheets

Entering single activities is useful for occasional use or for keeping detailed notes, but weekly timesheets are more streamlined for many entries. Use weekly timesheets to enter payroll-related timesheets and/or billable time that will be charged to customers.

ENTERING A SINGLE ACTIVITY

(Continued)

3. Press the **TAB** key to move to the Name field, and type the name of the employee or subcontractor whose time you are tracking.
4. Press the **TAB** key to move to the Customer:Job field, and type the name of the customer for whom you are tracking time. A window may appear, asking if you wish to use this employee's time to create paychecks. Click **Yes**. You can edit time at paycheck creation.
5. Press the **TAB** key to move to the Service Item field, and type the service item for which you are tracking time.
6. Press the **TAB** key to move to the Time field. Type the time in either hours and minutes, such as 2:15, or in hours and fractions of an hour, such as 2.25. To time an activity, click the **Start** button. The timer will start from the time you have entered until you click **Stop**, click **Pause**, or close the window.
7. Click the **Billable** check box if you need to charge this time back to the customer.
8. Click the **Payroll Item** down arrow, and choose the relevant payroll item if this time activity is for an employee. If you chose not to use time data to create paychecks, the Payroll Item field will not appear for this employee.
9. Press the **TAB** key to move to the Notes section, and type any notes pertaining to this time activity.
10. Click **Save & Close** (or click **Save & New** to continue adding time activities).

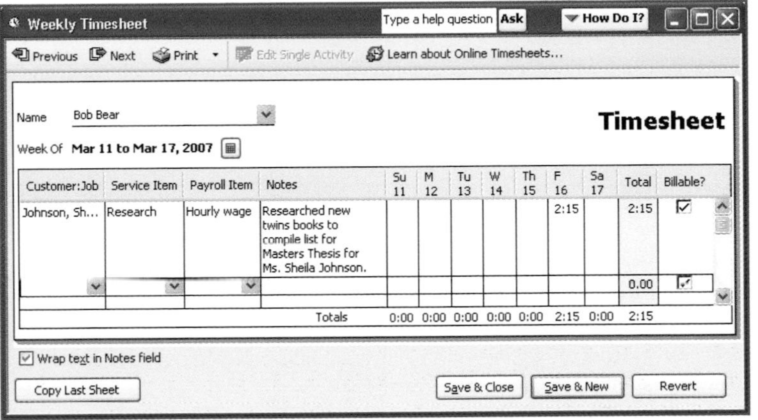

Figure 9-15: ***Make sure you are on the correct date before you start entering activities, or you will lose your information when you move to the correct date.***

To enter weekly timesheets:

1. Click the **Employees** (or **Customers**) menu, click **Enter Time**, and click **Use Weekly Timesheet**. The Weekly Timesheet window opens (see Figure 9-15).
2. Confirm or correct the date. Use the **Previous** and **Next** buttons at the top of the timesheet to move to earlier or later dates, respectively.
3. Click in the **Name** field, and type the name of the employee or subcontractor whose time you are tracking. As you will see, any single items entered appear in the weekly timesheet as well.
4. Press the **TAB** key to move to the Customer:Job field, and type the name of the customer for whom you are tracking time. If you are entering payroll hours, you can leave this field blank.
5. Press the **TAB** key to move to the Service Item field, and type the service item for which you are tracking time. If you are entering payroll hours, you can leave this field blank.
6. Click the **Payroll Item** down arrow, and choose the relevant payroll item if this time activity is for an employee set up to use time data for payroll.
7. Press the **TAB** key to move to the Notes field, and type any notes pertaining to this time activity. You can control how the text wraps by clicking the **Wrap text in Notes field** check box, located at the bottom.

8. Press the **TAB** key to move to the relevant fields for the days of the week. Type the time in either hours and minutes, such as 2:15, or in hours and fractions of an hour, such as 2.25.
9. If the time is to be charged back to the customer, make sure the billable column is checked, as it is in Figure 9-15. If the time is for payroll information only, click the **Billable** check box to clear the check.
10. Click **Save & Close** (or click **Save & New** to continue adding time activities).

Using weekly timesheets is the best way to enter payroll time data. When you next create a paycheck, QuickBooks will ask if you want to use the time data available.

Paying Taxes

Once you have tax items set up, QuickBooks tracks your taxes and gives you an easy way to pay everyone, including Uncle Sam, your local state agencies, your employees, and, of course, yourself. Your responsibilities as an employer include paying all withholdings on your scheduled basis, and QuickBooks makes this easy.

Review and Pay Payroll Taxes

Most companies need to pay payroll taxes at least quarterly, although some companies pay them monthly. Verify with your local tax agencies the frequency with which you need to pay any taxes. Before paying taxes, you can run a payroll report to review your payments, withholdings, and amounts due to tax agencies.

RUN A PAYROLL REPORT

To run a payroll report:

1. Click the **Reports** menu, click **Employees and Payroll**, and click **Payroll Summary**. A report is displayed similar to that pictured in Figure 9-16. Add the Payroll Summary report to your Icon bar for easy access and review.
2. Click the **Close** button when finished reviewing this report.

See Chapter 10 for information on customizing and memorizing reports.

TIP

Both federal and state (if using QuickBooks Enhanced payroll service) payroll forms are available for you to process, print, and mail. Click the **Employees** menu and click **Process Payroll Forms**.

Payroll Summary

Modify Report... | Memorize... | Print... | E-mail | Export... | Hide Header | Refresh

Dates: Last Calendar Quarter From 01/01/2007 To 03/31/2007 Columns Employee

3:07 PM
04/10/07

Butterfly Books and Bytes
Payroll Summary
January through March 2007

	Bob Bear			TOTAL		
	Hours	Rate	Jan - Mar 07	Hours	Rate	Jan - Mar 07
Employee Wages, Taxes and Adjustments						
Gross Pay						
Hourly wage	80	9.50	760.00	80		760.00
Hourly wage overtime (x1.5)	4.5	14.25	64.13	4.5		64.13
Total Gross Pay	84.5		824.13	84.5		824.13
Adjusted Gross Pay	84.5		824.13	84.5		824.13
Taxes Withheld						
Federal Withholding			-76.00			-76.00
Medicare Employee			-10.15			-10.15
Social Security Employee			-43.40			-43.40
AZ - Income Tax			0.00			0.00
Total Taxes Withheld			-129.55			-129.55
Deductions from Net Pay						
Dental Insurance (taxable)			-5.00			-5.00
Health Insurance (taxable)			-28.00			-28.00
Total Deductions from Net Pay			-33.00			-33.00
Net Pay	84.5		661.58	84.5		661.58
Employer Taxes and Contributions						
Federal Unemployment			5.60			5.60
Medicare Company			10.15			10.15
Social Security Company			43.40			43.40
AZ - Unemployment			0.00			0.00
Dental Insurance (company paid)			5.00			5.00
Health Insurance (company paid)			23.00			23.00
AZ Job Training Tax			0.70			0.70
Total Employer Taxes and Contributions			87.85			87.85

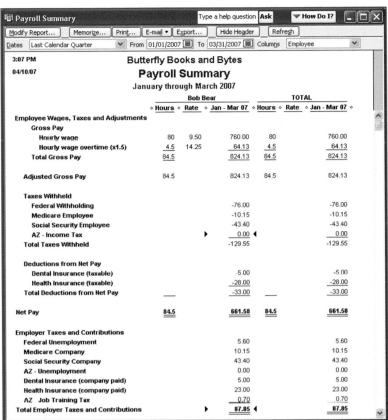

Figure 9-16: ***The Payroll Summary report gives you a quick and easy way to view your employee payroll information.***

PAY LIABILITIES

You can generate checks to pay taxes and other liabilities (such as insurance, garnishments, and so on).

To pay liabilities:

1. Click the **Employees** menu and click the **Payroll Center**. The Payroll Center opens as shown in Figure 9-17.
2. Click each item you wish to pay in the center Pay Scheduled Liabilities section to place a check mark in the leftmost column.
3. Click the **View/Pay** button. If a Choose Bank Account window appears, click the Account down arrow, select the appropriate account and click **OK**.

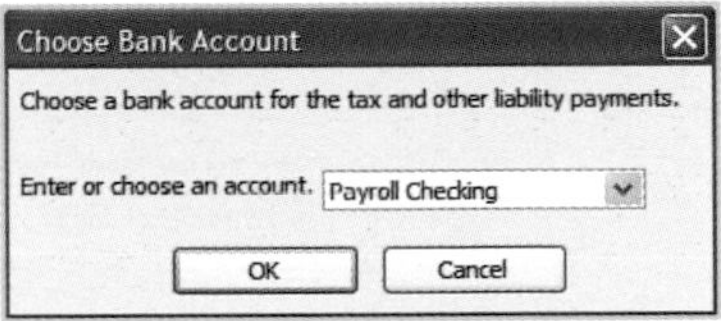

4. The Liability Payment window opens, as shown in Figure 9-18. If you chose more than one liability, click the **Save & Next** button to review all checks (Notice Payment 3 of 3 in the top-left corner of Figure 9-18). You can E-Pay now or print the checks now or later. If you are going to print them later, click the **To Be Printed** check box.
5. Click **Save & Close** for the last check (only option) to close the Liability Check window. A Payment Summary window will open.

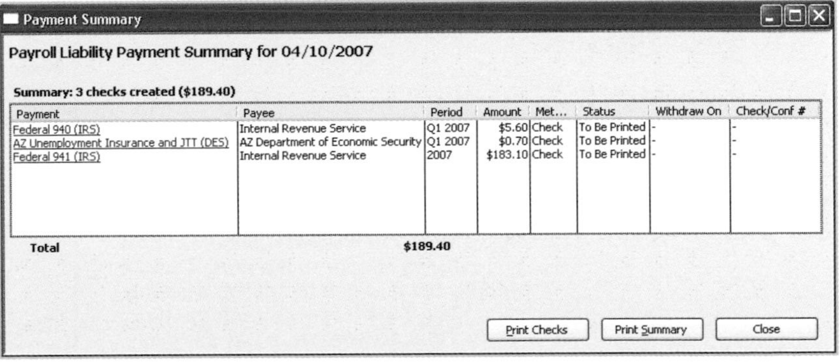
Payment Summary

Payroll Liability Payment Summary for 04/10/2007

Summary: 3 checks created ($189.40)

Payment	Payee	Period	Amount	Met...	Status	Withdraw On	Check/Conf #
Federal 940 (IRS)	Internal Revenue Service	Q1 2007	$5.60	Check	To Be Printed	-	-
AZ Unemployment Insurance and JTT (DES)	AZ Department of Economic Security	Q1 2007	$0.70	Check	To Be Printed	-	-
Federal 941 (IRS)	Internal Revenue Service	2007	$183.10	Check	To Be Printed	-	-

Total $189.40

Print Checks | Print Summary | Close

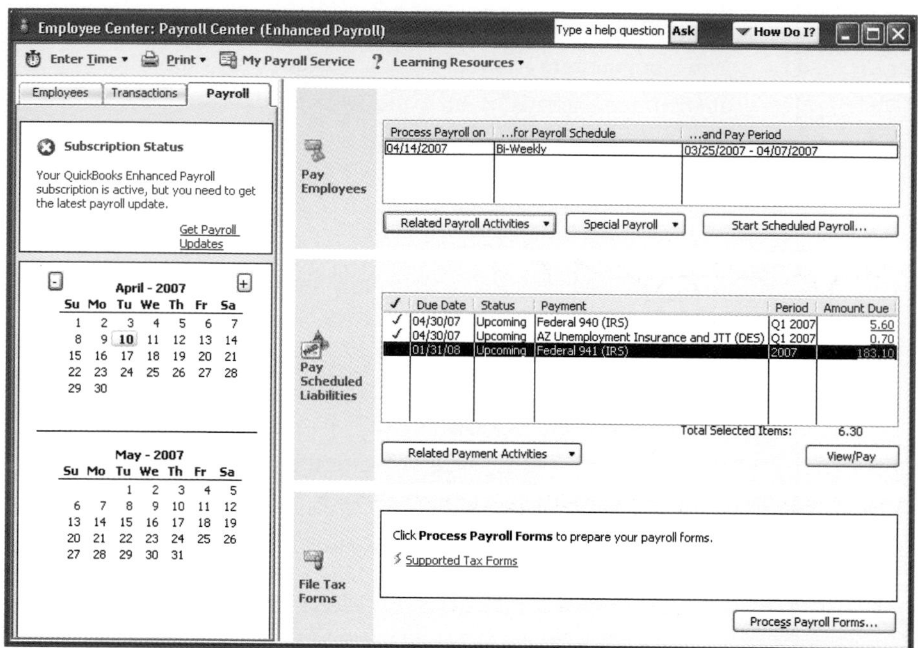

Figure 9-17: ***The Employee Center allows you to pay liabilities and file tax forms in addition to paying employees.***

6. Review the Payment summary window and make your choice to **Print Checks**, **Print Summary**, or **Close**. If you choose not to print checks now, you can click the **File** menu, click **Print Forms**, and click **Print Checks**. Be sure to select the correct account to see your checks.

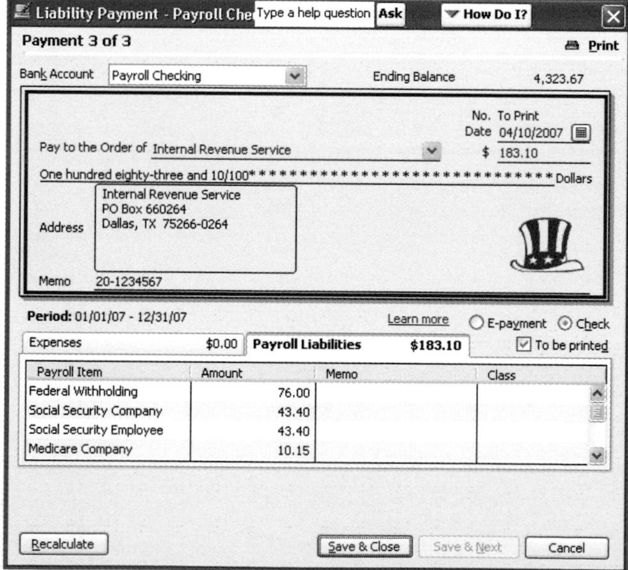

Figure 9-18: ***The Liability Check window looks similar to the Write Checks window, but it is tied to liability tracking. Don't write checks from the Write Checks window to pay liabilities.***

How to...

- *Use the Report Center*
- *Use the Report Menu*
- *Set Report Preferences*
- *Use the Button Bar*
- *Customize Reports*
- *Memorize Reports*
- *Use Memorized Reports*
- *Organize Memorized Reports*
- *Printing to a File*
- *Print Reports*
- *E-Mailing Reports in PDF or Excel Format*
- *Export Reports*

Chapter 10 Creating Reports

One of the most powerful features of QuickBooks is flexible, immediate reporting. Create a report almost as fast as you think about it from a wide assortment of preset reports, or customize any report to meet your company's needs. Then memorize it for easy report generation on a regular basis. In addition to standard reports, graphs are available for certain views, and all reports can be exported to Microsoft Excel, where they can be manipulated and have additional graphs generated. Reports can also be e-mailed in PDF format.

Create Company and Financial Reports

A paperless office is a wonderful thing. With QuickBooks, a click of the button changes a daily report to monthly or sorts clients from alphabetical order into their sales volume order. You can get immediate answers to questions without having printed a thing or waiting for accounting or data personnel.

CAUTION

Reports are only as accurate as the data from which they are created. Enter all of your information on a daily basis and make a commitment to accuracy.

TIP

Click the **More** link at the end of each report description on the Report Center for more detailed information.

Hover mouse over report icon to show report sample

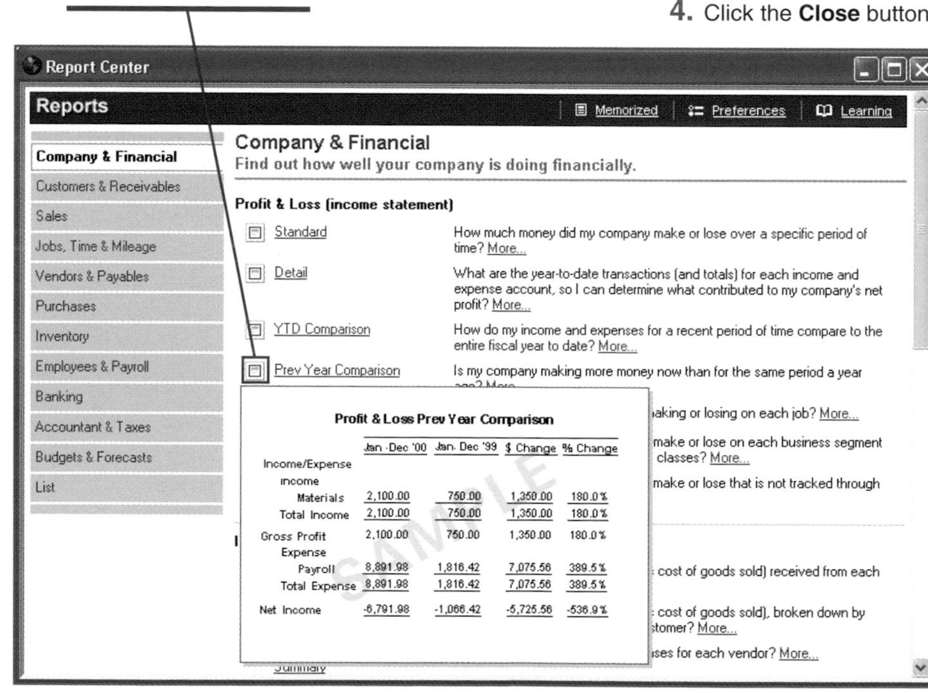

Figure 10-1: Move your mouse pointer over any of the small icons to see a sample report.

Use the Report Center

If you are unfamiliar with accounting terminology or are looking for a specific type of report, use the Report Center to preview sample reports and to create reports using your own data.

To view the Report Center:

1. Click the **Reports** menu and click **Report Center** (or click **Report Center** on the Navigation bar). The Report Center opens, as shown in Figure 10-1.
2. Click the different tabs on the left to see a detailed list of the reports available and a description of each.
3. Click the name of the report you want to create, for example, click **Standard** (under Profit & Loss on the Company & Financial tab). The report is displayed with default settings, as shown in Figure 10-2.
4. Click the **Close** button (the X in the upper-right corner) to close the report.

REPORT GROUPS

Reports are grouped into the following categories:

- **Company & Financial** includes traditional business reports, such as profit and loss, income and expense statement, balance sheet, and cash flow. Net Worth and Income and Expense can be viewed as graphs as well.
- **Customers & Receivables** includes accounts-receivable aging reports on overdue customers, customer balances, phone numbers and contact lists, and price lists reports.
- **Sales** includes reports broken down by customer, item, rep, and open sales orders as well as a Sales Graph.
- **Jobs, Time & Mileage** includes job profitability reports, job estimate versus actual reports, time reports, and mileage reports.
- **Vendors & Payables** includes accounts-payable aging reports on overdue bills, vendor balances, phone numbers and contact lists, 1099s, and sales tax reports.

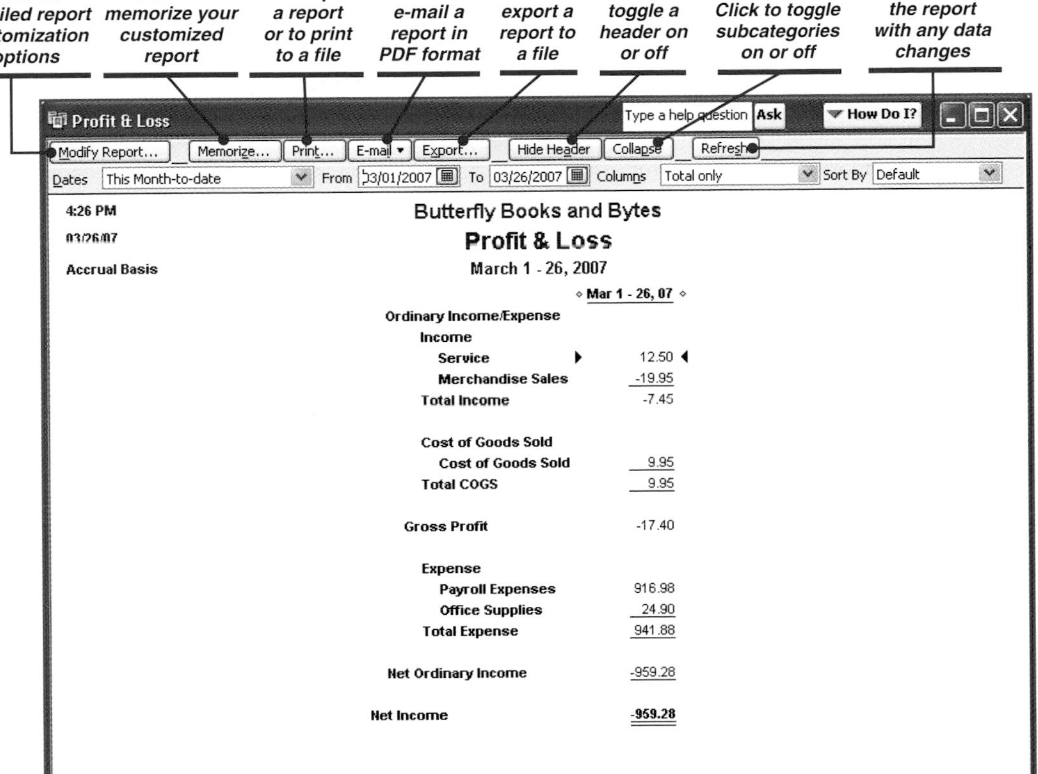

*Figure 10-2: **You can customize reports by using the buttons and drop-down menus at the top of each report window.***

- **Purchases** includes reports broken down by vendor, item, or purchase order.
- **Inventory** includes valuation and stock status reports, including pending builds (see Chapter 7 for more information on inventory).
- **Employees & Payroll** includes reports on payroll items, transactions, liabilities, employee earnings, employee withholdings, contact lists, and paid time off.
- **Banking** includes deposit reports; check reports, including missing checks; and reconciliation reports, including discrepancies.
- **Accountant & Taxes** includes reports on account activities, such as trial balances, general ledger, audit trail, journal, account listings, fixed asset listing, and income tax preparation information.
- **Budgets & Forecasts** includes budget overview reports, budgeted costs versus actual costs reports, budget profit and loss forecast overviews, and forecasted income versus actual income as well as a Budget vs. Actual Graph.
- **List** includes phone numbers and contact lists for all name groups, as well as lists of accounts, items, payroll items, fixed assets, terms, To Do items, and memorized transactions.
- **Industry Specific** reports in some versions of QuickBooks include customized reports for Contractors, Manufacturing & Wholesale, Professional Services, Retail, and Nonprofit.

TIP

Customize your report and then click the **View** menu and click **Add <Report Name> To Icon Bar** for quick access.

TIP

You can print any list while in the List window by clicking the **File** menu and clicking **Print List**. Try printing lists and then printing reports, and see which method you prefer.

4:33 PM	Butterfly Books and Bytes	
03/26/07	**Balance Sheet**	
Accrual Basis	As of March 26, 2007	
		Mar 26, 07
	ASSETS	
	Current Assets	
	Checking/Savings	
	Payroll Checking	4,338.42
	Checking	23,801.05
	Total Checking/Savings	28,139.47
	Accounts Receivable	
	Accounts Receivable	134.81
	Total Accounts Receivable	134.81
	Other Current Assets	
	Inventory Asset	448.00
	Total Other Current Assets	448.00
	Total Current Assets	28,722.28
	TOTAL ASSETS	**28,722.28**
	LIABILITIES & EQUITY	
	Liabilities	
	Current Liabilities	
	Accounts Payable	
	Accounts Payable	397.86
	Total Accounts Payable	397.86
	Other Current Liabilities	
	Payroll Liabilities	255.40
	Sales Tax Payable	14.05
	Total Other Current Liabilities	269.45
	Total Current Liabilities	667.31
	Total Liabilities	667.31
	Equity	
	Retained Earnings	100.20
	Opening Bal Equity	30,433.06
	Net Income	-2,478.29
	Total Equity	28,054.97
	TOTAL LIABILITIES & EQUITY	**28,722.28**

Figure 10-4: ***When you move from a different accounting system to QuickBooks, running a balance sheet for the same date in both systems is a good way to ensure that your new system is correctly set up.***

Use the Report Menu

Create reports and graphs from the Report menu on a regular basis. Your version of QuickBooks may have different reports than seen here, so the best way to learn what each report does is to run it.

1. Click the **Reports** menu and click the grouping you want to use, for example, **Company & Financial**, as shown in Figure 10-3.
2. Click the report name you want to run, such as **Balance Sheet Standard**. The report window opens (see Figure 10-4).
3. Review the report and click the **Close** button (the X in the upper-right corner) when finished.

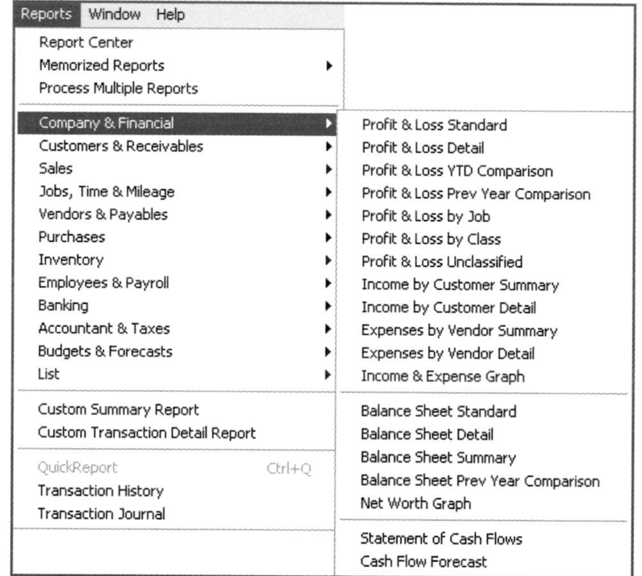

Figure 10-3: ***Run any report by clicking it.***

TIP

Zoom in by double-clicking any number in a report to see either a subreport of the transactions that make up an amount or the transaction itself. Keep double-clicking subsequent reports that open to zoom into the transaction in greater detail.

COMMON REPORTS

Commonly used reports in QuickBooks include the following:

- **Profit and Loss Statement** (located under Company & Financial) lists all income and expenses, and then calculates the difference, showing your profit (or loss). View year-to-date (YTD) comparisons or previous-year **comparisons** to see trends in your business. This report is also known as an Income Statement.
- **Balance Sheet** (located under Company & Financial) shows a snapshot of your business on a specific date. The current value of assets, liabilities, and equity (the difference between assets and liabilities) is shown. Equity is also considered the net worth of the business.
- **Employee, Vendor, or Customer Contact List** (located under Employee, Vendor, or Customer) lists the names, addresses, and phone numbers, as well as specific related fields, of whichever group you choose. Each contact list is located under the related grouping.
- **Payroll Reports** (located under Employees & Payroll) list the wages and taxes paid on paychecks, which is useful to have on hand when filing forms at the end of each tax period.
- **Sales Reports by Item, Customer, or Rep** (available under Sales) allows you to see where sales are the strongest. A sales graph shows you a pictorial representation, with both a pie graph and a bar chart that you can customize according to item, customer, or rep.
- **Budget Reports** (located under Budget & Forecasts) reflect where you stand in relation to your budget, thus allowing you to evaluate your business's success against your plan and to consider alternatives, such as adjusting income and expenses or altering your budget.

GRAPHING INFORMATION

In addition to printed reports, you can create graphs to see a pictorial representation of your data. As with reports, you can double-click any (graphical) total to open a subgraph or subreport summarizing how that total was calculated. You can then double-click items in that subreport to zoom into the actual transactions.

1 2 3 4 5 6 7 8 9 10

Figure 10-5: Click the Income button at the bottom of the graph to change the pie chart display from expense to income accounts.

To create a graph-based report:

1. Click the **Report** menu and click the grouping you want to use, for example, **Company & Financial**.
2. Click **Income & Expense Graph**. The graph is displayed, as shown in Figure 10-5.
3. Review the graph and click the **Close** button (the X in the upper-right corner) when finished.

Navigate and Modify Reports

Standard reports in QuickBooks are based on default settings that most people use; however, your business may require different settings. You can modify any report at any time to get the information you need. Memorize reports for recurring use, and add a report to the Icon bar for frequent use.

Set Report Preferences

QuickBooks contains a number of preferences that you can set to affect all reports. Reports & Graphs (used as an example here) have both My Preferences and Company Preferences (see Chapter 8).

To set report preferences:

1. Click the **Edit** menu and click **Preferences**. The Preferences window opens.
2. Click **Reports & Graphs** on the left (see Figure 10-6).
3. Select from among the following settings:
   - **Prompt Me To Modify Report Options Before Opening A Report** opens the Modify Report window each time a report is run. This is useful if you always customize a report; otherwise, this feature may slow you down. Try it if you are unsure. You can always turn it off again.
   - **Refresh Automatically** will re-run the report when any change is made in QuickBooks that affects that report. If you are on a network or have a large, slow data file, you can choose to be prompted to refresh or simply not refresh while you're looking at a report. Each report window has a Refresh button that you can click at any time.

TIP

Right-click any item in a graph to see the dollar amount of the corresponding section. Double-click any item in the graph to zoom in to a more detailed graph or report.

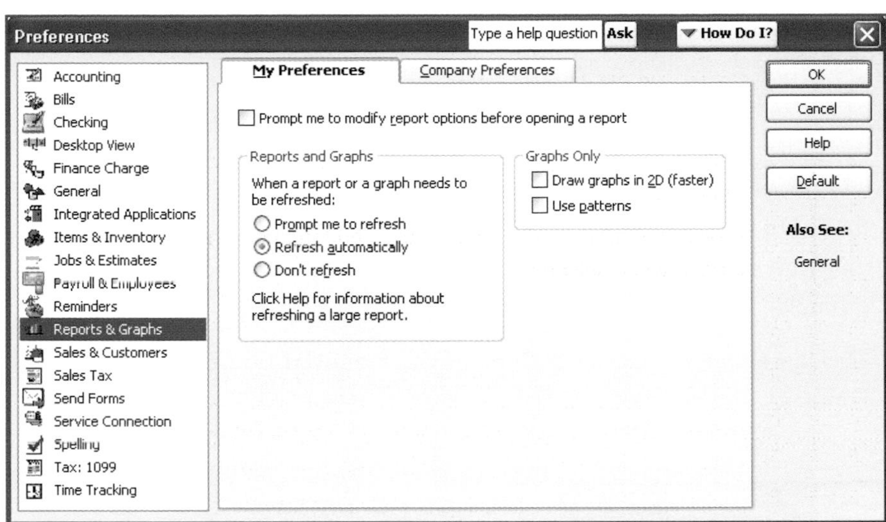

Figure 10-6: ***You can modify reports according to personal preferences as well as company preferences.***

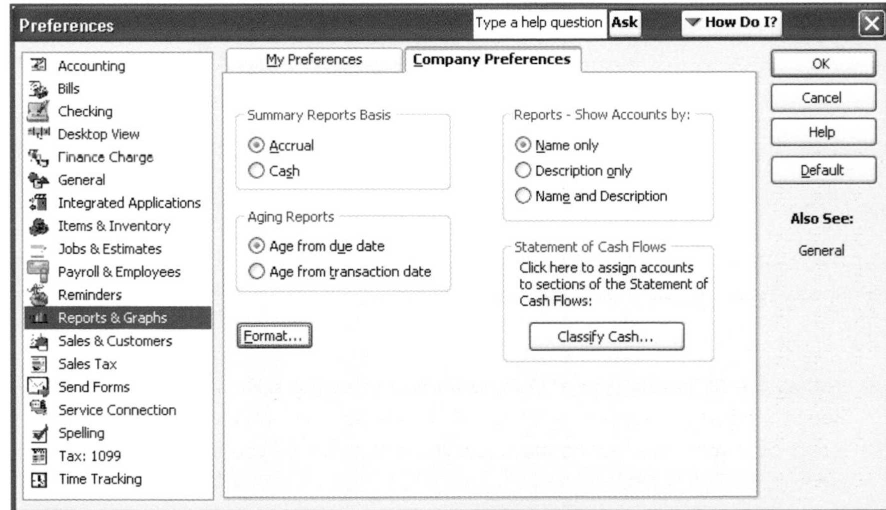

Figure 10-7: ***Changing the default settings here changes the settings of all reports, with the exception of memorized custom reports.***

- **Graphs** can be drawn in two dimensions (2-D) or in patterns instead of in full color (see Figure 10-5 for an example of a full-color graph). This is useful if you're printing reports on a black-and-white printer instead of a color printer. You can change this feature when printing, and then change it back when you are finished.

4. Click the **Company Preferences** tab. You'll see the choices presented in Figure 10-7. Select from the following:

   - **Summary Reports Basis** affects summary reports only. Selecting the Accrual option shows sales as income when you enter a sale and bills as expenses when you enter a bill, regardless of whether invoices or bills have been paid. Selecting the Cash option shows sales as income when you receive payments and bills as expenses when you pay them. This preference doesn't affect individual transaction-based reports or 1099 reports, which are always on a cash basis.
   - **Aging Reports** sets the date to calculate the number of overdue days on aging reports. Each invoice has a transaction date and a due date. The due date may be 30 days later if the customer is net 30. You can age from either the date the transaction occurred or the due date.
   - **Show Accounts by Name Only** is the most common setting and makes the report easy to read. Use the description (or both) if you prefer. The description used will be the one you entered when you set up the account in the Chart of Accounts.
   - **Classify Cash** allows you to change where accounts appear in any given section of a report. Only change this on the advice of an accountant.

5. If you clicked **Classify Cash**, click **Cancel** to close the window without making any changes.

6. Click the **Format** button. The Report Format Preferences window opens. Any changes you make here will affect all reports. The choices are the same for all reports (see "Customize Reports" later in this chapter for more information).

NOTE

You can change sales tax liability reports in the Sales Tax section of the Preferences window.

CAUTION

In a multiuser setting, only the Administrator user can change company preferences, but he or she must be in single-user mode to do so. Click the **File** menu and click **Switch To Single-User Mode** before changing company preferences.

7. Click **Cancel** to close the window without saving your changes, or click **OK** if you have made changes you want to save. You are returned to the Preferences window.
8. Click **OK** to save your preferences and close the window.

Use the Button Bar

At the top of every report in QuickBooks is a Button bar, as seen in Figure 10-8. To view and experiment with report settings (using the Profit & Loss report as an example):

Click the **Reports** menu, click **Company & Financial**, and click **Profit & Loss Standard**. The Profit & Loss Standard report is displayed.

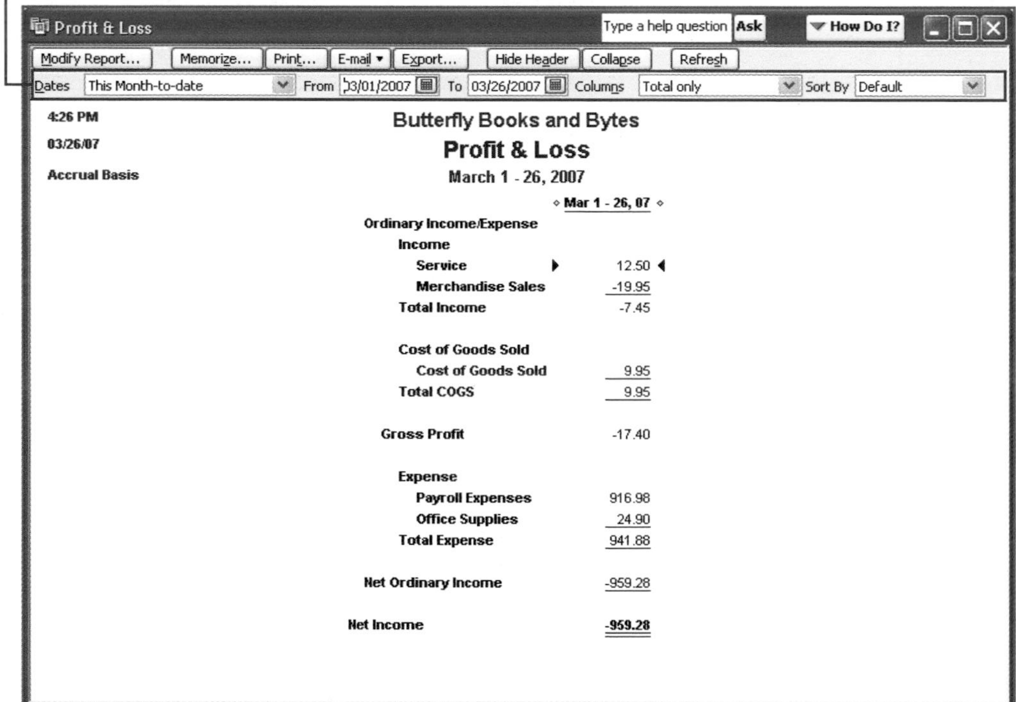

***Figure 10-8:** Fields with down arrows enable you to change the report immediately. If you set custom dates, click the report to have the date range take effect.*

CHANGE THE DATE RANGE

In the bottom row of the Button bar, the Dates down arrow includes commonly used preset date ranges, such as Today, This Week, This Month, This Fiscal Quarter, This Fiscal Year, This Fiscal Year-to-Date, Last Week, Last Month, and so on.

To change the date range:

1. Click the **Dates** down arrow, and select the date range you want.

   –Or–

1. Click in the **From** field, and select a date.
2. Click in the **To** field, and select a date.
3. Click anywhere in the report to refresh the report and use the new dates.

TIP

Sorting in client-related reports allows you to see your largest and smallest clients (by income amount).

CAUTION

After making any changes, be sure to preview your report before saving or printing it. You may need to resize columns to accommodate larger fonts, or the font size might be too large to fit on the page or too small to read.

VIEW REPORT COLUMNS

Most reports open with only the current total column displayed unless they are a comparative report (comparing a current period to another period), but you can use the Columns field to see sublevels of data in your date range. You can view your data broken down into periods, such as Day, Week, Month, Quarter, and so on; or by different topics, such as Customer:Job, Rep, Payee, Terms, and so on. Each report will have different choices.

SET THE SORT BY FIELD

The Sort By field allows you to sort by different items.

Click the **Sort By** down arrow, and click a field.

Typically, summary reports can only be sorted by account or by amount. Detailed reports can be sorted by any of the fields.

RESIZE COLUMNS

Small diamonds separate each column in a report. By dragging these diamonds, you can shrink the columns to fit on your page or expand them to show all data.

To resize an account column:

Move your mouse pointer over the diamond to the right of the account column name, and click and drag to the desired size.

To resize all data columns at once:

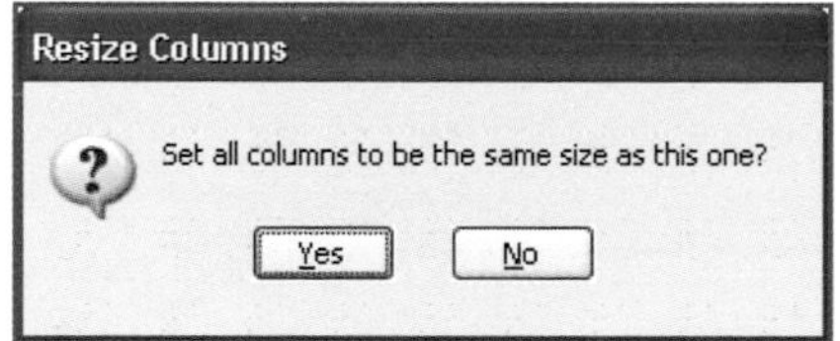

1. Move your mouse pointer over the diamond to the right of the column name, and click and drag to the desired size. When you release the mouse button, a dialog box appears, asking if you want to make all the columns the same size.
2. Click **Yes** if you want to make all columns the same size, or click **No** if you have one column that needs to be a different size from the others.

Customize Reports

In addition to the quick changes you can make using the Button bar, you can make a variety of changes to each report. Each change you make to an individual report will affect only that report, and your changes will be lost

1 2 3 4 5 6 7 8 9 10

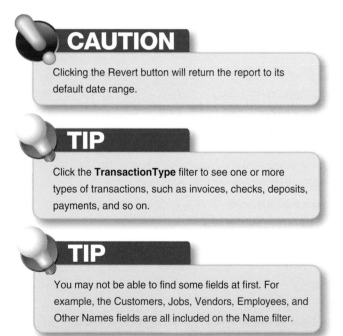

Figure 10-9: The ability to modify a report according to date, columns, or sort order is available in the Modify Report window, as well as on the Button bar.

CAUTION

Clicking the Revert button will return the report to its default date range.

TIP

Click the **TransactionType** filter to see one or more types of transactions, such as invoices, checks, deposits, payments, and so on.

TIP

You may not be able to find some fields at first. For example, the Customers, Jobs, Vendors, Employees, and Other Names fields are all included on the Name filter.

if you close the report without memorizing it. To make global changes to all reports, see the section "Set Report Preferences" earlier in this chapter.

To customize any report:

1. Click the **Modify Report** button. The Modify Report window opens, as seen in Figure 10-9.
2. Click the tab that corresponds to the area you want to modify, and make your changes. If you want the Modify Report window to open every time you run a report, choose that option in the Preferences window (see "Set Report Preferences").

EDIT THE DISPLAY

The best way to learn how any option affects your report is to run a report, and then change one item at a time to see the corresponding result.

1. With any report open, click the **Modify Report** button. The Modify Report window opens with the Display tab active.
2. Choose any of the following options:
   - Click the **Dates** down arrow to choose preselected dates, or type specific dates in the From and To fields.
   - Click the **Accrual** or **Cash** option to indicate which basis you would like the report to display.
   - Click the **Display Columns By** and **Sort By** down arrows to choose the desired options. You can also choose to sort by ascending (0–9, A–Z) or descending (Z–A, 9–0) order.
   - Click the desired additional columns in the Add Subcolumns For area to display comparison or percentage information.
3. Click the **Advanced** button to see additional choices:

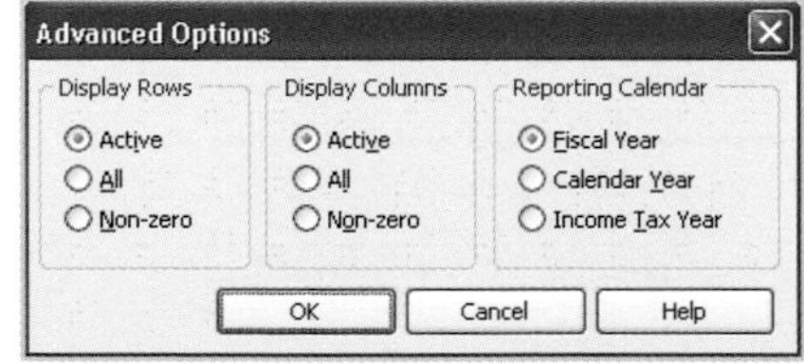

- In the Display Rows area, **Active** is selected by default. Click **All** to see inactive accounts in addition to active accounts, or click **Non-Zero** to hide accounts with no activity for the selected period.

- In the Display Columns area, **Active** is selected by default. Click **All** to see inactive accounts in addition to active accounts, or click **Non-Zero** to hide accounts with no activity for the selected period.
- In the Reporting Calendar area, **Fiscal Year** is selected by default. Click **Calendar Year** to use the range of January 1–December 31, or click **Income Tax Year** if it is different from your fiscal and calendar years.

4. Click **OK** when finished to close the Advanced Options window.
5. Click **OK** when finished to close the Modify Report window.

FILTER REPORT CONTENT

The Filters tab on the Modify Report window is a powerful feature. It allows you to control what data is shown by limiting (filtering) the data used to generate the report. There are approximately 50 filters representing all the fields in QuickBooks, including accounts, names (which includes items in the Customers, Jobs, Vendors, and Employees Lists), dates, statuses, vendor type, customer type, and custom fields. Don't choose too many filters, however, or you won't have any data for your reports.

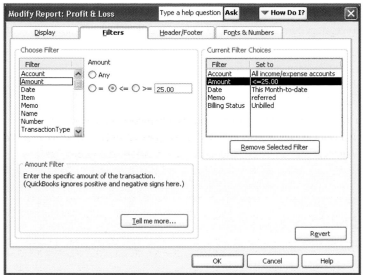

Figure 10-10: Experiment with various filters to create custom memorized reports.

1. With any report open, click the **Modify Report** button. The Modify Report window opens.
2. Click the **Filters** tab, as seen in Figure 10-10.
3. In the Choose Filter area (on the left), scroll through the list and click a filter. Each filter will have a variety of choices, including one or more of the following:
   - A drop-down list of choices to further refine the filter (such as when using the Accounts or Names filter)
   - Equal To, Less Than, or Greater Than options (for example, in Figure 10-10, with the Amount filter selected, amount options appear to the right)
   - Date range fields (when using the Date filter)
   - Text fields (when using the Memo or Number filter)
   - Status options (when using the Billing Status or Cleared filter)
4. To deselect a filter, click the relevant name in the Current Filter Choices area (located on the right side of the window, as seen in Figure 10-10), and click the **Remove Selected Filter** button.
5. Click **OK** when finished to save your changes and close the Modify Report window.

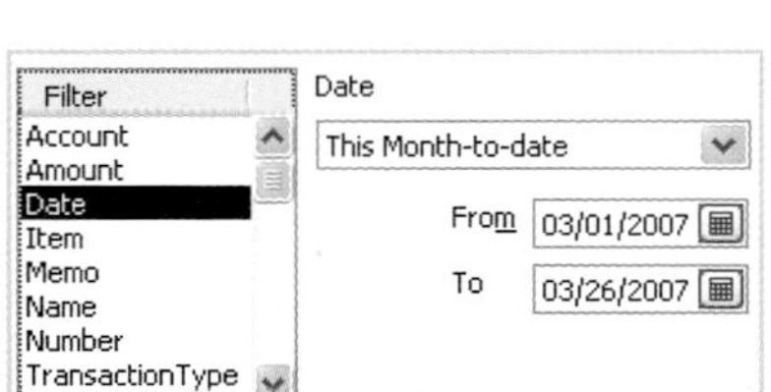

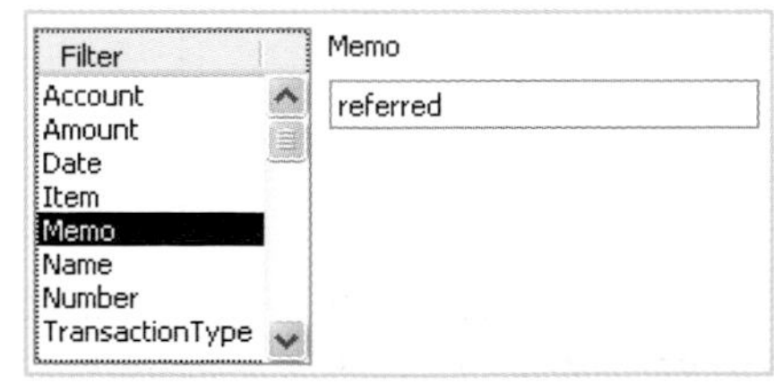

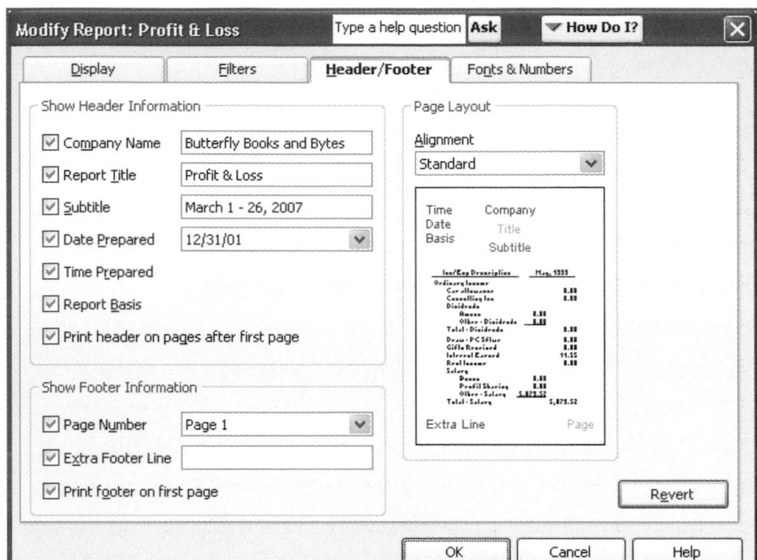

***Figure 10-11:* Use the small sample report to guide you in placing each section of the header and footer.**

TIP

You can use custom fields from name lists to create specific reports by filtering for that customized field. Scroll all the way down in the Filter list to find your customized fields.

Change the default report settings in the Preferences window. Click the **Edit** menu, click **Preferences**, and then click **Reports & Graphs**.

MODIFY REPORT HEADERS AND FOOTERS

Headers and footers appear at the top or bottom of a page, respectively. You can include headers and footers on all pages or have a header on just the first page and/or a footer on all pages thereafter.

1. With any report open, click the **Modify Report** button. The Modify Report window opens.
2. Click the **Header/Footer** tab, as seen in Figure 10-11.
3. Change any section by clicking in the relevant field and typing the new text, or by choosing an item from the related drop-down list. To prevent any section of the header or footer from printing, click the relevant check box to deselect it.
4. Click **OK** when finished to save your changes and close the Modify Report window.

MODIFY FONTS AND NUMBERS

Fonts and numbers can be set so that your reports reflect your company's preferences.

1. With any report open, click the **Modify Report** button. The Modify Report window opens.
2. Click the **Fonts & Numbers** tab, as seen in Figure 10-12.
3. In the Change Font For list, located on the left, click the report element for which you would like to change fonts. An example will appear to the right, showing the font color, size, and type currently in place for that report element.
4. Click the **Change Font** button. A dialog box appears, from which you can change the following properties:

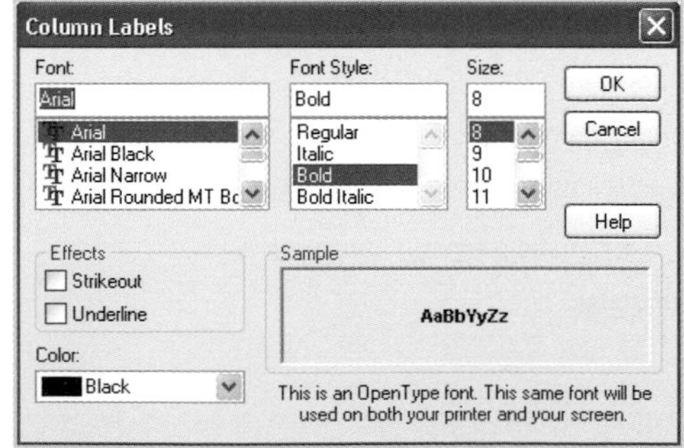

TIP

You can right-click Reports to change the font of the item you're right-clicking on.

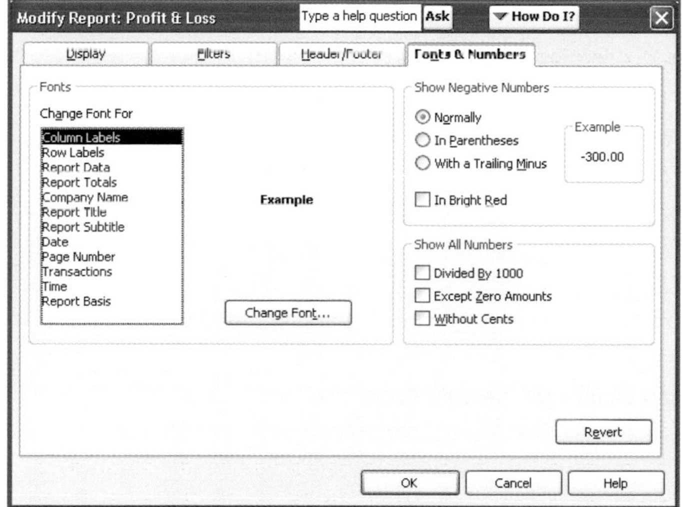

***Figure 10-12:* Make changes to fonts and numbers, and then click OK to see the result.**

TIP

Memorize a report if you're not sure you might need it again. It's easier to delete a memorized report than to remember all the specific changes you may have made if you have to run the report again.

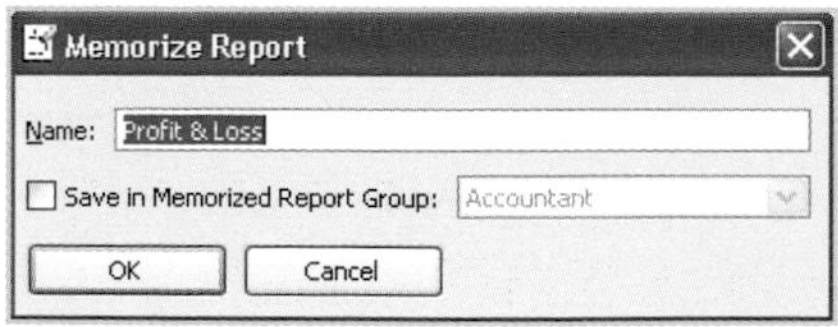

- **Font** is the specific typeface used—in other words, the "look" of the text and numbers on the report. Click each type to see a preview of what it will look like in the lower-right area of the dialog box.
- **Font Style** displays text in bold, italics, or regular typeface.
- **Size** is measured in points, and 72 points is equal to one inch. The most common sizes for reports are 8, 10, and 12, with 8 being the smallest readable to most people. QuickBooks limits your size choices to between 6 and 60.
- **Effects** include strikeout (~~example~~) and underline (example).
- **Color** can be used to emphasize or customize reports if you have a color printer.

5. Click **OK** to apply your choices to the element you selected and close the dialog box. A dialog box may appear, asking if you want to change all related fonts. Click **Yes** to have all related fonts in the report change to the same style.
6. Customize how numbers are displayed by selecting from among the following options on the right side of the Fonts & Numbers tab (see Figure 10-12):
   - In the **Show Negative Numbers** area, you can choose to display negative numbers normally, in parentheses, or with a trailing minus (the minus sign is on the right rather than on the left). Click the **In Bright Red** check box if you want to call attention to negative numbers and you use a color printer.
   - In the **Show All Numbers** area, you can choose to show all numbers divided by 1,000 (for large numbers), suppress zero amounts, and only display whole dollar amounts.
7. Click **OK** when finished to save your changes and close the Modify Report window.

Memorize Reports

When you memorize reports, you are memorizing the settings, not the data. Each time you open a memorized report, you will get the latest data. Each time you close a report after making changes, QuickBooks will ask if you want to memorize the report. Click **No** if you made changes for a single time only or made a mistake.

To memorize reports at any time:

1. Click the **Memorize** button at the top of the report you want to memorize. The Memorize Report dialog box appears with the current name of the report highlighted.
2. Edit the report name or type a new name, such as Profit & Loss - modified.
3. Click **OK** to memorize the report.

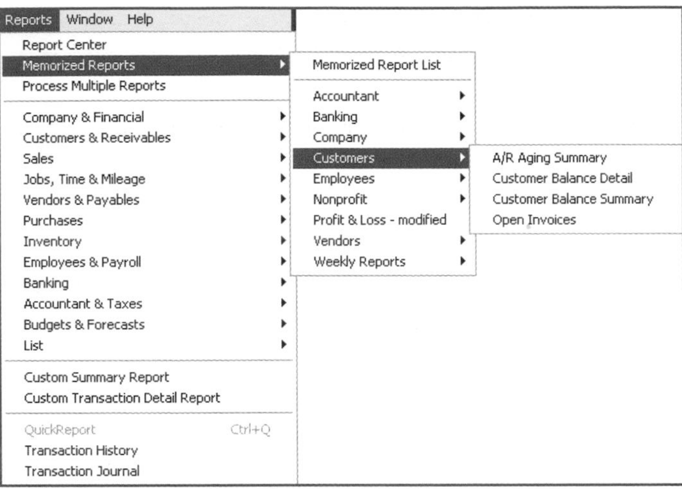

Figure 10-13: From the Memorized Reports List, you can open a report saved to a memorized group, such as Accountant, Banking, or Company.

TIP

Click the **Save In Memorized Group** check box if you want to add the report to an existing group or to a custom group you have added.

Use Memorized Reports

When you memorize a report, it is added to your Reports menu, either directly under the Memorized Reports submenu or under the custom grouping you chose. You can open each memorized report individually or open a group of memorized reports.

DISPLAY A SINGLE MEMORIZED REPORT

To display a single memorized report:

Click the **Reports** menu, click **Memorized Reports**, and click the report you want to run, as shown in Figure 10-13. The report is displayed.

RUN A GROUP OF MEMORIZED REPORTS

To run multiple reports:

1. Click the **Reports** menu and click **Process Multiple Reports**. The Process Multiple Reports window opens (see Figure 10-14).
2. Click the **Select Memorized Reports From** down arrow, and click the group, for example, **Company**. The report area, in the lower half of the screen, displays all the reports in that memorized group with the reports already selected.

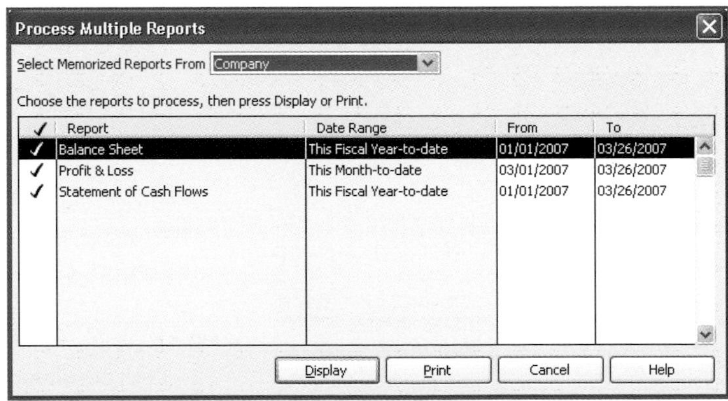

Figure 10-14: All reports in a group are selected by default.

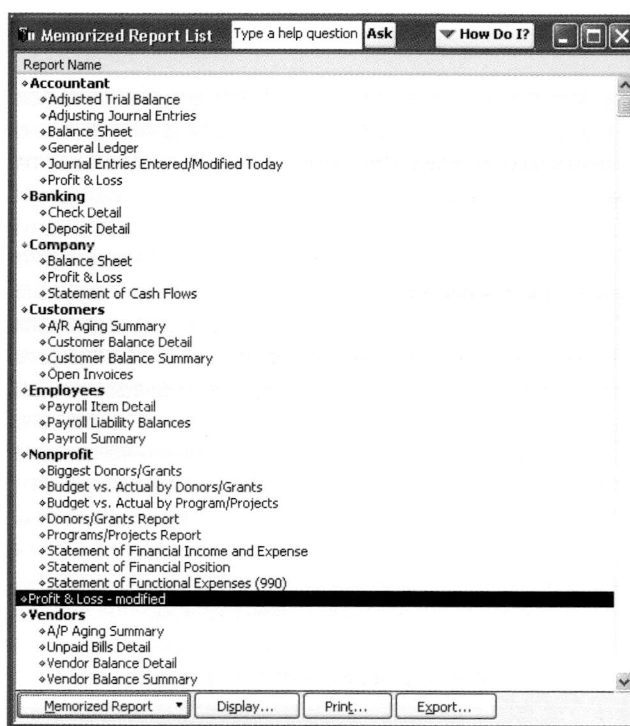

***Figure 10-15:* Move reports to groups by dragging the diamonds up, down, left, or right.**

You can also choose <All Reports> from the drop-down list and then select any number of individual reports to run at once.

3. Click the **Display** button (or click **Print** if you want the reports to be sent directly to the printer without previewing them). The reports are run and the Process Multiple Reports window closes.
4. Review the reports. When finished, you can close the windows or print the reports (if you didn't already do this in Step 3).

Organize Memorized Reports

If you customize and memorize reports often, over time, those reports may be difficult to find in a single list. Fortunately, you can organize your memorized reports according to topics that make sense for your business.

To access the Memorized Report List:

> Click the **Reports** menu, click **Memorized Reports**, and click **Memorized Report List**. The Memorized Report List is displayed, as shown in Figure 10-15.

Custom groups can be added to the Reports menu, and reports can be moved to different groups using the Memorized Report List, which is similar to other lists found throughout QuickBooks. See Chapter 3 for more tips on working with lists.

CREATE A NEW GROUP

To create a new group:

1. Click the **Memorized Report** menu button (located at the bottom of the screen), and click **New Group**. The New Memorized Report Group dialog box appears.

2. Type the name of your new group, such as <u>Weekly Reports</u>.
3. Click **OK**. The group is added to your Memorized Report List.

TIP

QuickBooks comes with standard memorized reports, but you can change these. When you close it, QuickBooks will ask if you want to replace the existing report with the modified one.

TIP

You can change the QuickBooks standard memorized reports or your own customized memorized reports. Simply open a memorized report and make your preferred changes. When you close the report, QuickBooks will ask if you want to replace the existing report with the modified one.

QUICKSTEPS

PRINTING TO A FILE

In addition to exporting and printing reports, you can print directly to a file, which is useful for transferring information to another program.

1. Click the **Print** button on any report window. The Print Reports dialog box appears, as shown in Figure 10-16.
2. In the Print To area, click the **File** option.
3. Click the down arrow located to the right of the File option, and select the preferred file type:
   - **ASCII Text File** keeps the layout intact but removes all formatting and saves the file with a .txt file extension.

Continued . . .

4. Click the **Close** button (the X in the upper-right corner) to close the dialog box.
5. Refer to Chapter 3 for more information on moving items in a list.

EDIT MEMORIZED REPORT NAMES

To edit the names of your reports:

1. Open the Memorized Report List, right-click the report you want to edit, and click **Edit Memorized Report**. The Edit Memorized Report dialog box appears.

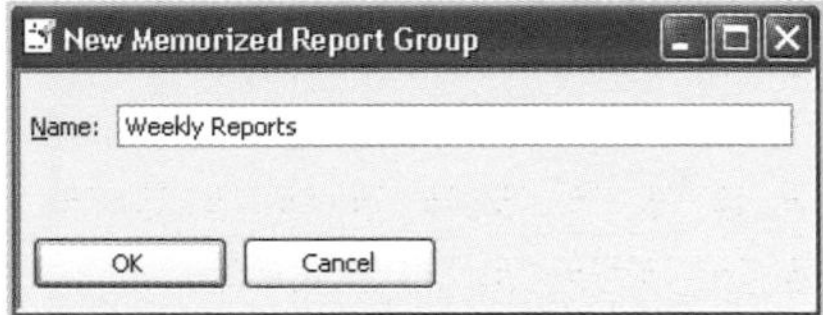

2. Type a new name for the report. Click the **Save In Memorized Report Group** check box, click the down arrow, and choose the new group that you want this report to be a part of, if desired.
3. Click **OK** to save the new name.

Print, E-Mail, and Export Reports

Viewing reports on your computer screen is a fast, easy way to see how your business is doing. However, most businesses need to distribute reports as well, and some may need to export information into another program. You can do all of that using QuickBooks. At the top of any report window on the Button bar are the Print, E-Mail, and Export buttons (next to the Modify Report and Memorize Report buttons). Click any of these to open the related dialog boxes.

Print Reports

Printing a report is the most common way of distributing information. To print a report:

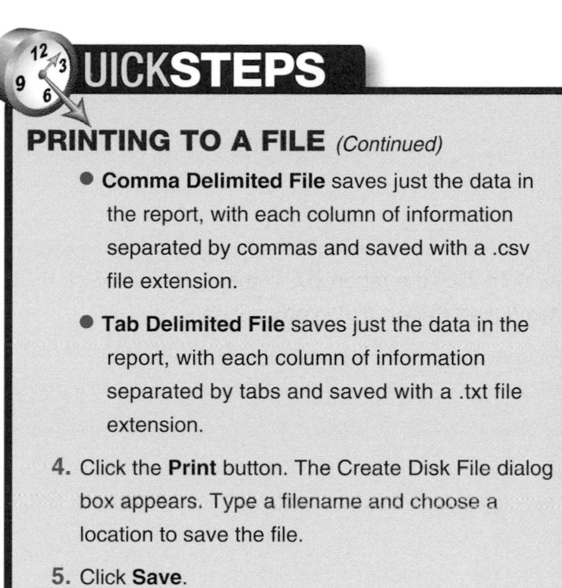

QUICKSTEPS

PRINTING TO A FILE *(Continued)*

- **Comma Delimited File** saves just the data in the report, with each column of information separated by commas and saved with a .csv file extension.
- **Tab Delimited File** saves just the data in the report, with each column of information separated by tabs and saved with a .txt file extension.

4. Click the **Print** button. The Create Disk File dialog box appears. Type a filename and choose a location to save the file.
5. Click **Save**.

1. Click the **Print** button on any report window. The Print Reports dialog box appears, as shown in Figure 10-16.
2. In the Print To area, click the **Printer** option and choose from among the following options:
   - Click the **Printer** down arrow to select an alternate printer if the default printer is not the one you want to use.
   - Click the **Options** button if you want to change settings specific to your printer. A separate dialog box appears. Click **OK** when finished to close that dialog box.
   - In the Orientation area, click the **Landscape** option to change the page orientation to horizontal. Portrait (vertical orientation) is the default selection.
   - In the Page Range area, click the **Pages** option and type the page numbers you want to print if you don't want to print all pages in a report.
   - In the Page Breaks area, click the **Smart page breaks** and **Page break after each major grouping** check boxes if you have a long report and want to make it easier to read by providing "natural" breaks. (This may make the report print on more pages.)
   - Click in the Number of copies box and edit to print multiple copies of the report.
     - Collate is a toggle box. When checked and multiple copies of the report are being printed, reports print one after the other. When Collate is unchecked, all page ones are printed, then all page twos, etc.
     - Click the **Fit Report To** check box, and type the number of pages wide in the field, for example, 1, to force QuickBooks to resize the type to a smaller size if the report content is too wide. This may make the type too small to read if the report is very wide, but it is useful for reports that are just slightly too wide. Use the Landscape orientation or select a larger number of pages wide if the report is not readable.
     - Click the **Print In Color** check box to toggle this option on or off.
3. When finished, click the **Preview** button to see how the report will look when printed, as shown in Figure 10-17.
4. If the preview is how you want the report to look, click **Print**. The report is sent to the printer, and the preview window closes. If the report does not look how you want it, click **Close** and make further adjustments as needed.

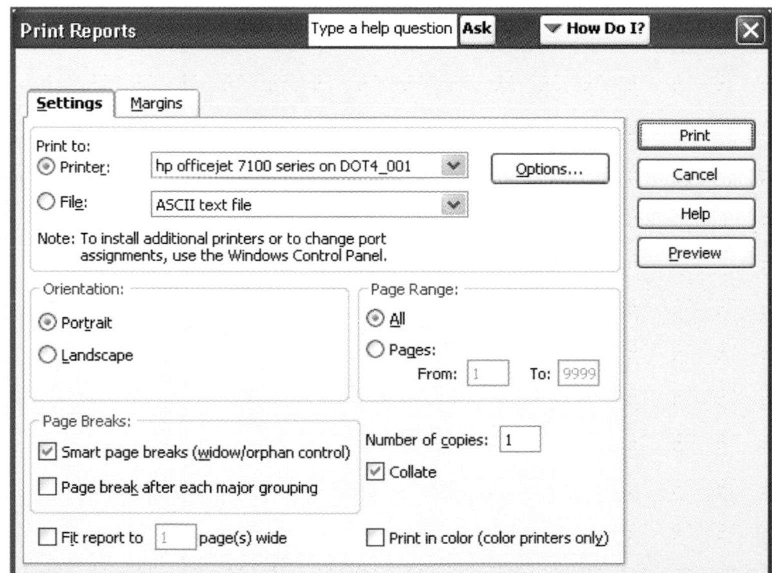

Figure 10-16: Click Print if you have a short report and don't need to worry about formatting.

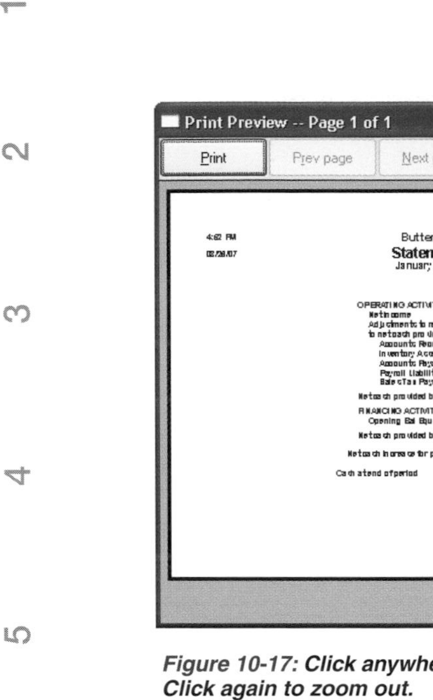

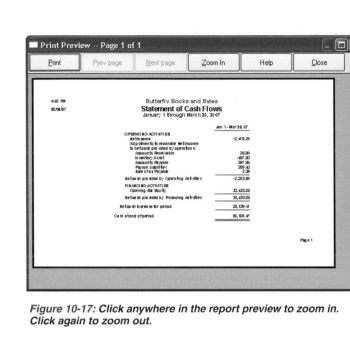

Figure 10-17: Click anywhere in the report preview to zoom in. Click again to zoom out.

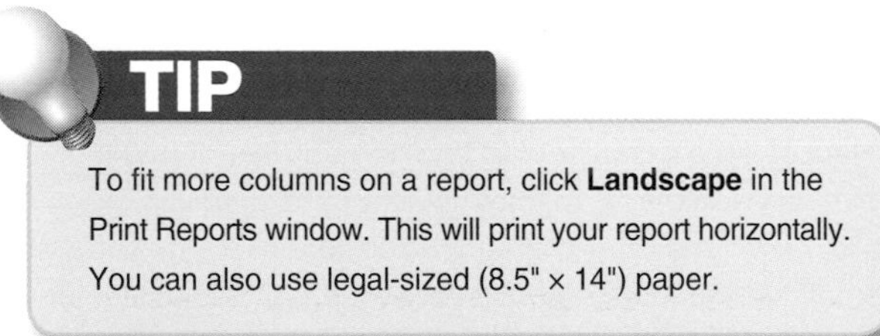

TIP

To fit more columns on a report, click **Landscape** in the Print Reports window. This will print your report horizontally. You can also use legal-sized (8.5" × 14") paper.

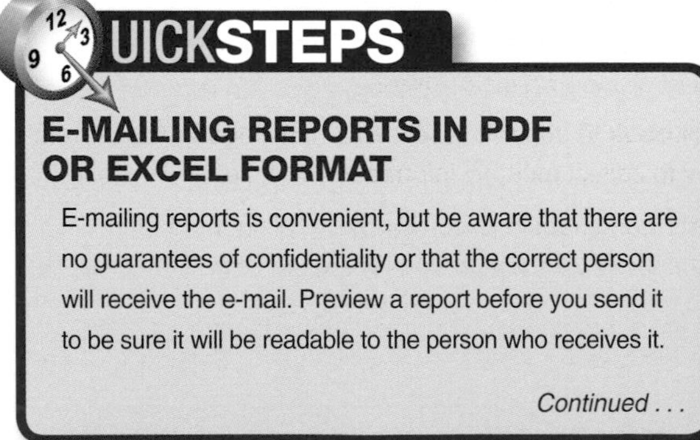

QUICKSTEPS

E-MAILING REPORTS IN PDF OR EXCEL FORMAT

E-mailing reports is convenient, but be aware that there are no guarantees of confidentiality or that the correct person will receive the e-mail. Preview a report before you send it to be sure it will be readable to the person who receives it.

Continued . . .

Export Reports

QuickBooks has a number of links to the Microsoft Office suite of products, including the Letters and Envelopes Wizard covered in Chapter 8, which sends information to Word. Report information can be sent directly to Microsoft Excel, a spreadsheet application. Although QuickBooks has a variety of report customization options available, for raw data manipulation, exporting reports to Excel allows you to create detailed budgets, create projection estimates, create "What If?" scenarios, perform more detailed analysis, and import to or compare other programs' data.

BASIC EXPORTING

To export a report:

1. Click the **Export** button on any report window. The Export Reports window opens, with the **A New Excel Workbook** option selected by default, as shown in Figure 10-18.

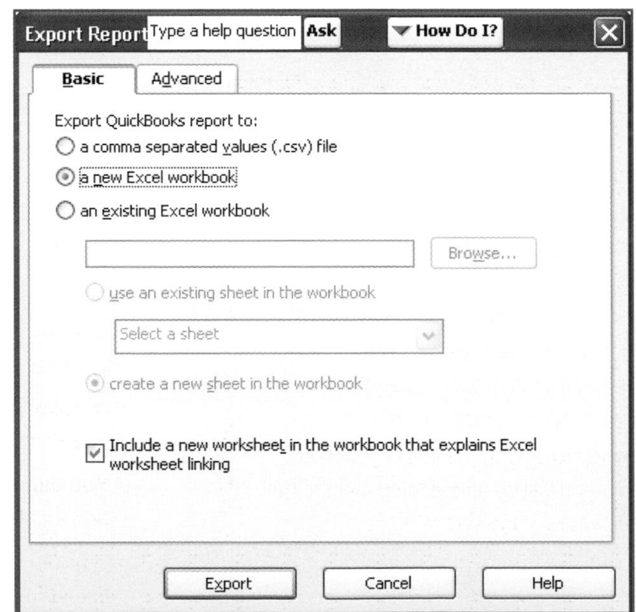

Figure 10-18: You must have Microsoft Excel installed to export information to Excel files.

1 2 3 4 5 6 7 8 9 10

QUICKSTEPS

E-MAILING REPORTS IN PDF OR EXCEL FORMAT *(Continued)*

To e-mail reports:

1. Click the **E-Mail** button on any report window. Click one of the following:
   - **Send Report as Excel** Allows the person receiving the report to manipulate it, but that person must have Excel.
   - **Send Report as PDF** Prevents the person receiving the report from manipulating it,but Acrobat Reader is a free program.
2. Click **OK** if a security warning appears. The Edit E-Mail Information window opens, as shown in Figure 10-19.
3. In the To field, type the e-mail address of the person to whom you are sending the report.
4. In the Cc (Carbon Copy) field, type the e-mail addresses of anyone else to whom you would like to send the report.
5. In the Bcc (Blind Carbon Copy) field, type the e-mail addresses of anyone to whom you want to send the report without the original recipient seeing their e-mail addresses.
6. Edit the default e-mail text to add any pertinent information, such as the purpose of the attached report or any information that is needed to understand the report's significance.
7. Click the **Send Now** button. If this is your first time sending, you will be asked to connect to the Internet and enter your e-mail address.

You have the option to send invoices and other forms later, but reports are always sent immediately.

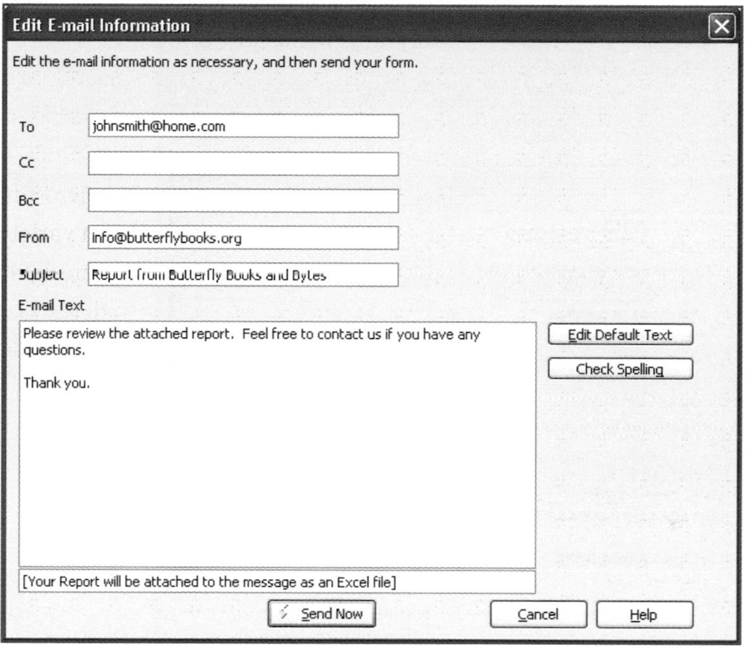

***Figure 10-19:** Send a report to yourself before sending it to others to see how it appears.*

2. Click the **Export** button to transfer the report to a new Excel file. QuickBooks will open Excel and create a new workbook, as seen in Figure 10-20. Alternatively, you can choose either of the remaining options in the Export Reports window:
   - Click **a comma separated values (.csv) file** to create a file for import into any other data program, such as a Microsoft Access database.
   - Click **an existing Excel workbook** to add this report as a new page in any current Excel file. This is a good way to collect monthly information in a file.

   You can also choose to include a worksheet in Excel that will explain the export process by clicking the relevant check box at the bottom of the window.
3. From Excel, you can choose to print, view, or save the file. Click the **Close** button (the X in the upper-right corner) to close Excel. You can choose to save the file or not.

	A	B	C	D	E	F	G
1						Jan 1 - Mar 26, 07	
2			OPERATING ACTIVITIES				
3				Net Income		-2,478.29	
4				Adjustments to reconcile Net Income			
5				to net cash provided by operations:			
6					Accounts Receivable	26.89	
7					Inventory Asset	-497.80	
8					Accounts Payable	397.86	
9					Payroll Liabilities	255.40	
10					Sales Tax Payable	2.35	
11			Net cash provided by Operating Activities			-2,293.59	
12			FINANCING ACTIVITIES				
13				Opening Bal Equity		30,433.06	
14			Net cash provided by Financing Activities			30,433.06	
15		Net cash increase for period				28,139.47	
16	Cash at end of period					**28,139.47**	
17							
18							
19							

Figure 10-20: Data exported to Excel is a copy of the current report's information and can be manipulated without affecting the original QuickBooks data.

TIP

You can also export customer data and other items from QuickBooks by clicking the **File** menu, clicking **Utilities**, and then clicking **Export**, which will display additional options.

ADVANCED EXPORTING FEATURES

You can also customize the appearance and content of your exported file.

1. Click the **Export** button on any report window. The Export Reports window opens. Click the **Advanced** tab to see the options shown in Figure 10-21.
2. Choose from among the following:
   - Click the formatting options to choose whether to include formatting information in Excel or to use Excel's default font (the first area).
   - Click the Excel options to set the initial Excel preferences for this report page (the middle area).
   - Click the printing options to determine how the page will print in Excel (the bottom area).
3. Click **Export** to send the file to Excel or to a .csv file, whichever you chose on the Basic tab.

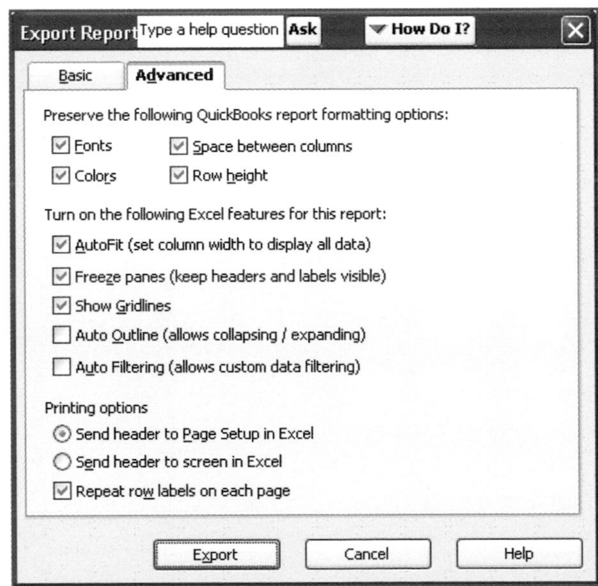

Figure 10-21: To just export the report data, clear the top four formatting check boxes.

Index

Numbers

Symbol

A

B

C

D

E

F

G

H

I

J

P

Q

R

S

T

U

V

W

Y